CHERYL DUNN
THE WHILES

Just as long as I have been searching for meaningful compositions and striking light on the streets of NY, I have been searching my archive to find that special shot I took 15, 20 years ago or even yesterday. I organize imagery using descriptive words, dates, names and locations. For instance, I'll search "BROADWAY" or "BIRD" or "CROSSWALK." The groupings that emerge are always fascinating to me. The random, connective threads, sometimes disparate, tell a new story. These stories are about how we move within a cityscape, communicate, love, fight, dance and survive. The streets are like a canvas where a piece of wood in a trash can becomes a beautiful sculpture, where the rooftops are a spiritual respite from the streets — yet still part of the same pulse, the same club. The way we move through public space — walking, dancing, skating, or even fighting — has a distinct rhythm, a pace that belongs distinctly to NYC. This is THE WHILES NEW YORK CITY.

Published by Blurring Books
BlurringBooks.com
@BlurringBooksNYC

Blurring Books

First Edition / First Printing

Printed in China

ISBN – 978-1-963814-30-9

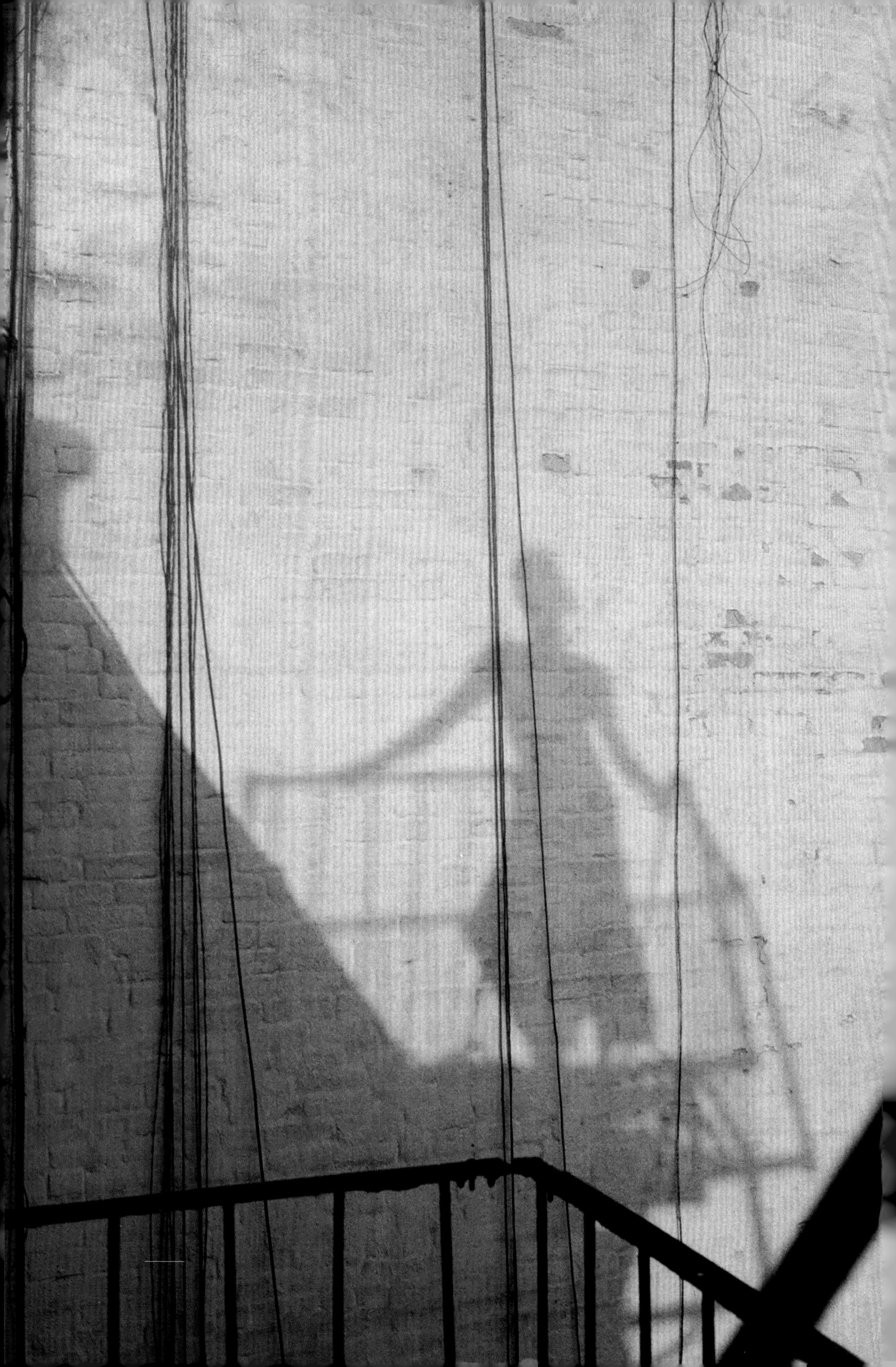

BIRD
BOX
BRIDGE
BROADWAY
BUNNY
CALL
COP
CROSSWALK
DOG
EAST VILLAGE
FIDI
FIREWORKS
FLASH
GIRL
GOD
HAND
JOE
LONELY
LOVE
MATTRESS
RAT
ROOFTOP
SIGN
SLEEPING MEN
SMILE
SMOKE
SPILL
TIRE
TRAIL
TV
USA
WET
YANKEES

WORDS FROM

D.V. De VINCENTIS

Cheryl Dunn has always moved across the surface of her landscapes like a master gamer fleet of foot, familiar enough with the topography to navigate quickly, but with the constantly refreshing eye required to spot and capture the gems and prizes in the terrain of the game — her images. Dunn's frames do not document so much as state entire ideas of hers, or articulate wordless declarations of her subjects.

Like few other species, humans find comfort in associations, in linkage, in groupings. Sets of things that make sense together satisfy one of our primary desires, that of order. Transfixed by communities of many kinds, Dunn seeks and finds groupings within frames: concert goers in nights of absolute unison, kid cliques appropriating blocks as they trespass them, random curbside refuse that seems to gather itself to pose for Dunn's lens. In a sense, Dunn has been conjuring combinations for decades.

In this volume, though, Dunn takes a step forward with the explicit editorial approach of arranging her images by the associations she finds between them. In so doing, she winds up saying something entirely new and unexpected, and finds a new act of her storytelling. The groupings in this volume not only scratch our primal itch for order, their proximity generates an alchemy among them; they cause each other to expand gracefully while remaining unruly. These almost-montages compound what Dunn says into more than the sum of their eloquent parts.

There's often wit in Dunn's work, and in this collection there is no lack of her sly observation that can only be shared with the rest of us by stopping the world with a still frame, something that can only be done with a photograph, and only by a maker with the innate intelligence and hopeless love for the world around them, an image-maker like Dunn.

BIRD

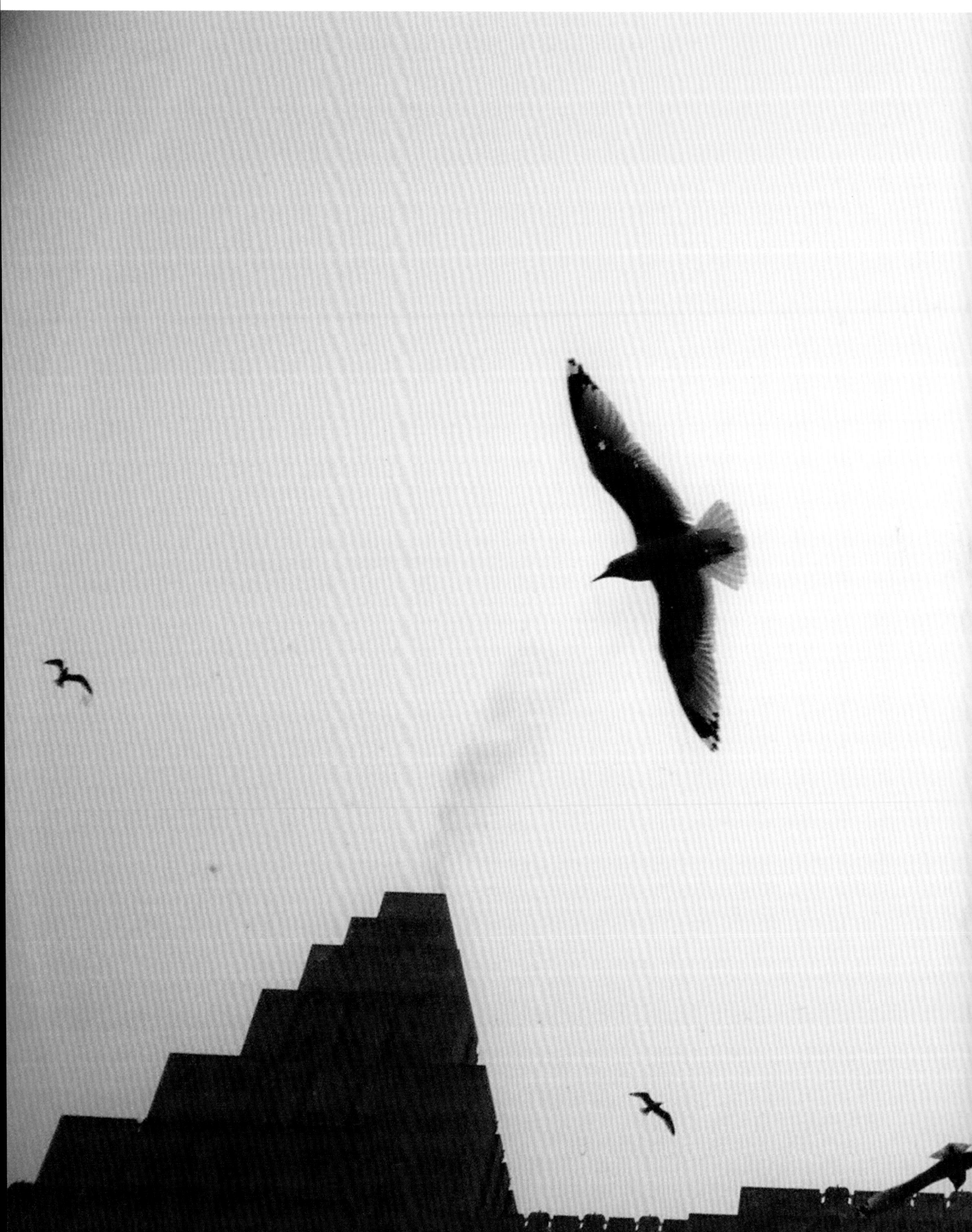

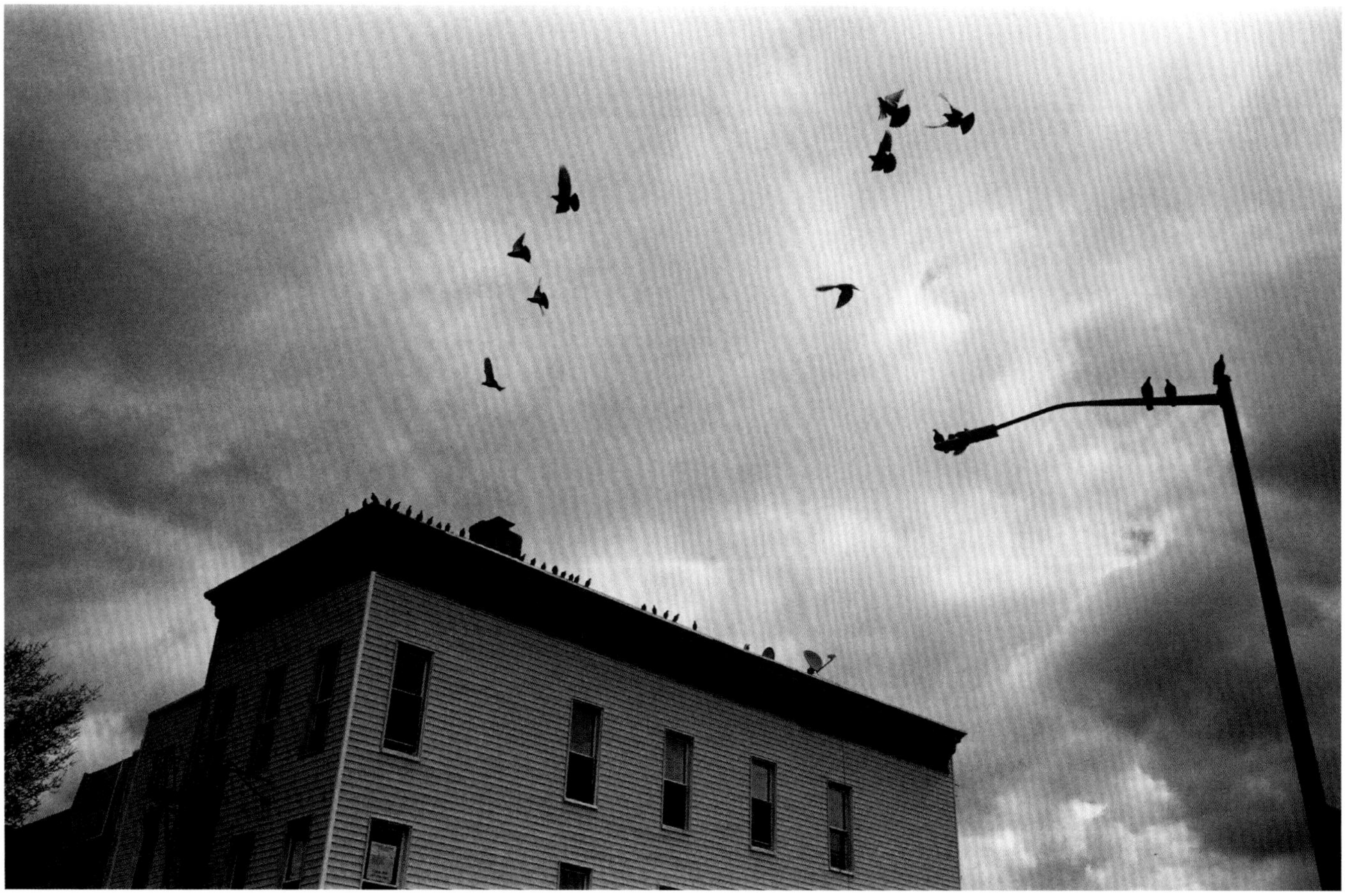

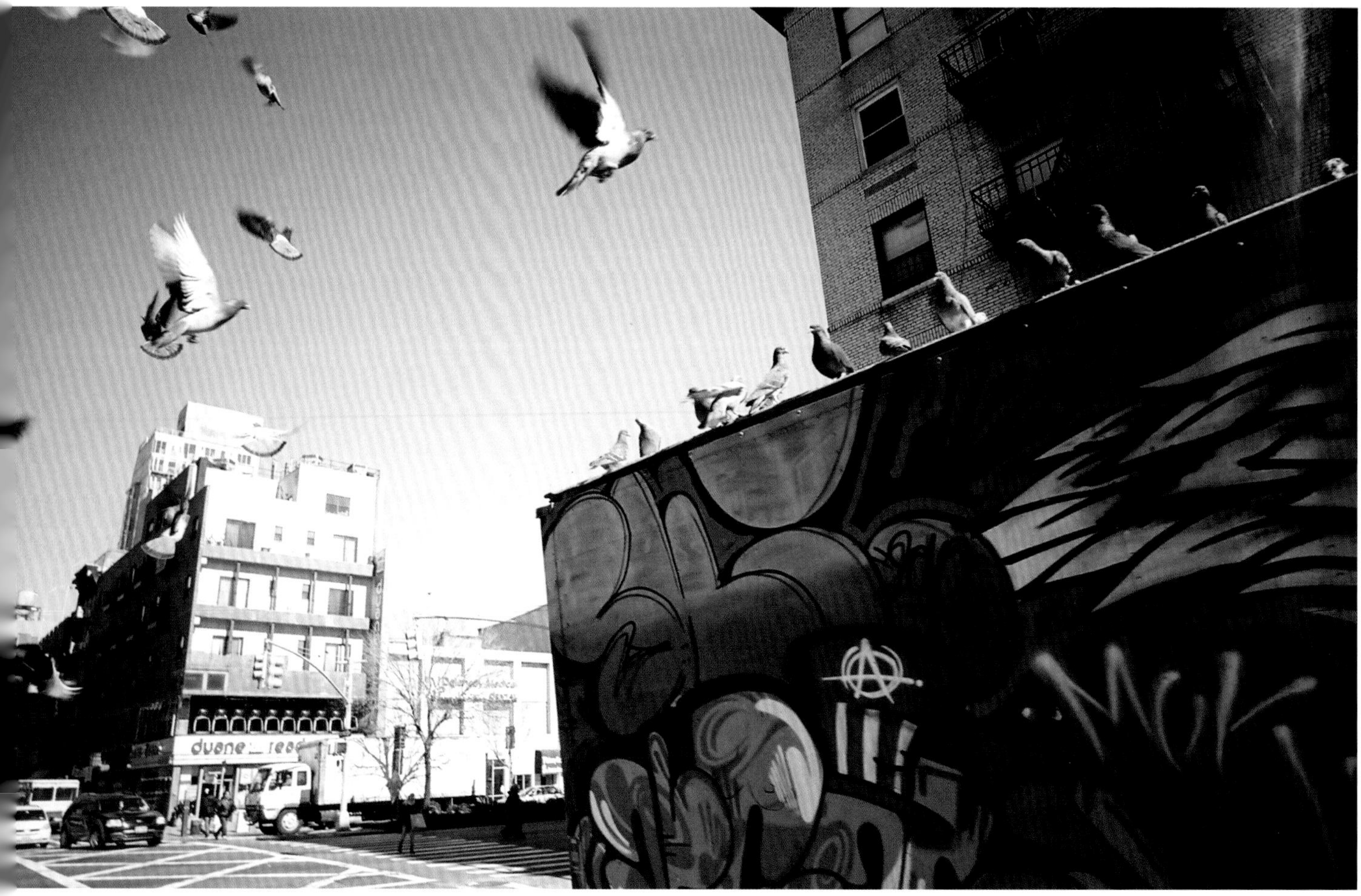

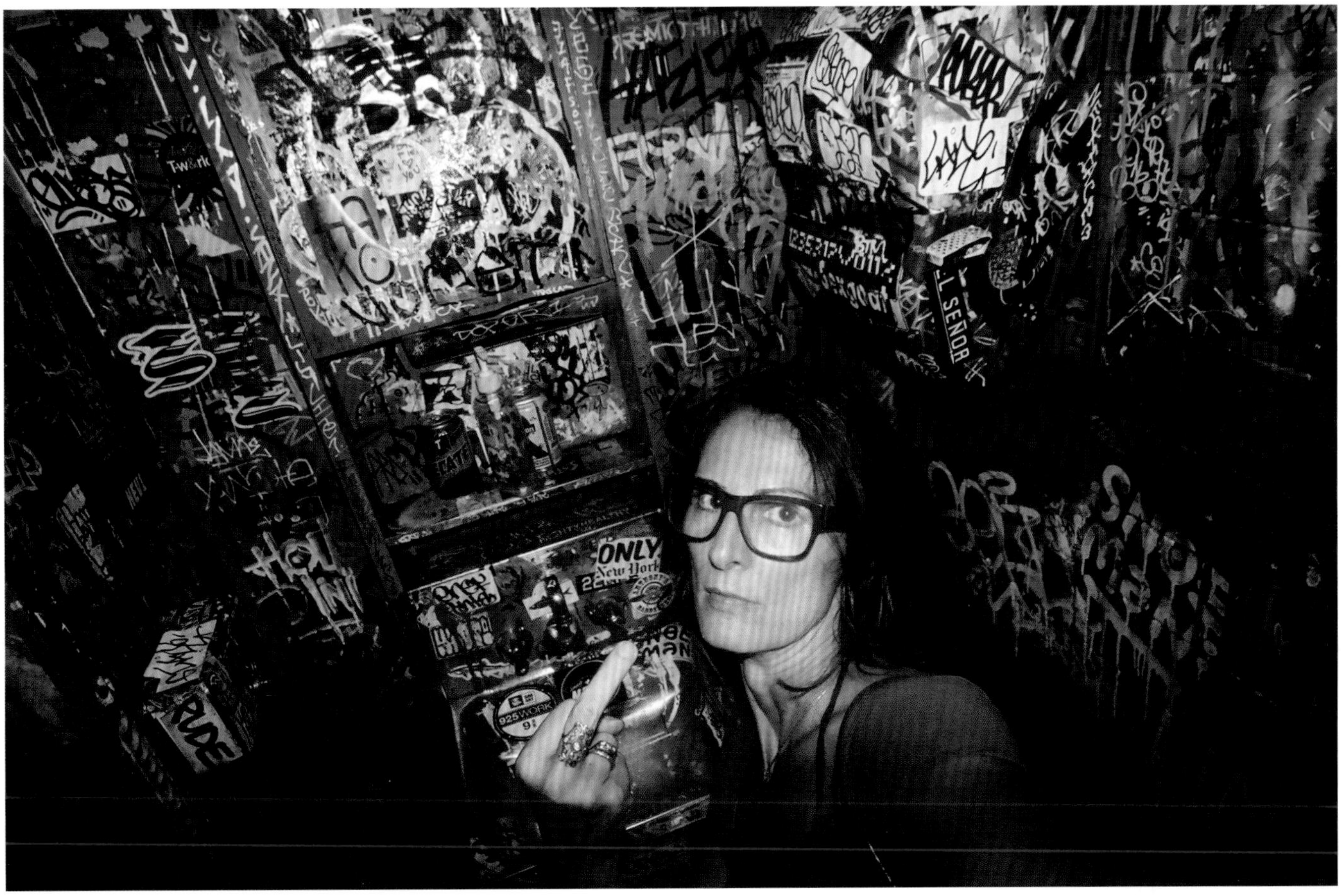
ONLY
New York
925WORK
RUDE

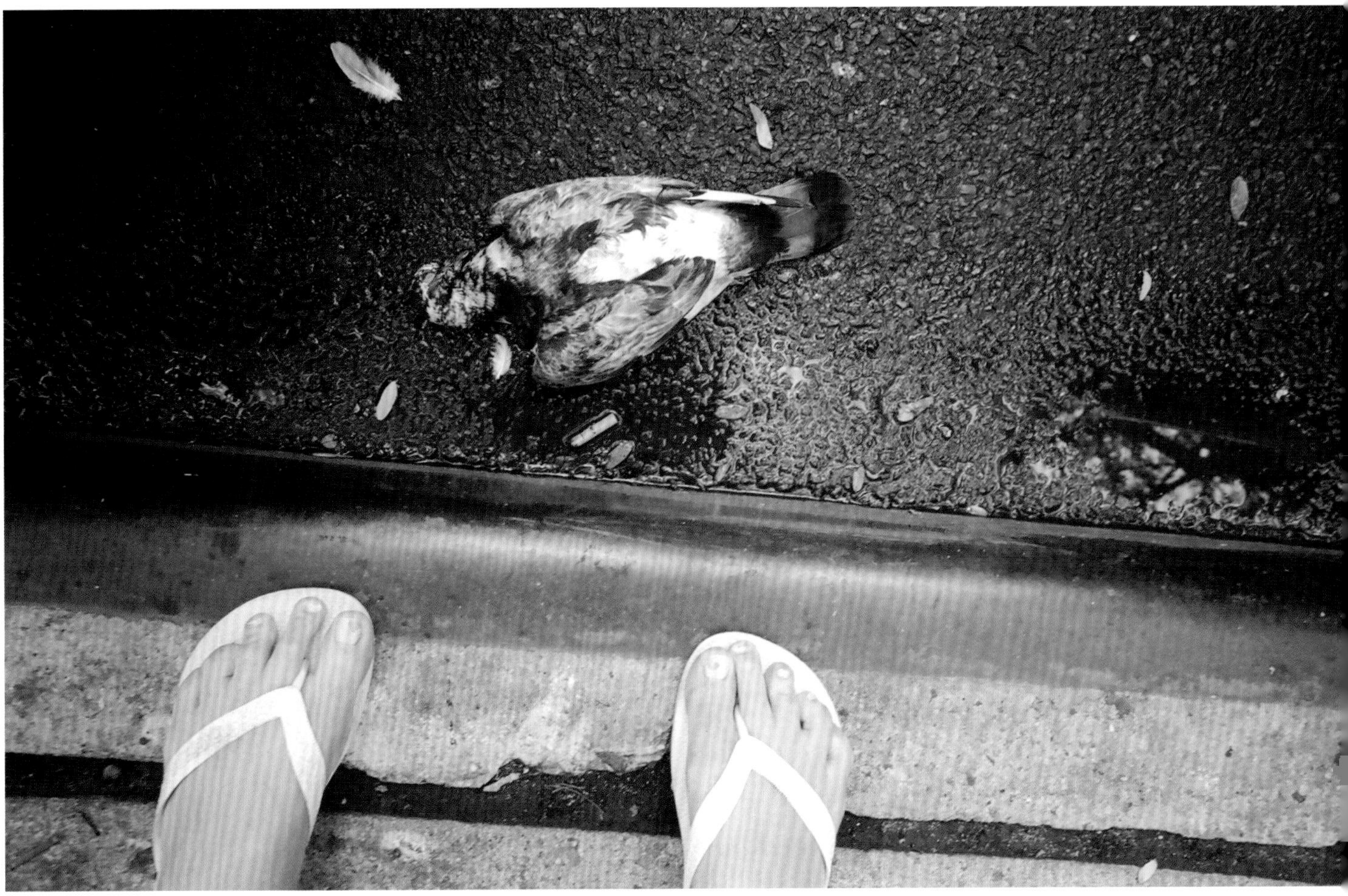

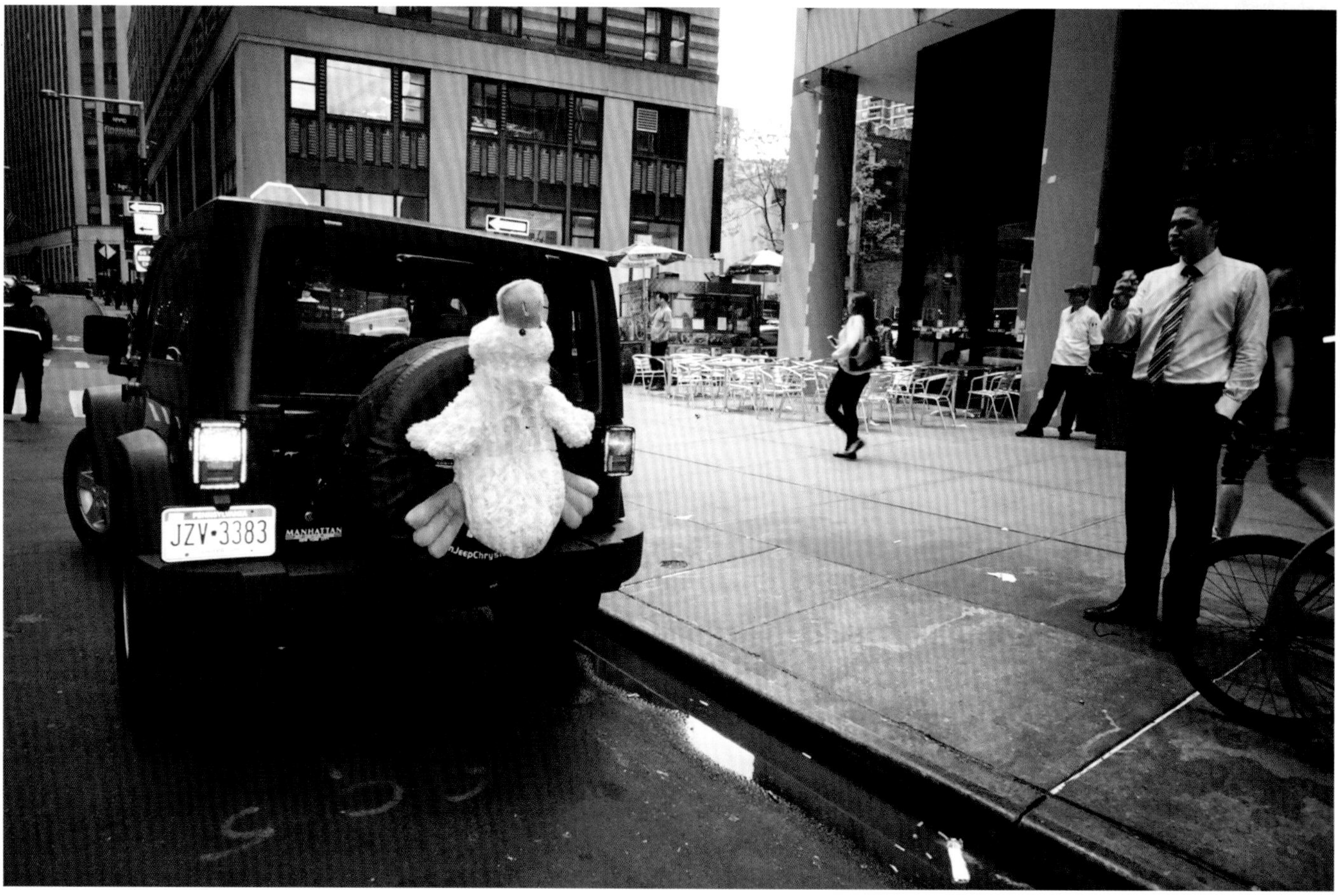

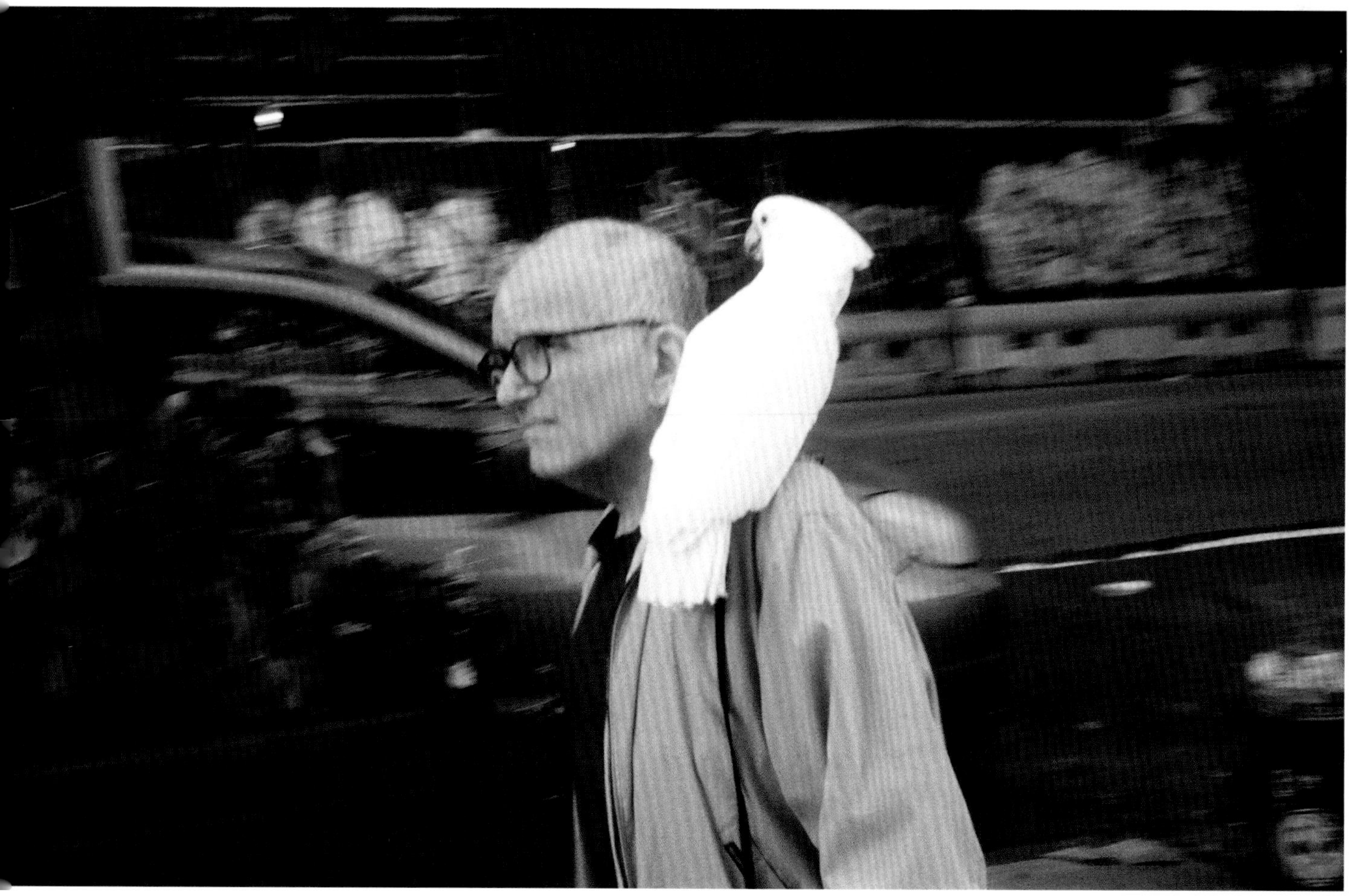

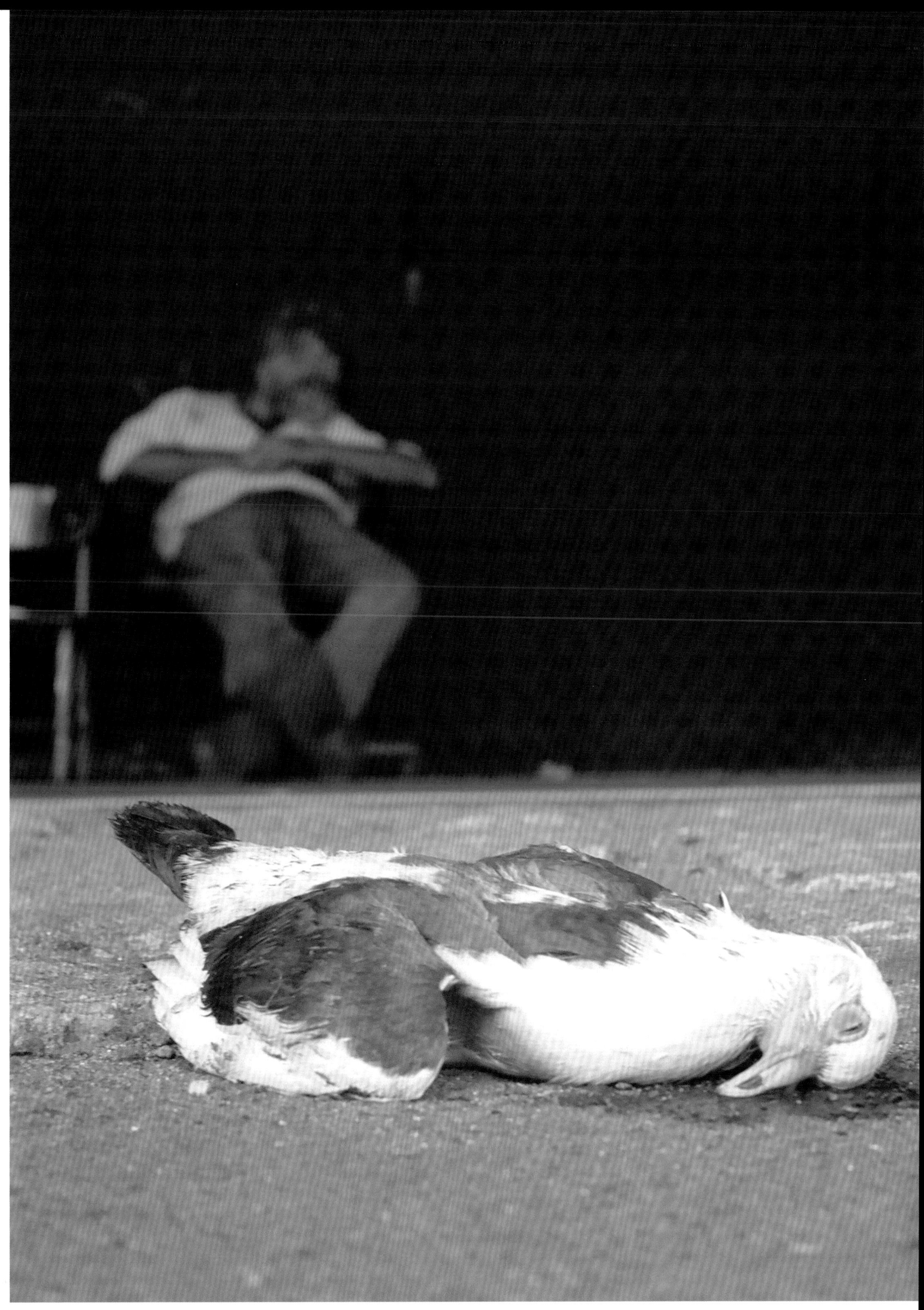

BOX

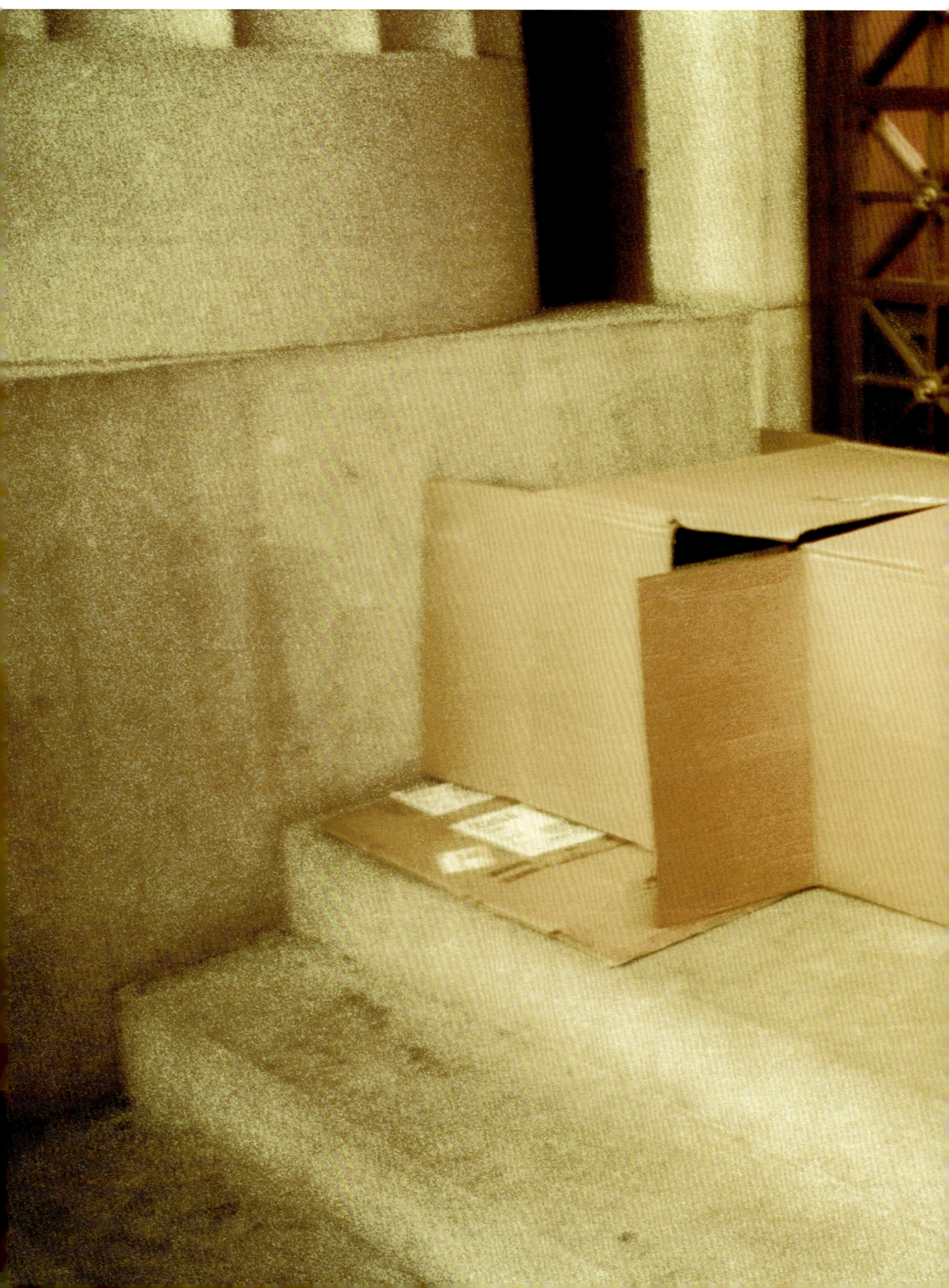

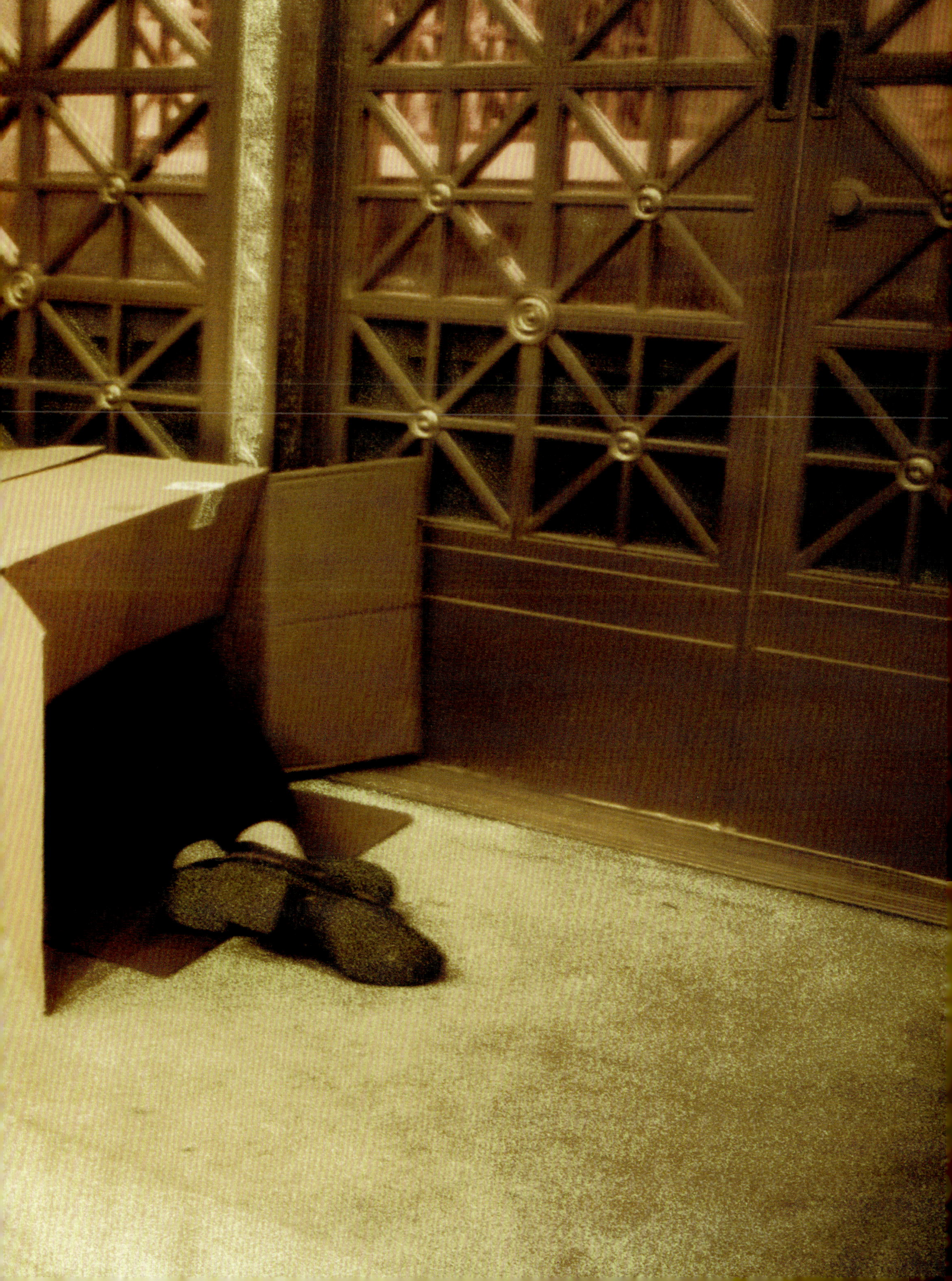

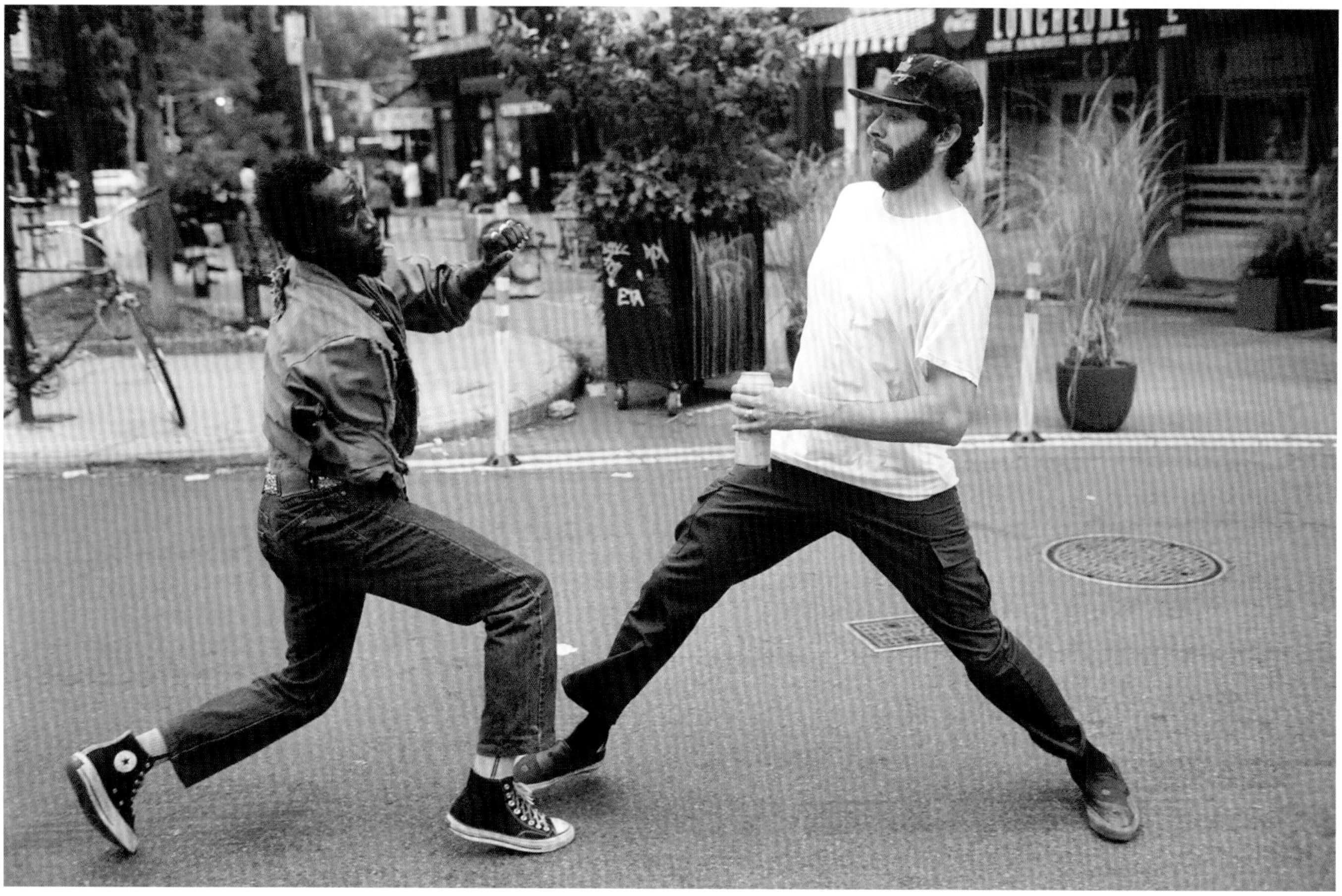

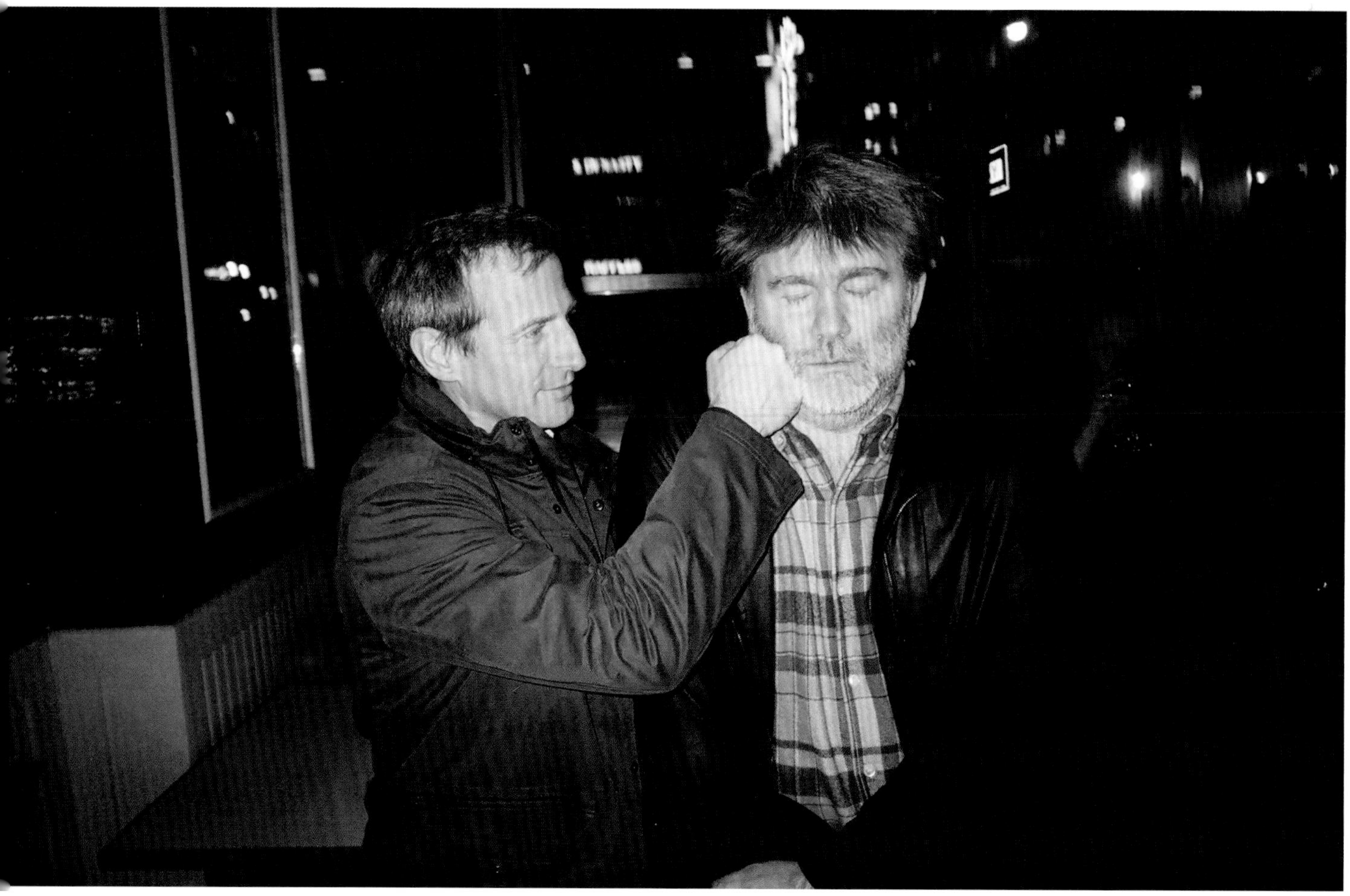

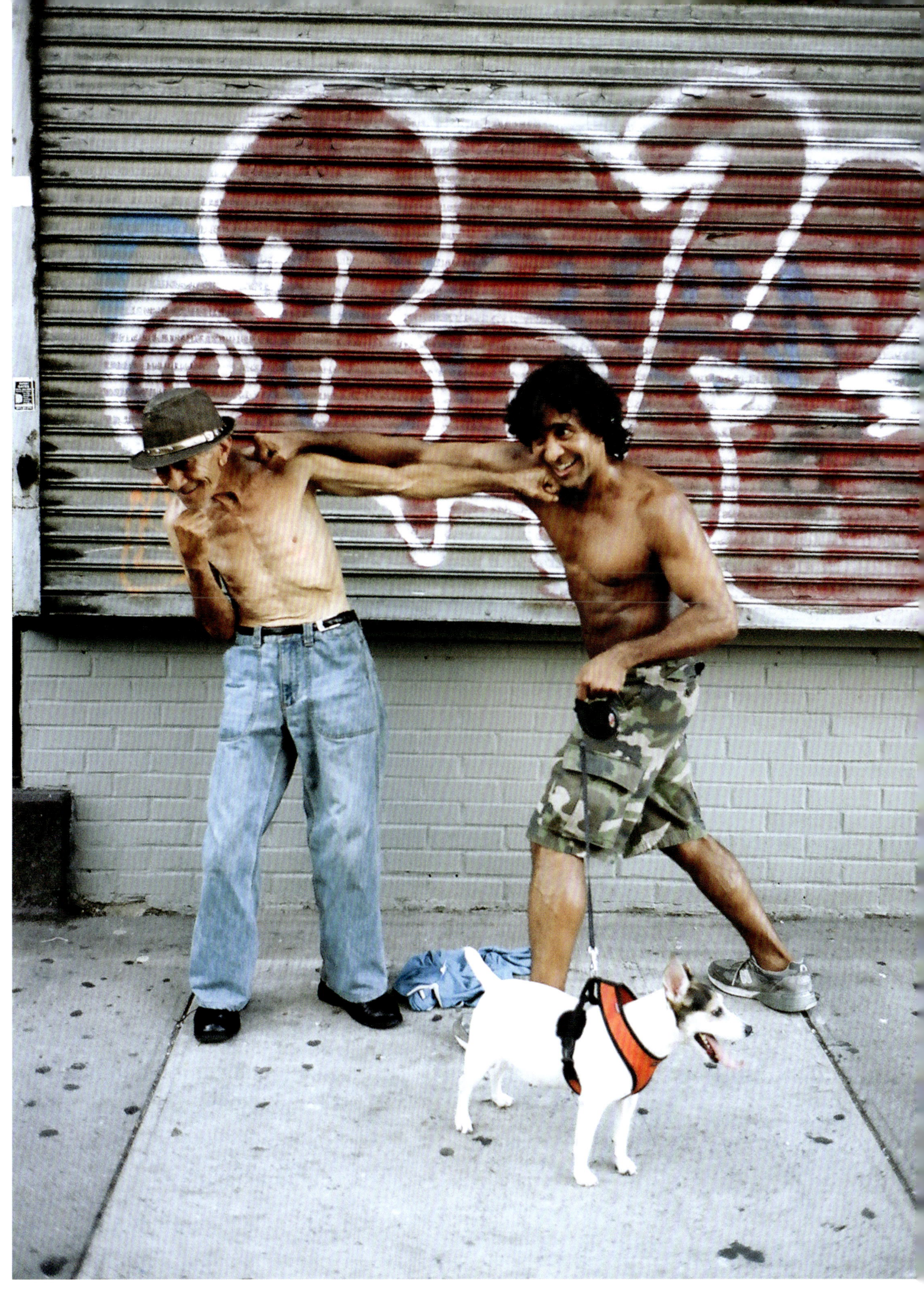

BRIDGE

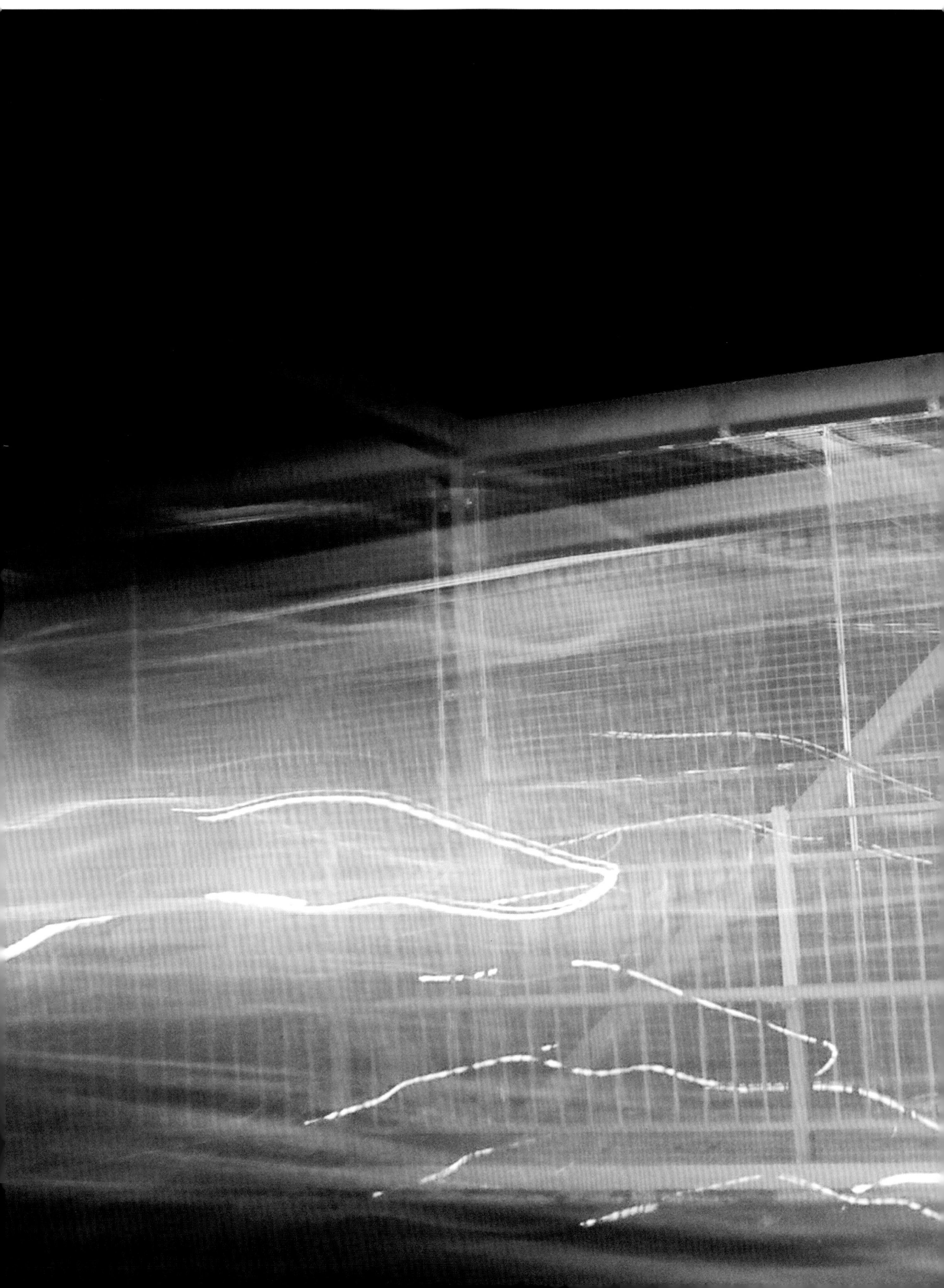

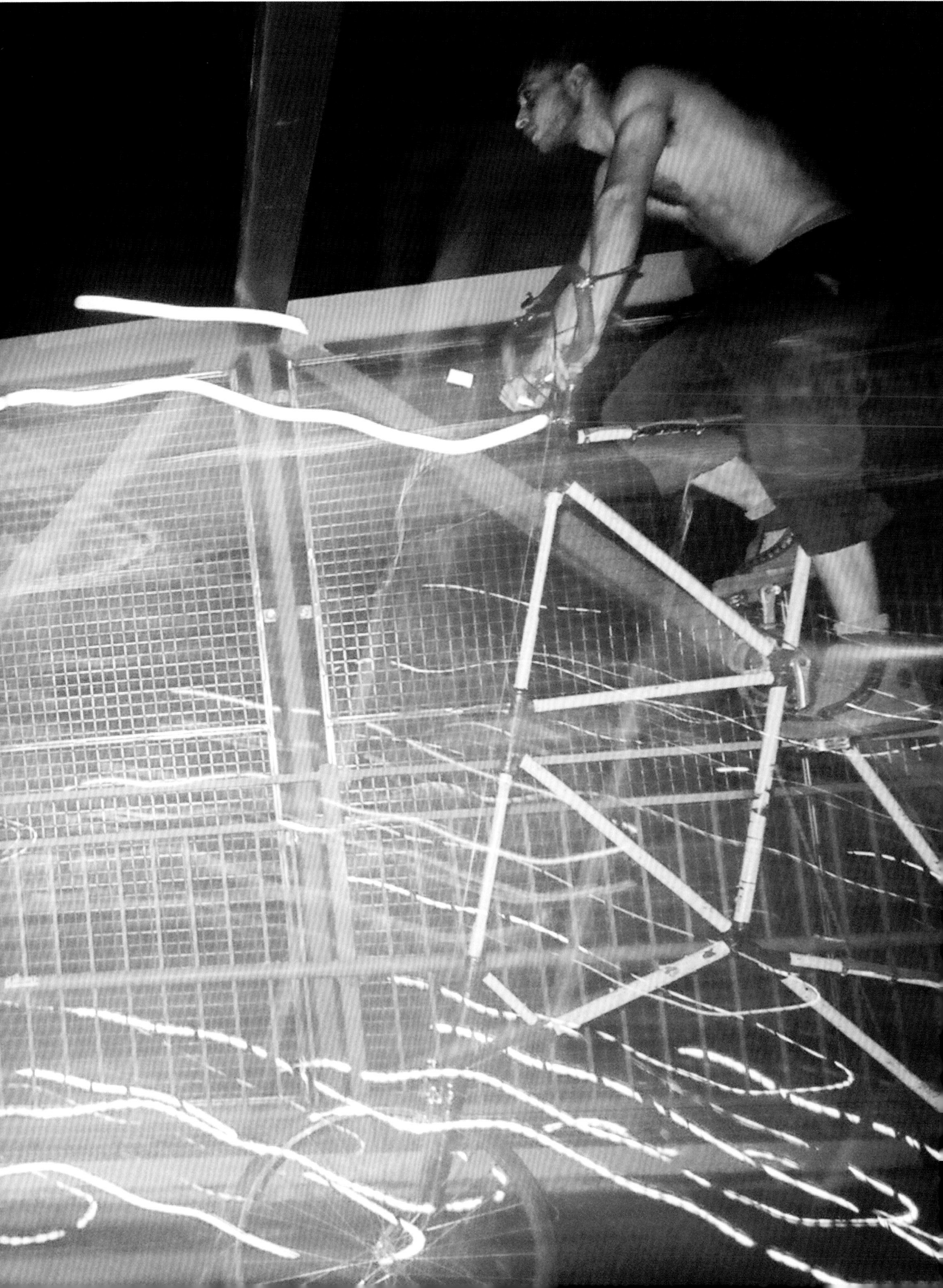

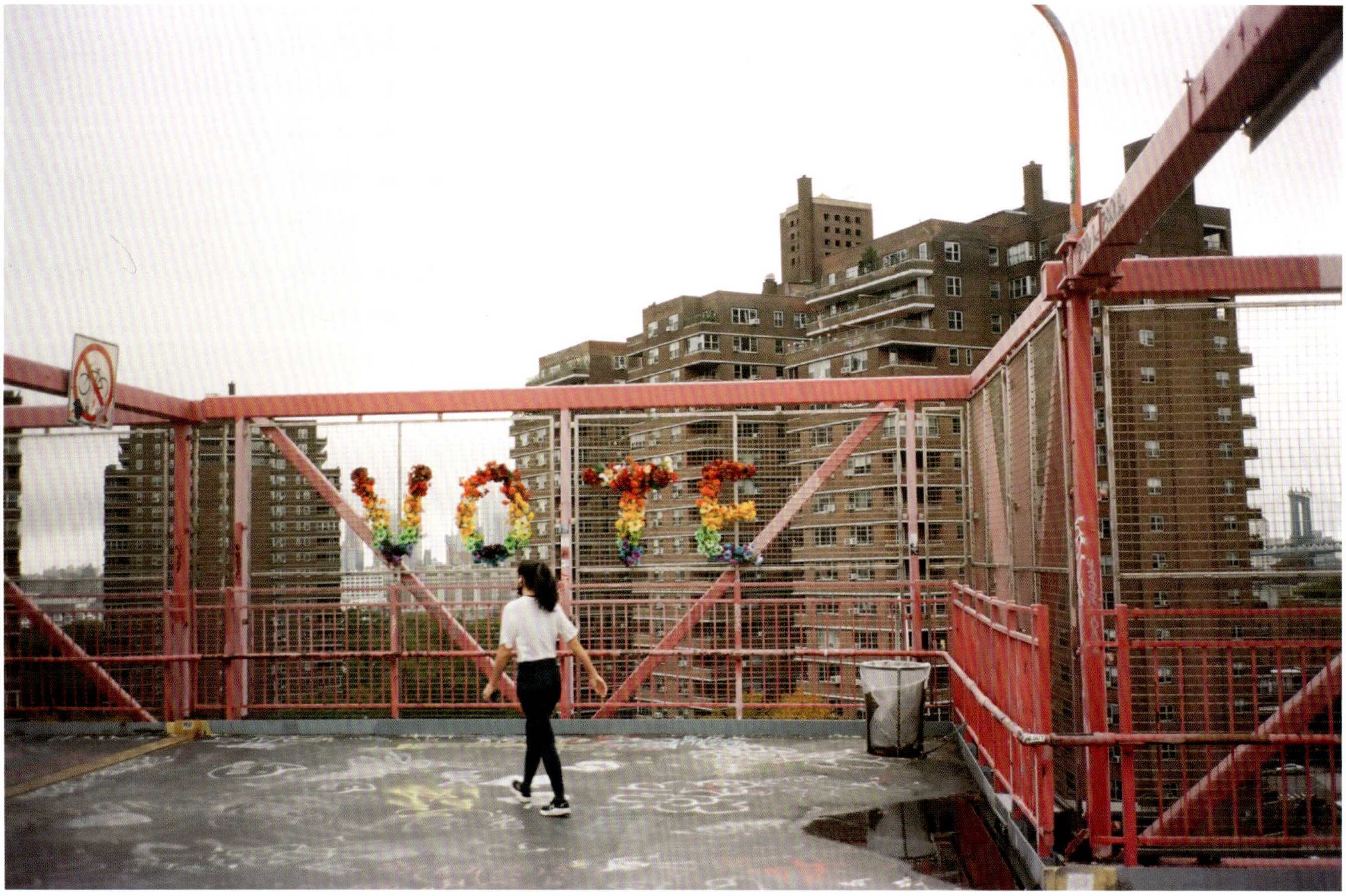

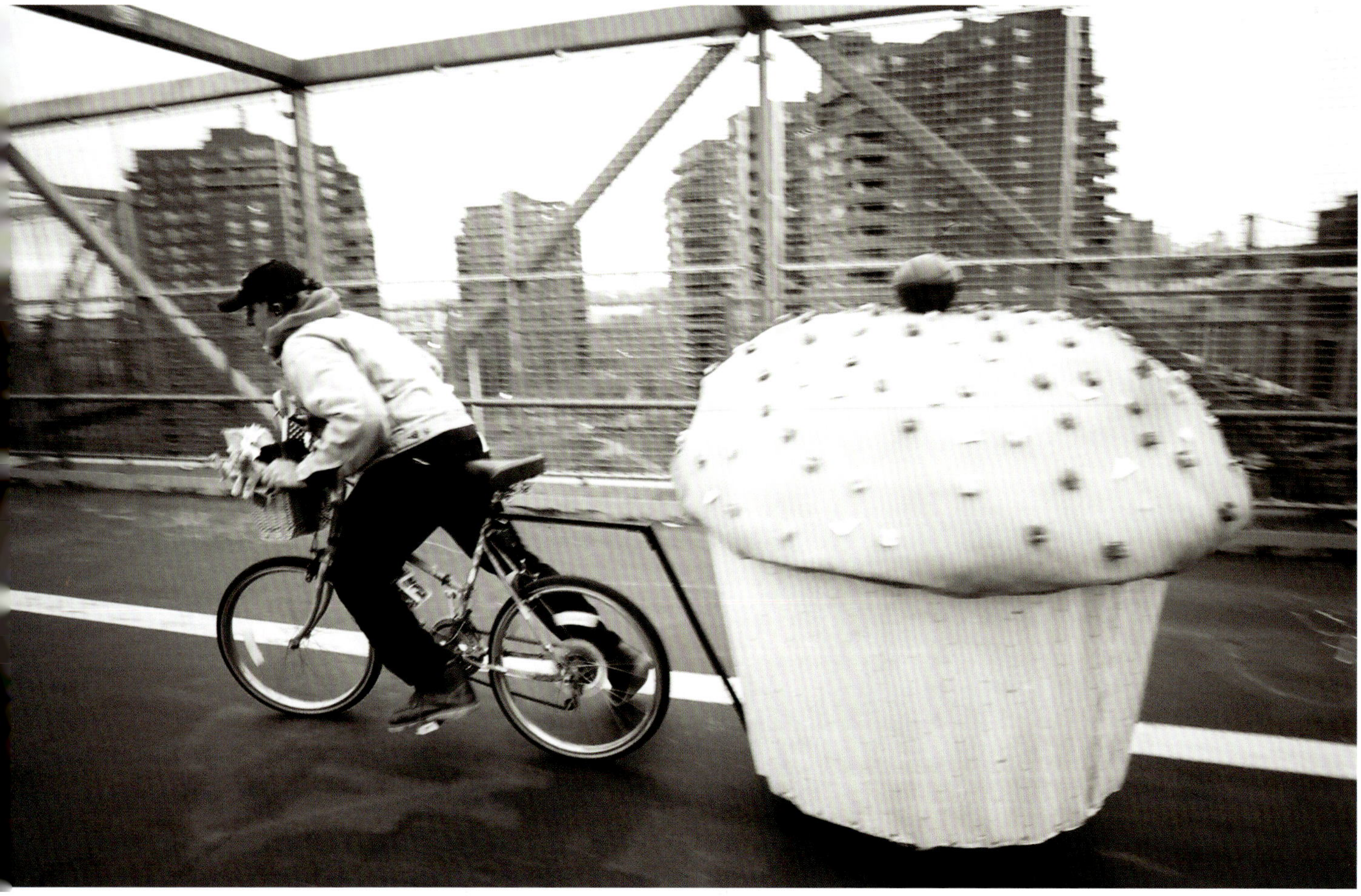

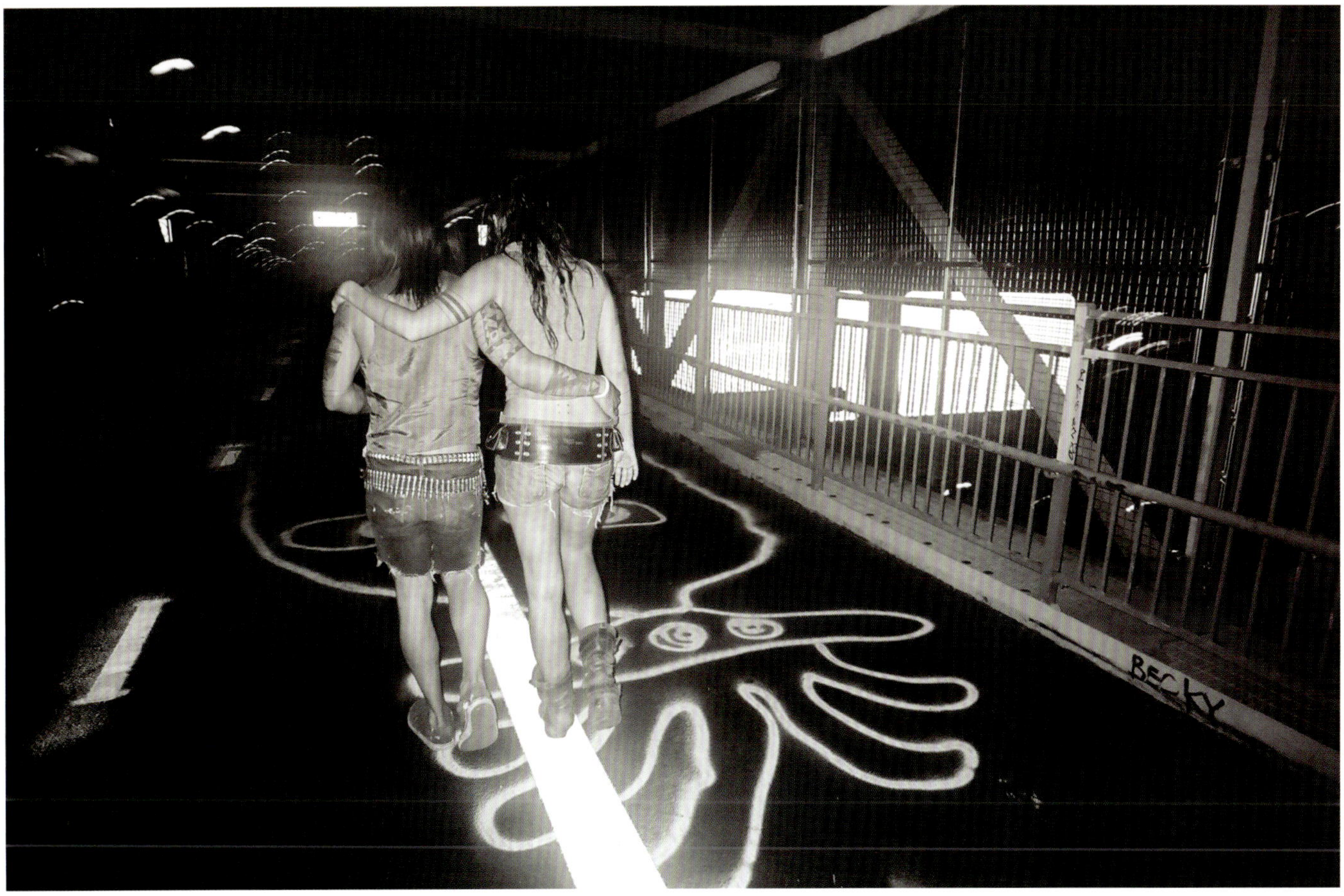

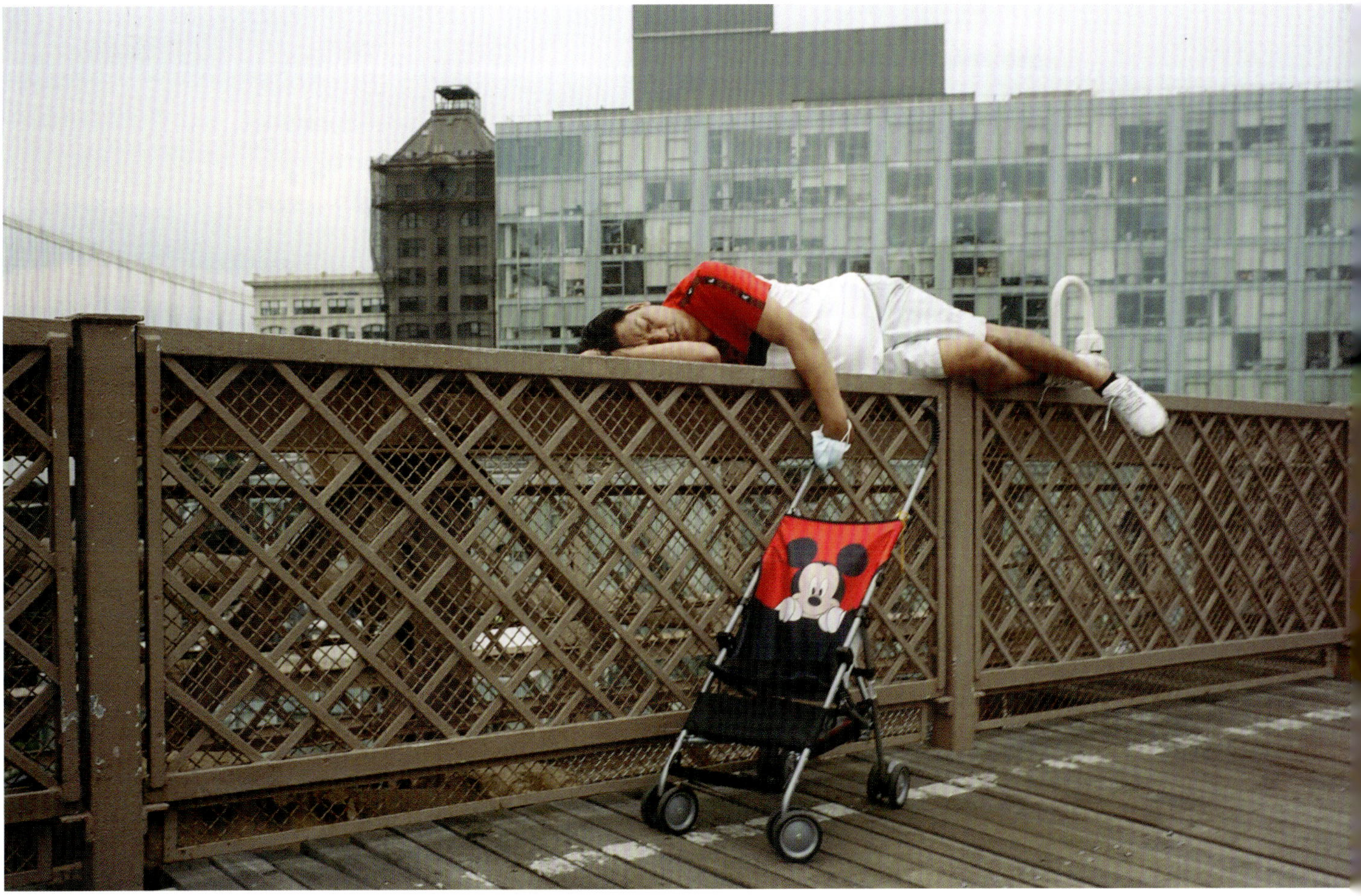

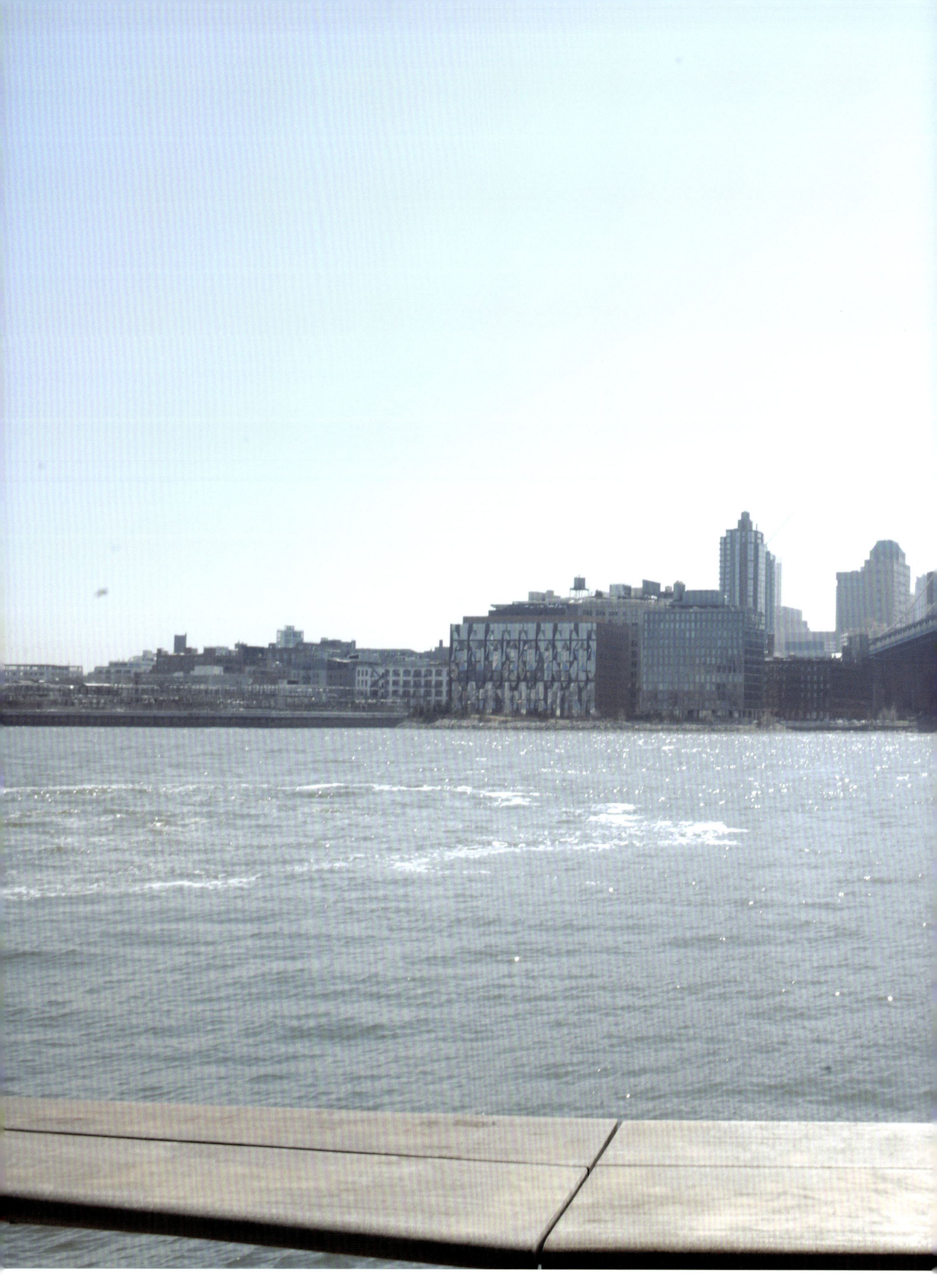

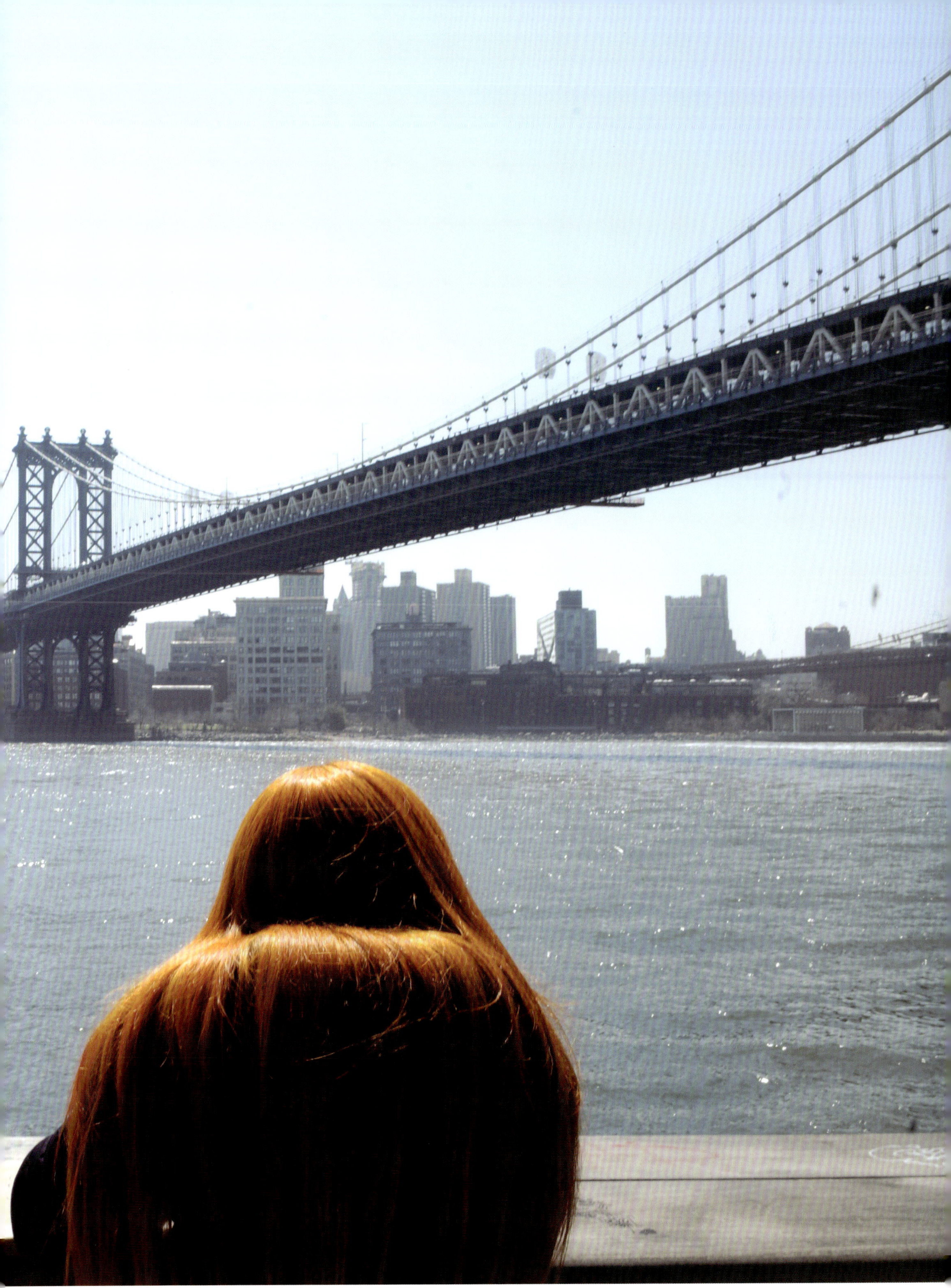

BROADWAY

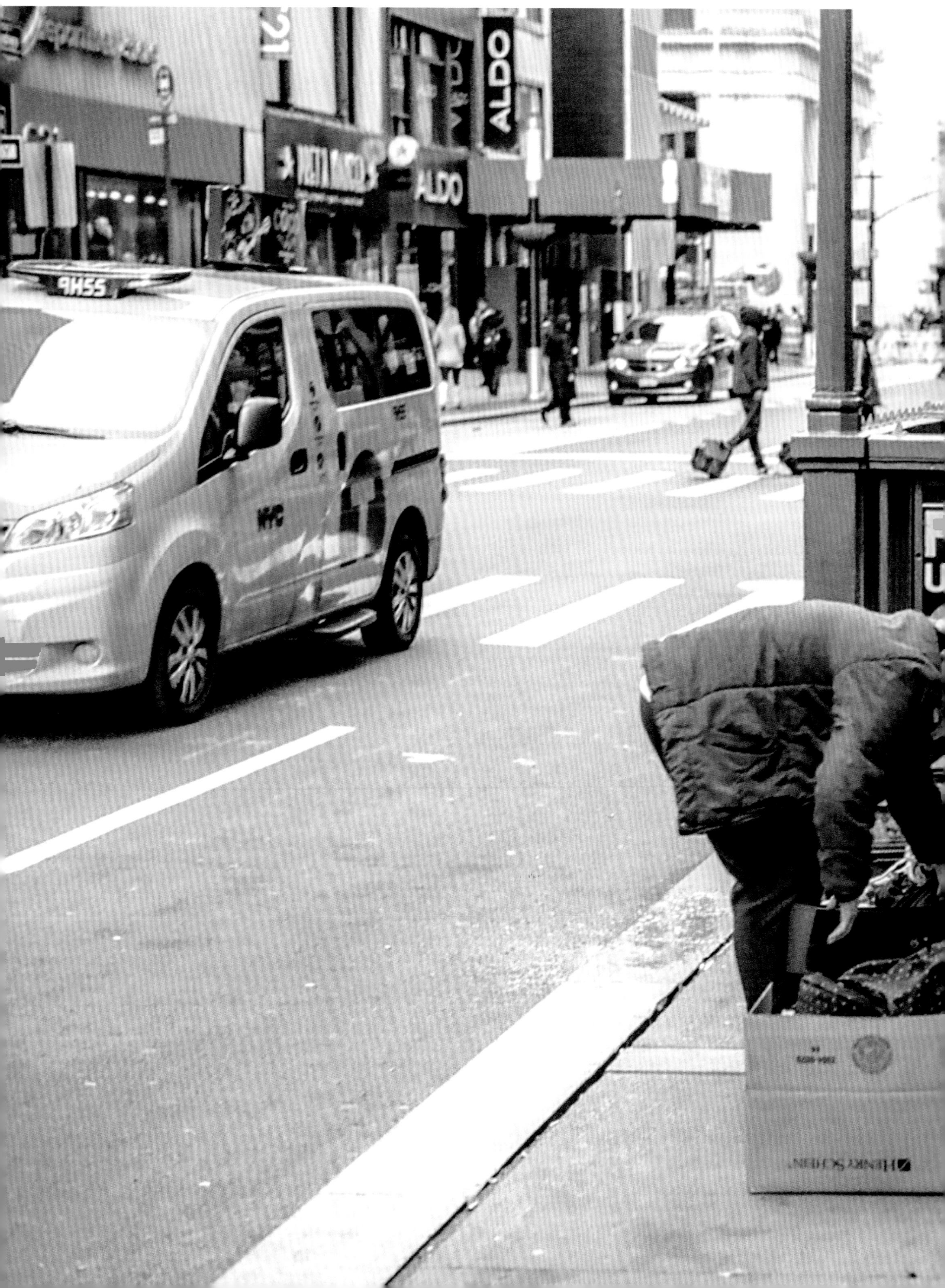

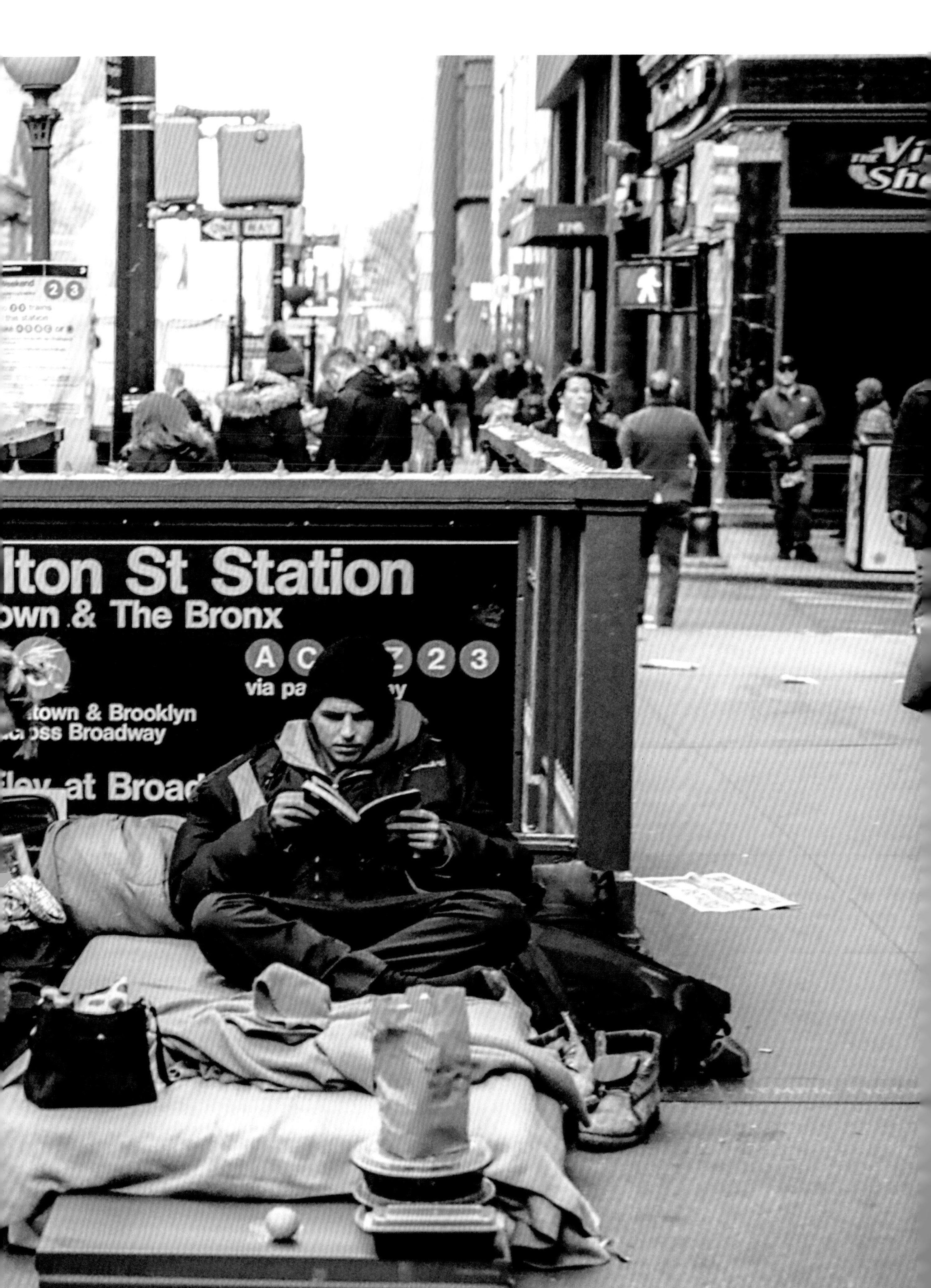
lton St Station
own & The Bronx
A 2 3
town & Brooklyn
ss Broadway
at Broad

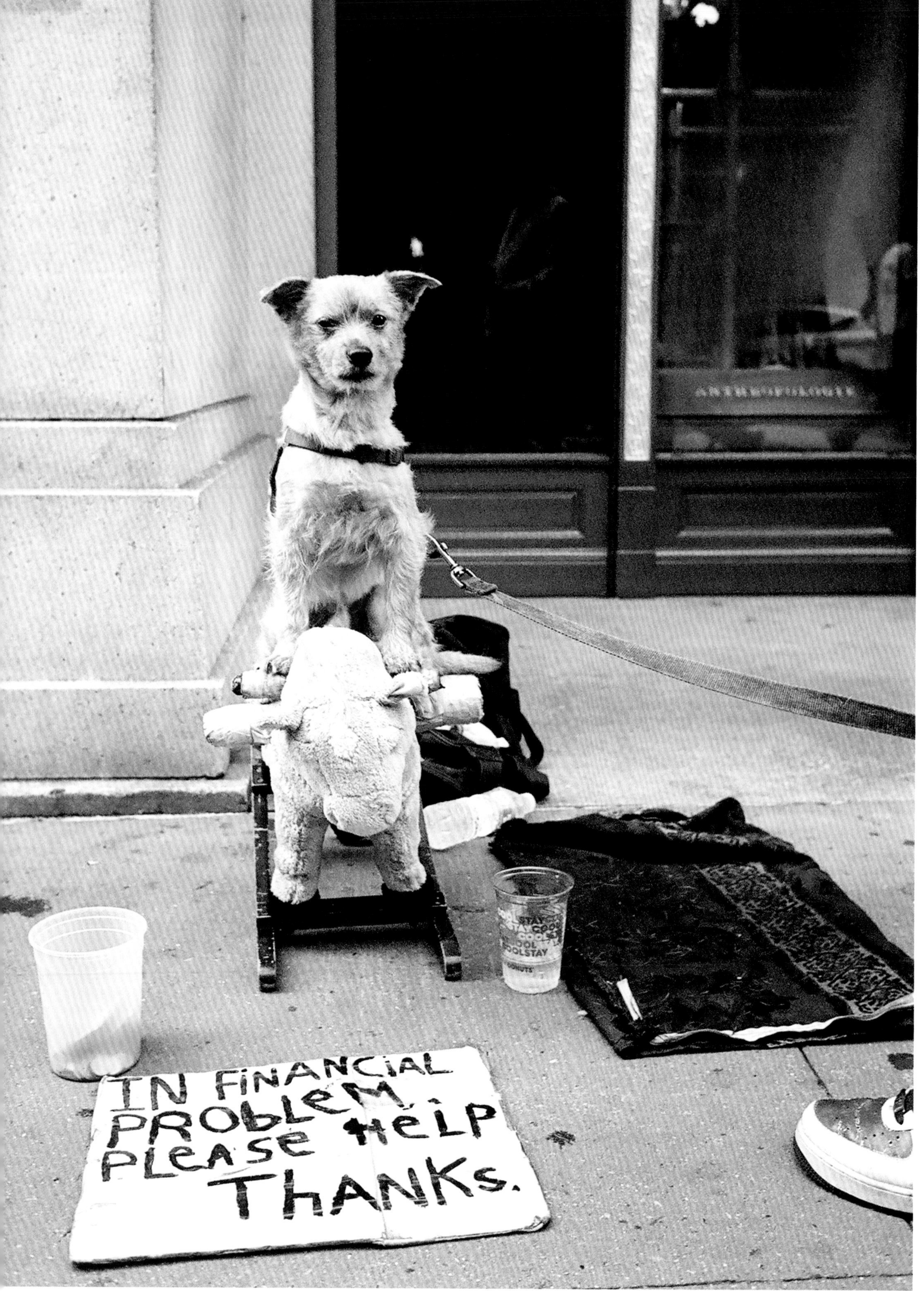
IN FINANCIAL
PROBLEM.
PLEASE HELP
THANKS.

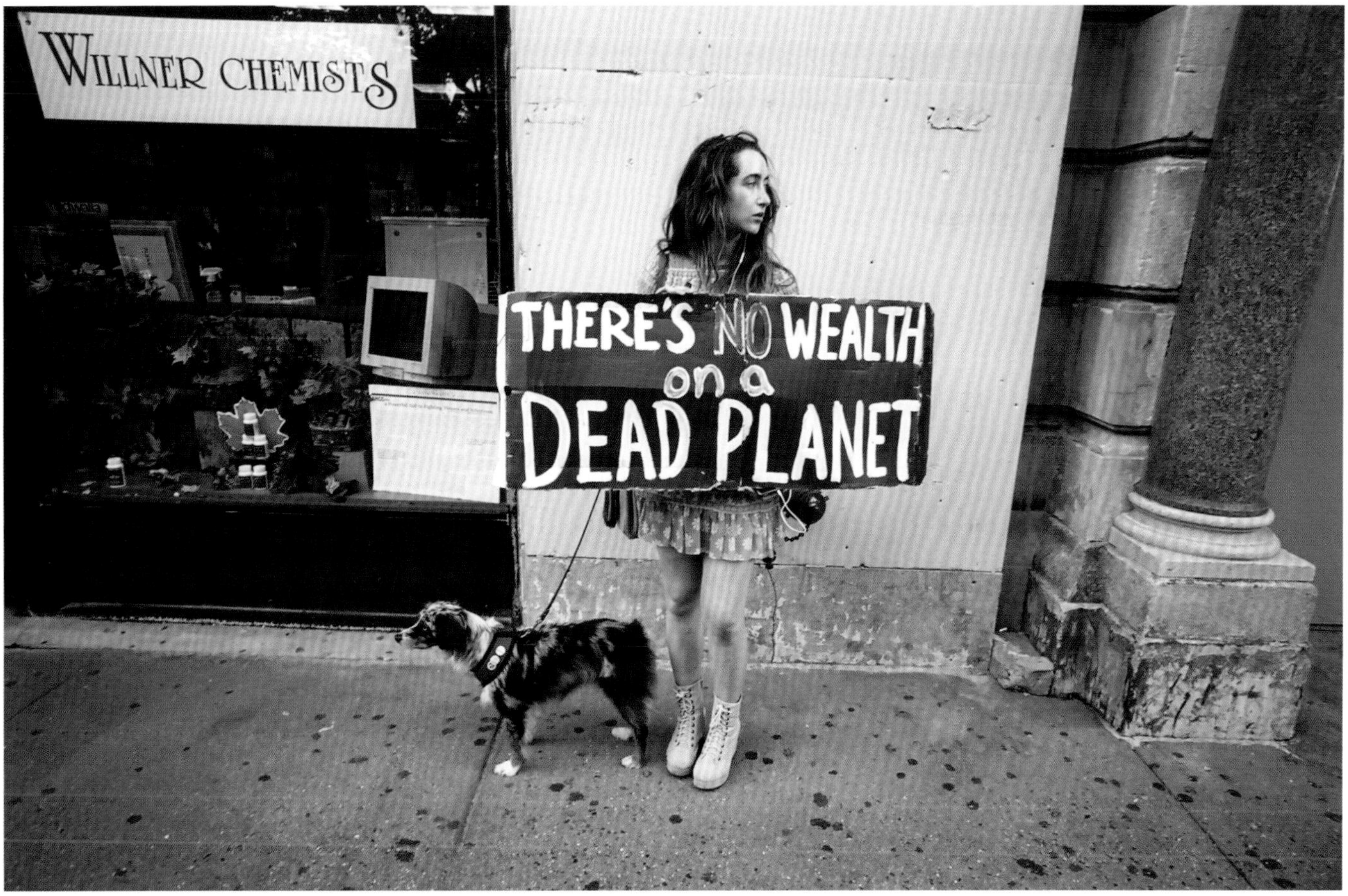
WILLNER CHEMISTS
THERE'S NO WEALTH
on a
DEAD PLANET

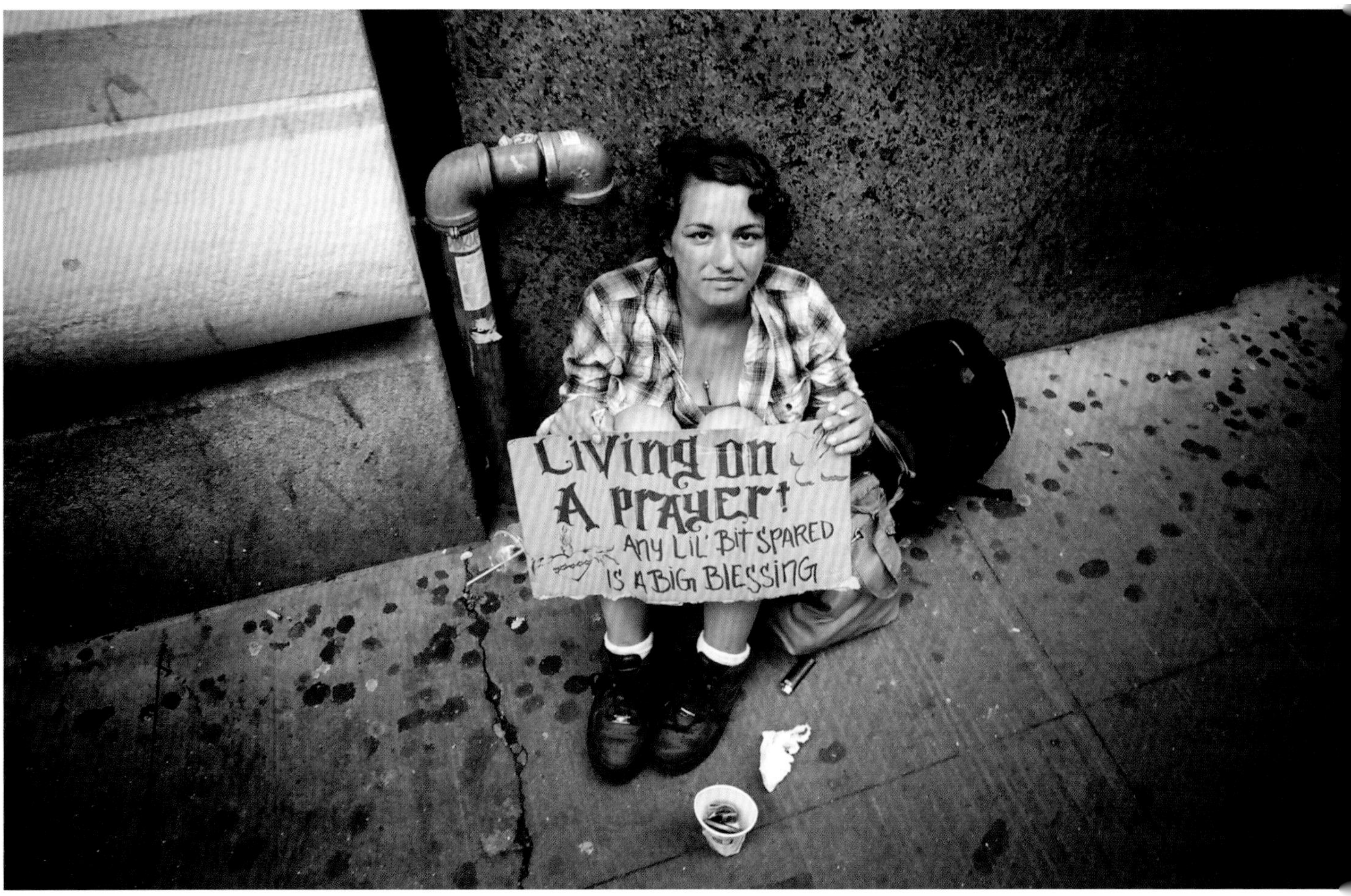
Living on
A prayer!
Any Lil' Bit Spared
Is A Big Blessing

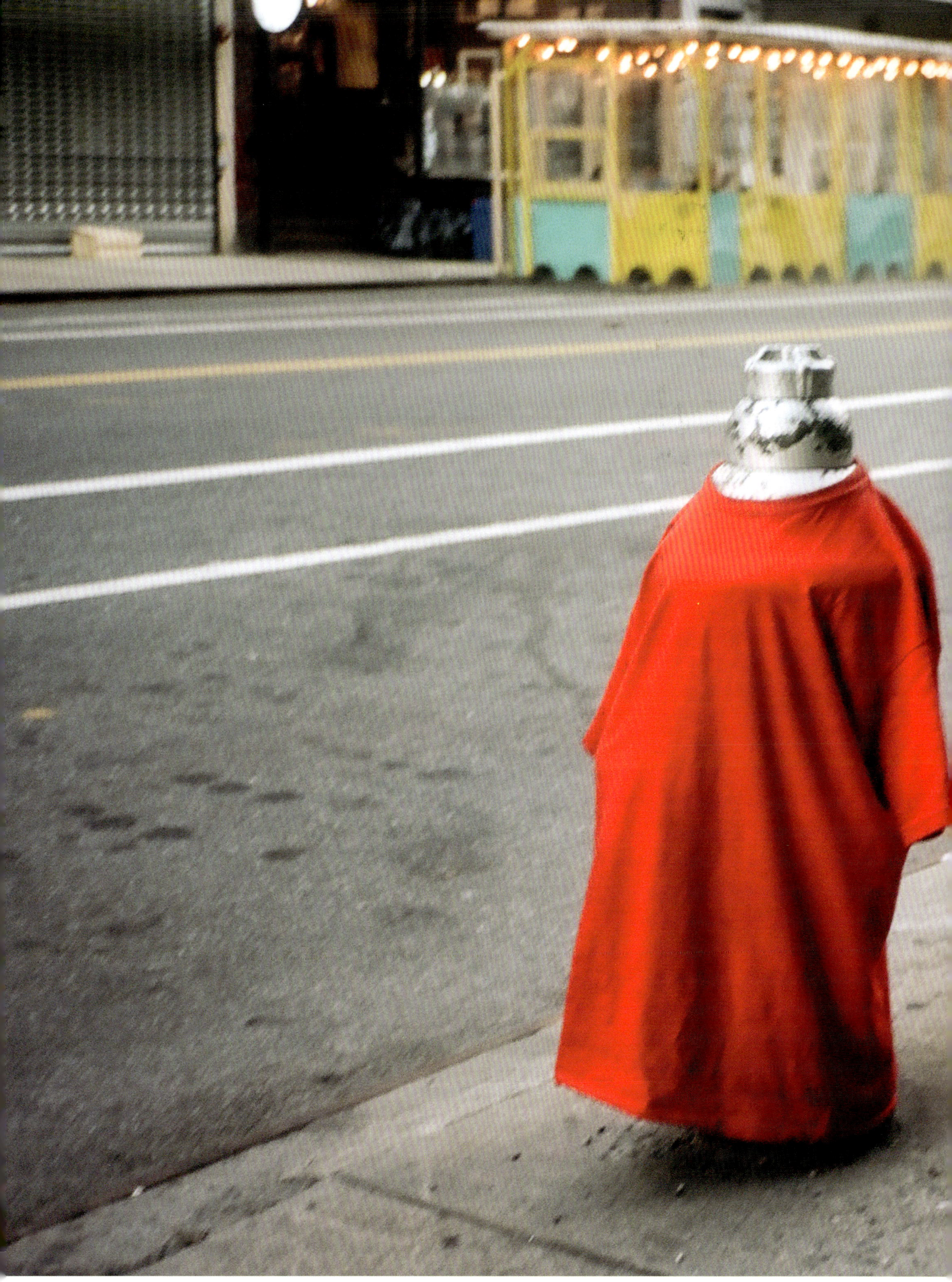

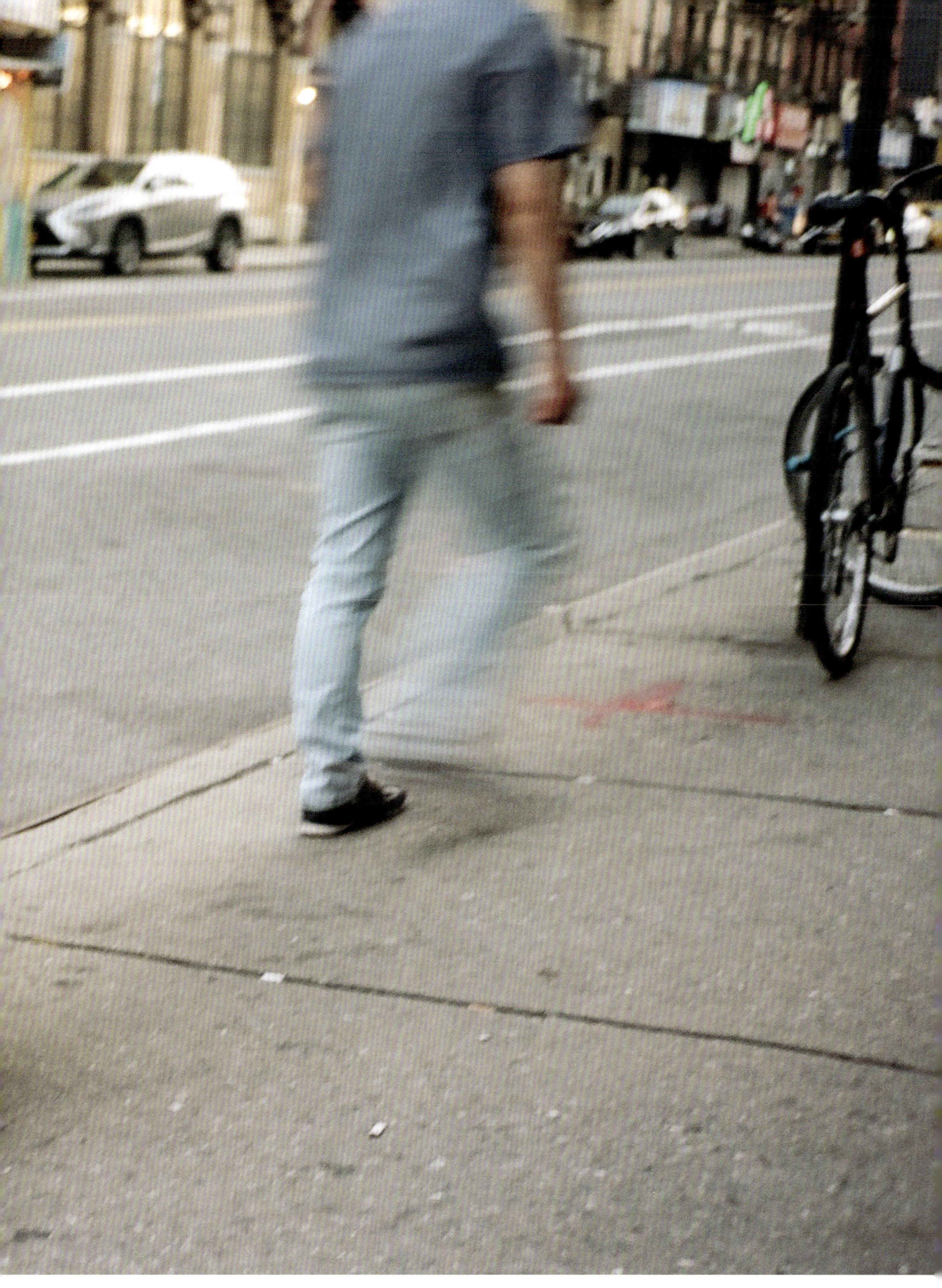

BUNNY

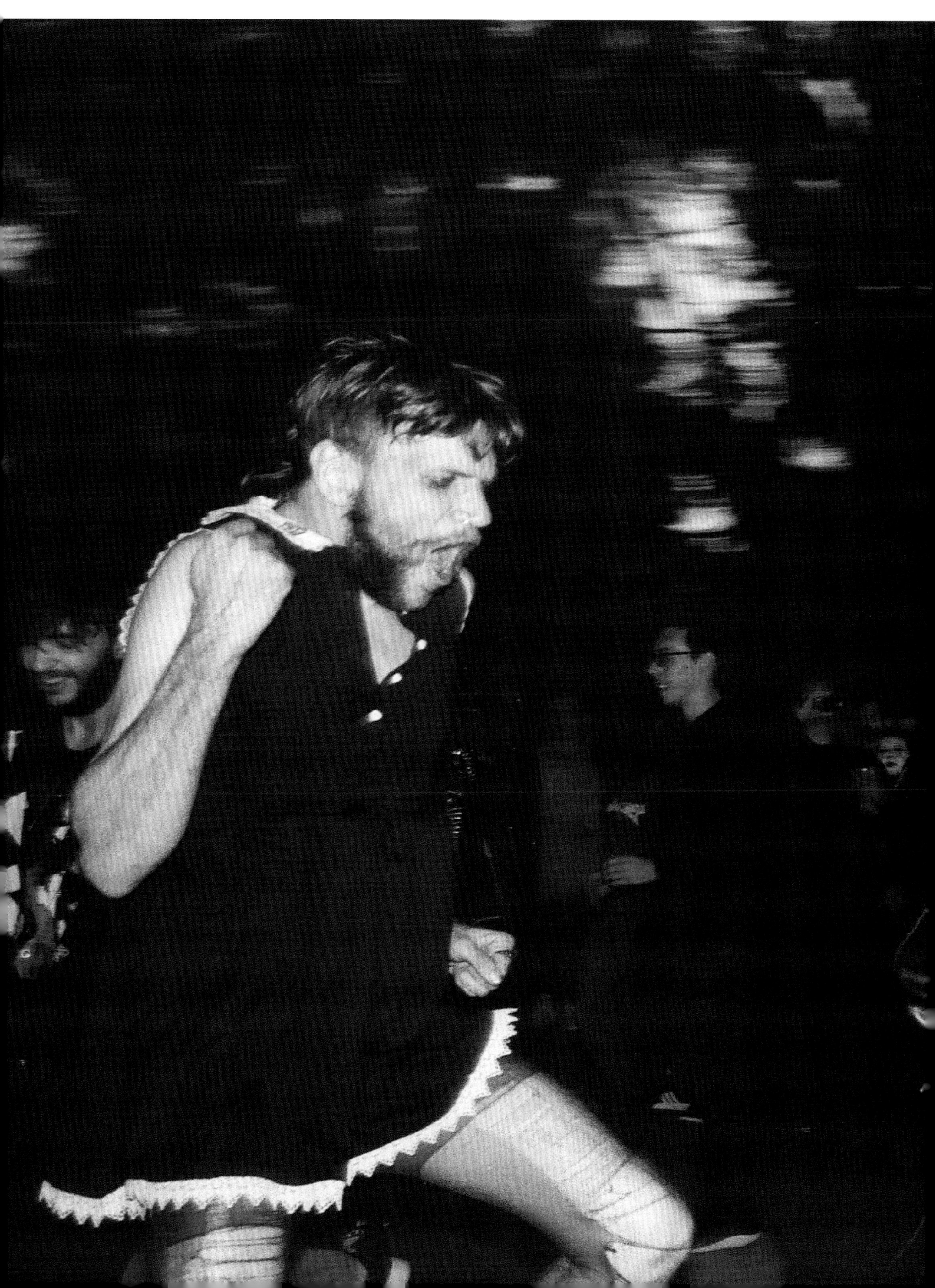

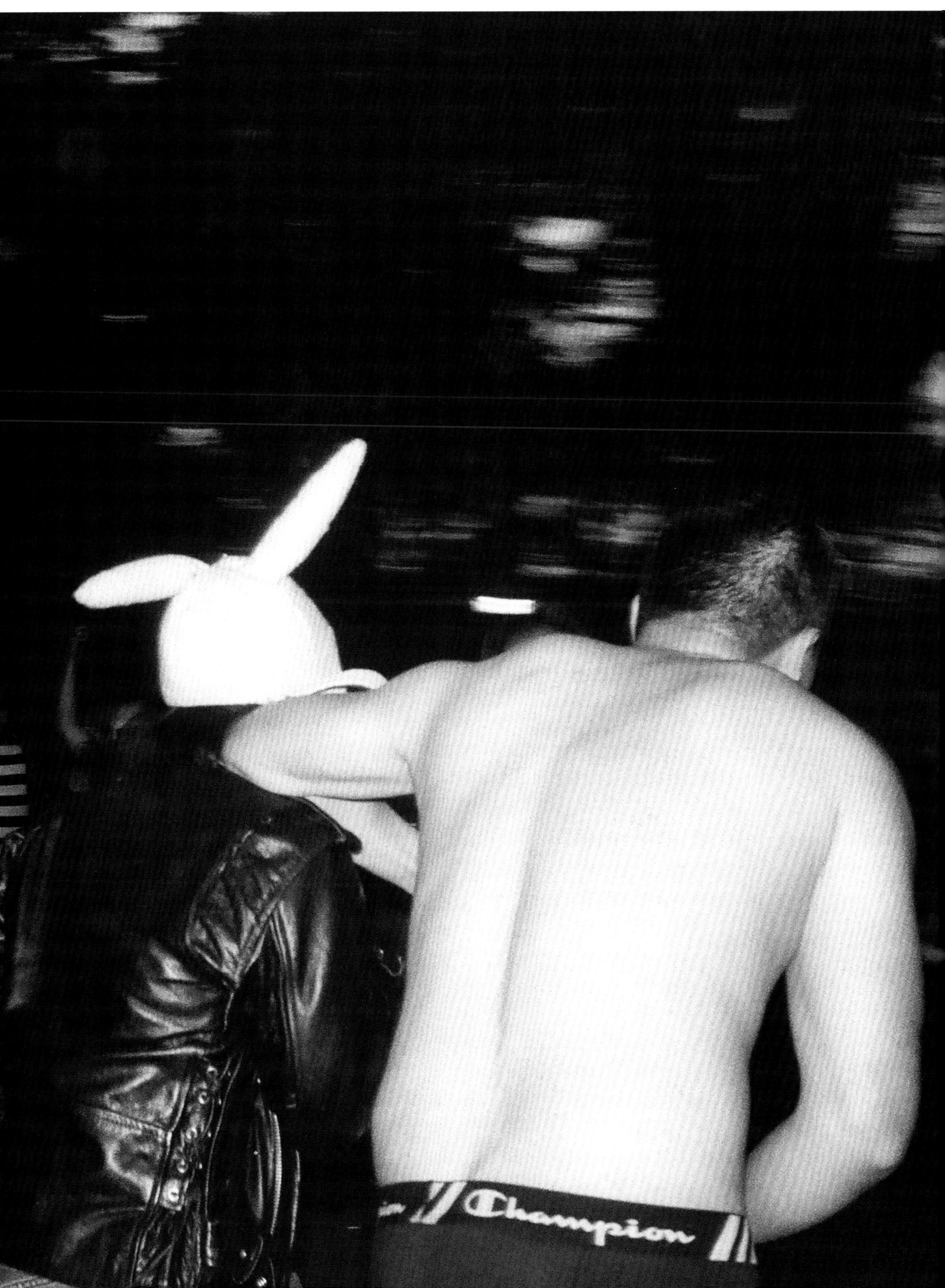
Champion

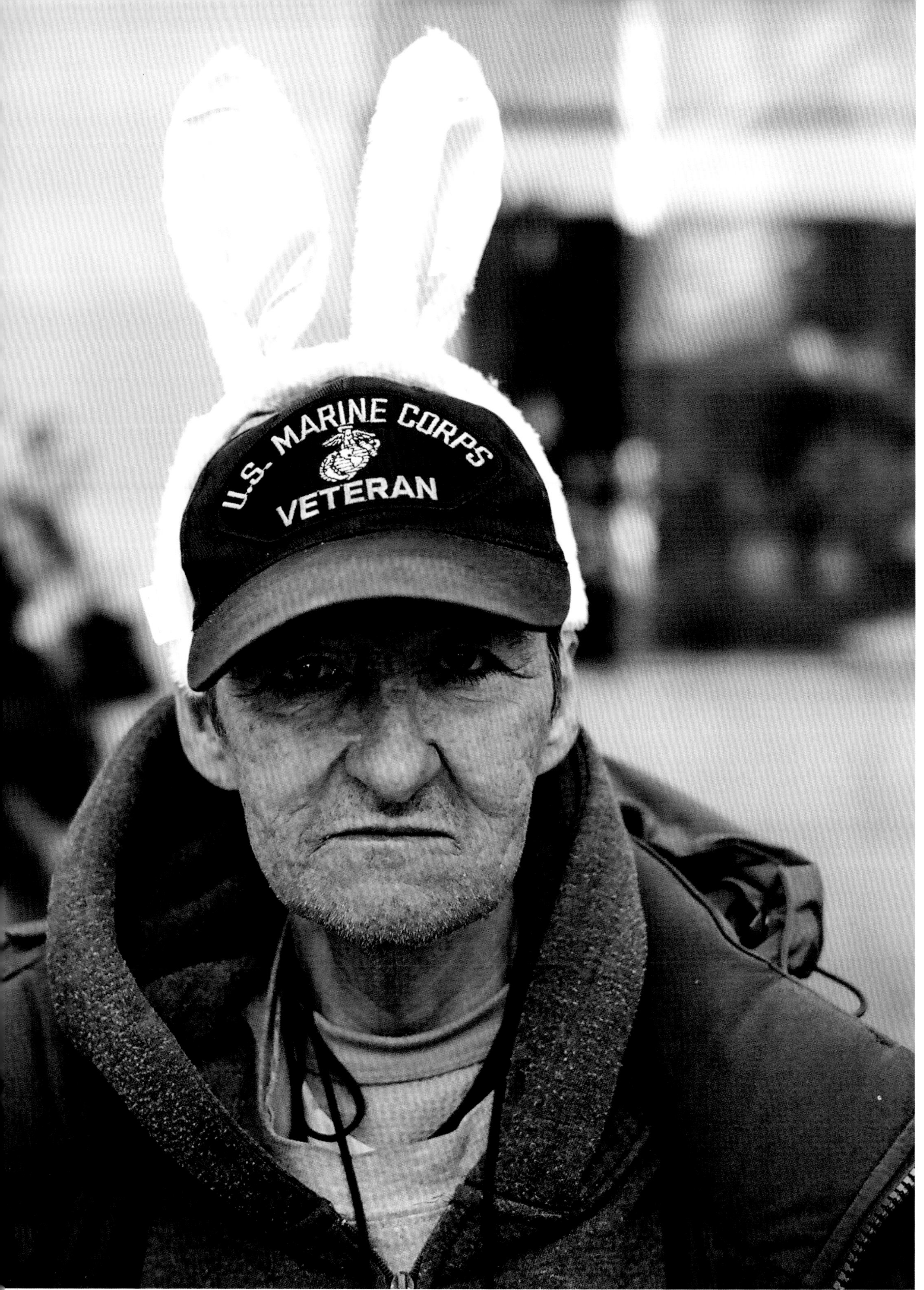
U.S. MARINE CORPS
VETERAN

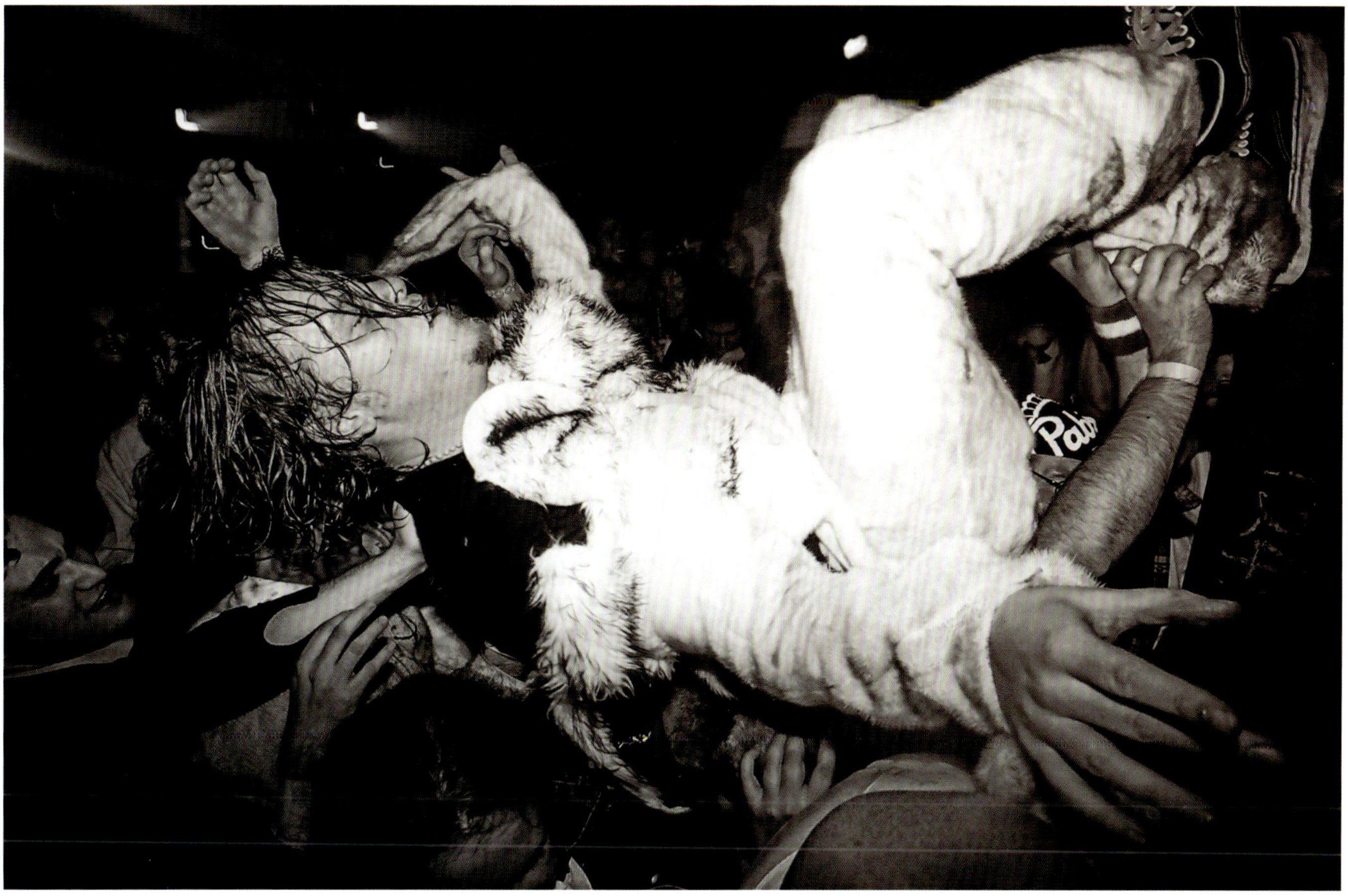

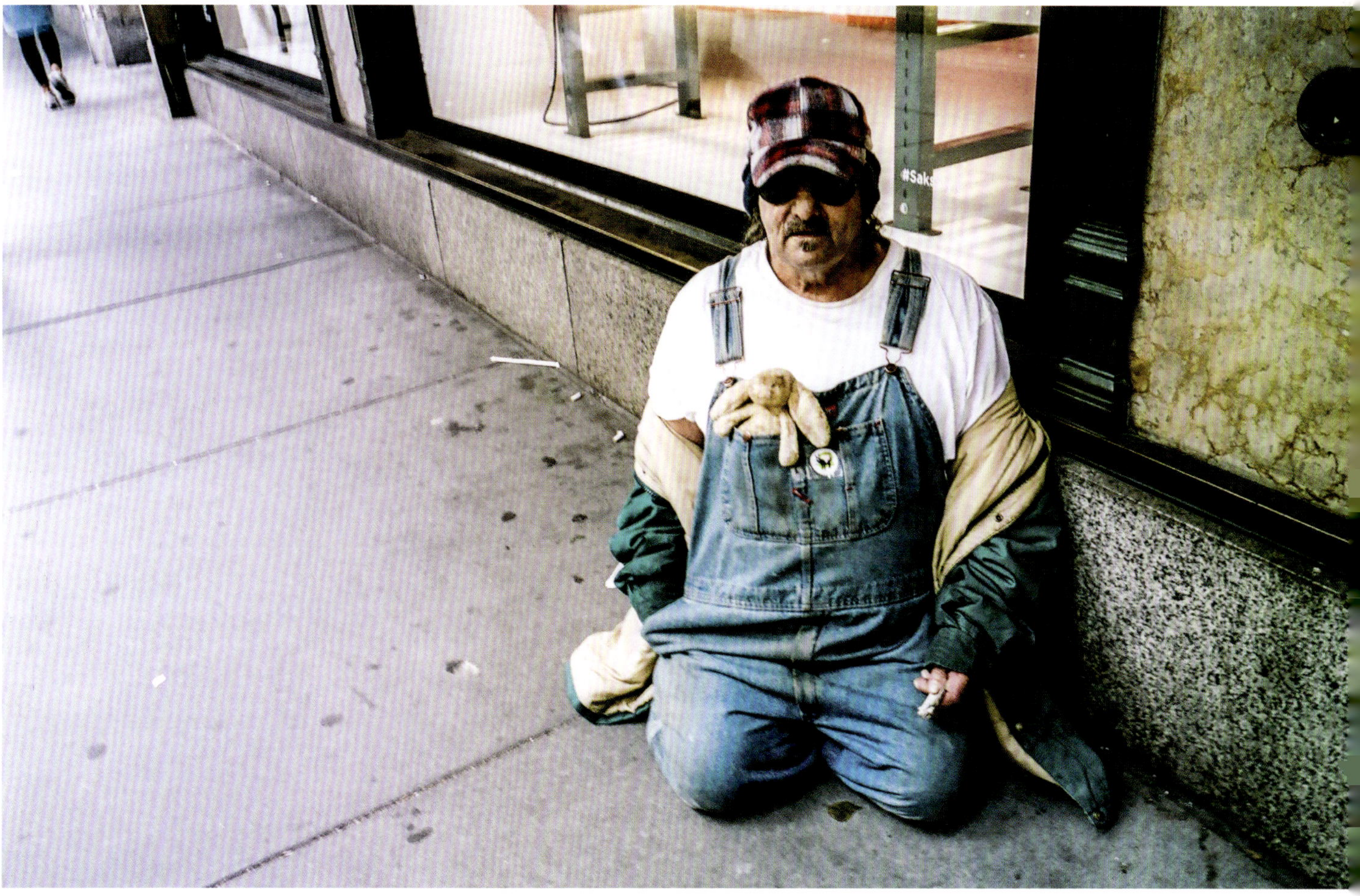

CALL

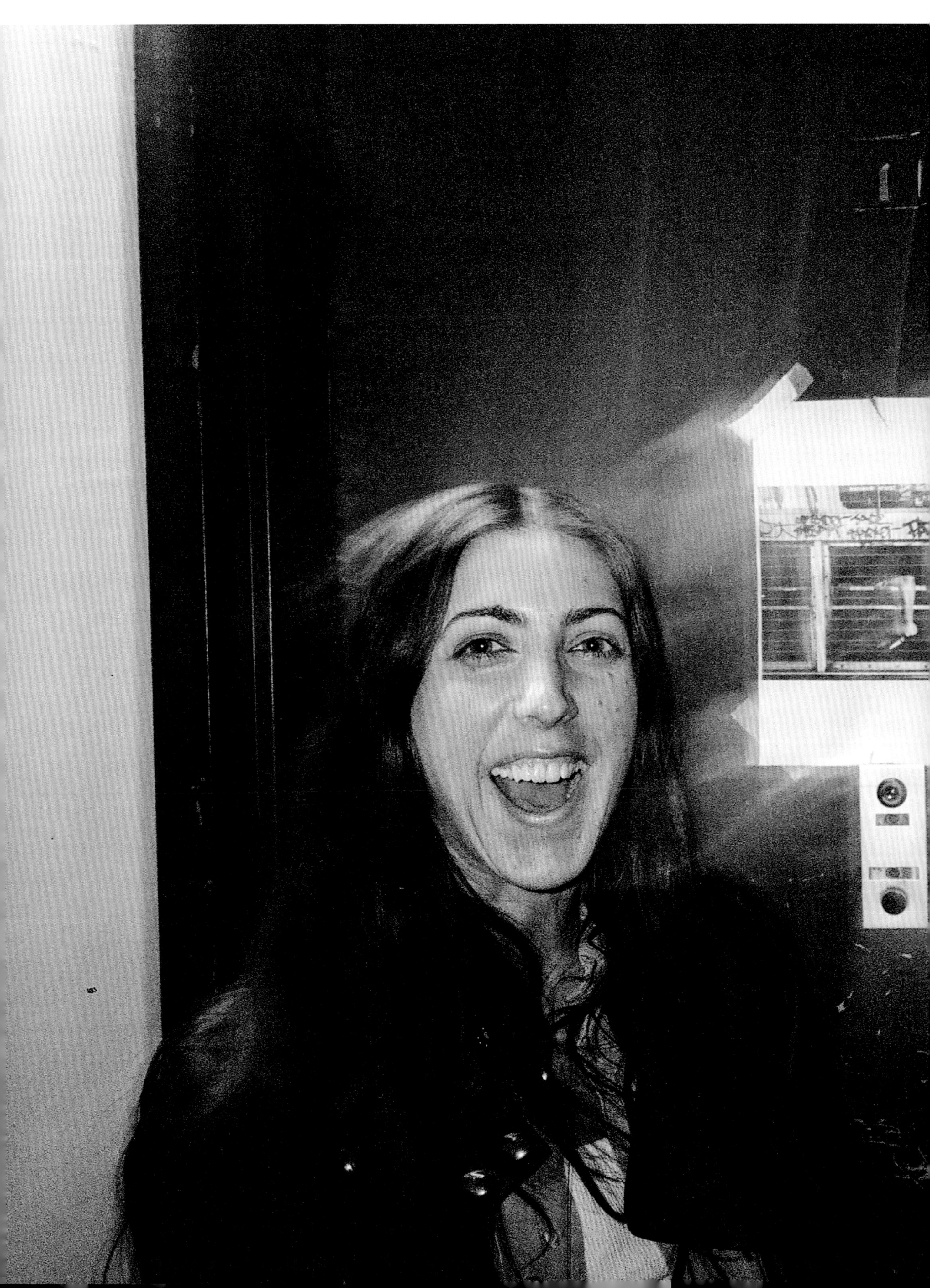

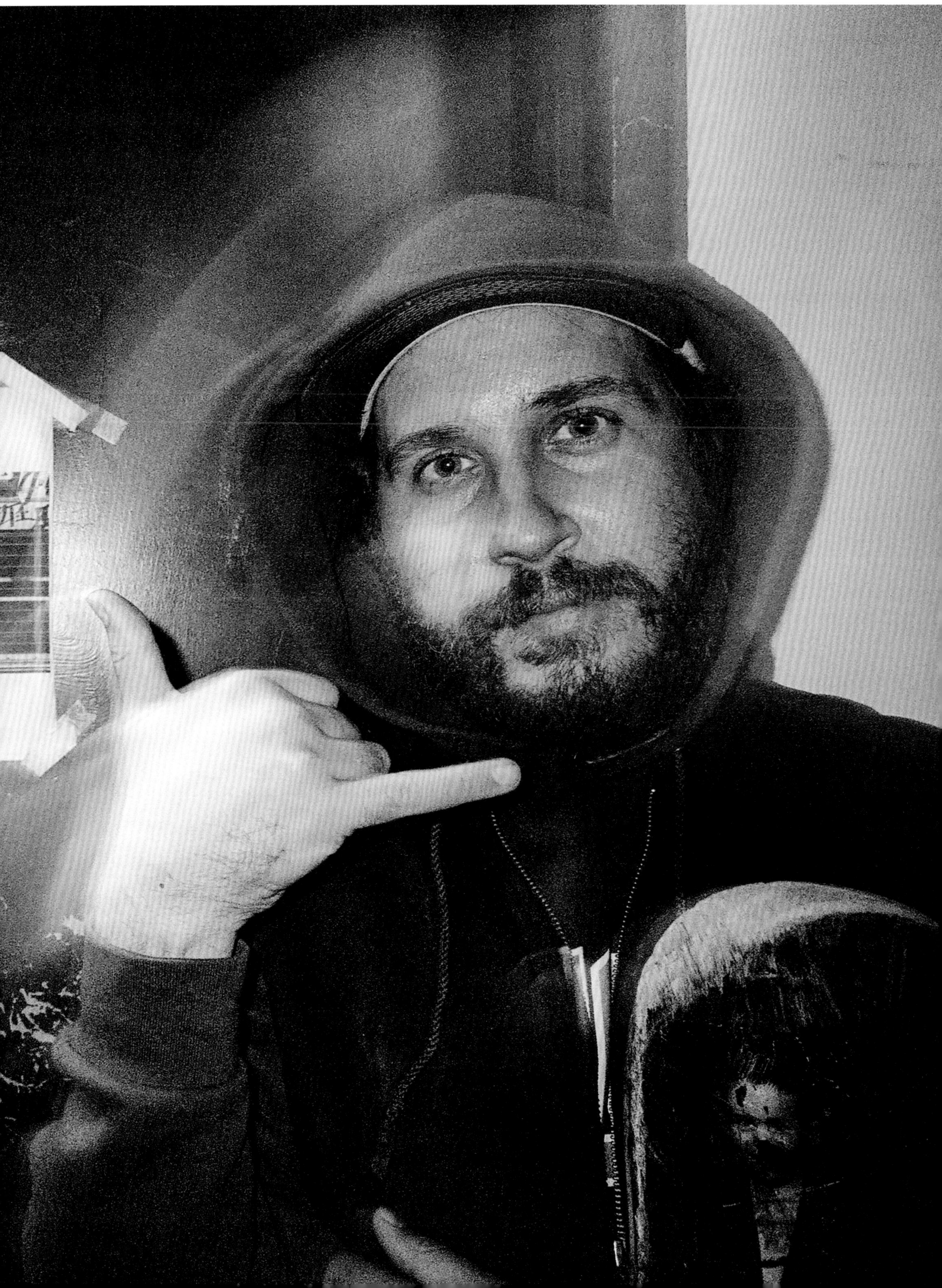

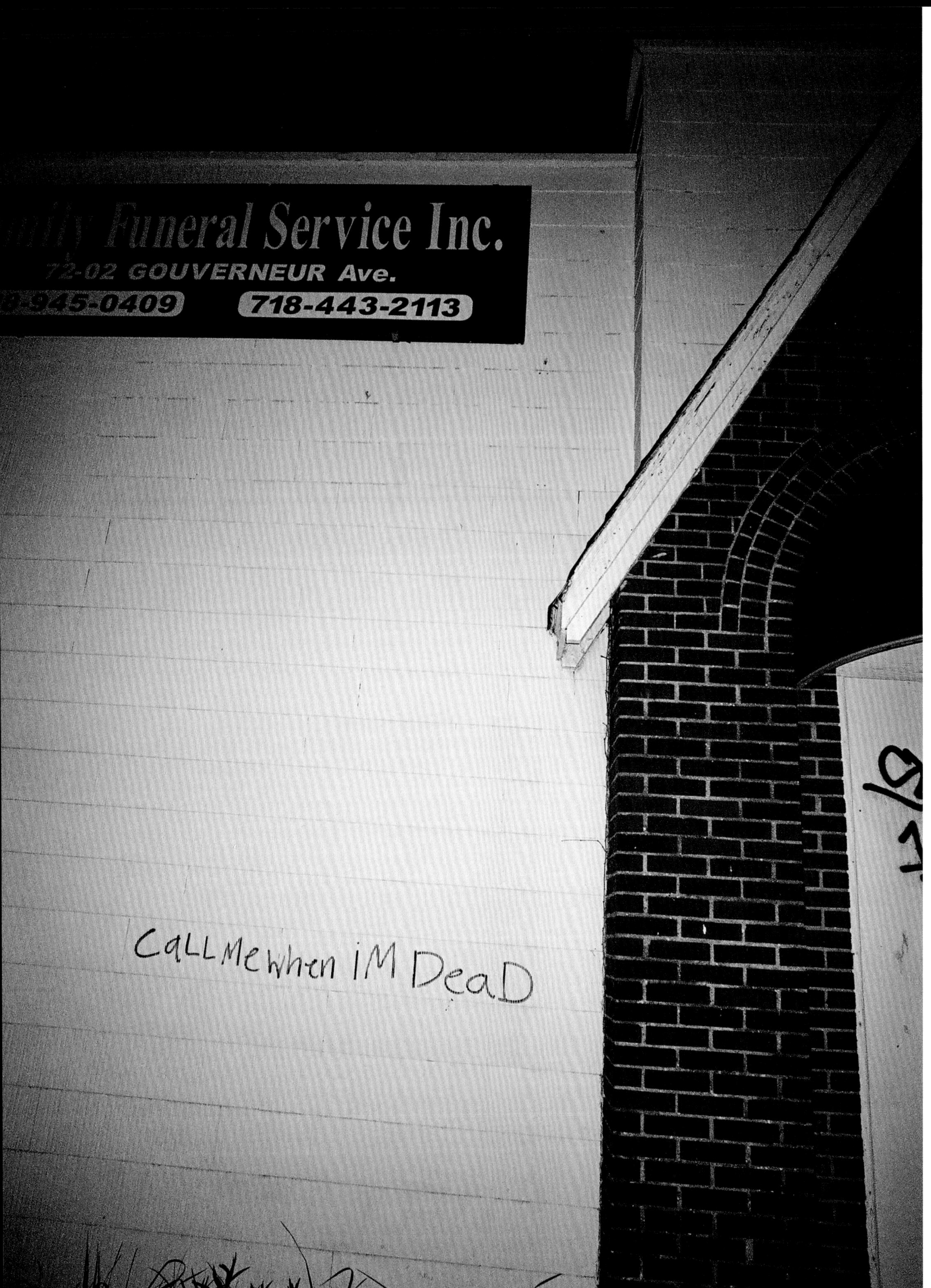
Funeral Service Inc.
72-02 GOUVERNEUR Ave.
945-0409
718-443-2113
CaLL Me When IM DeaD

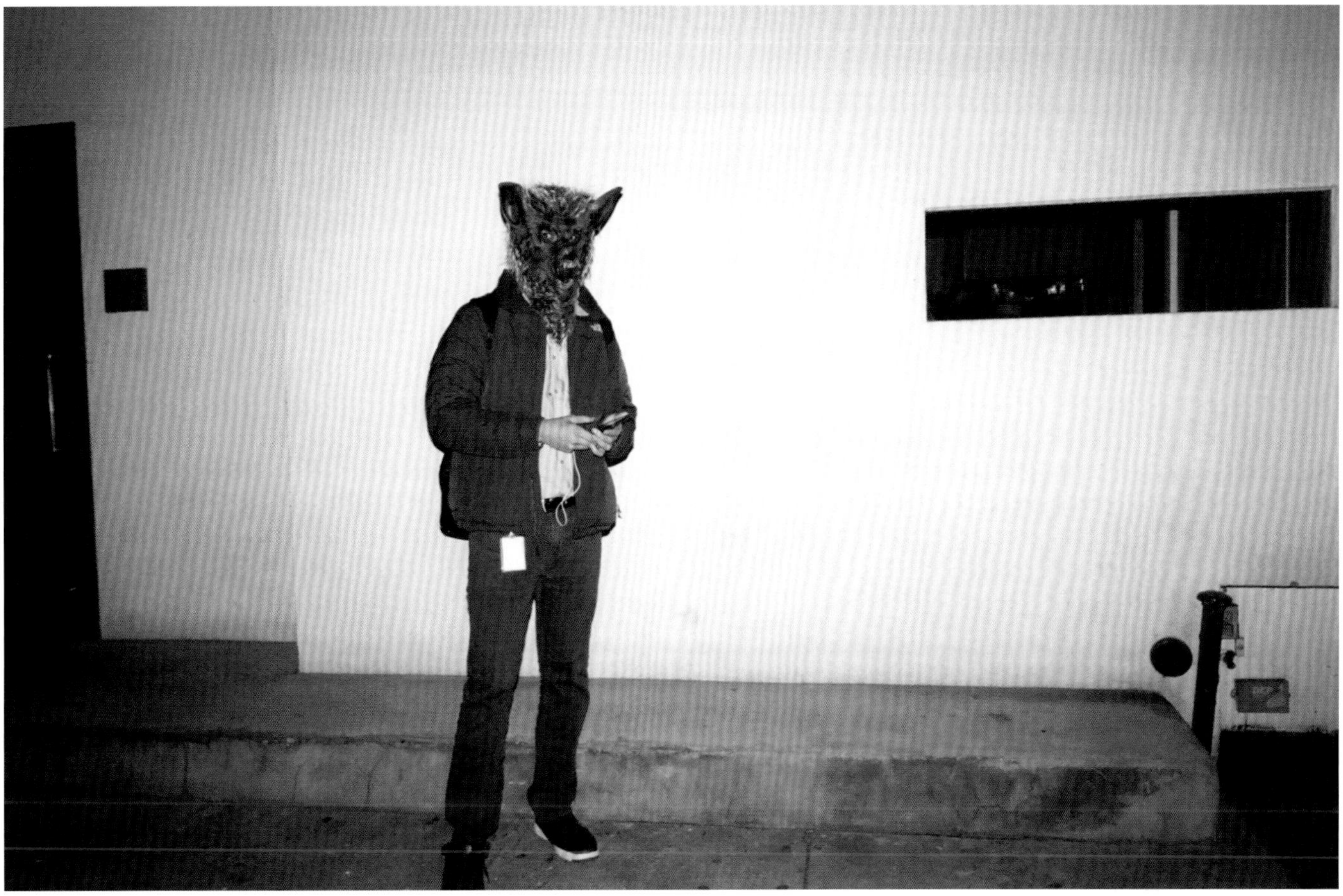

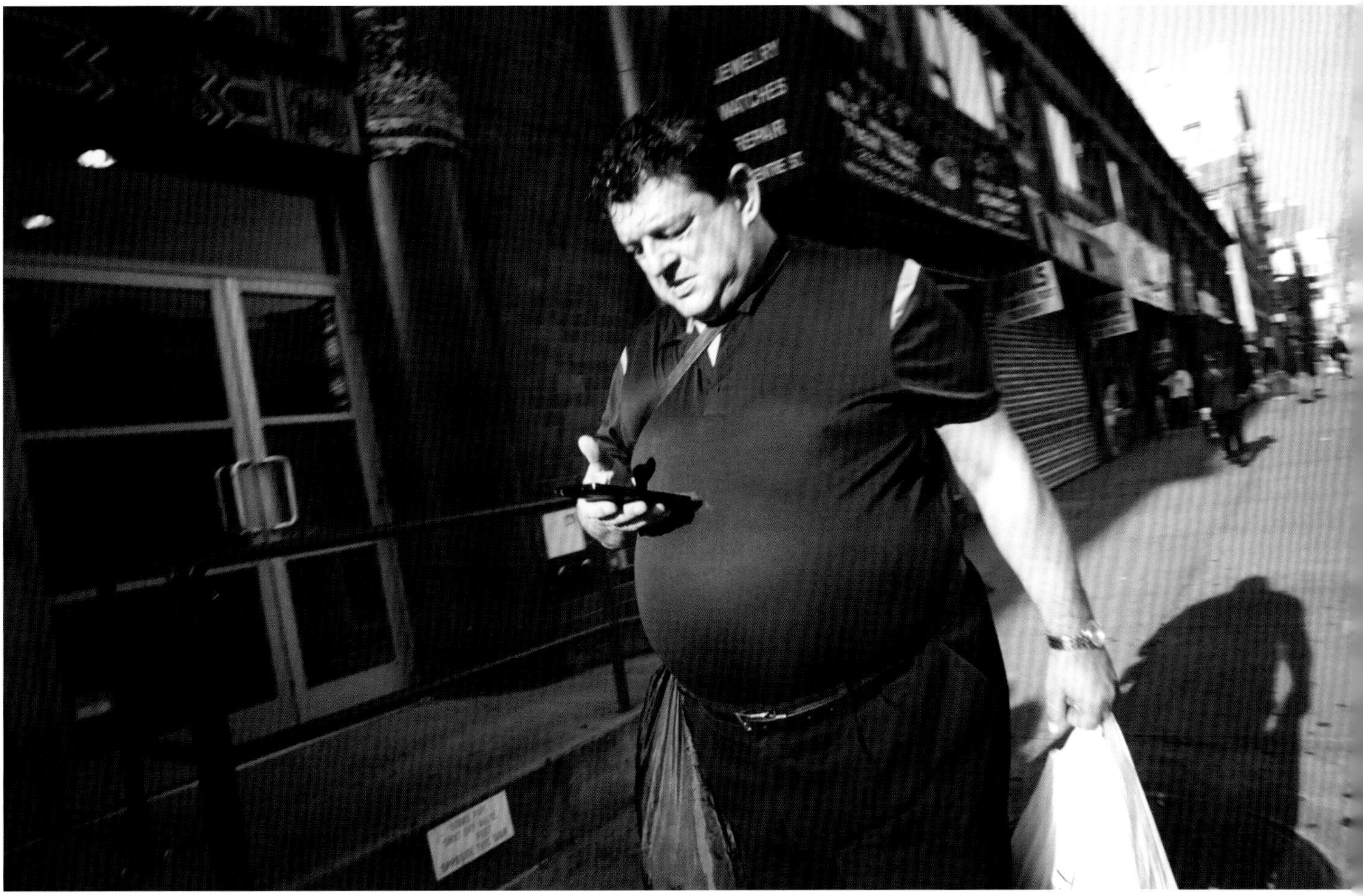
JEWELRY
WATCHES
REPAIR

COP

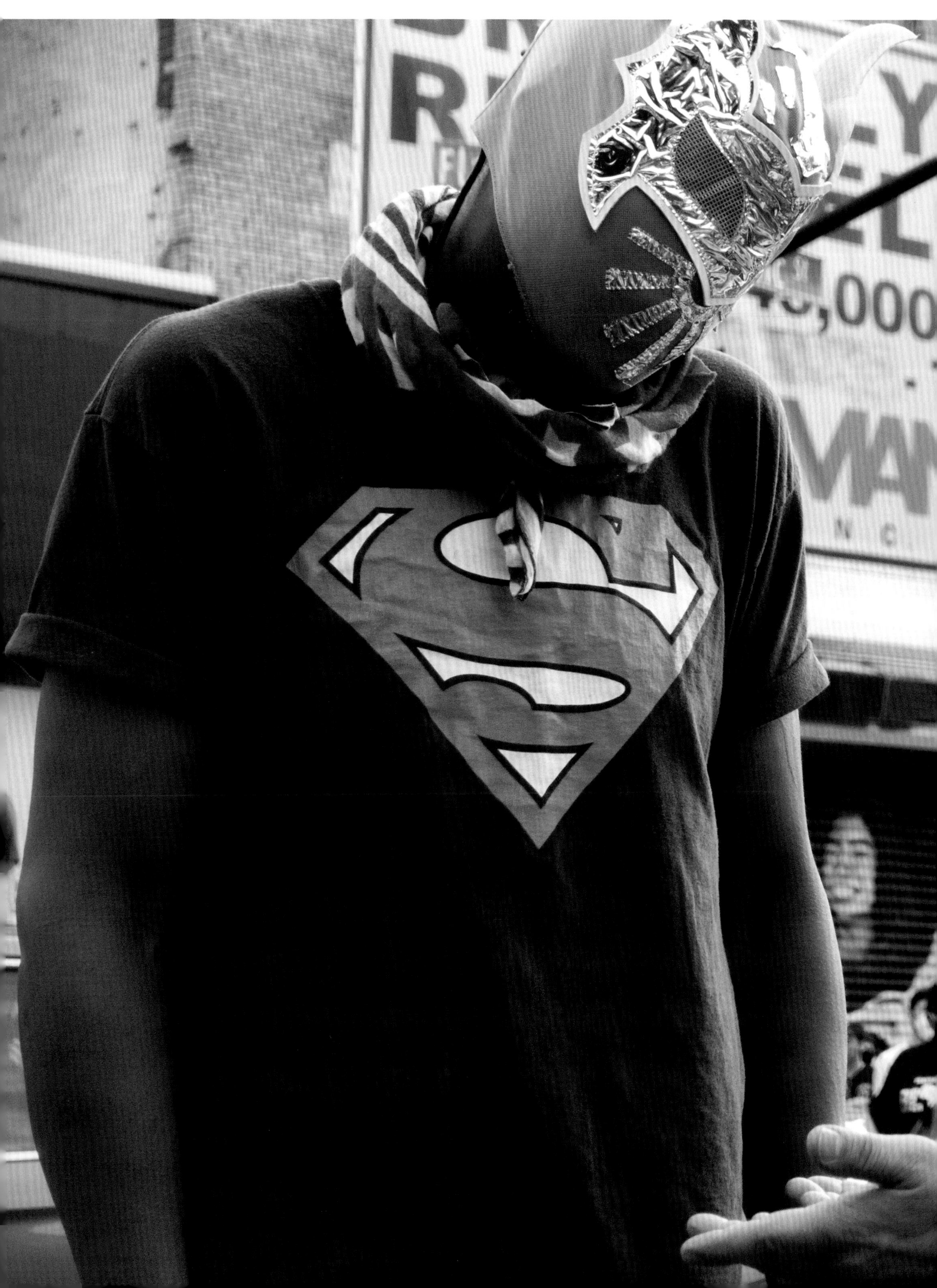

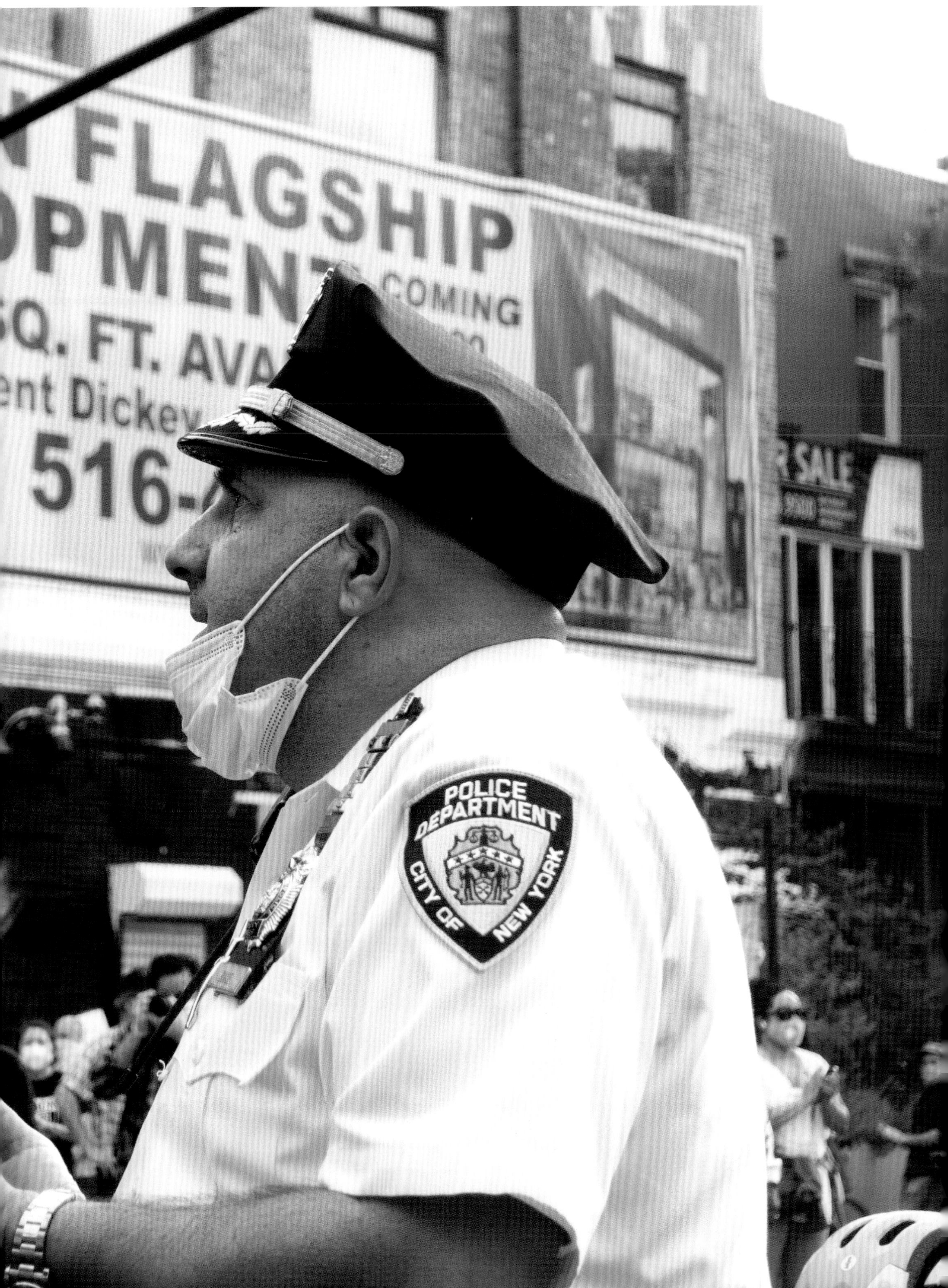
FLAGSHIP
OPMENT
COMING
SQ. FT. AVA
ent Dickey
516-
POLICE DEPARTMENT
CITY OF NEW YORK
R SALE

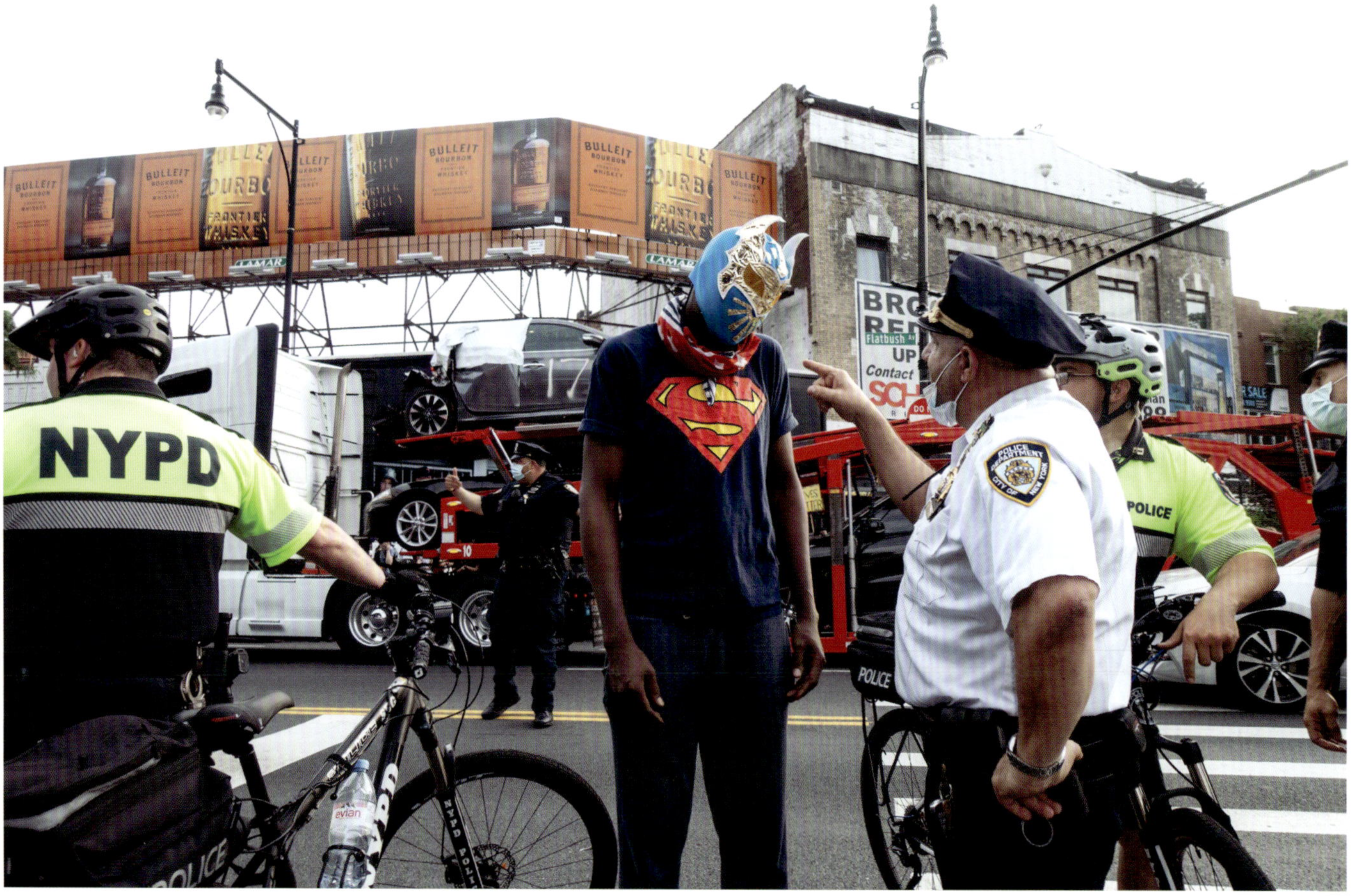

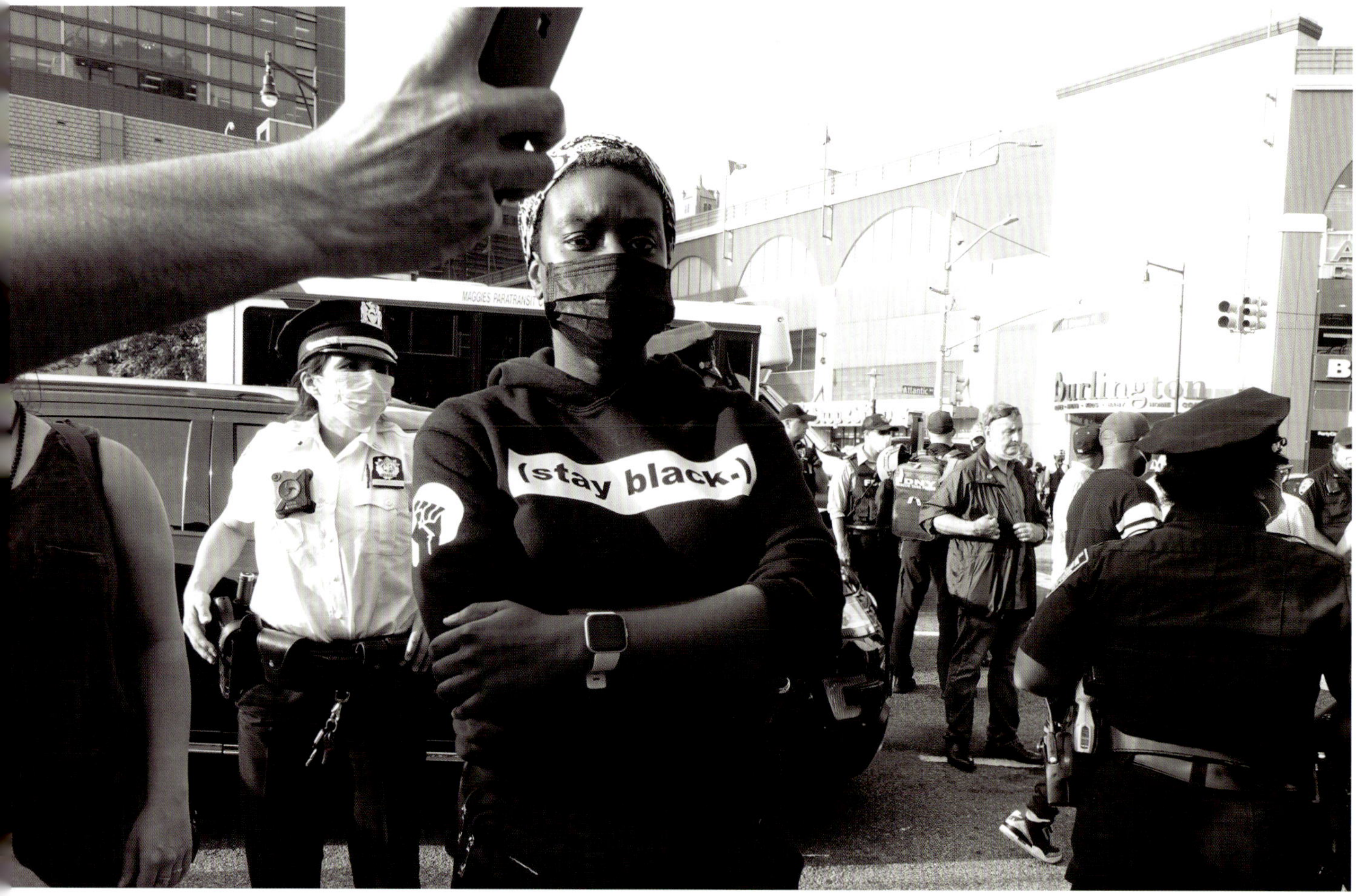

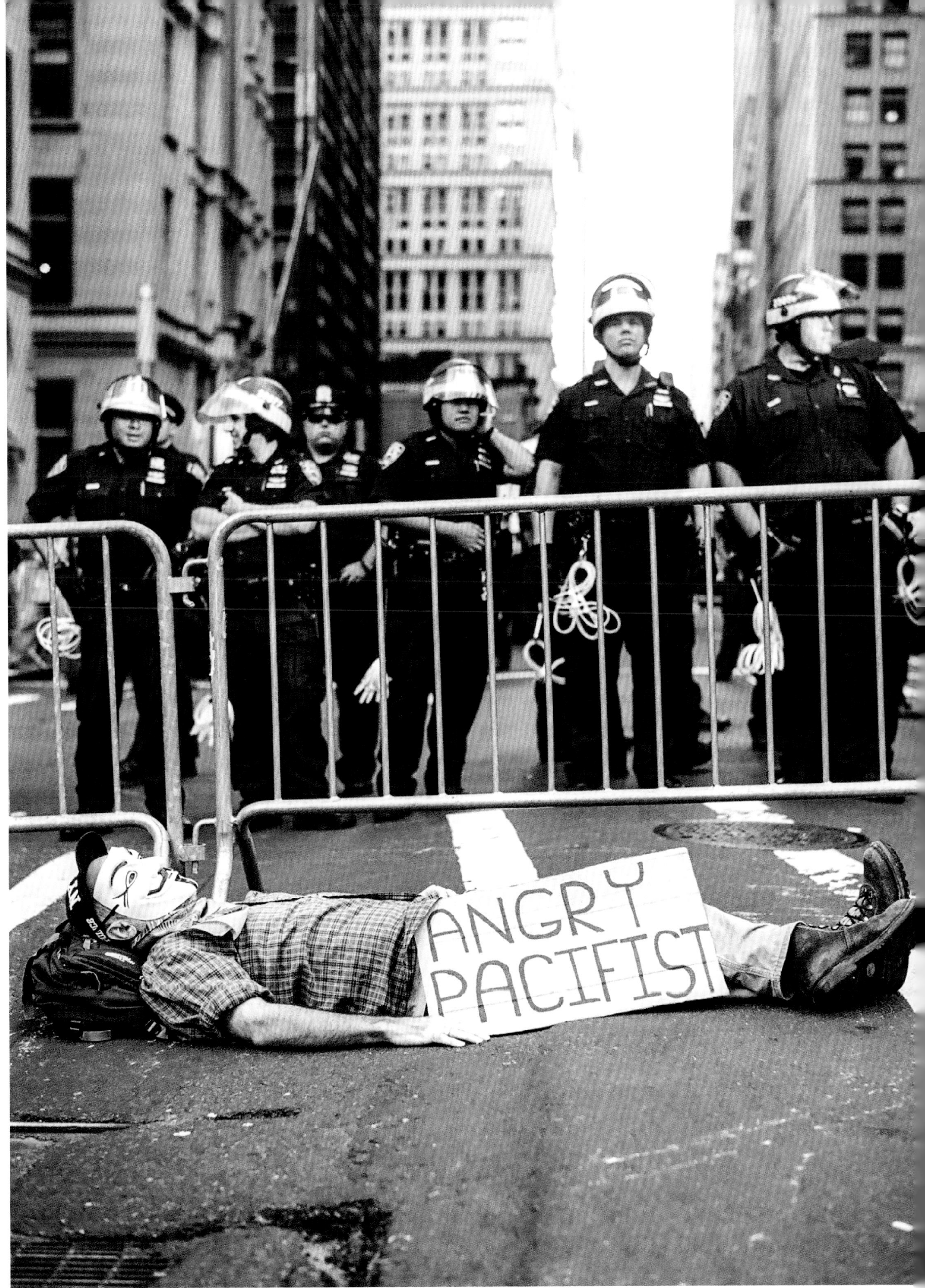
ANGRY
PACIFIST

CROSSWALK

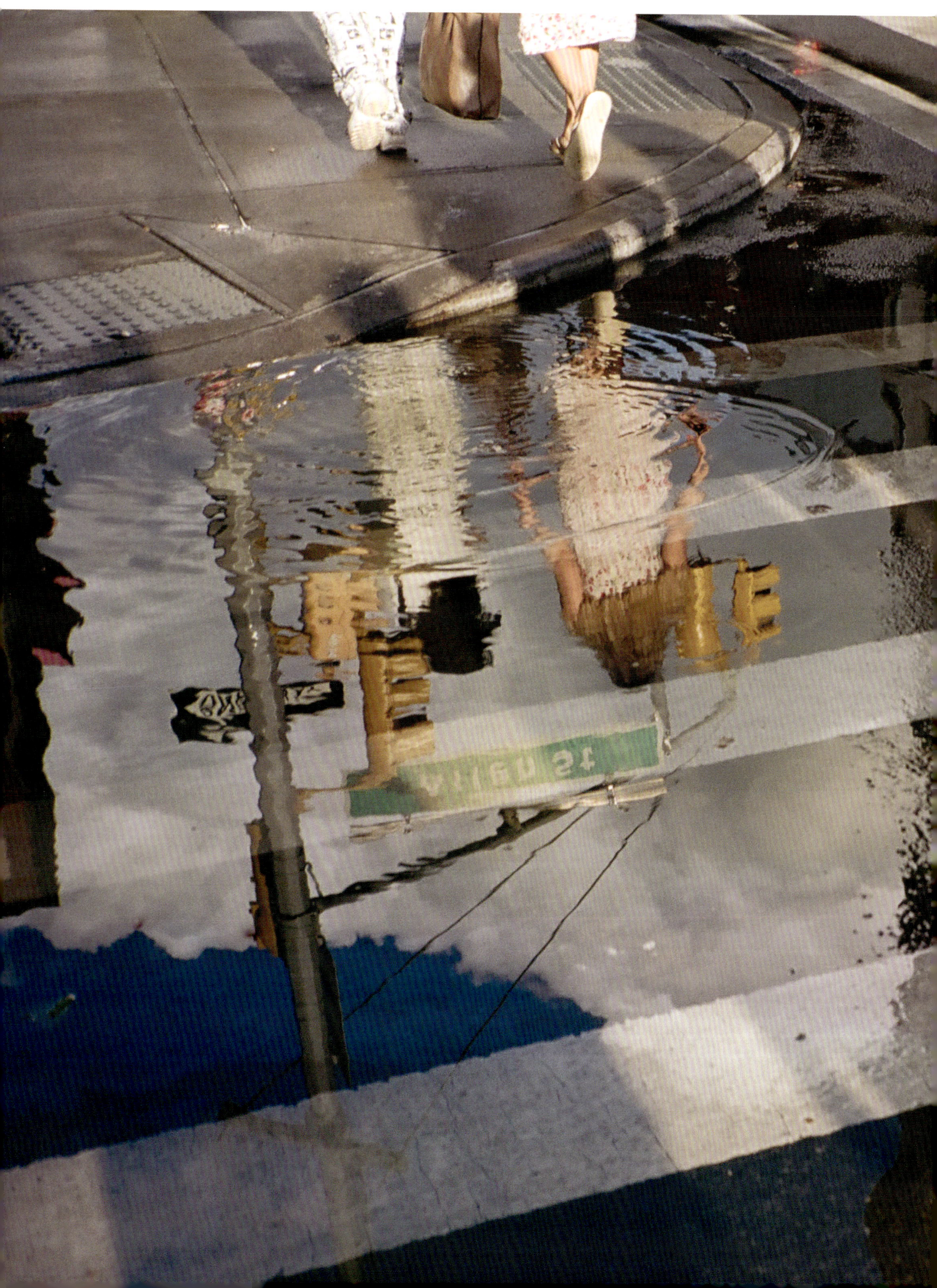

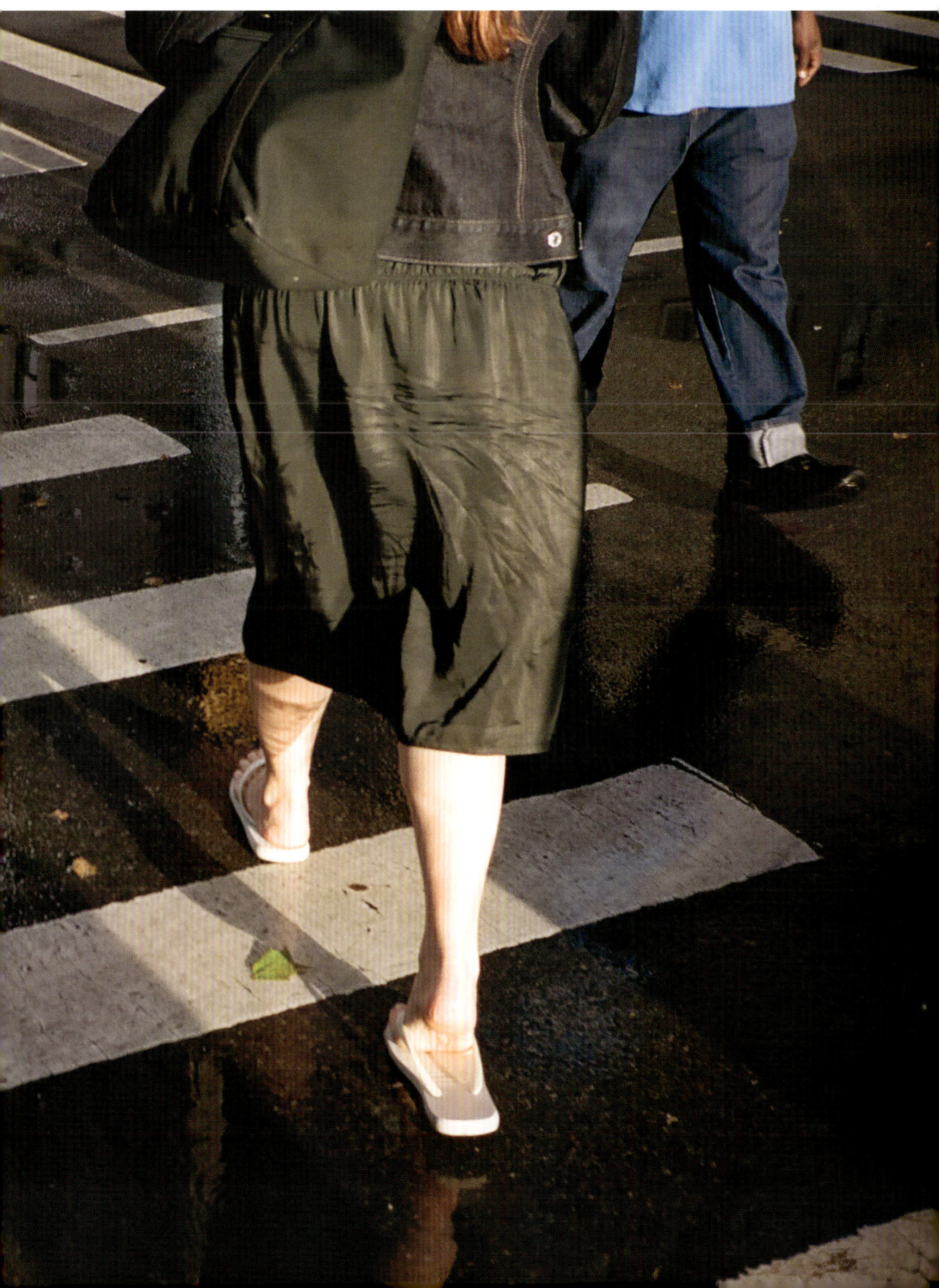

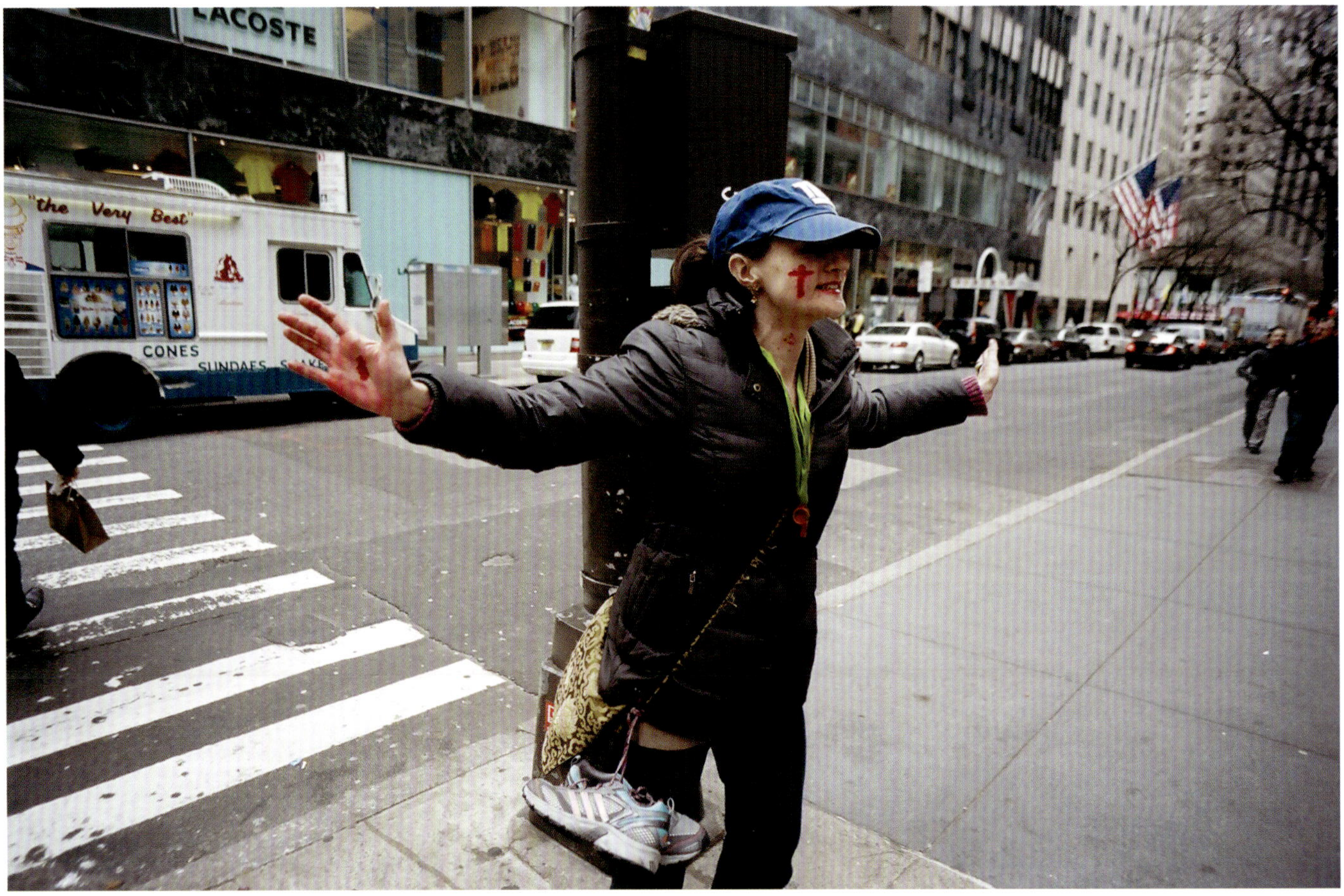
LACOSTE
"the Very Best"
CONES

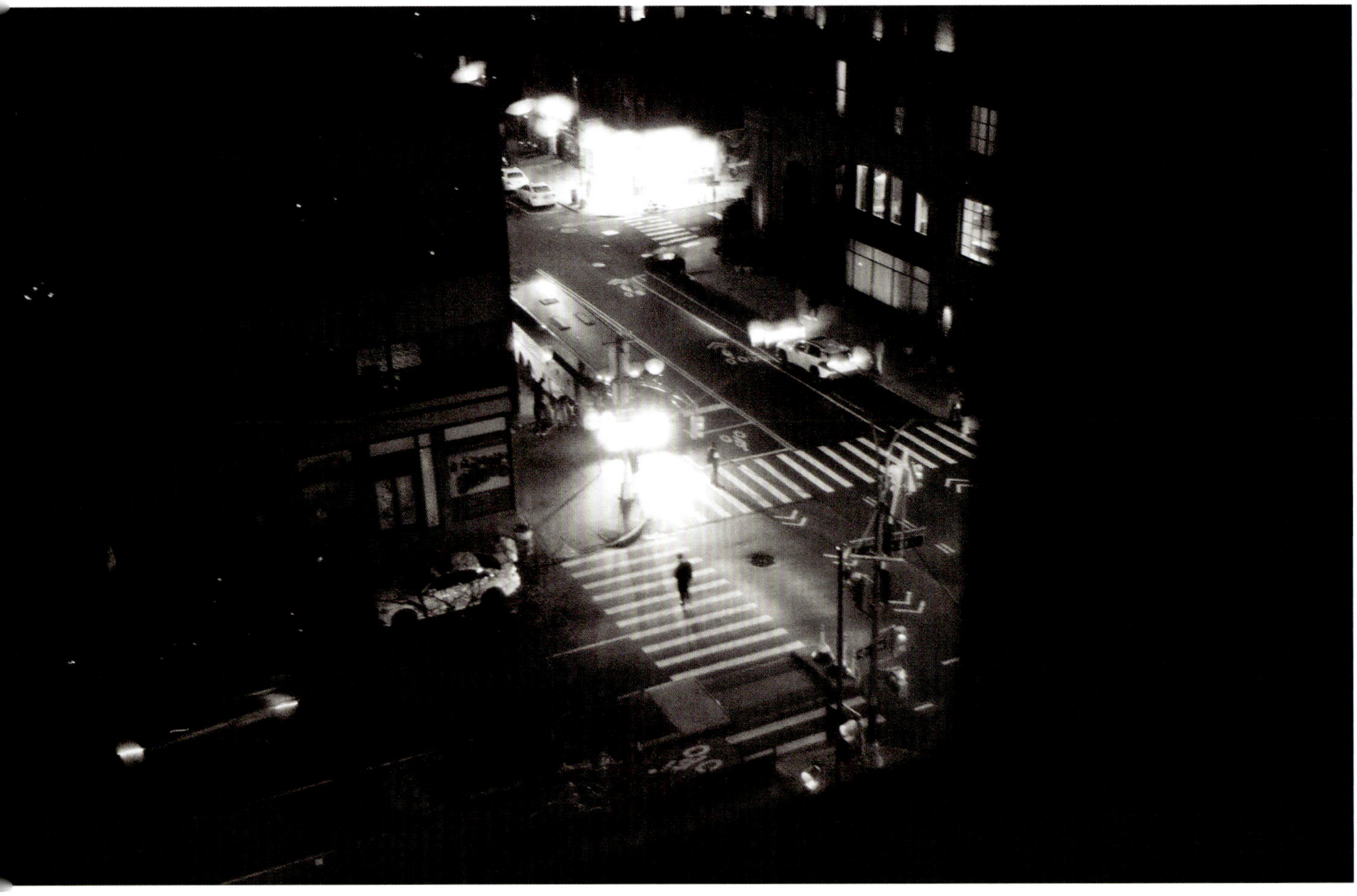

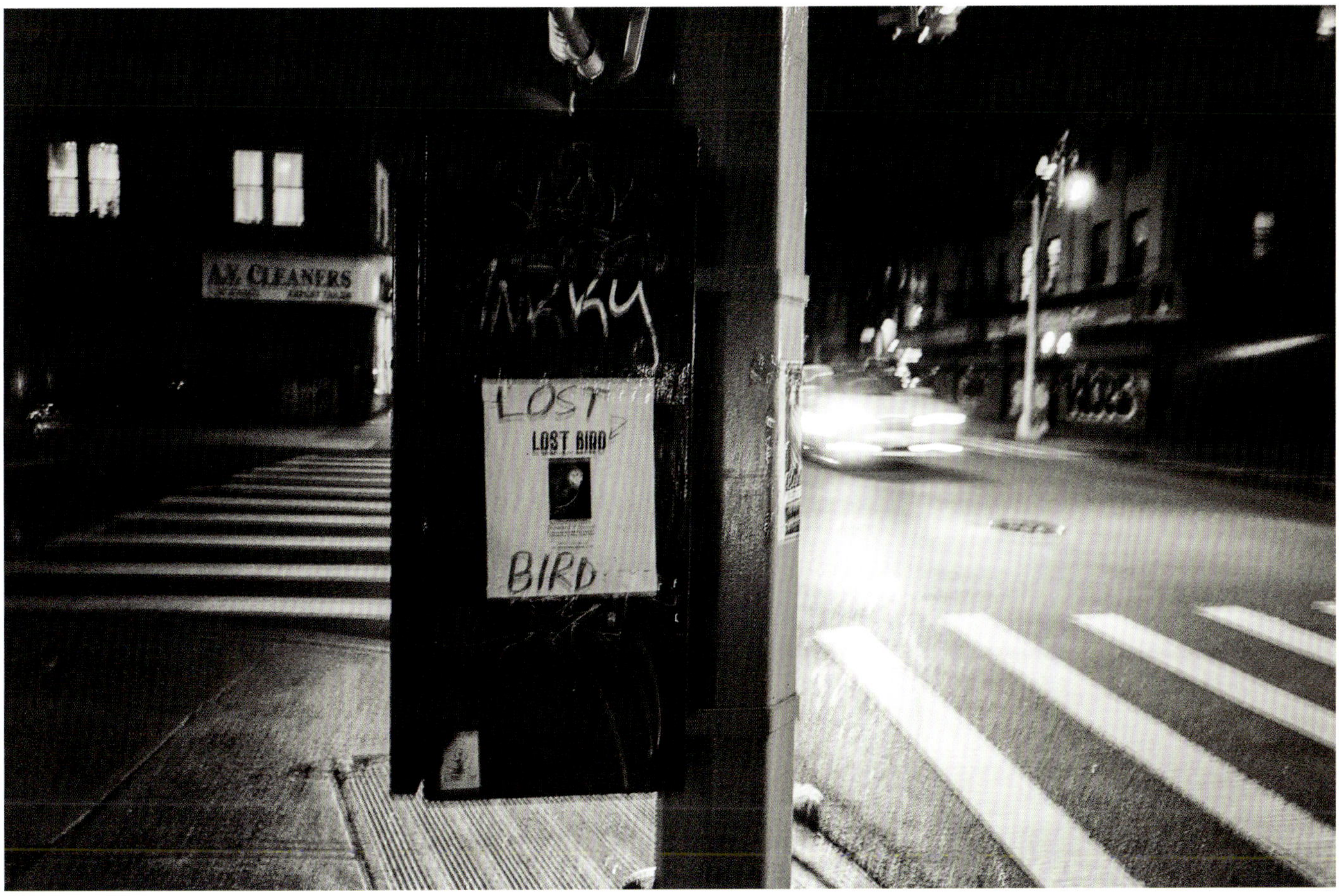
A.Y. CLEANERS
LOST
LOST BIRD
BIRD

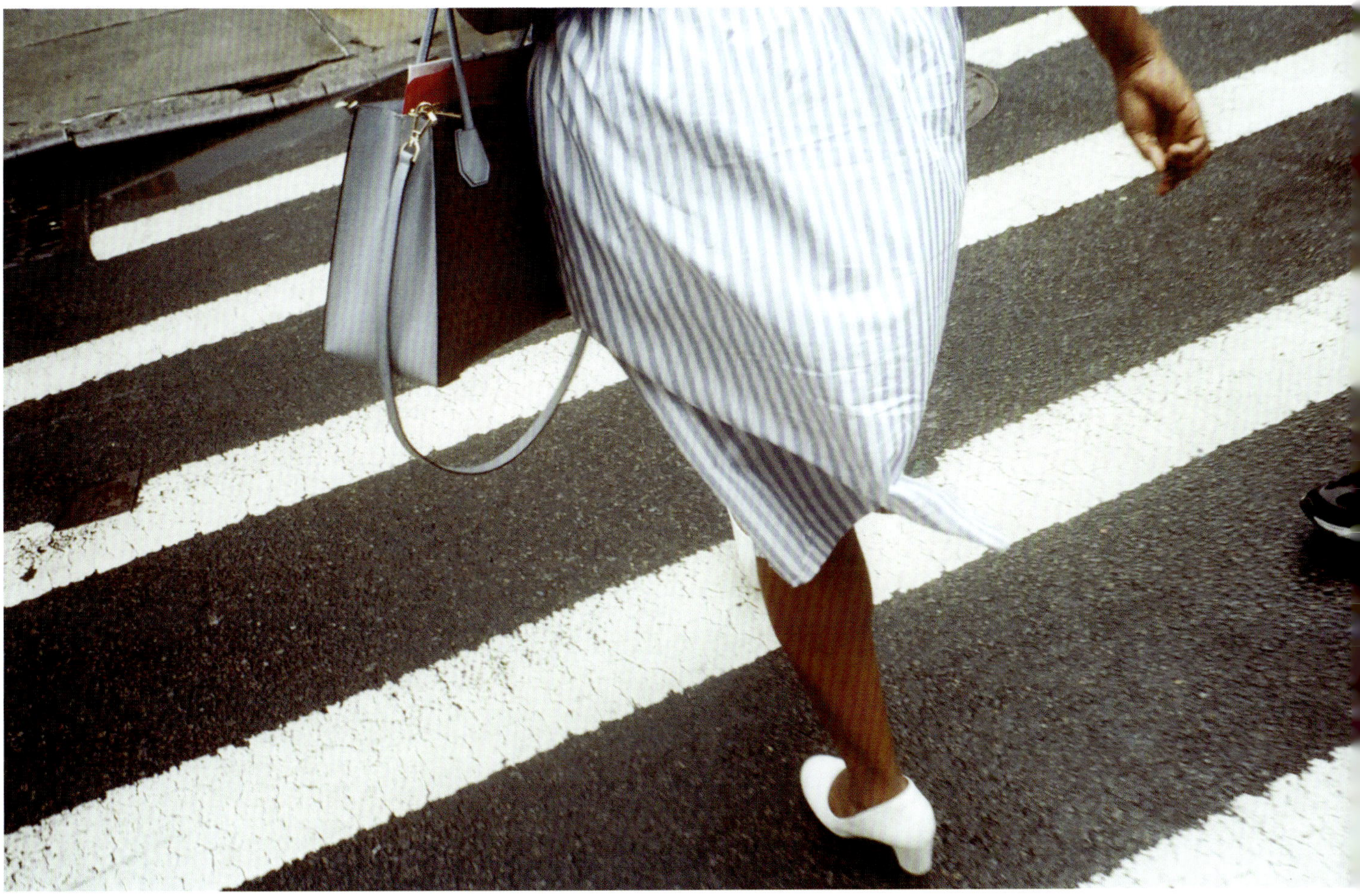

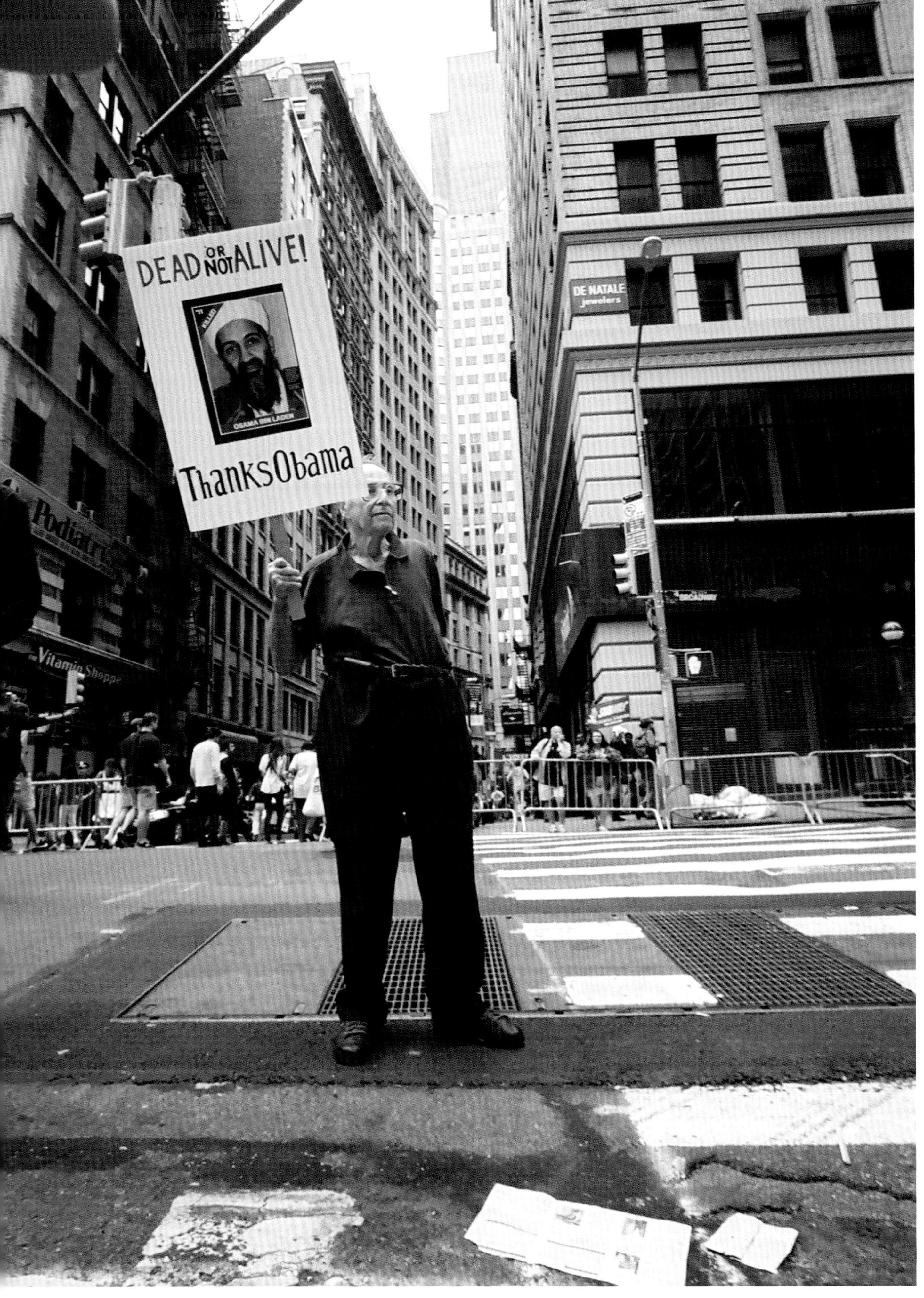
DEAD OR NOT ALIVE!
KILLED
OSAMA BIN LADEN
Thanks Obama
DE NATALE
jewelers
Podiatry
Vitamin Shoppe
BROADWAY

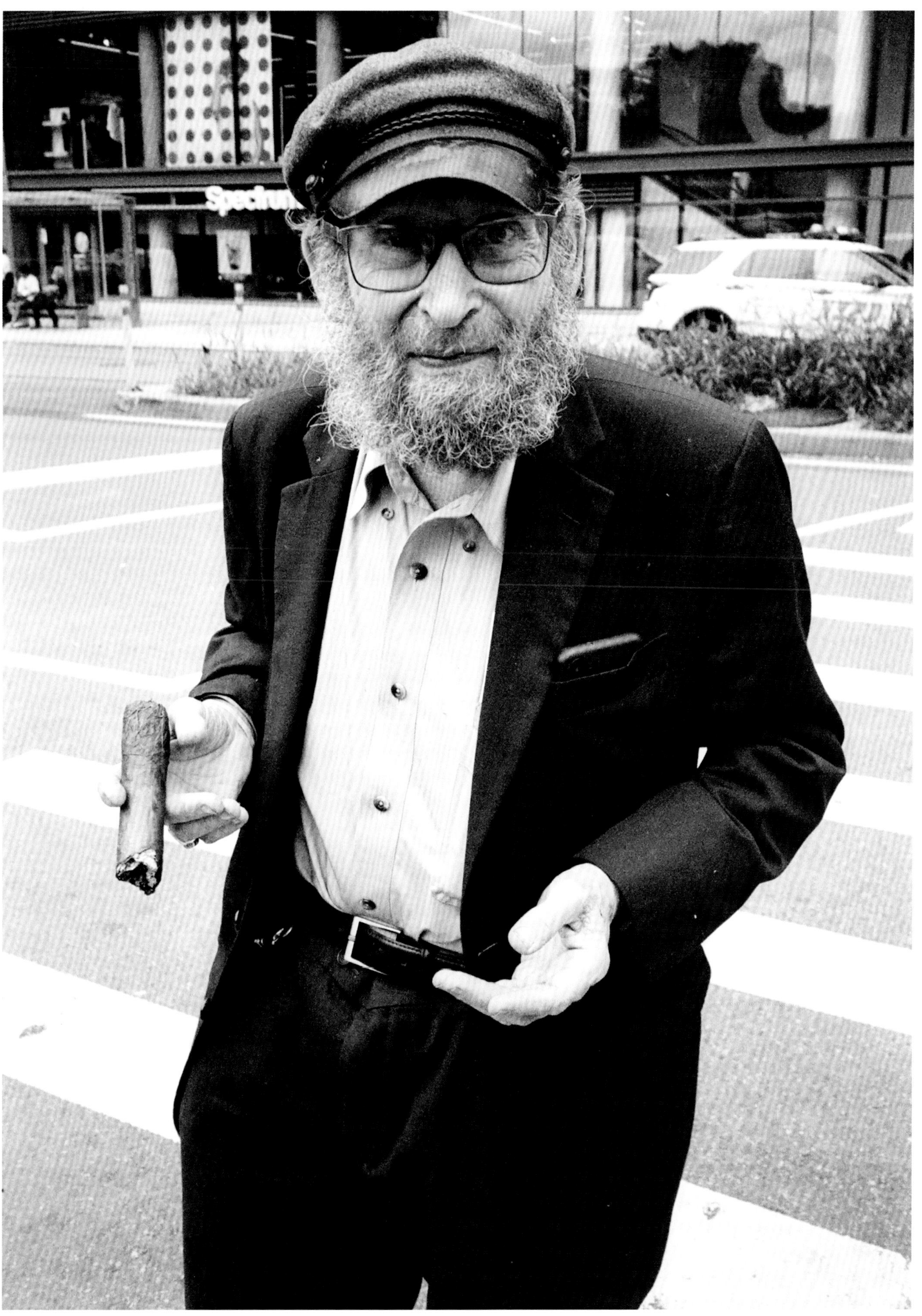

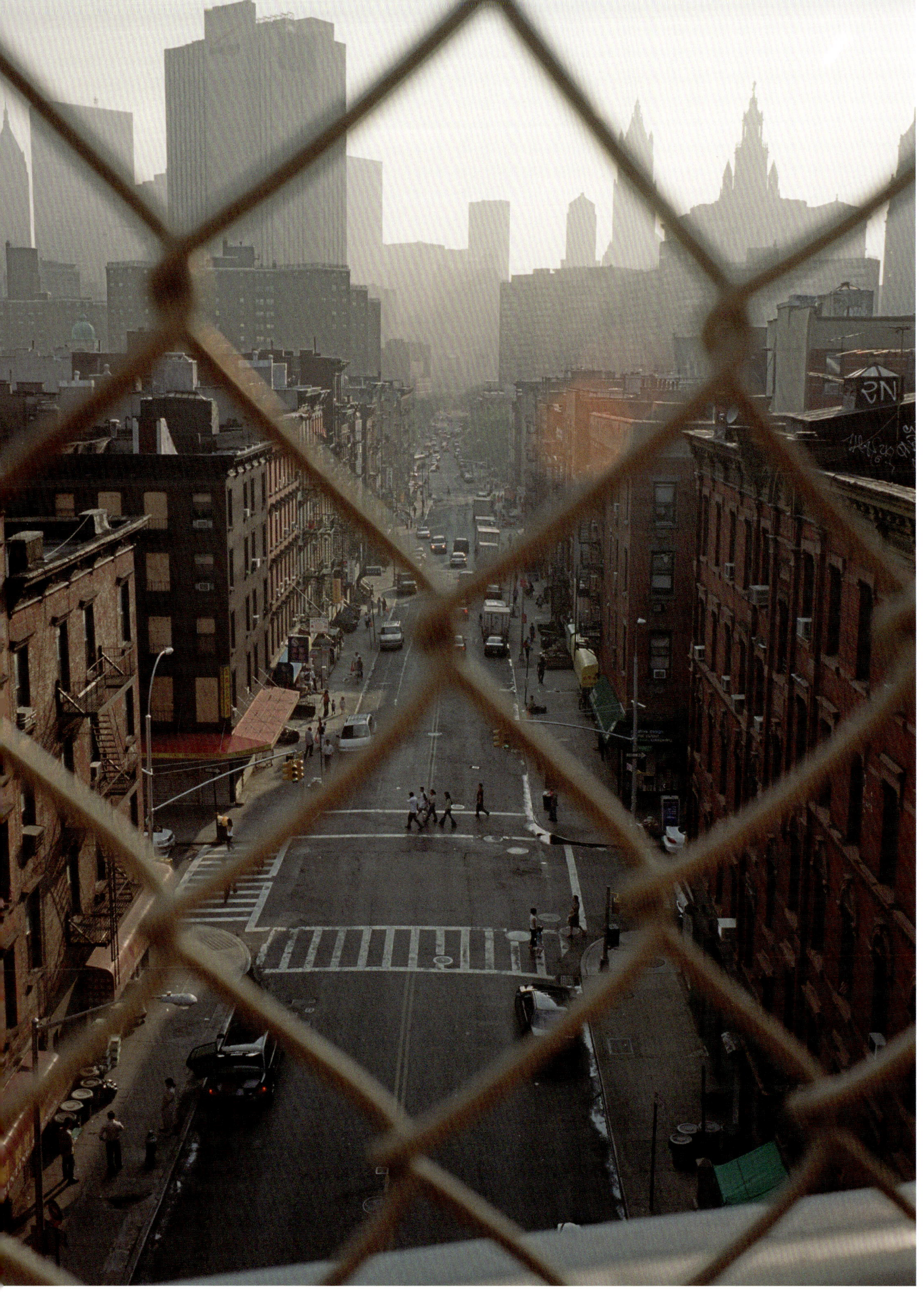

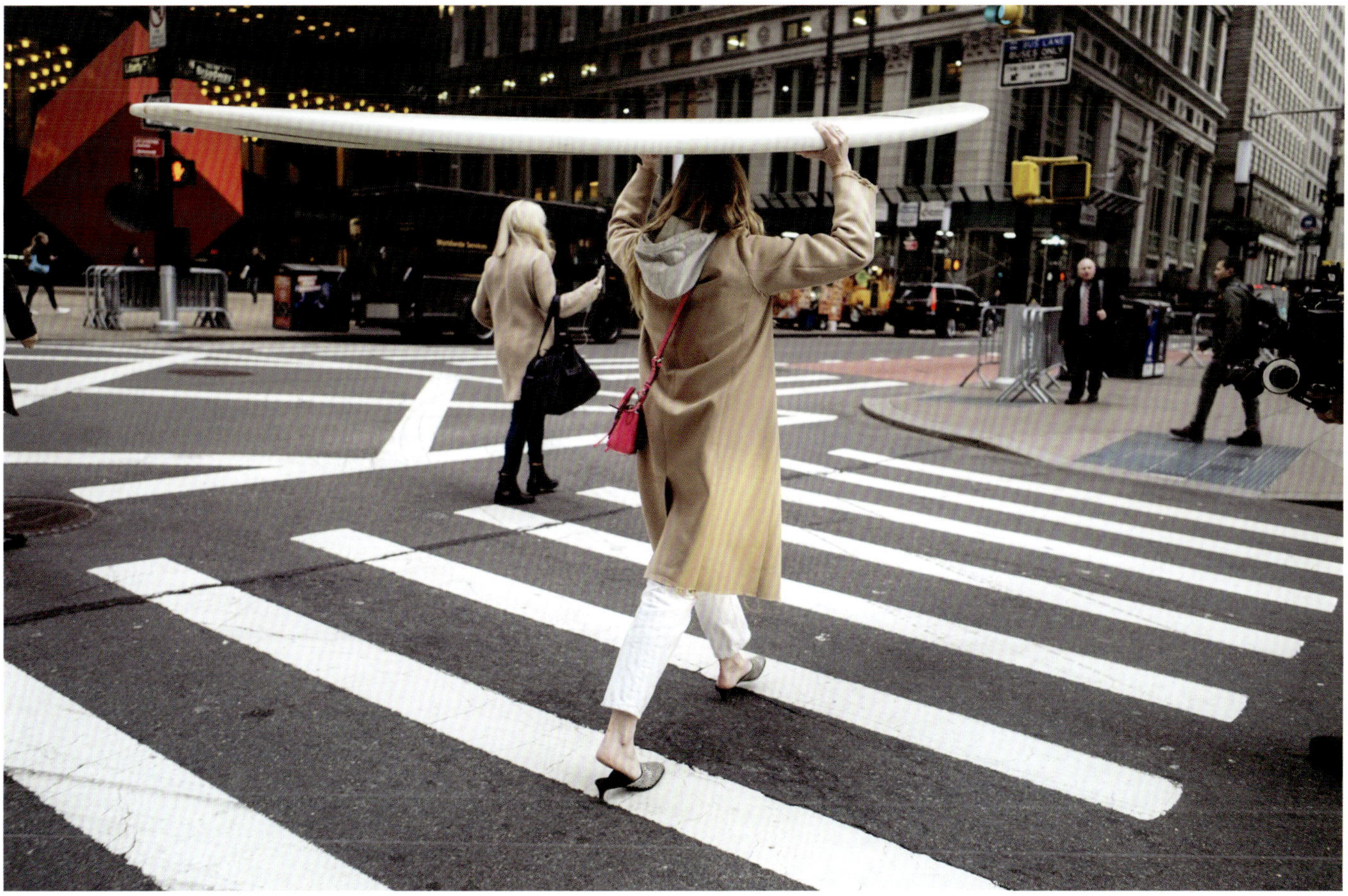

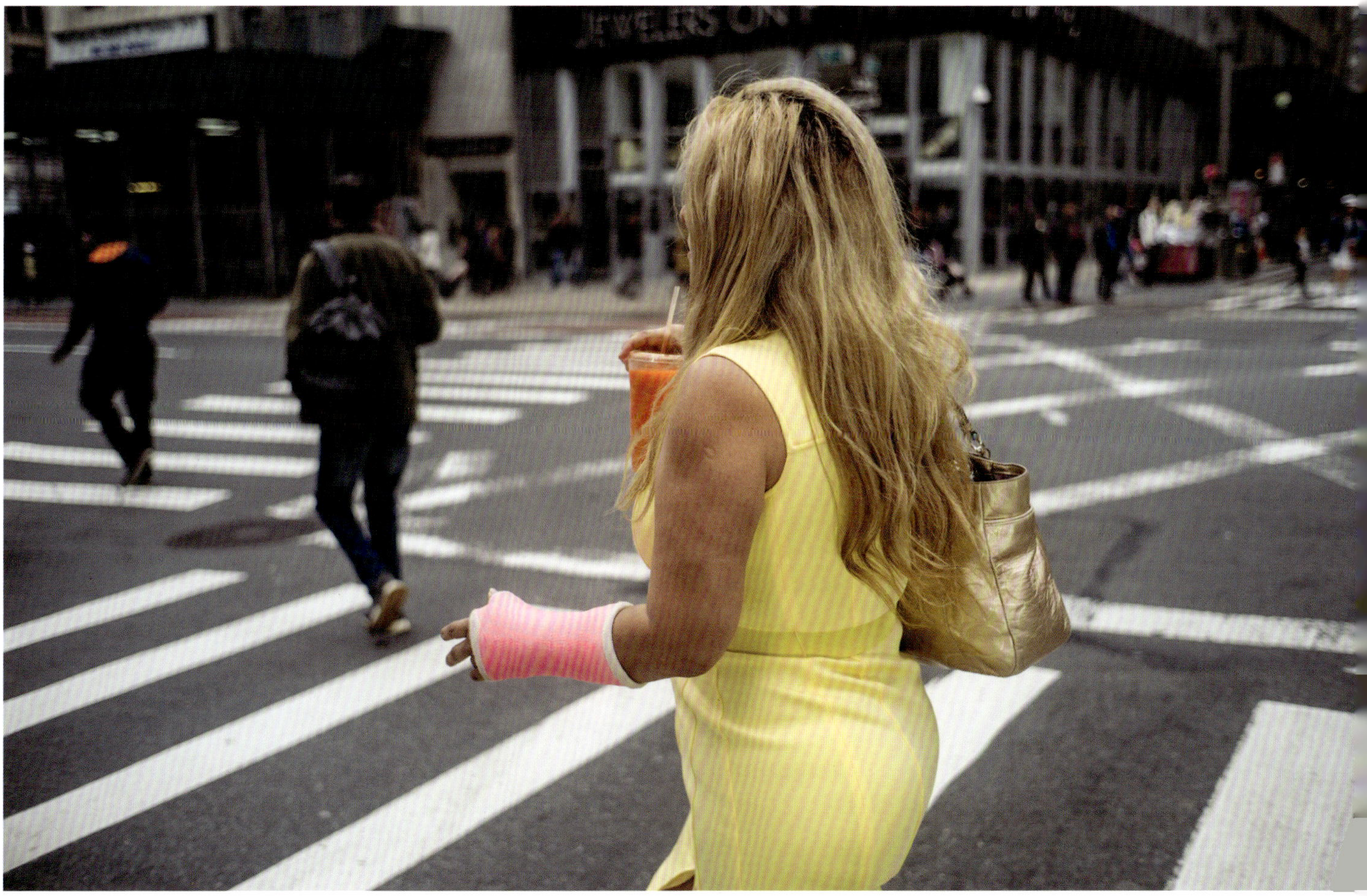

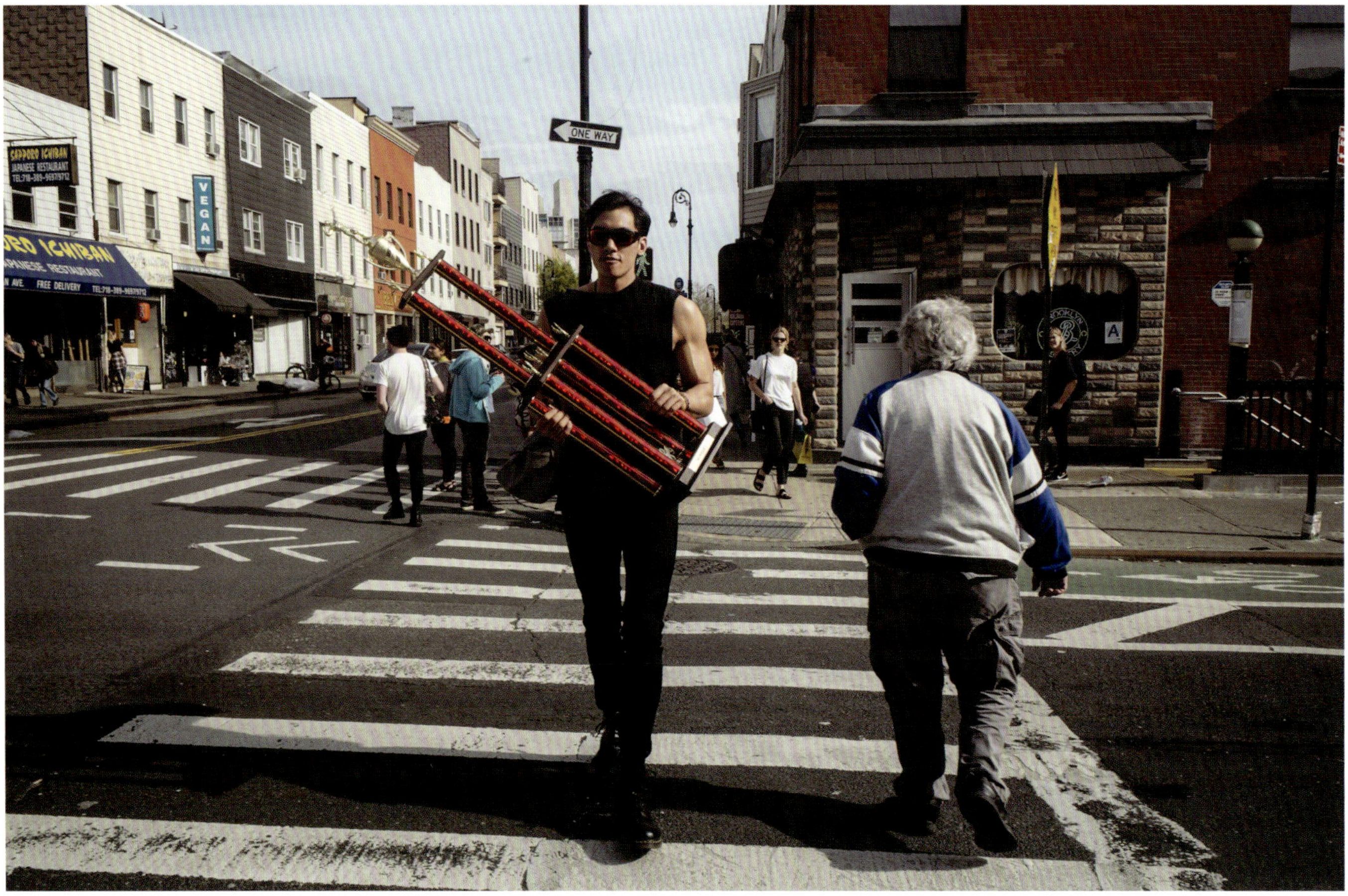

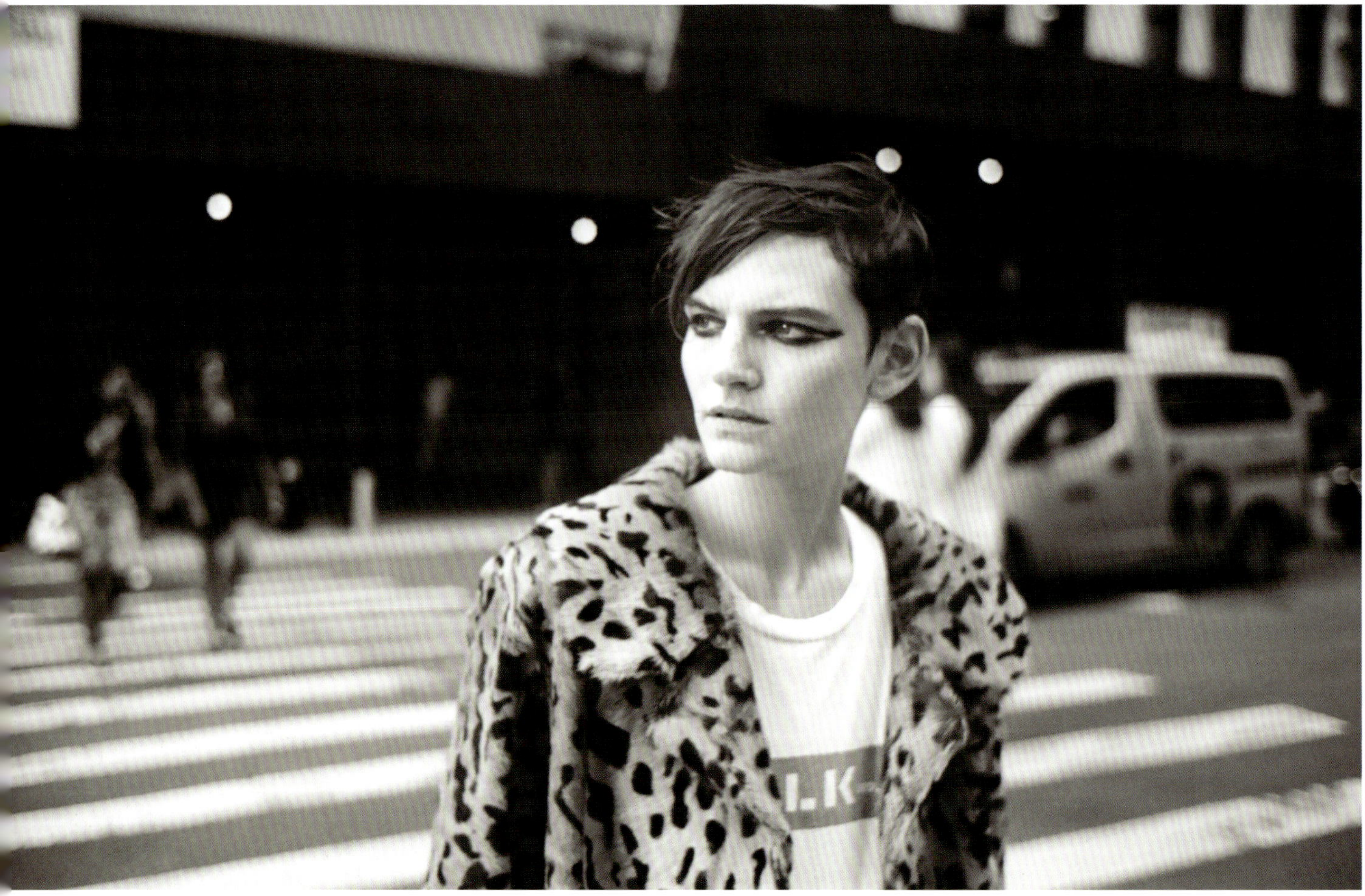

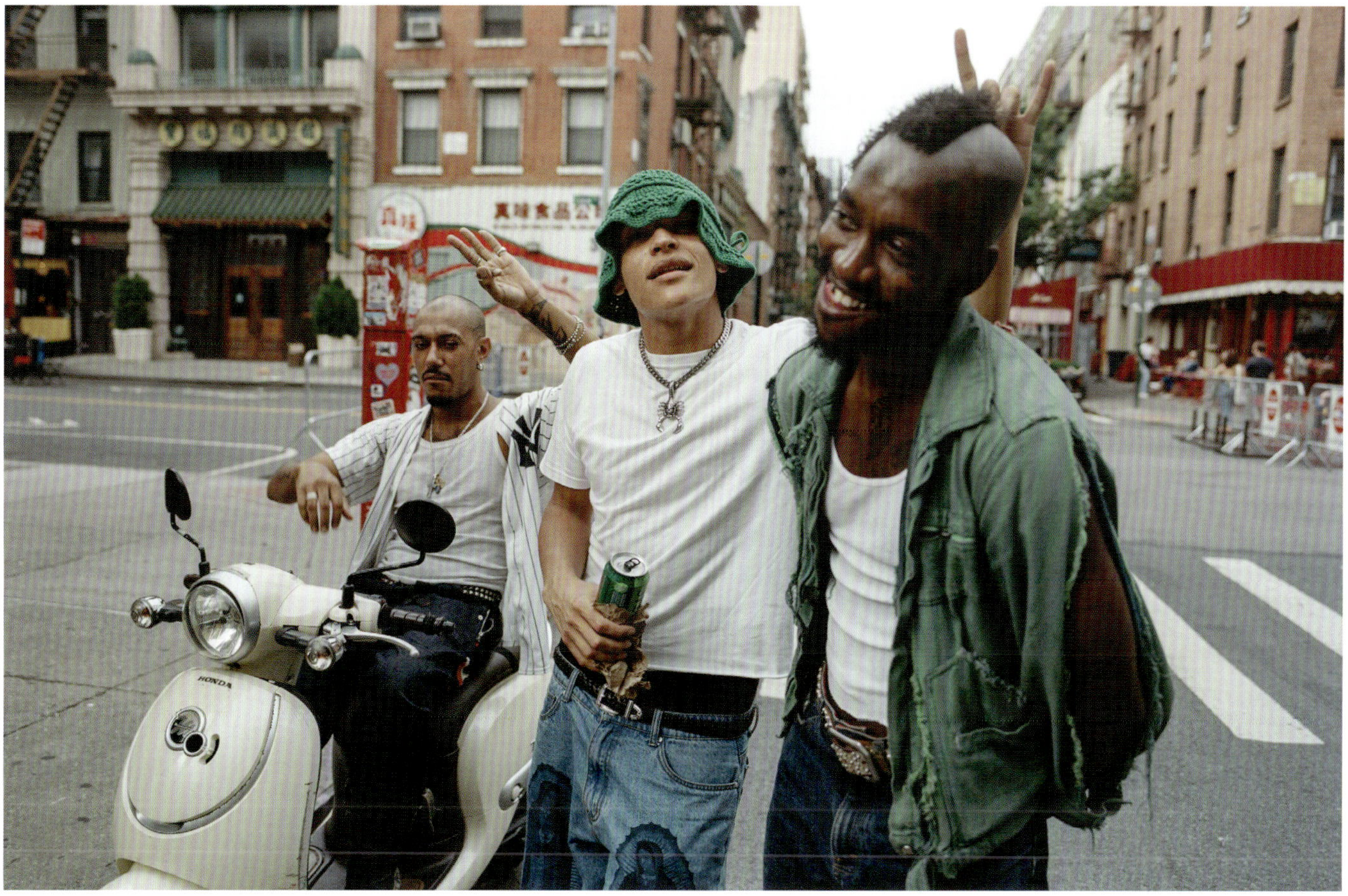

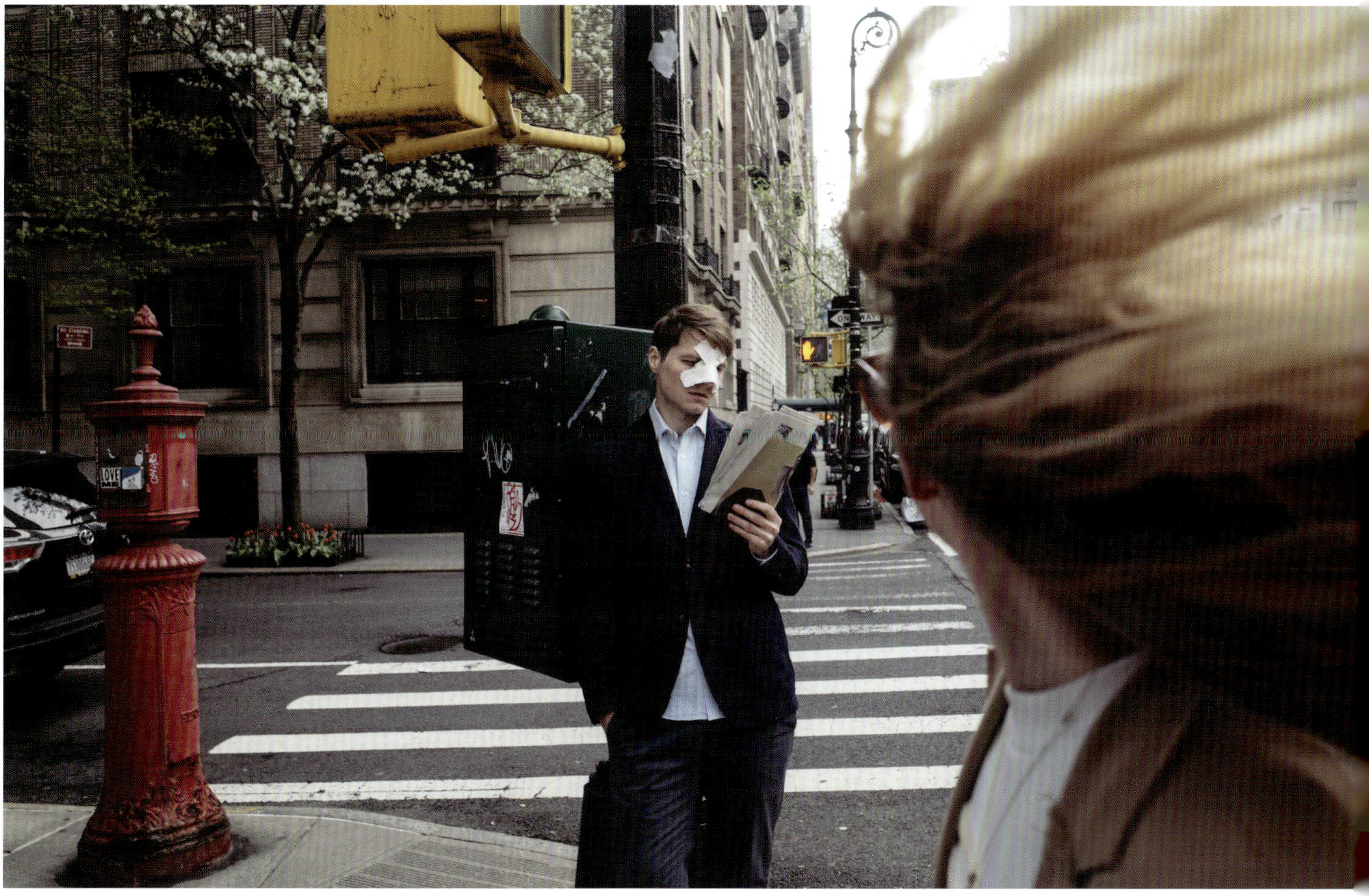

DOG

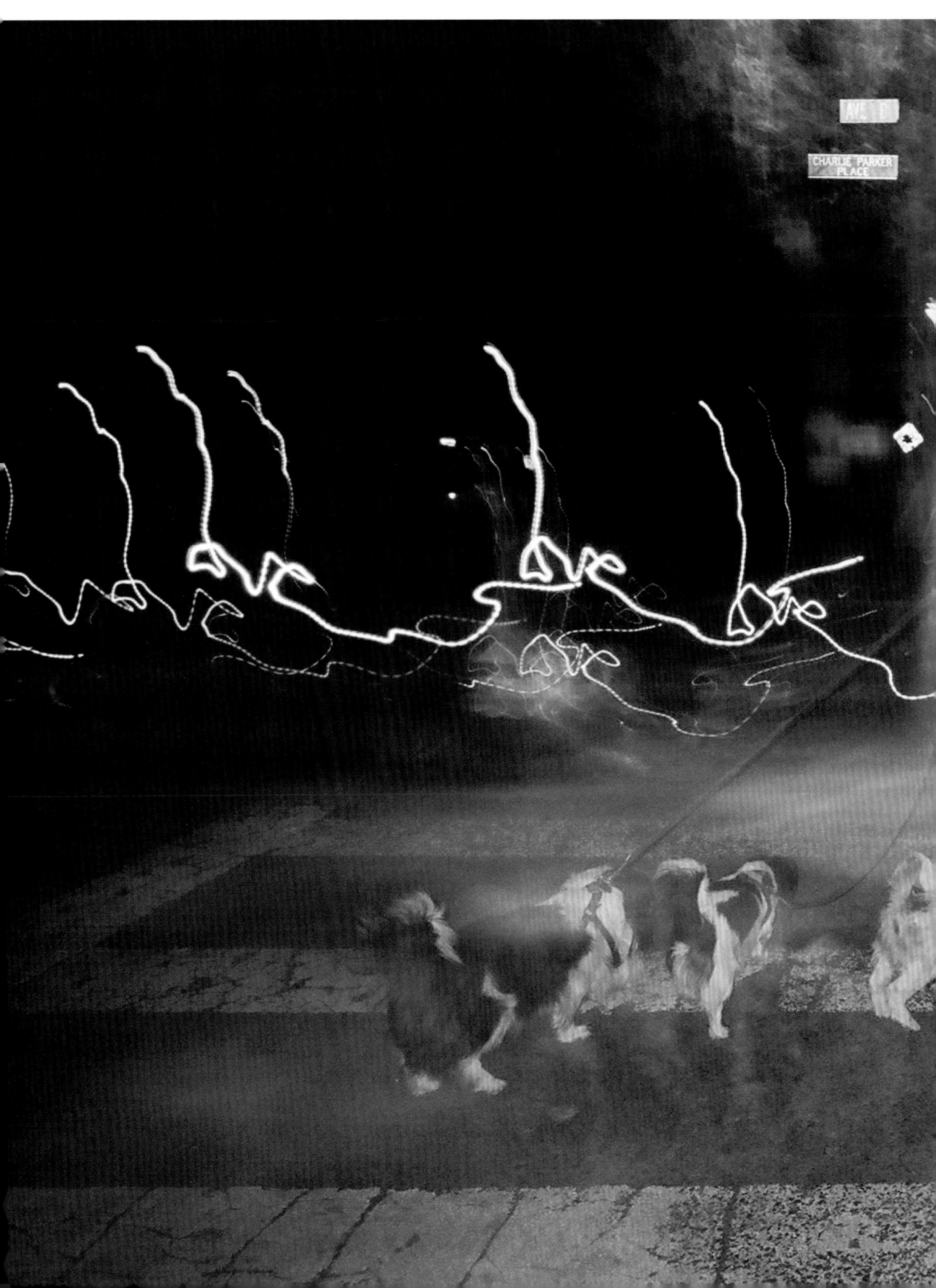

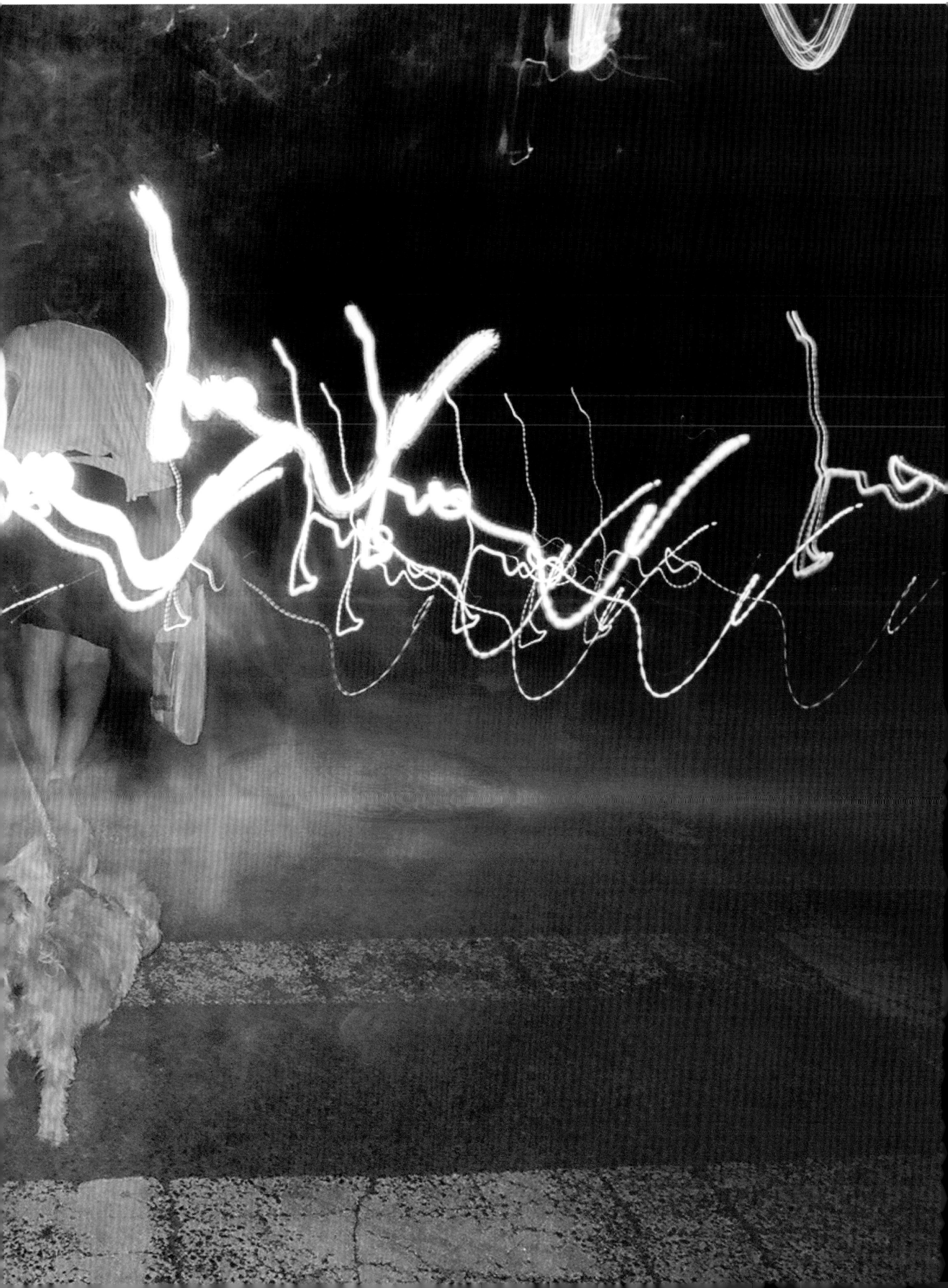

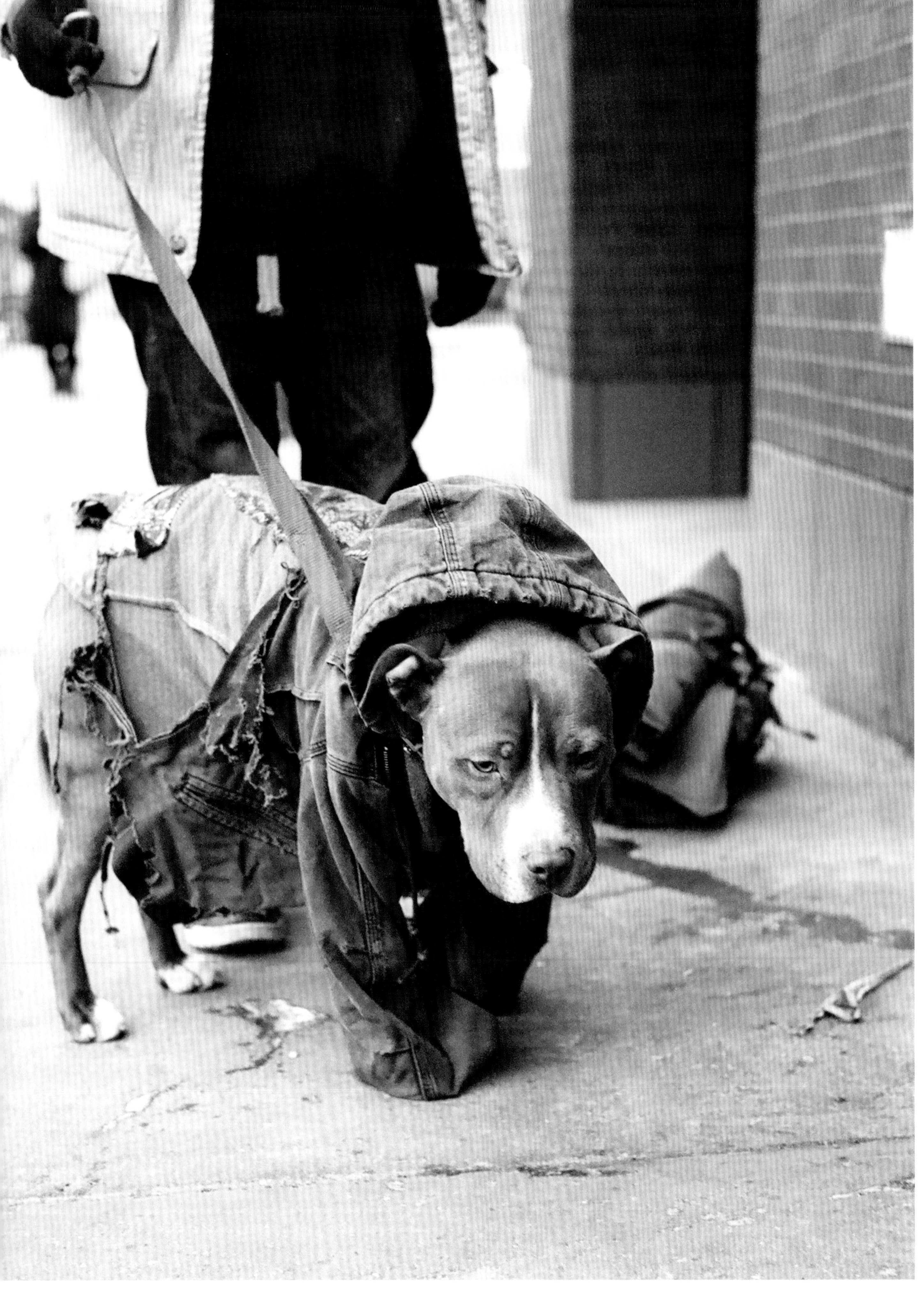

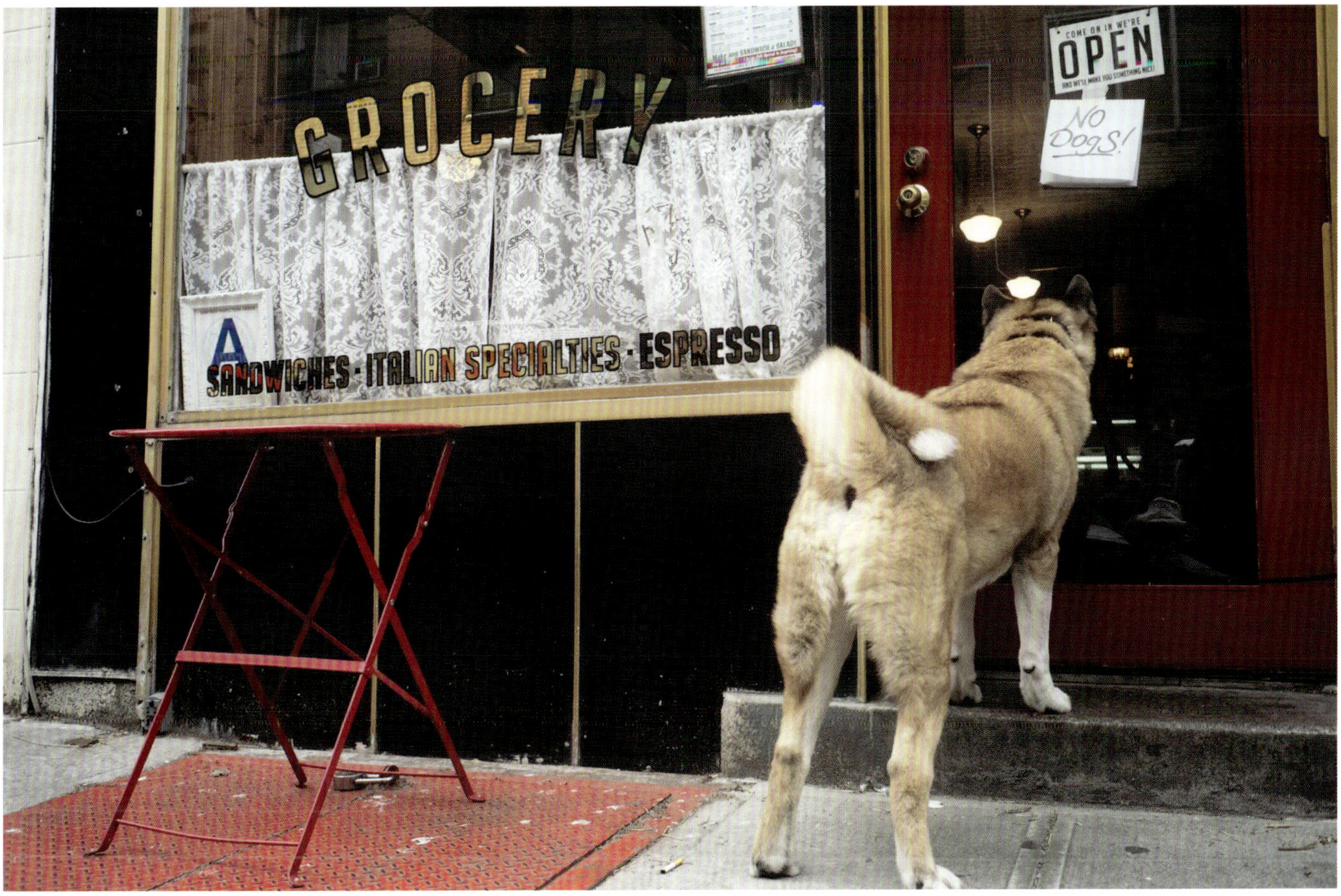
GROCERY
SANDWICHES · ITALIAN SPECIALTIES · ESPRESSO
OPEN
NO DOGS!

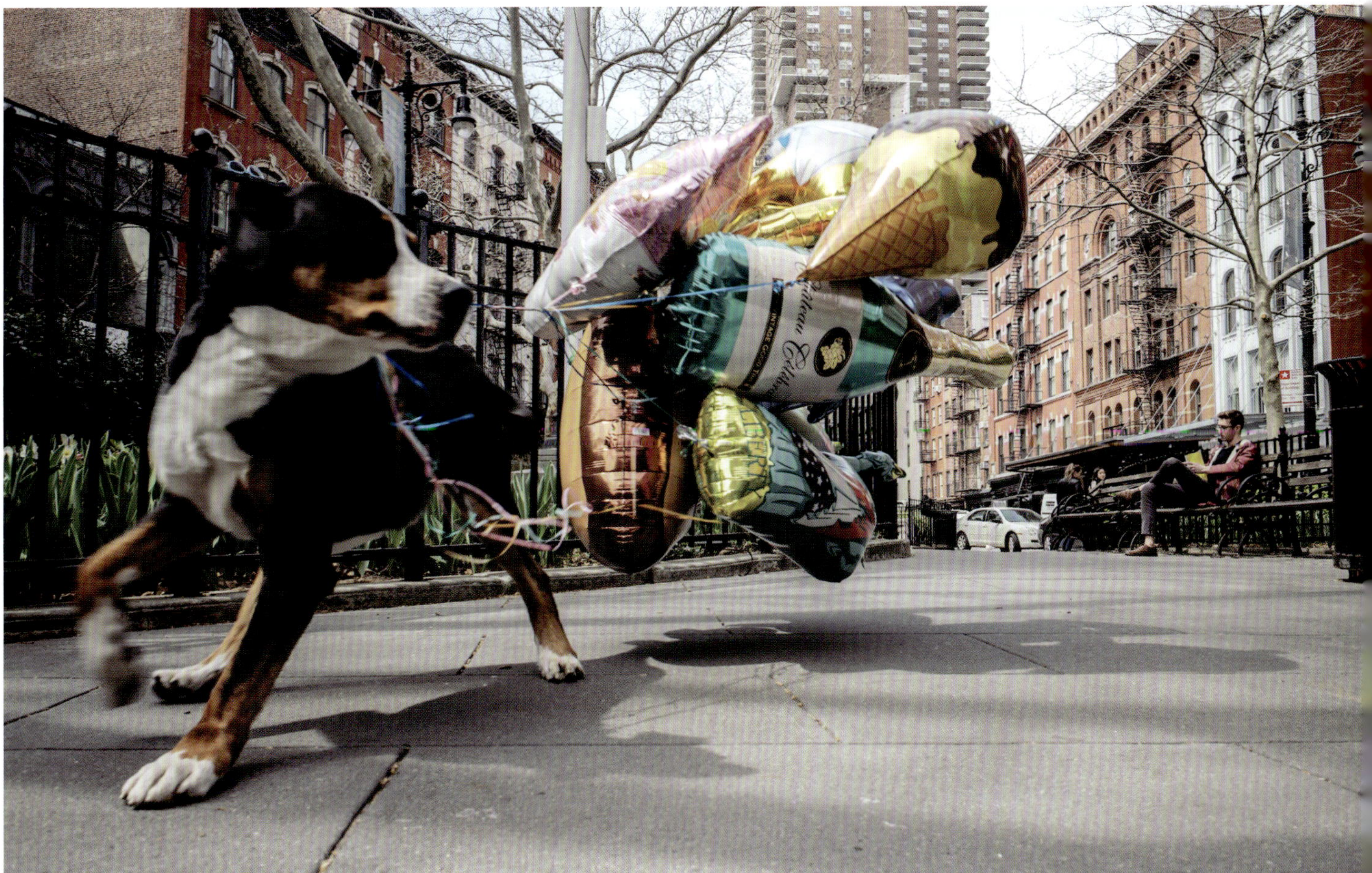

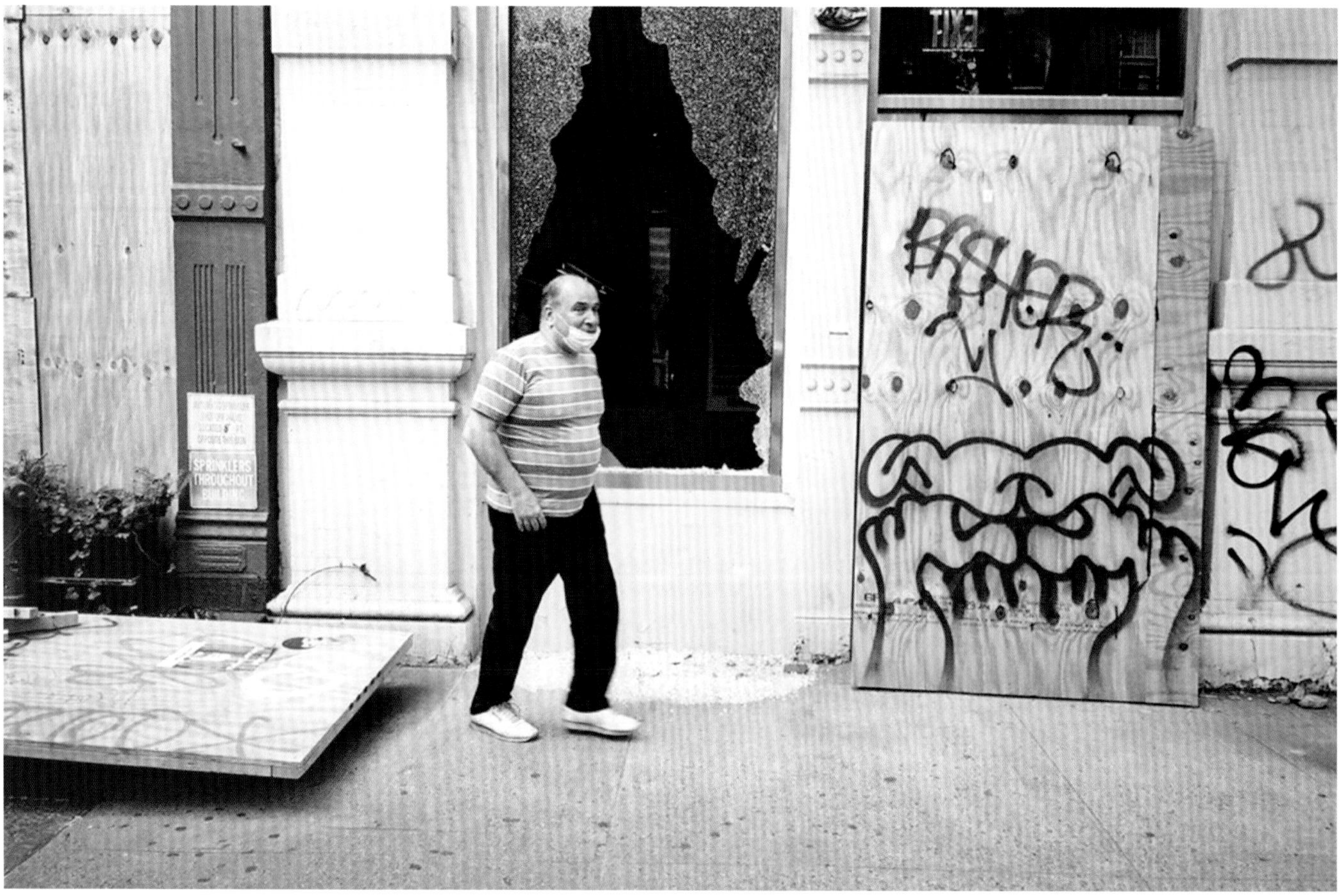

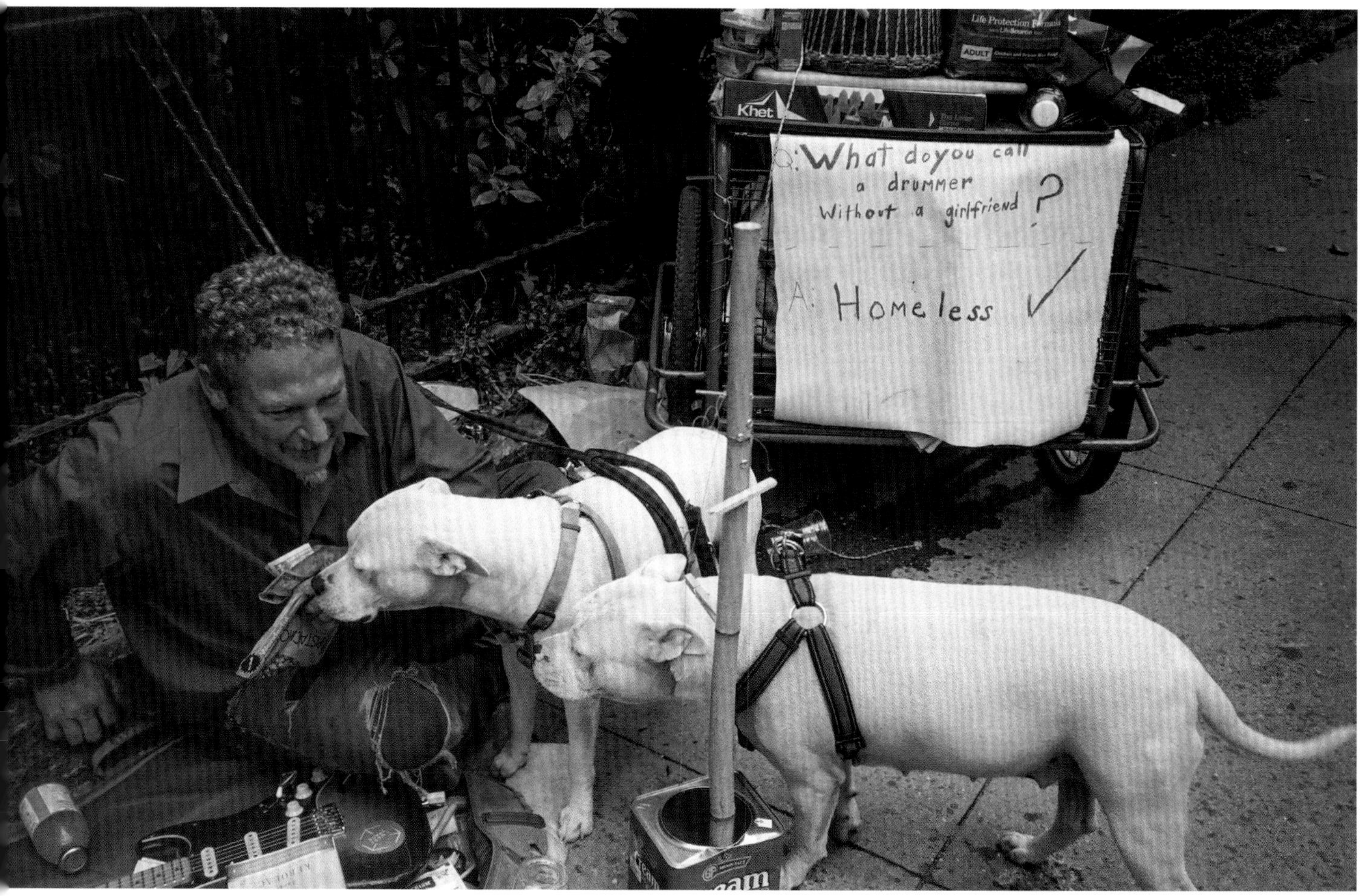

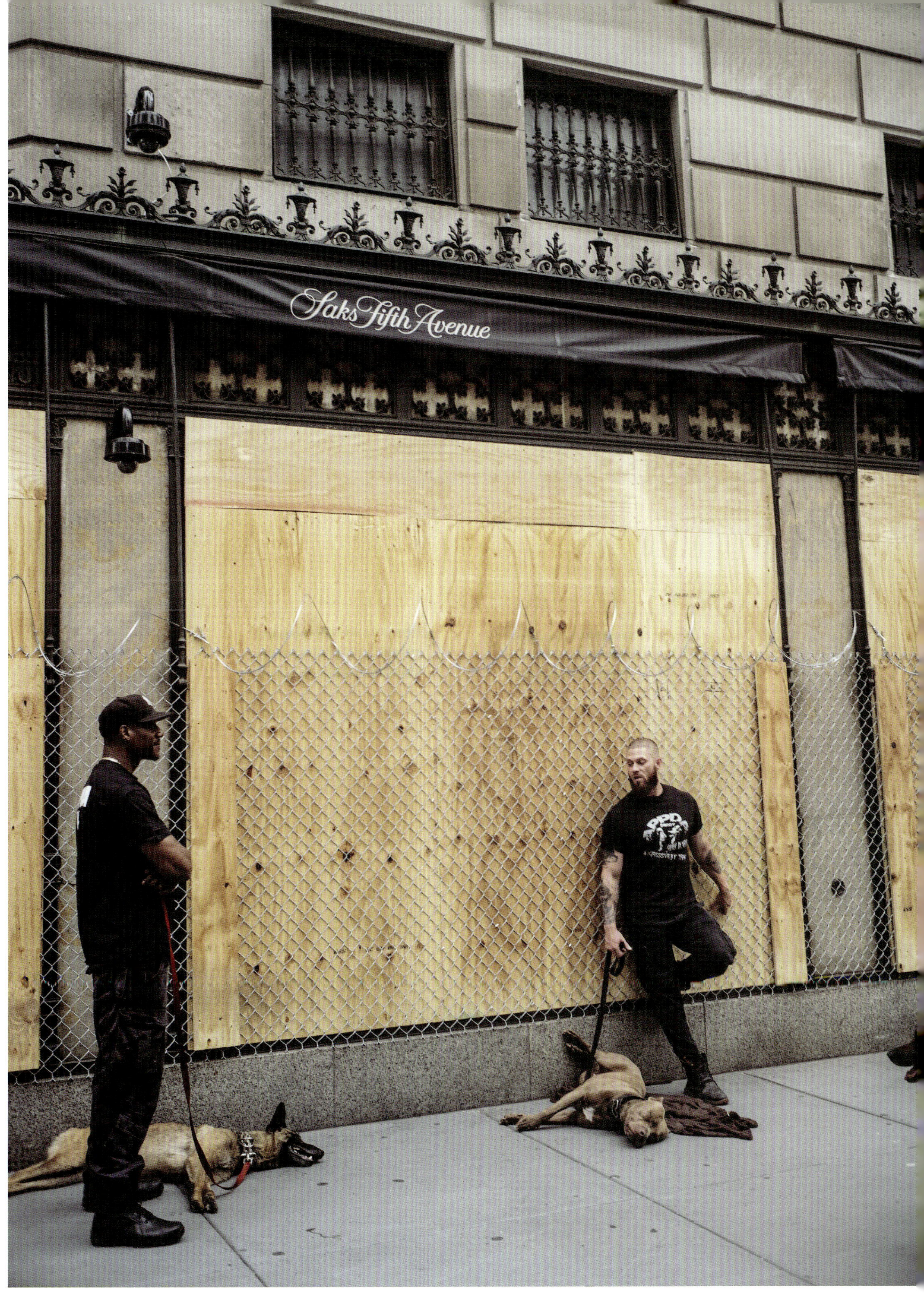
Saks Fifth Avenue

EAST VILLAGE

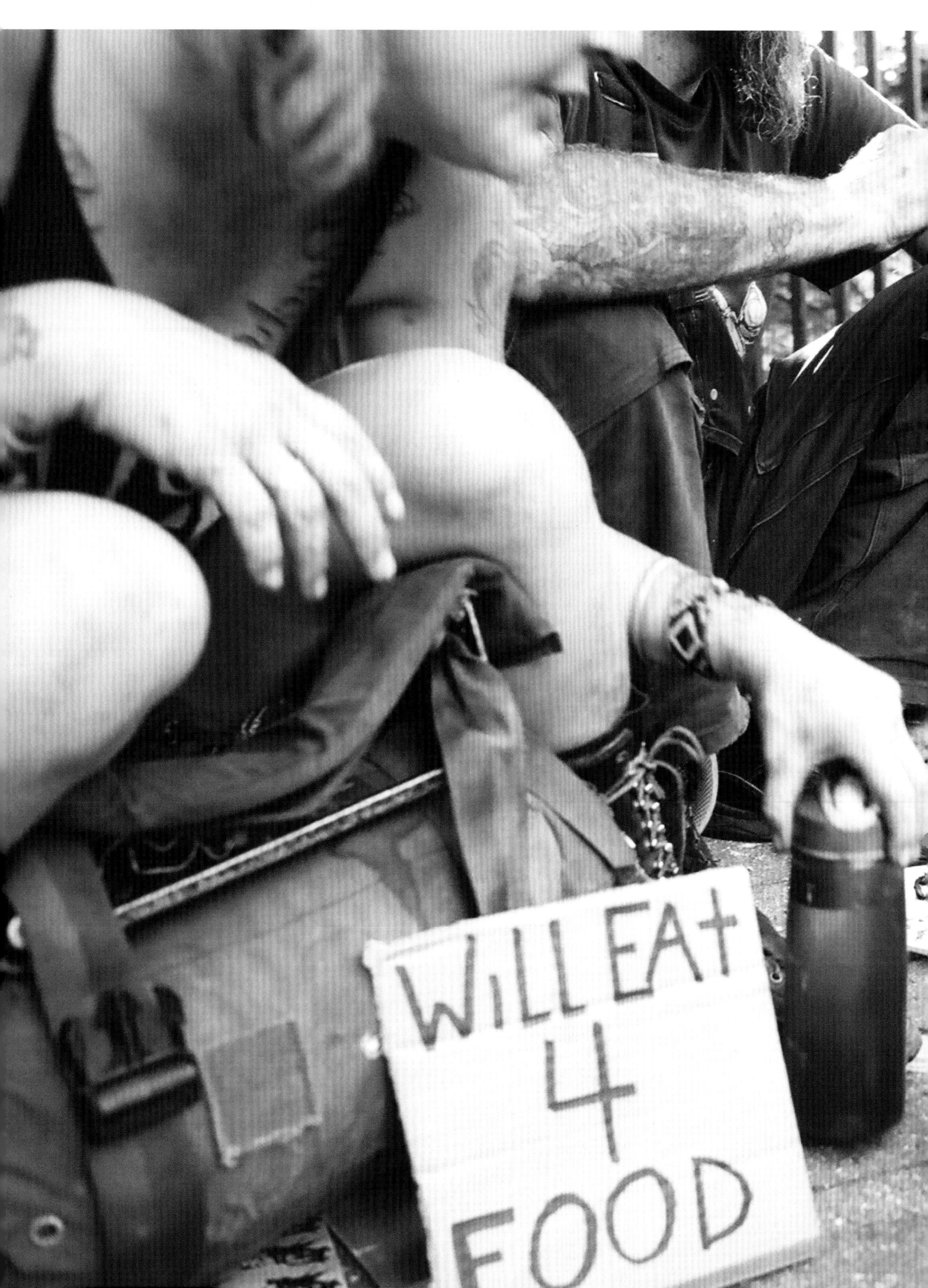

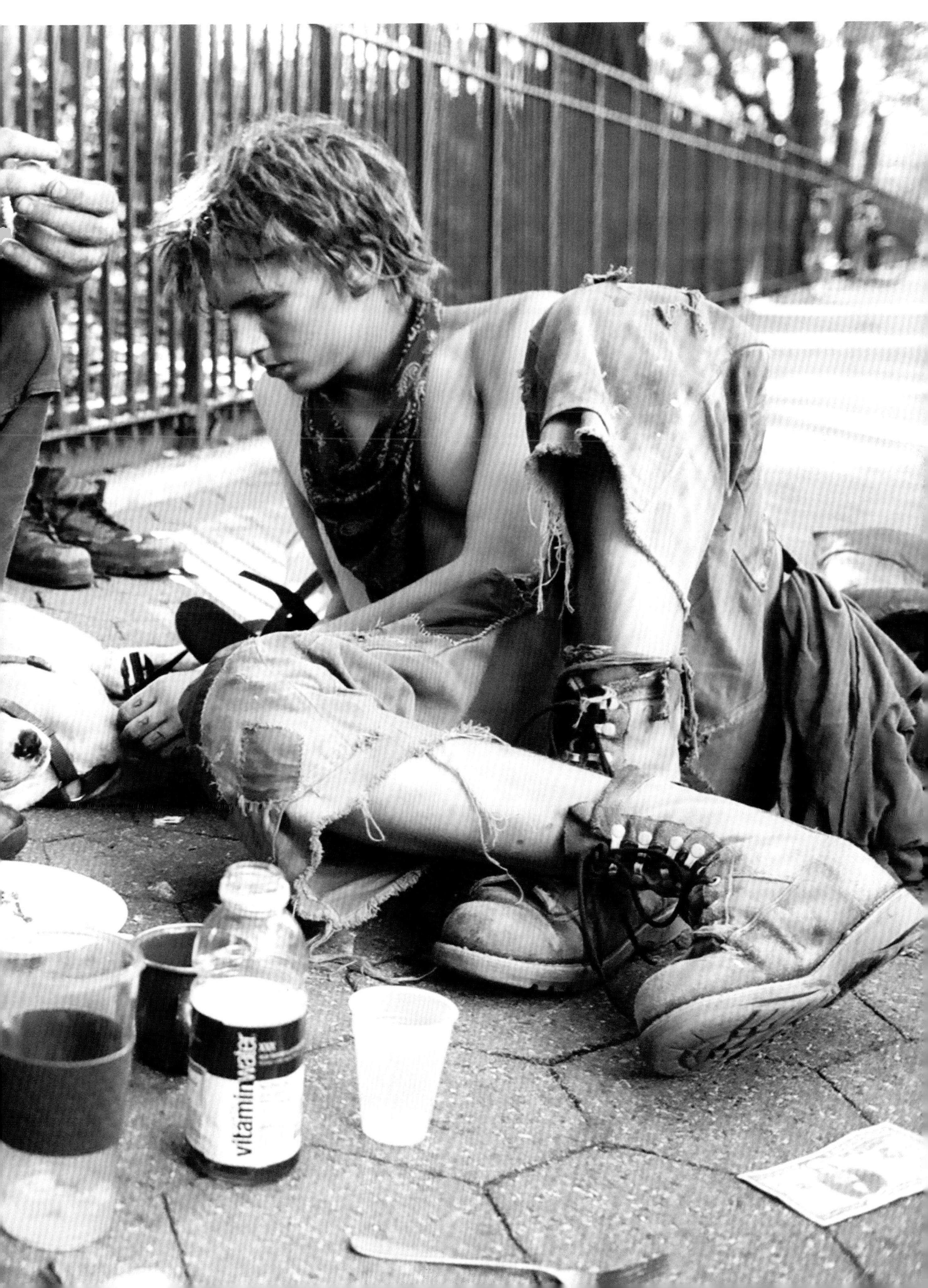
vitaminwater

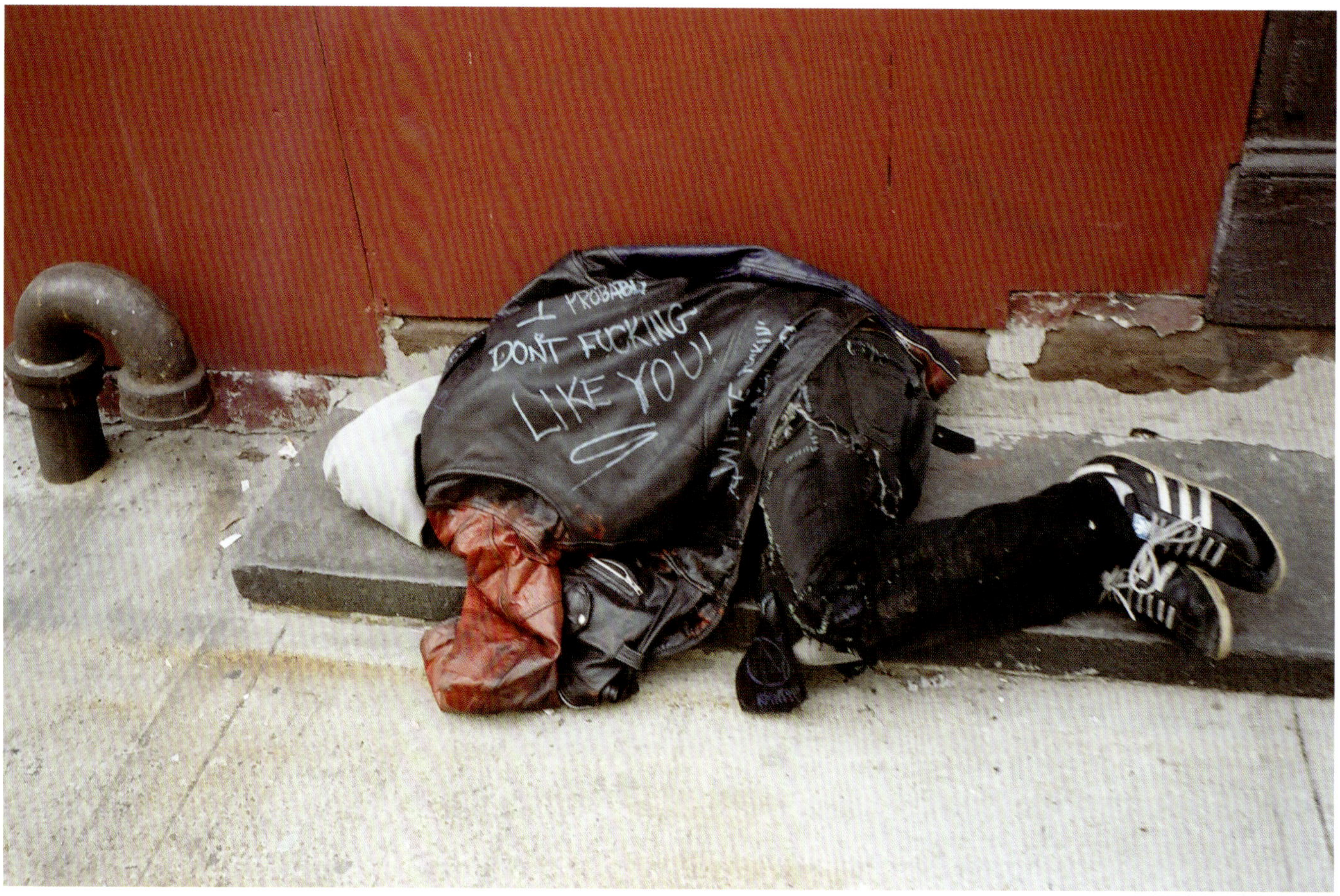
I PROBABLY
DONT FUCKING
LIKE YOU!

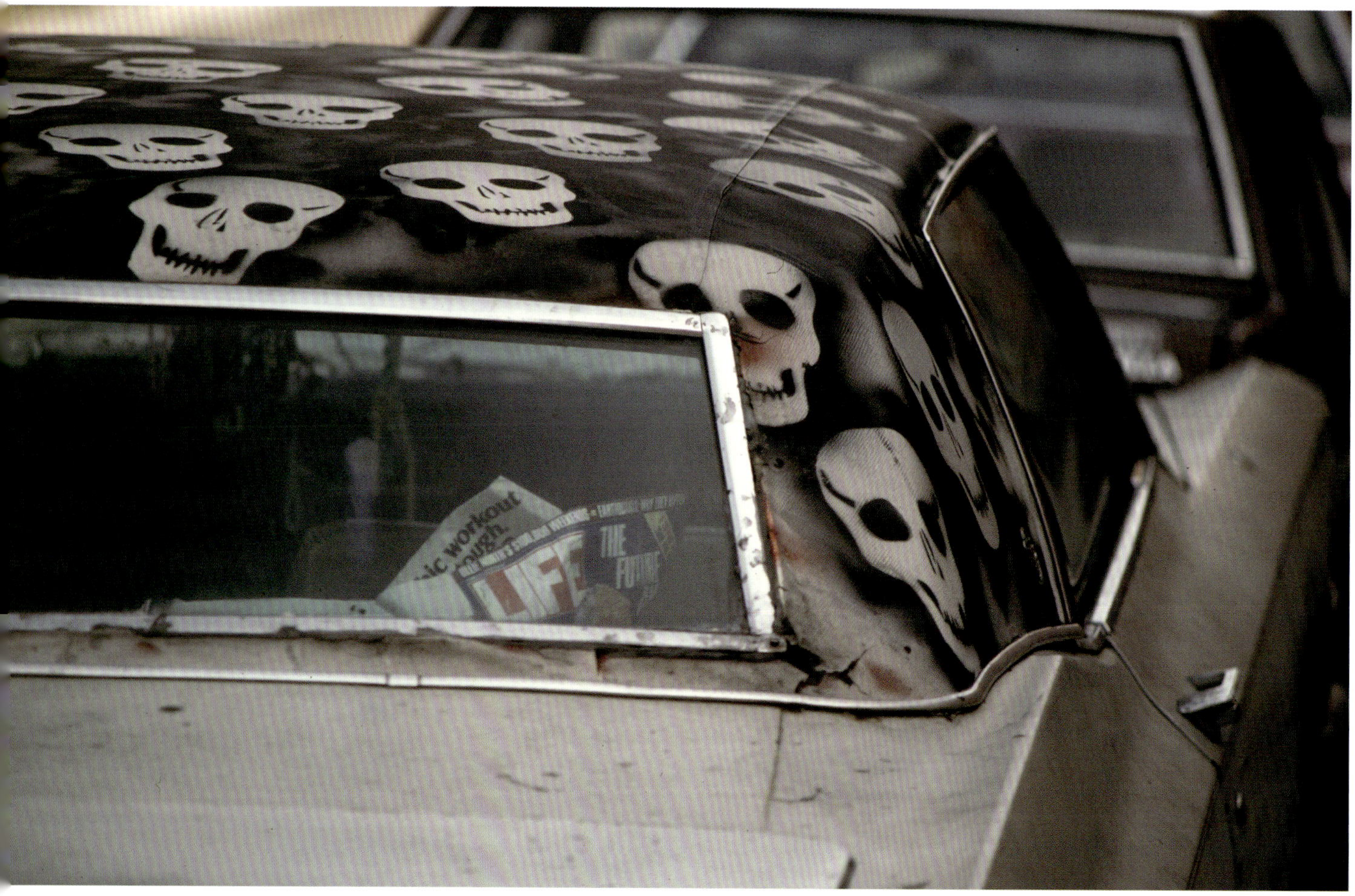
THE FUTURE

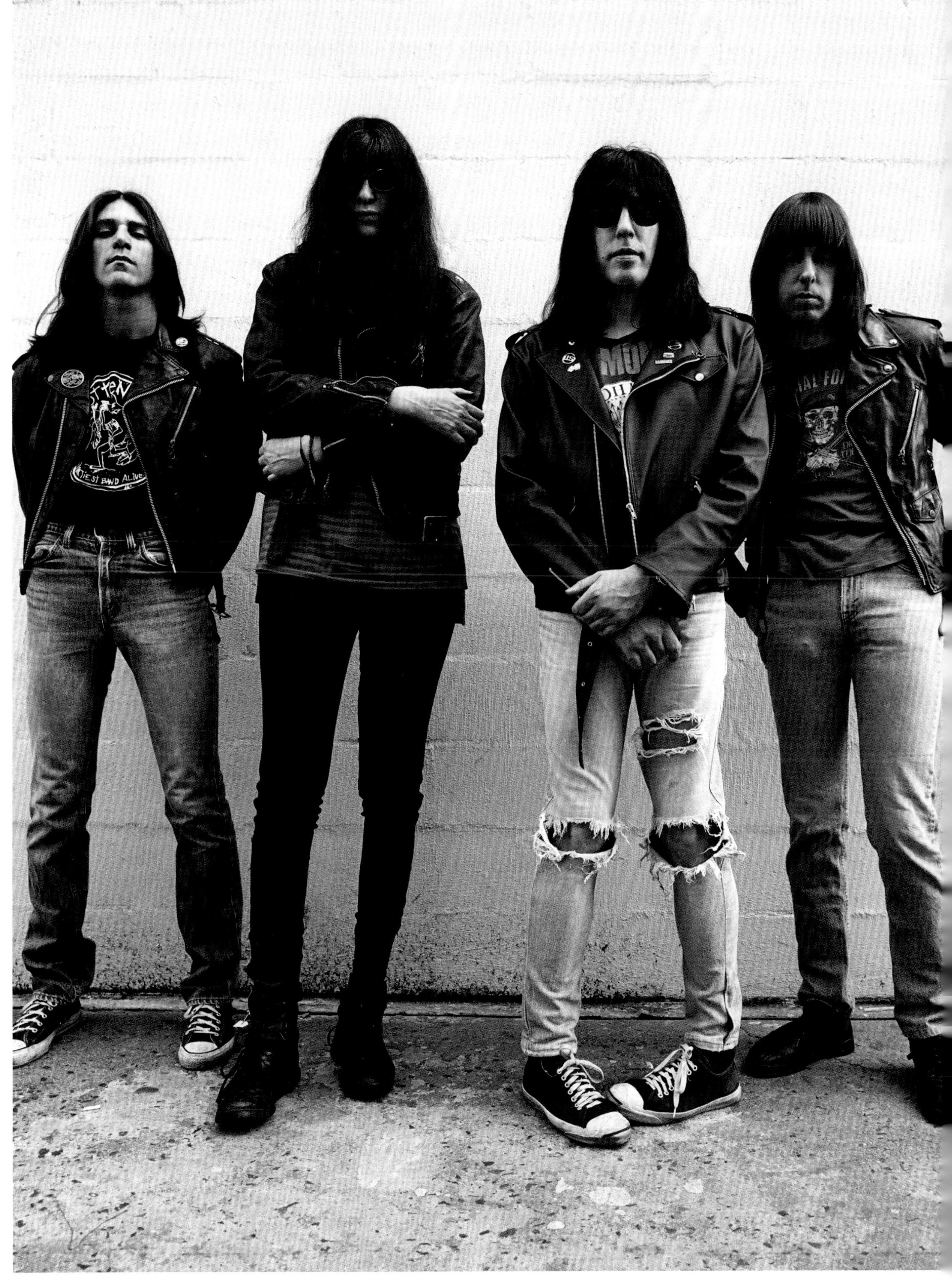

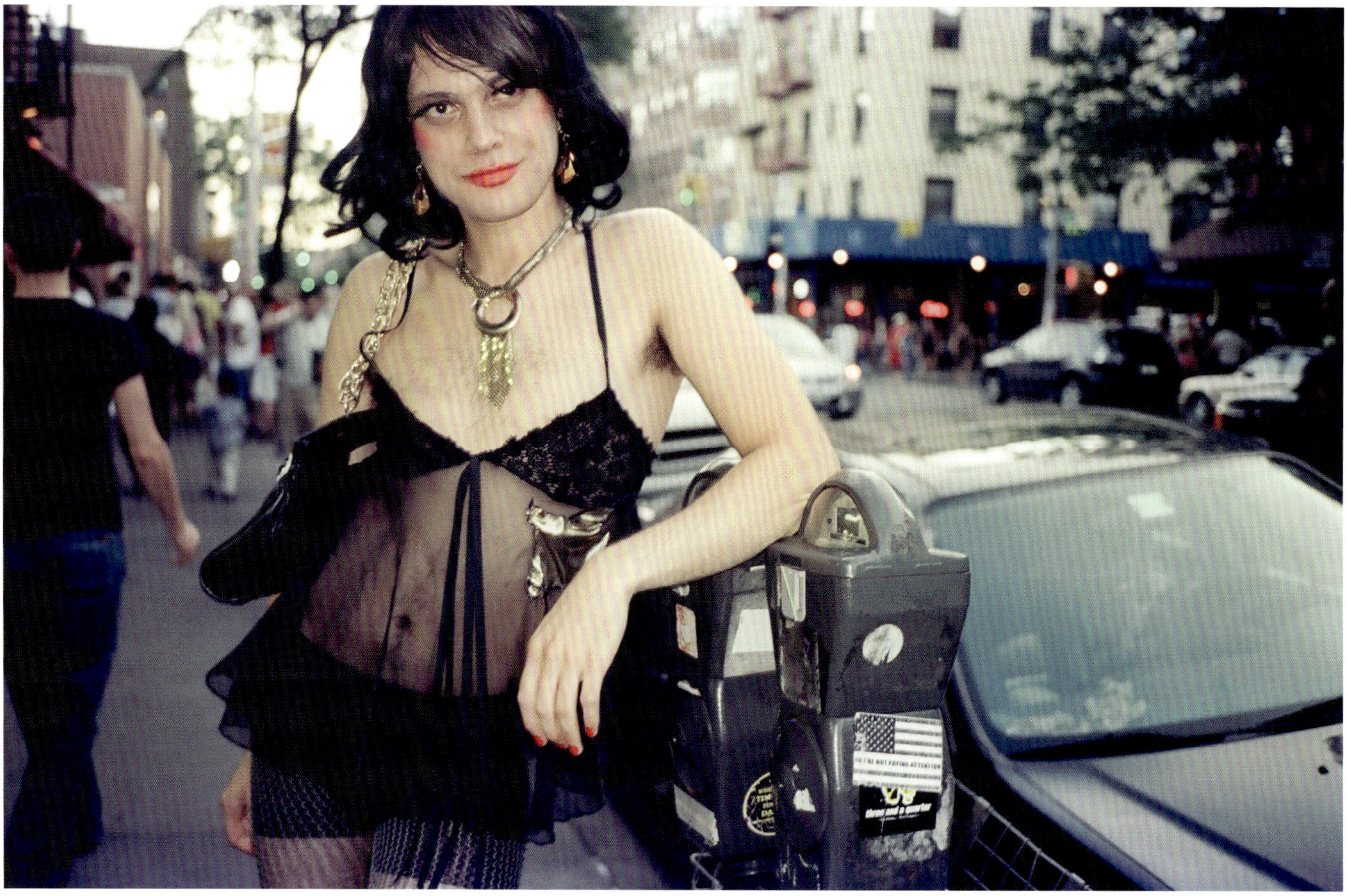

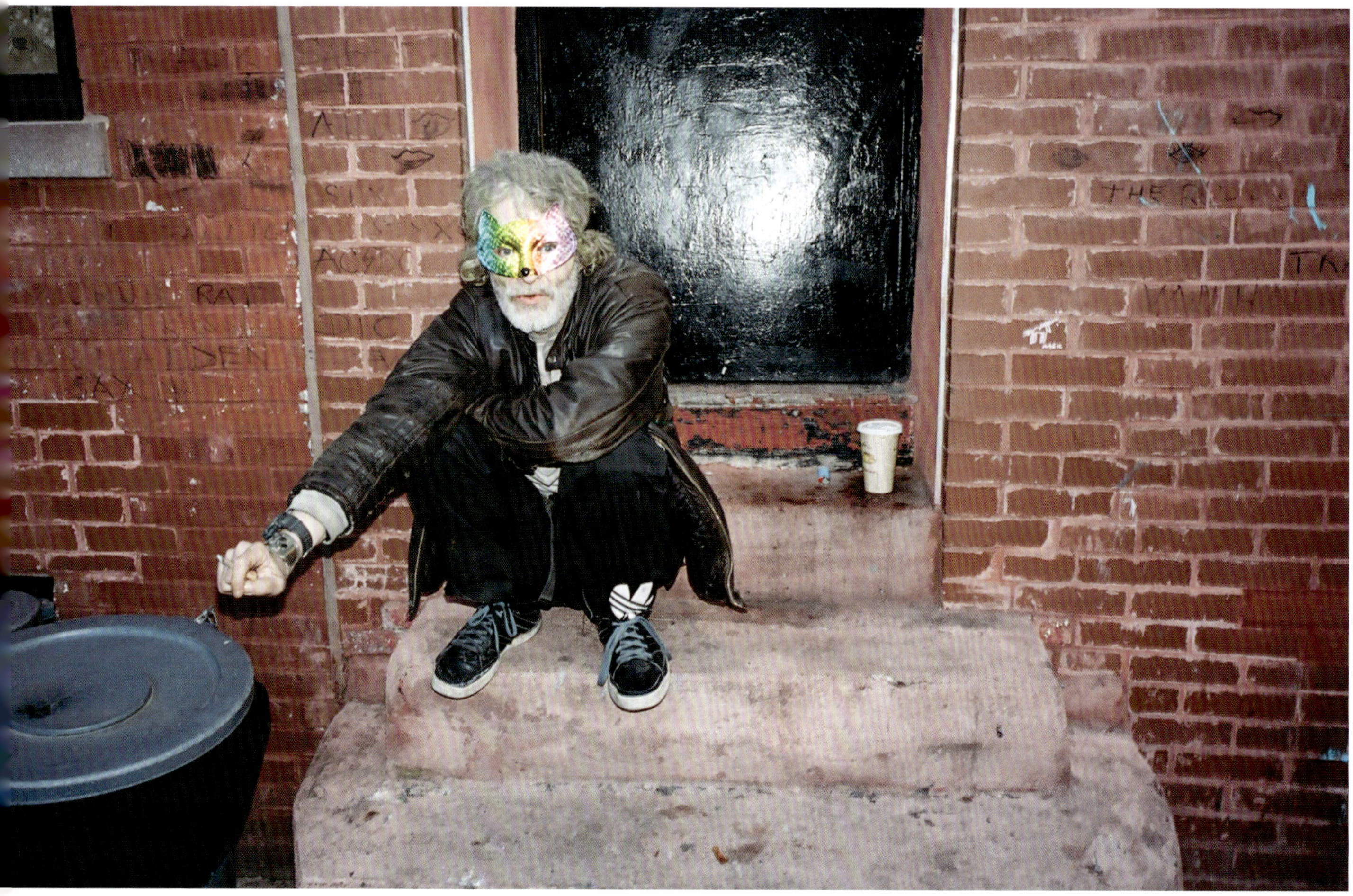

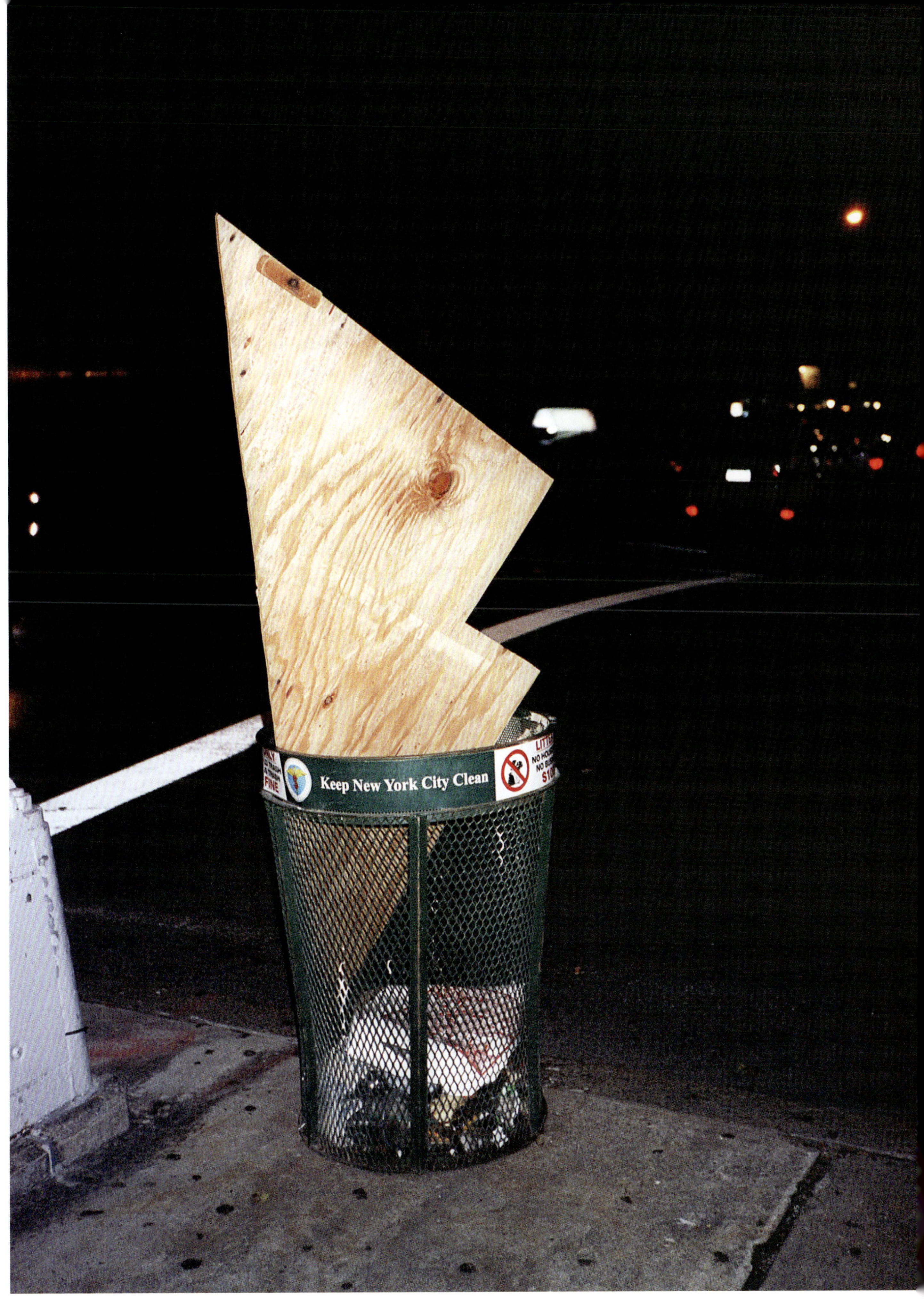
Keep New York City Clean

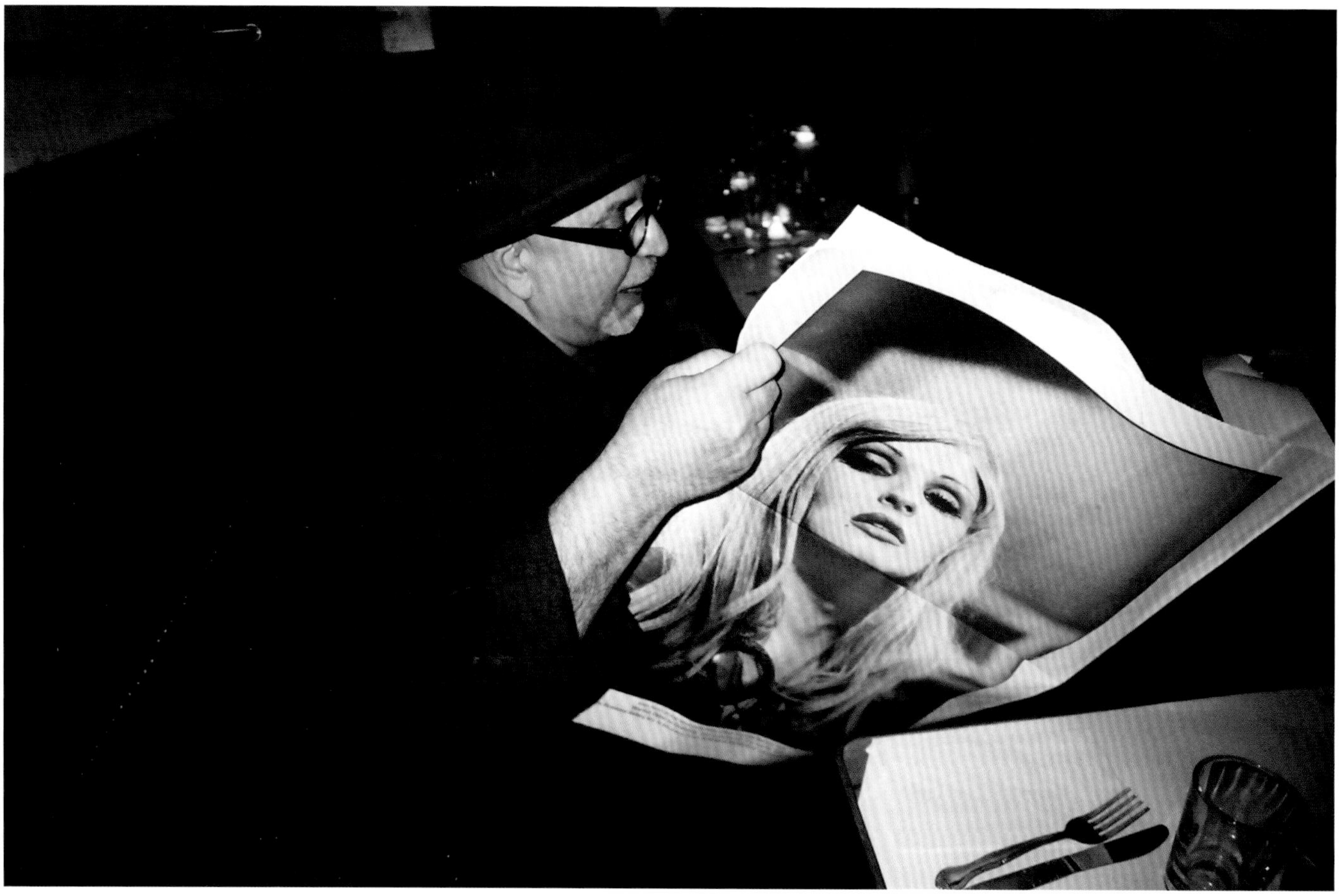

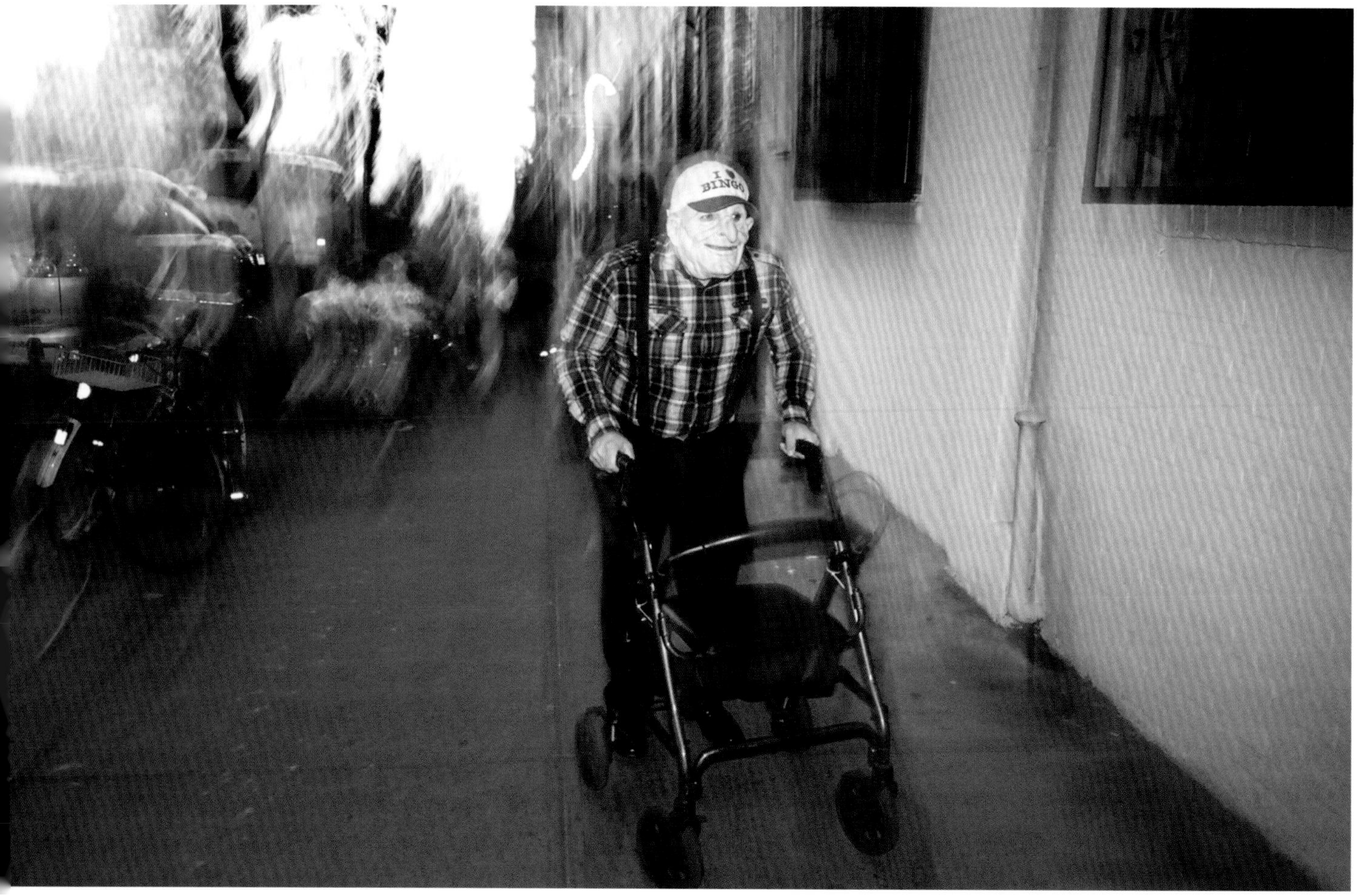

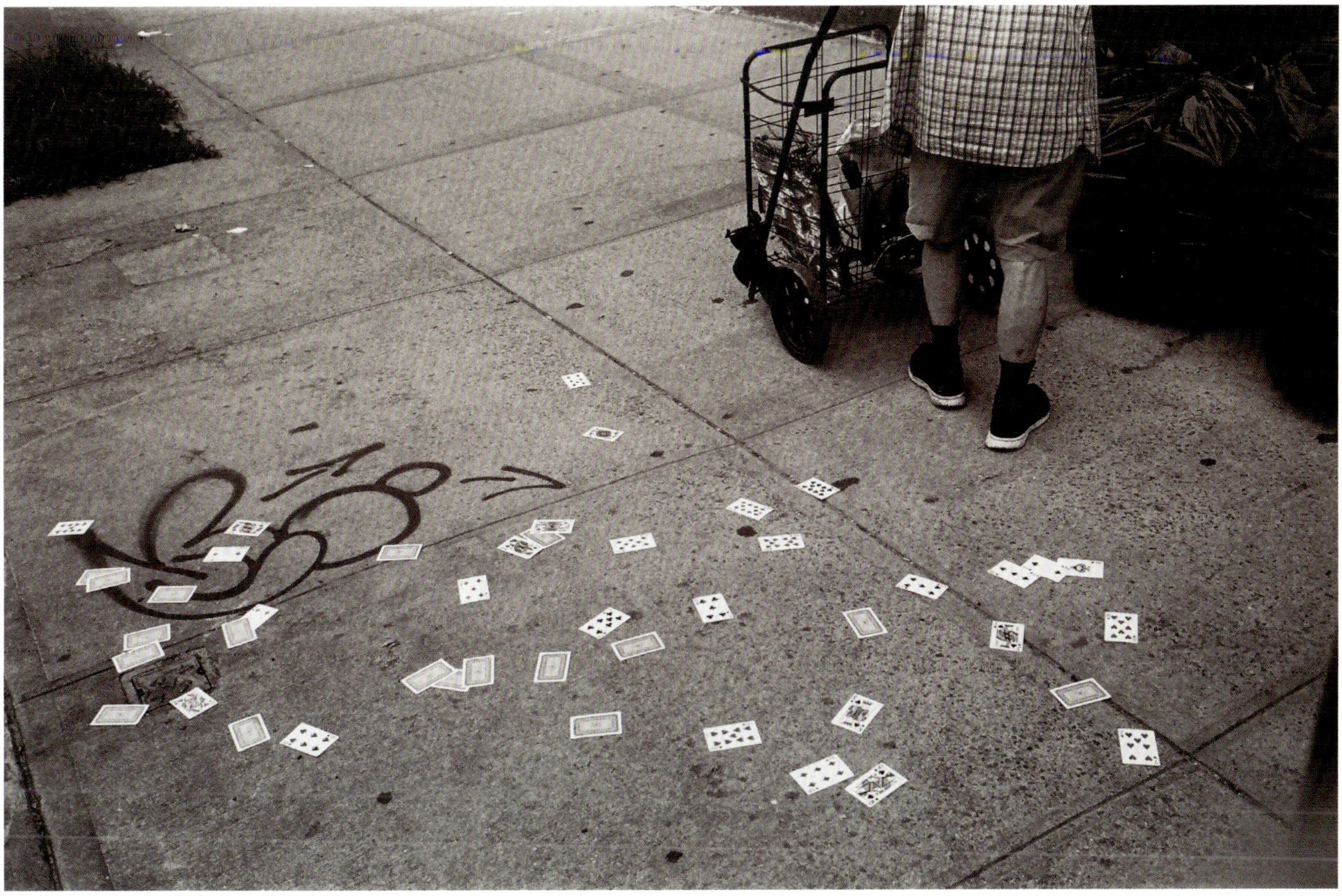

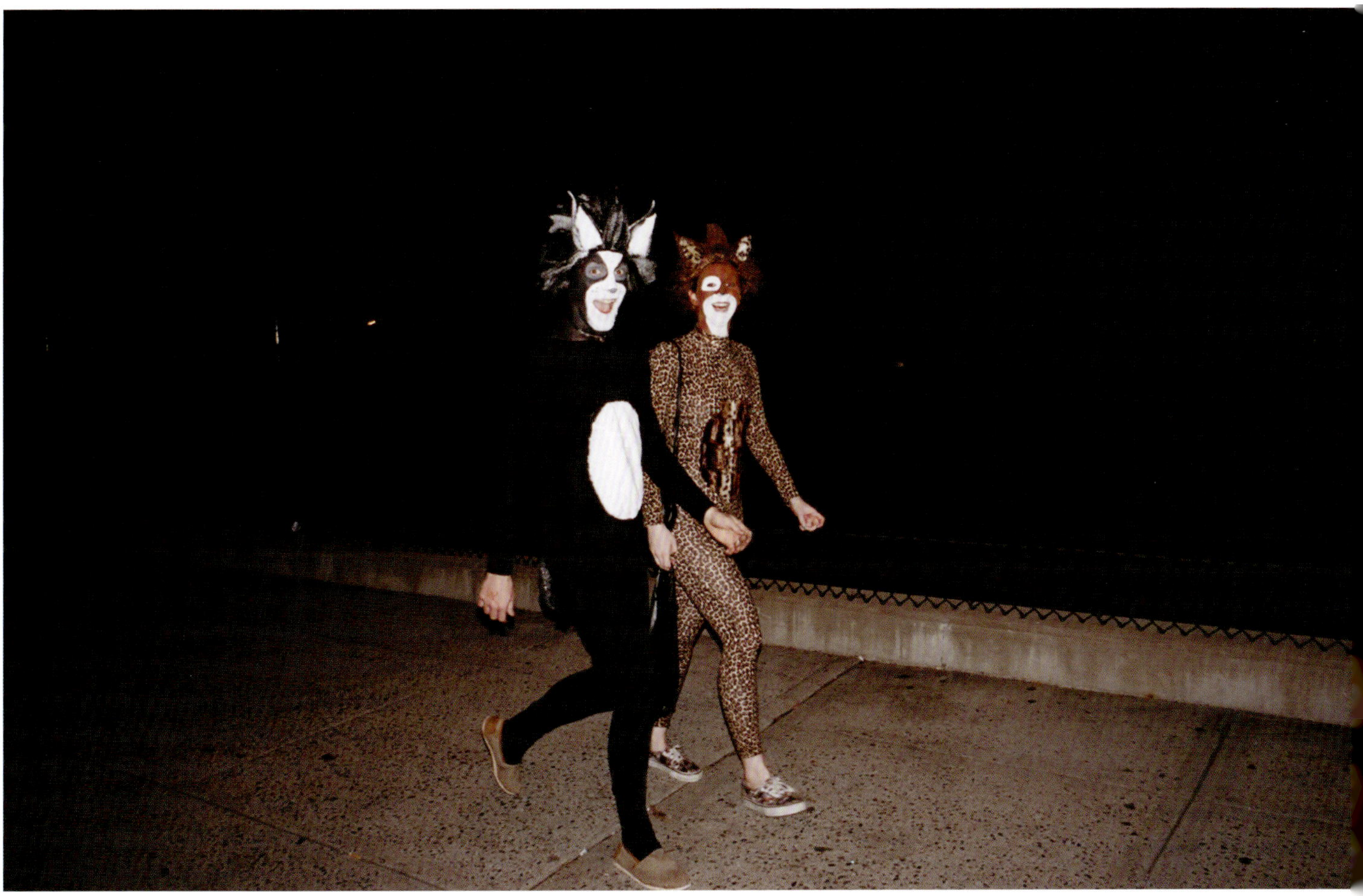

FIDI

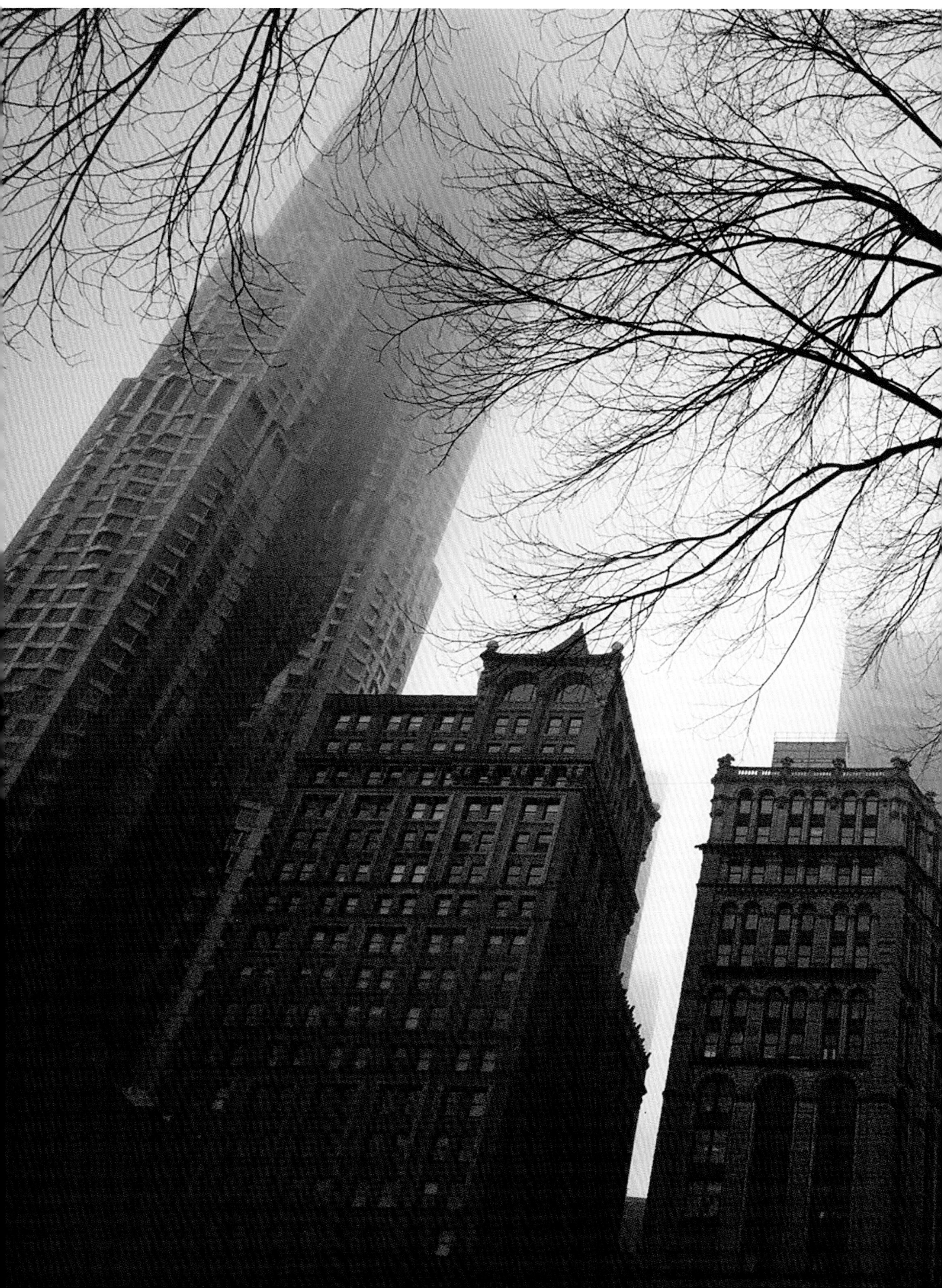

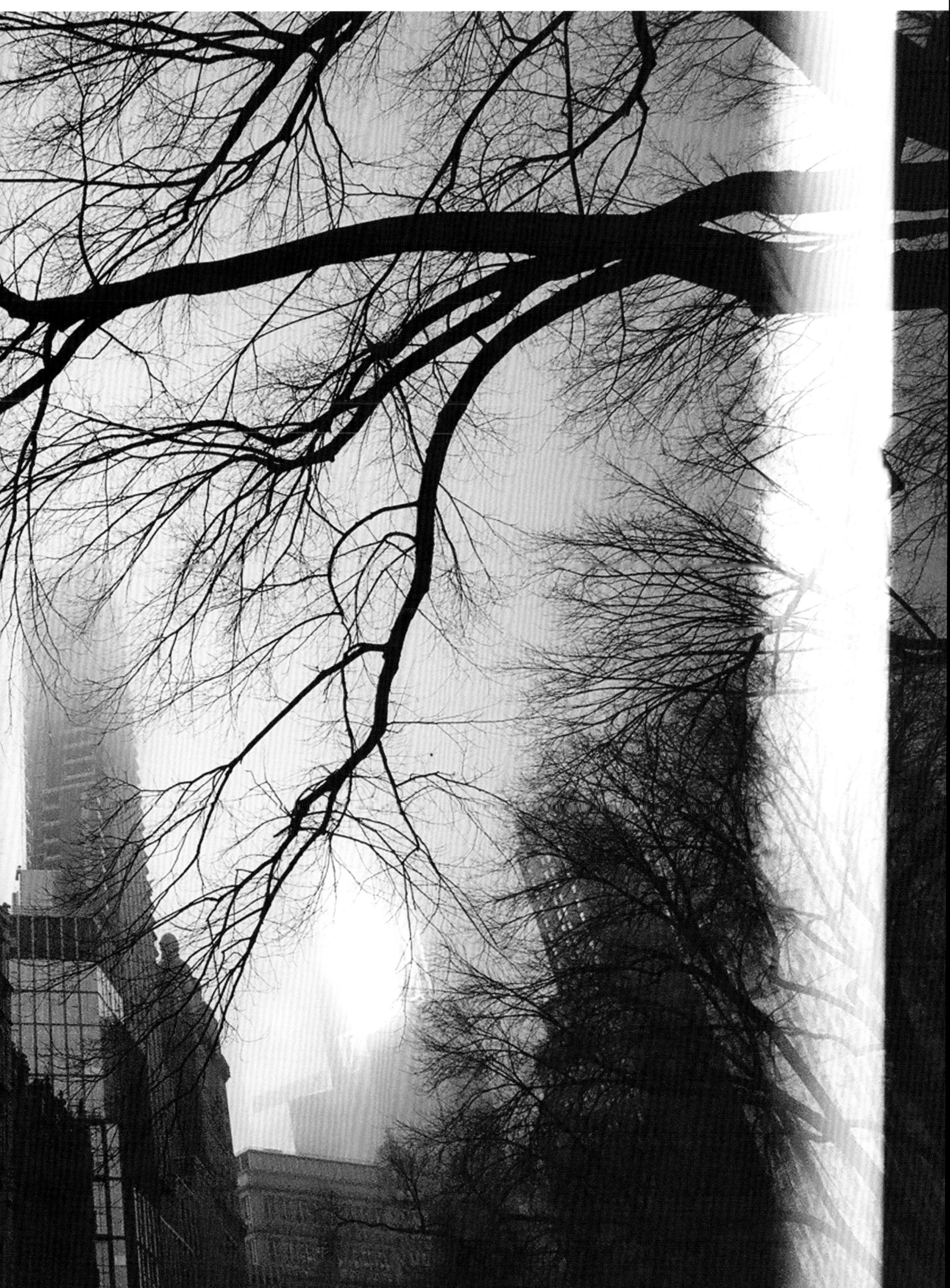

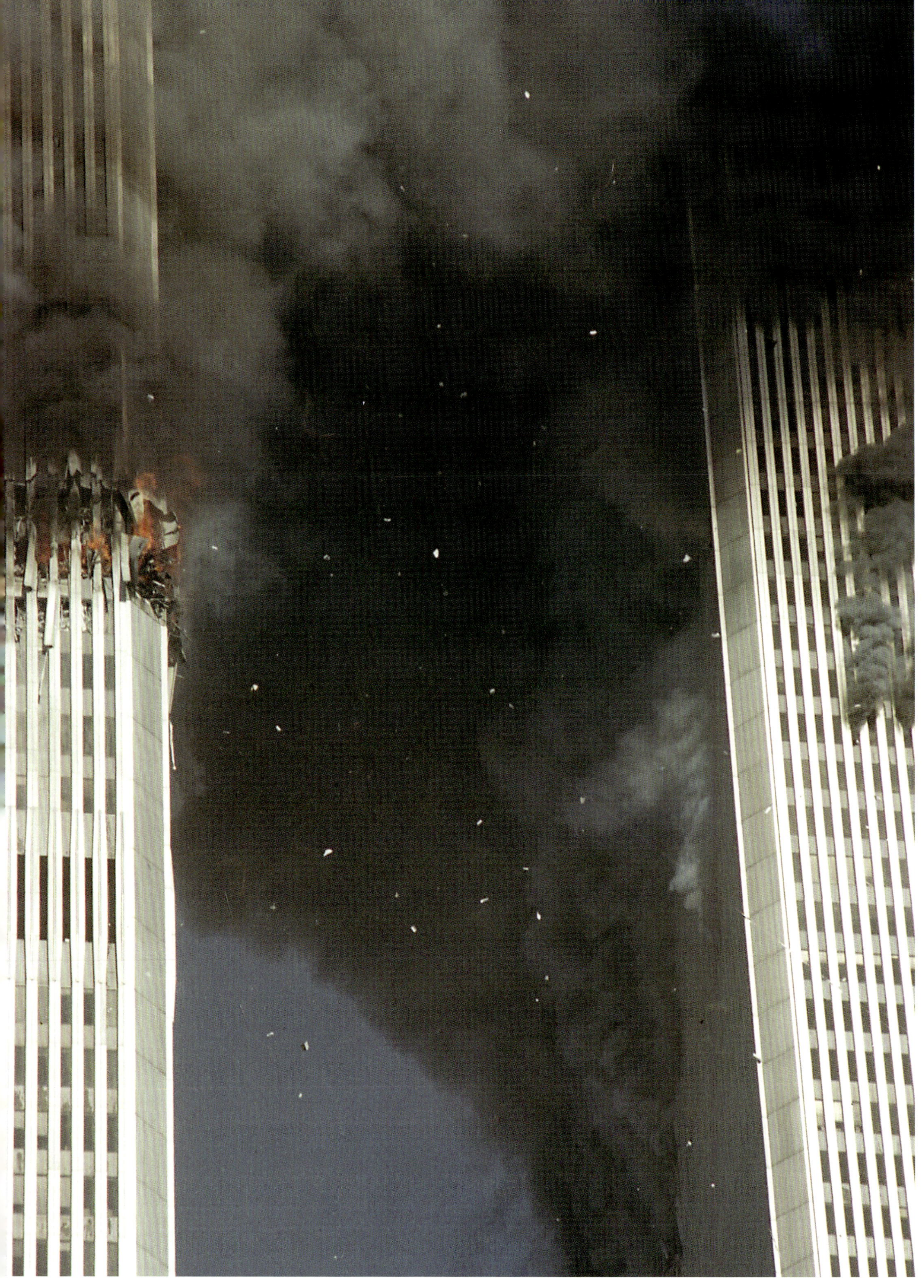

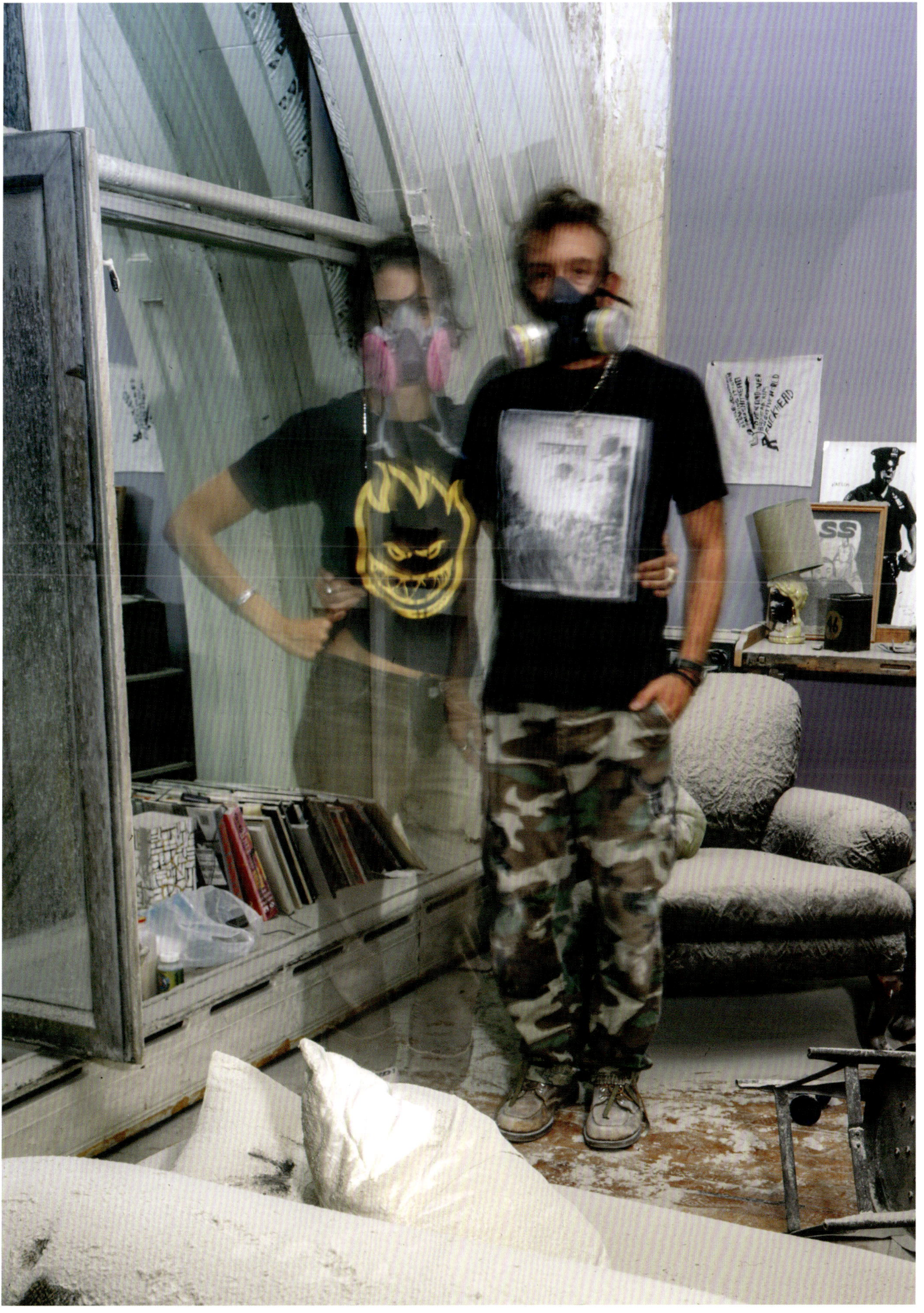

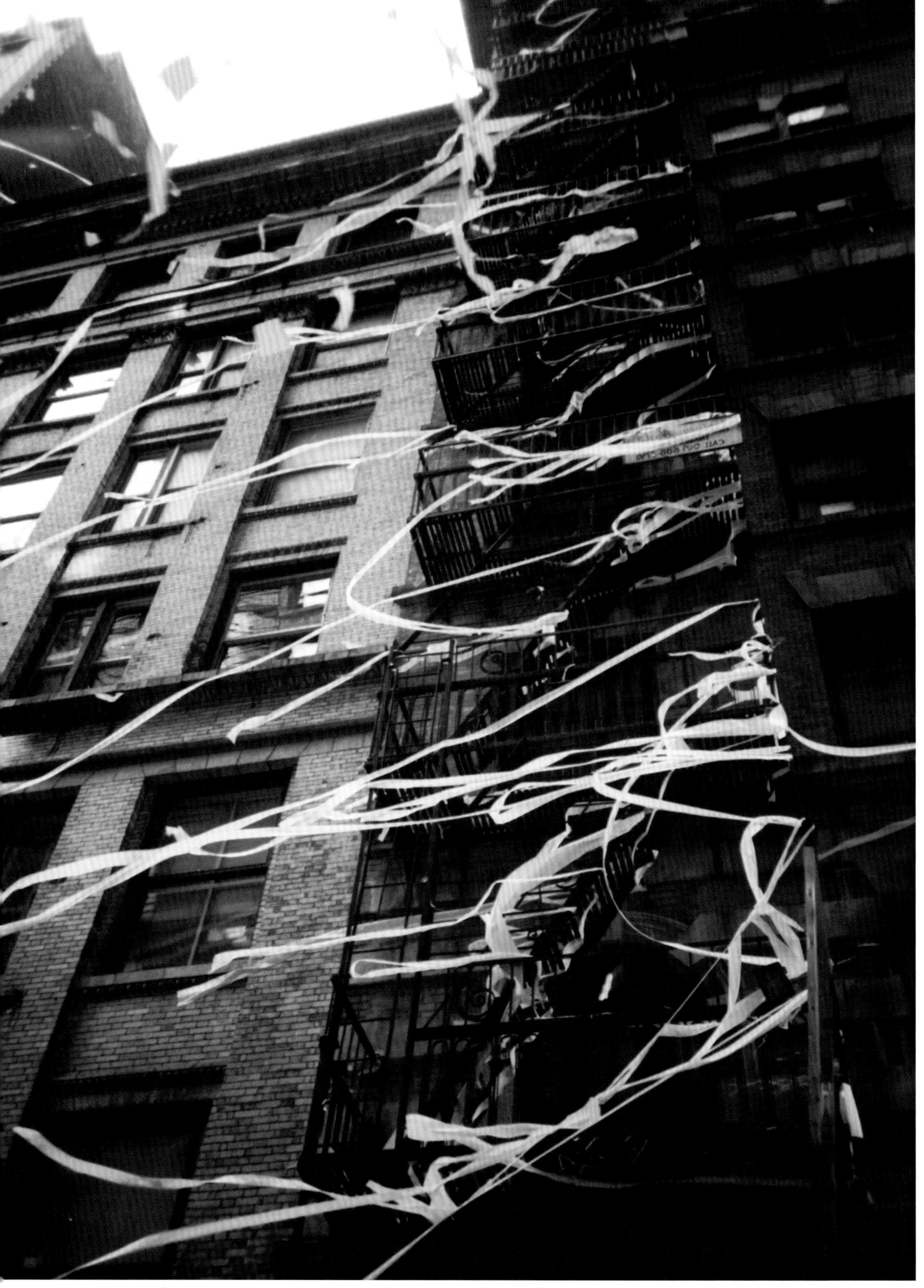

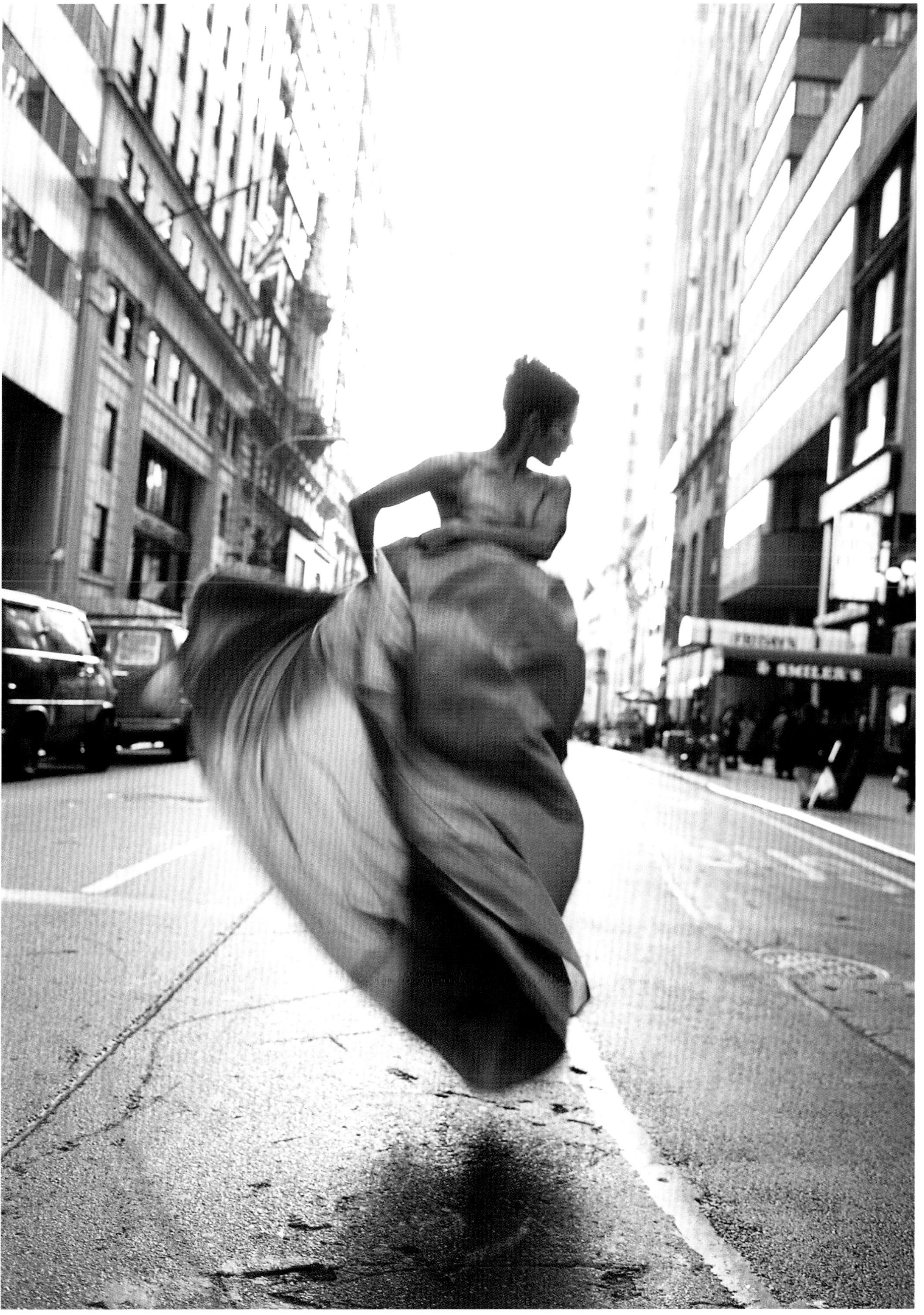

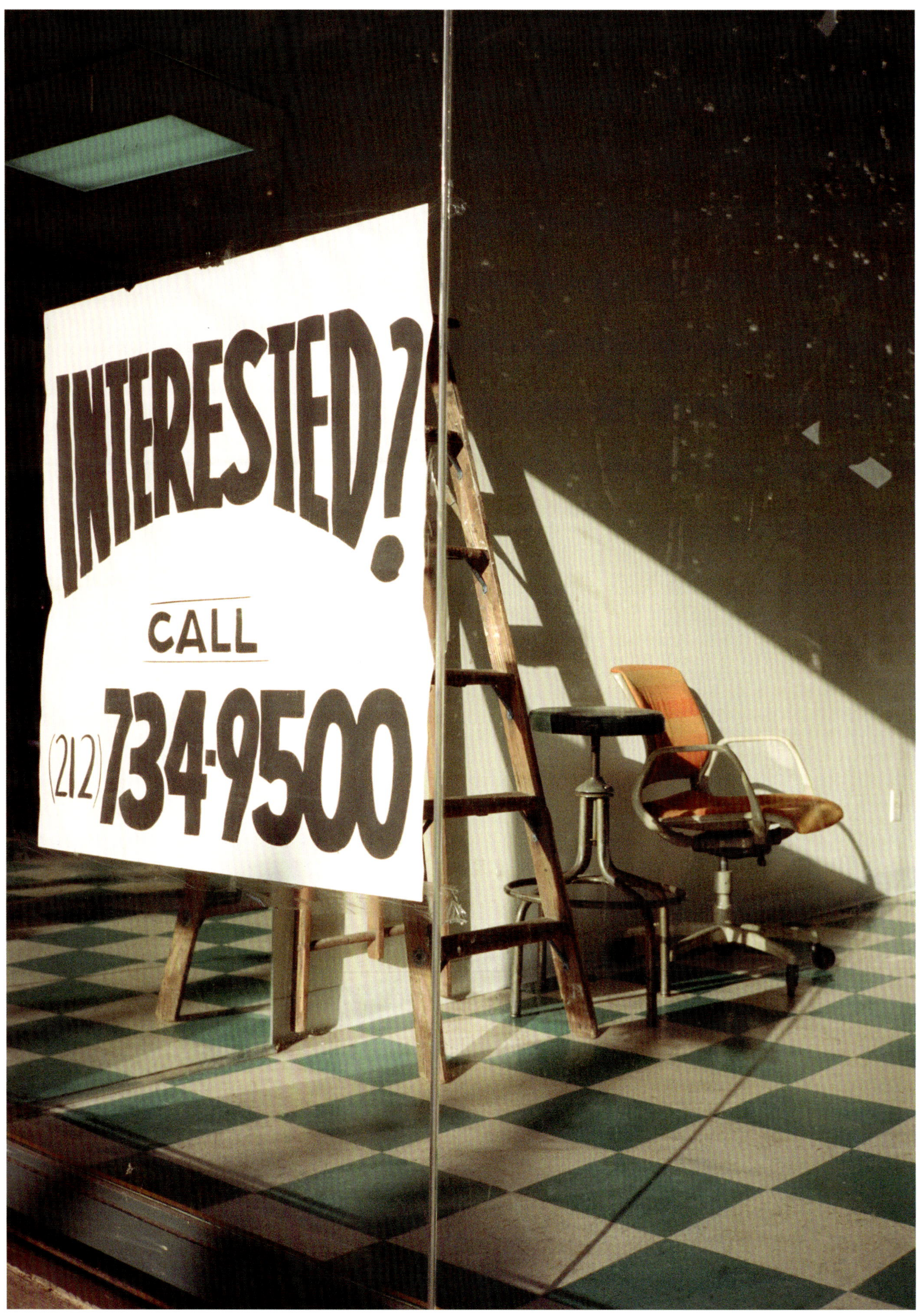
INTERESTED?
CALL
(212) 734-9500

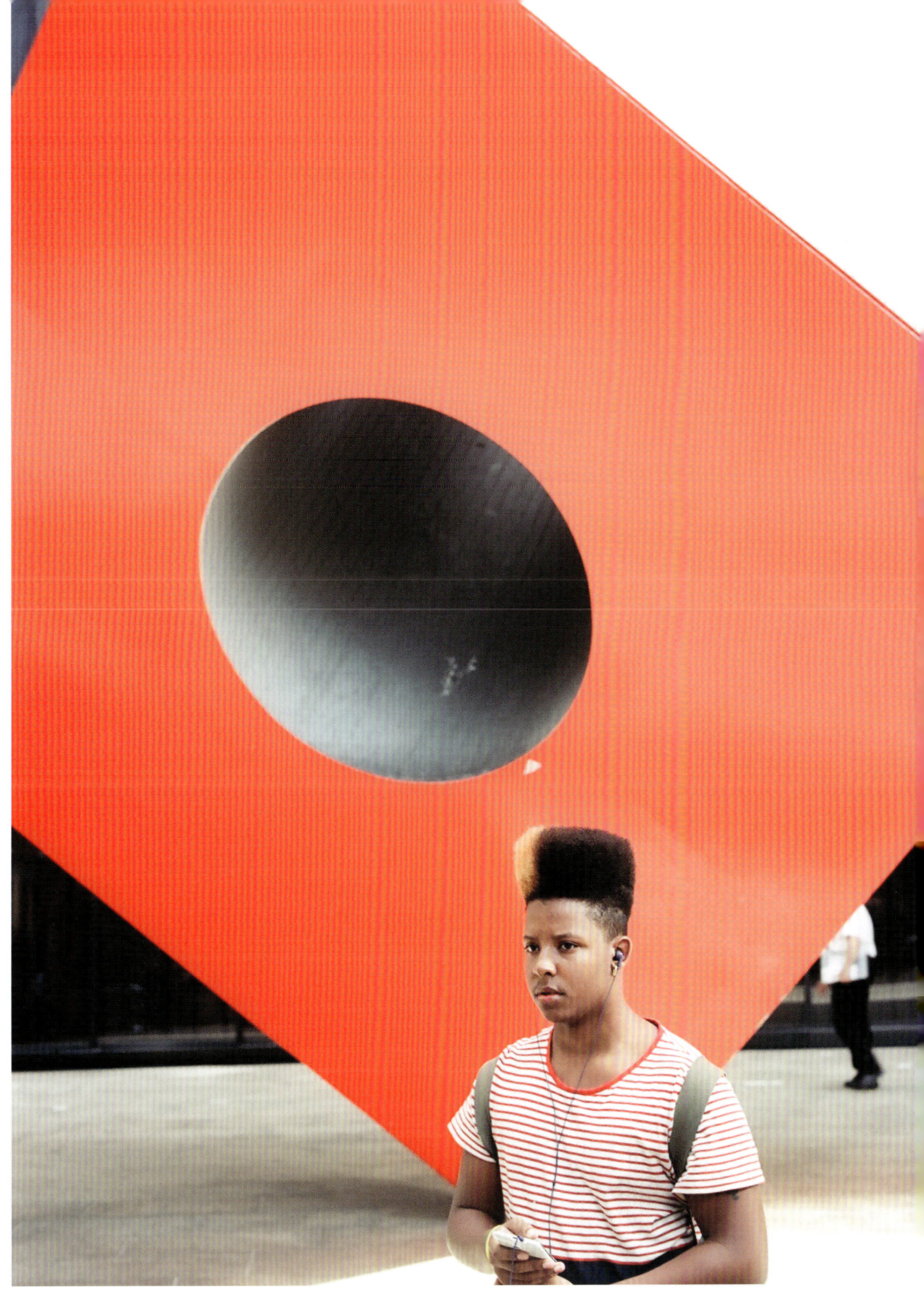

FIREWORKS

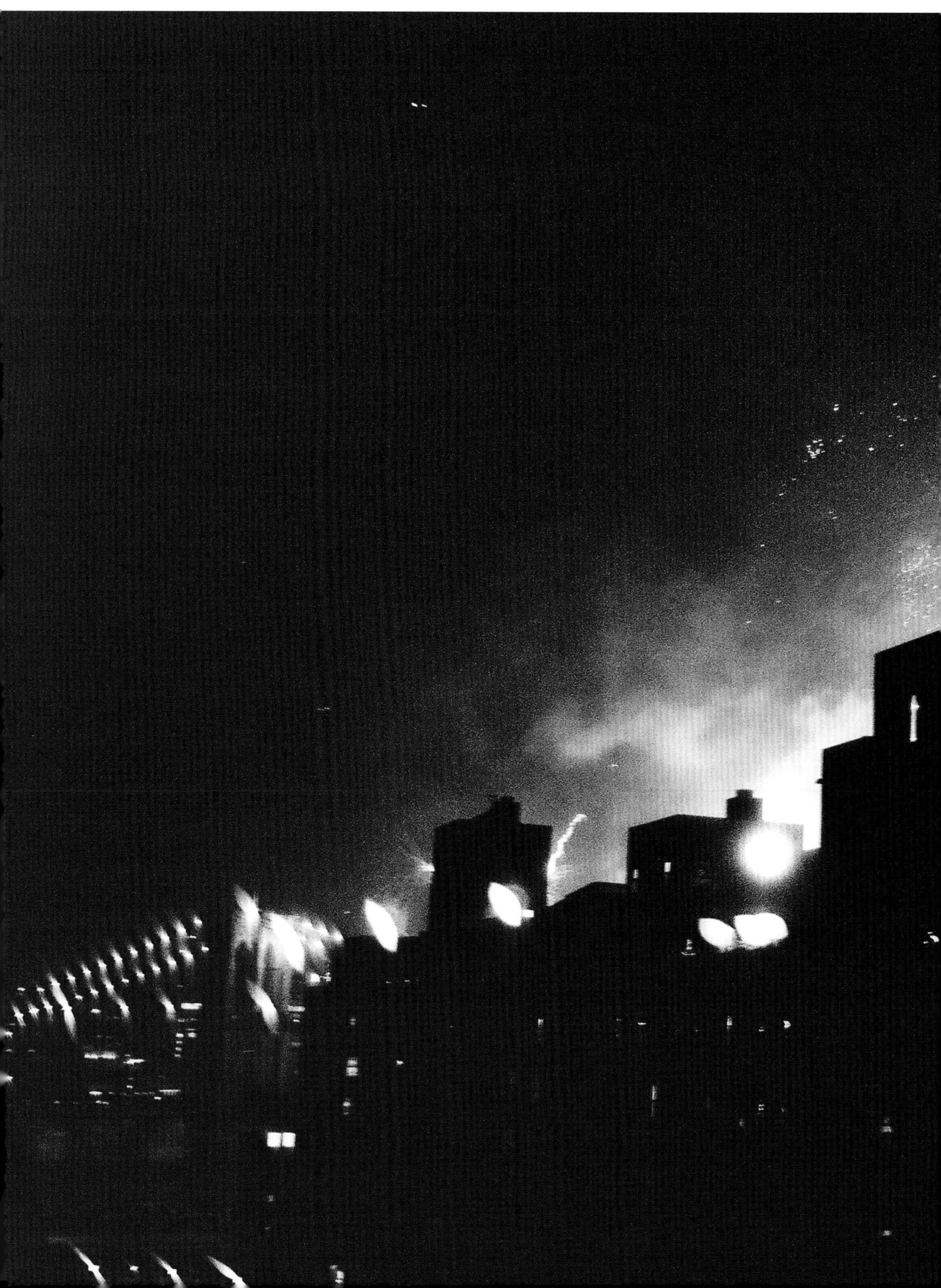

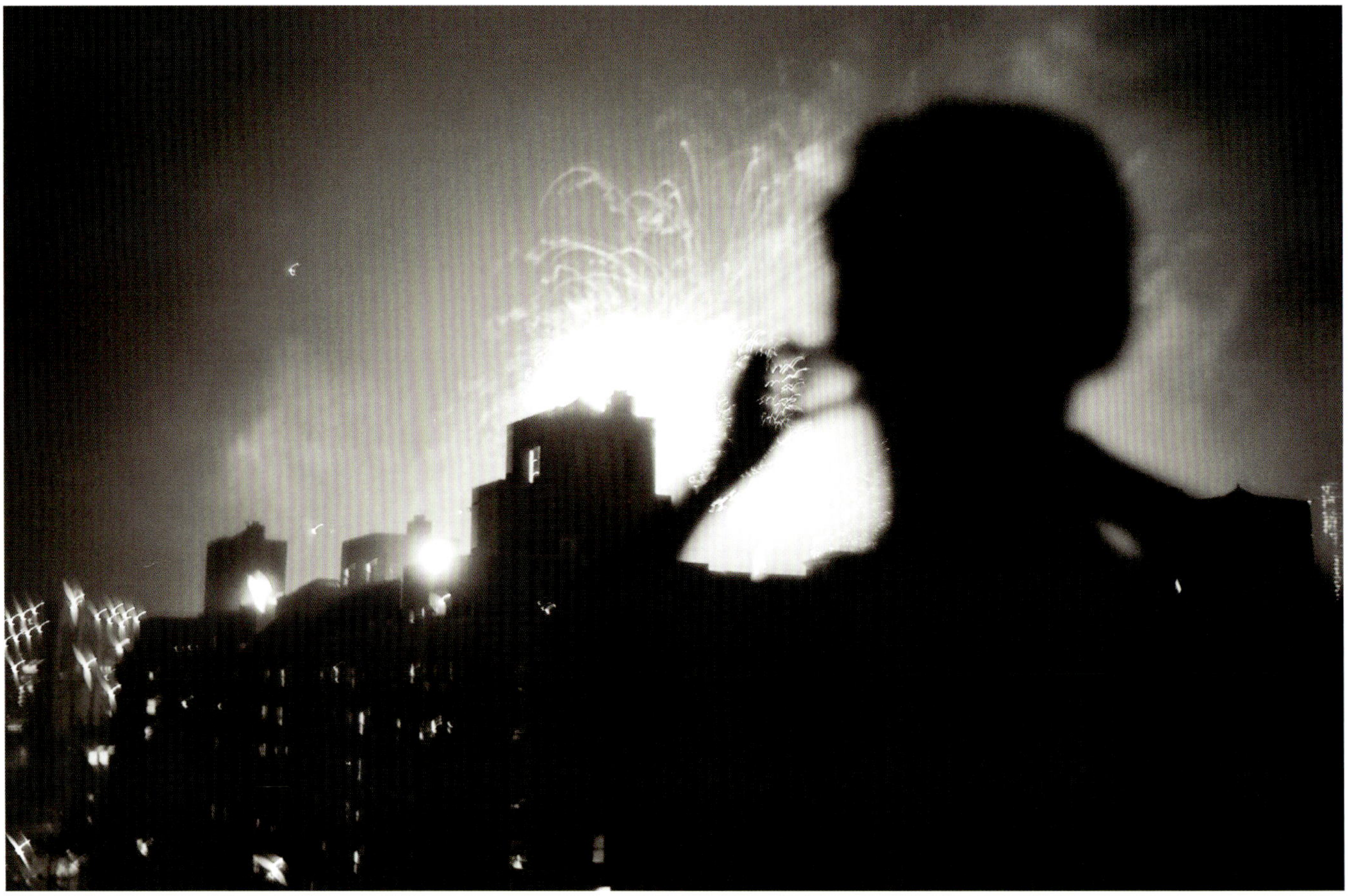

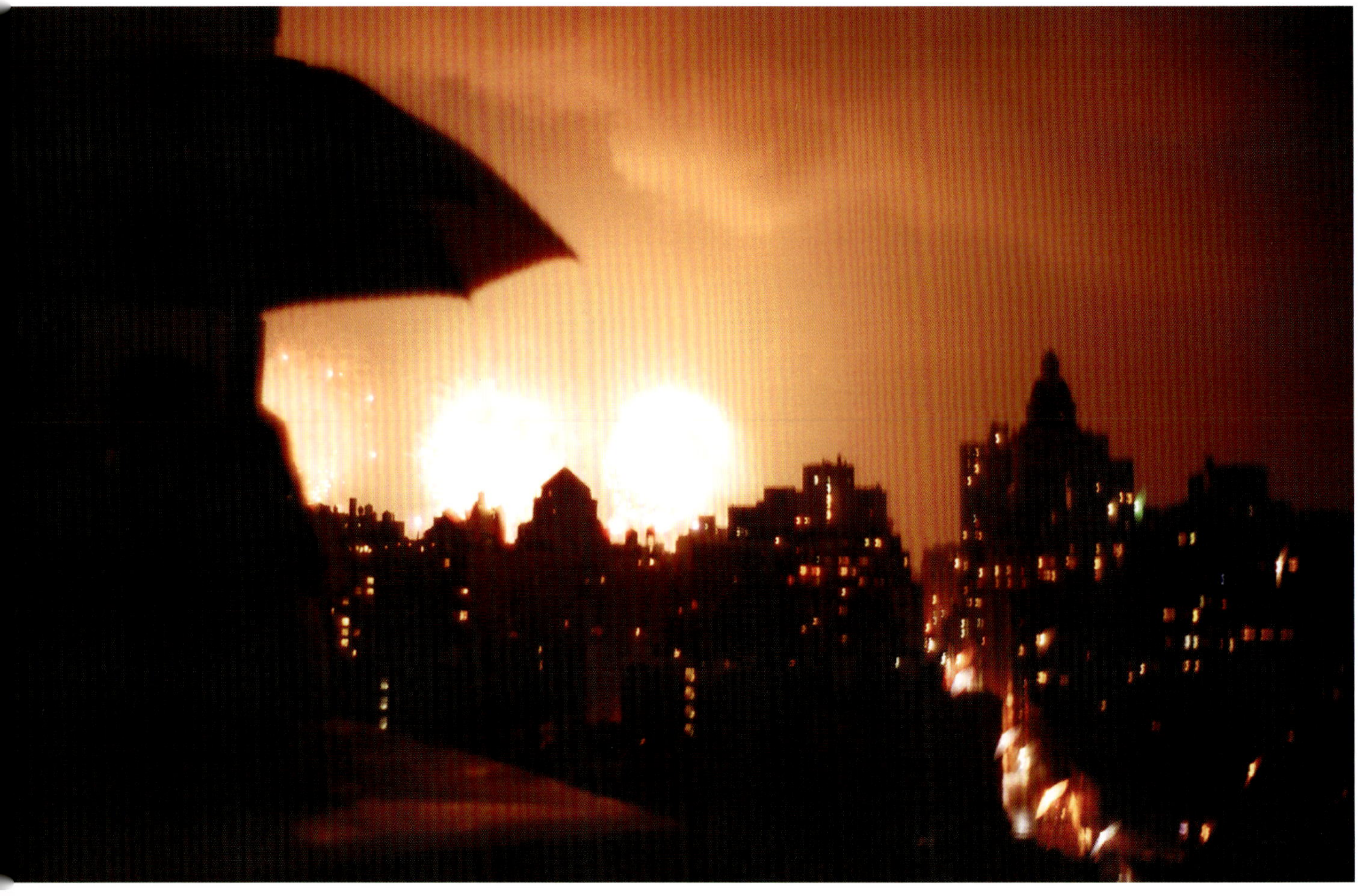

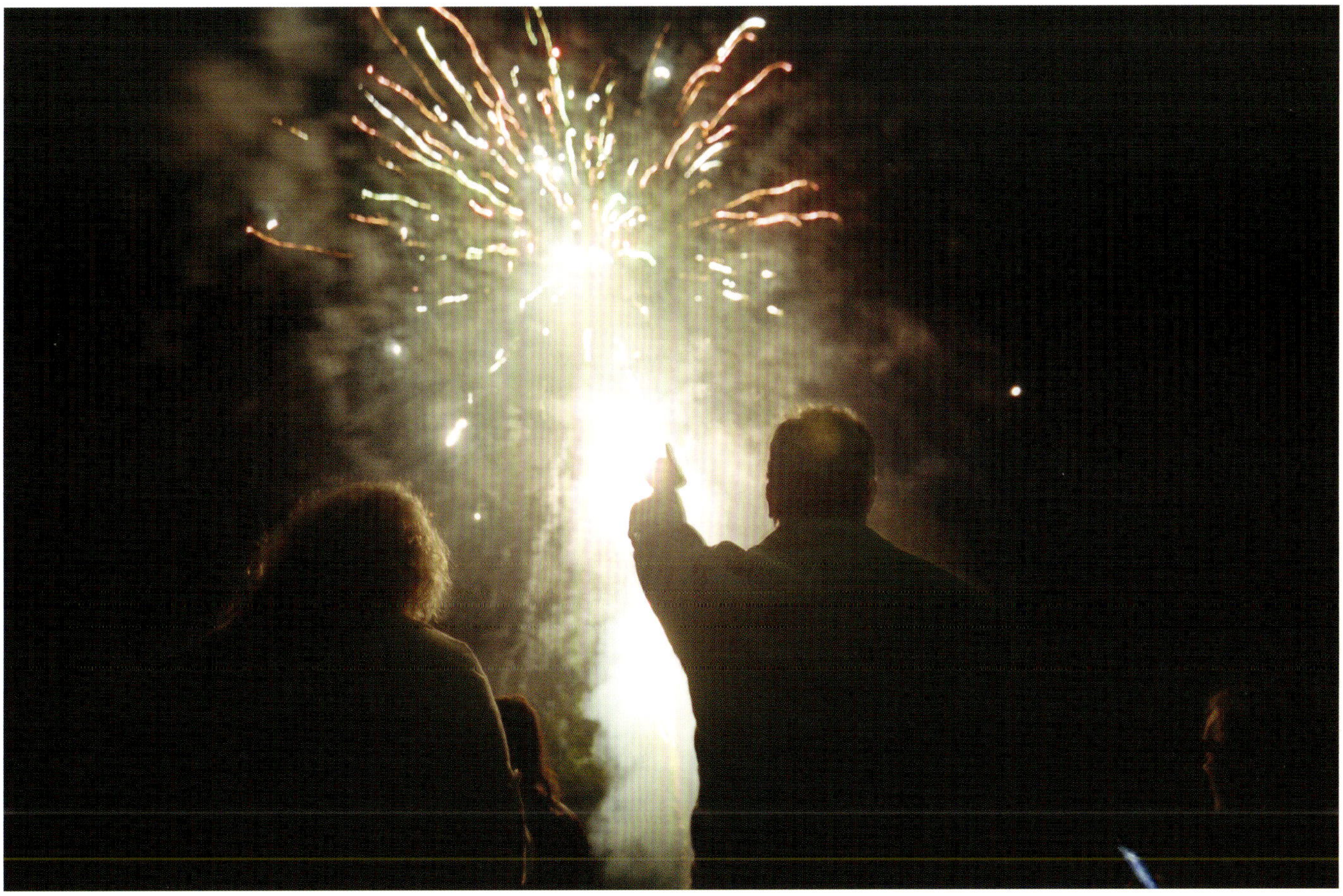

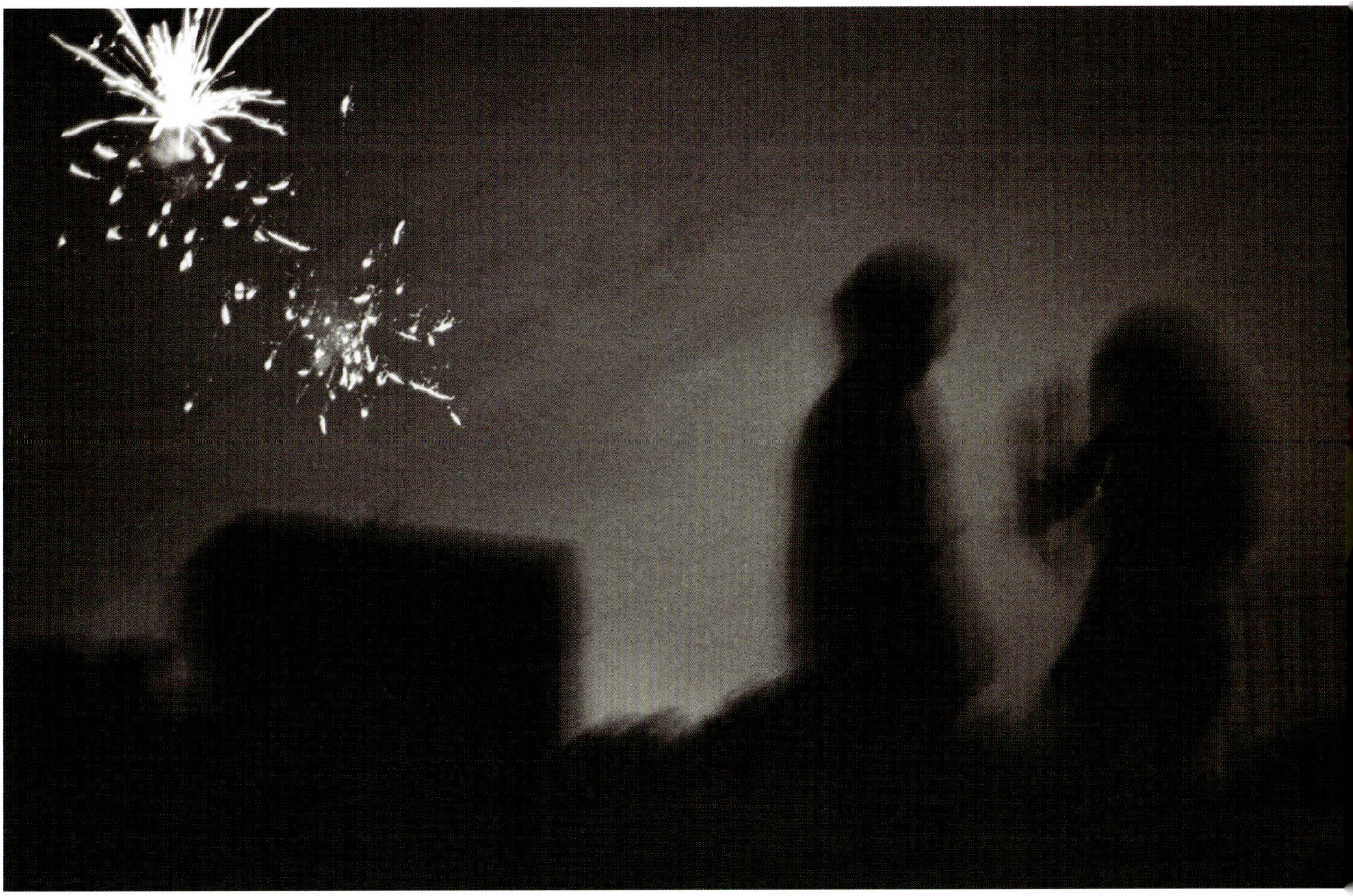

FLASH

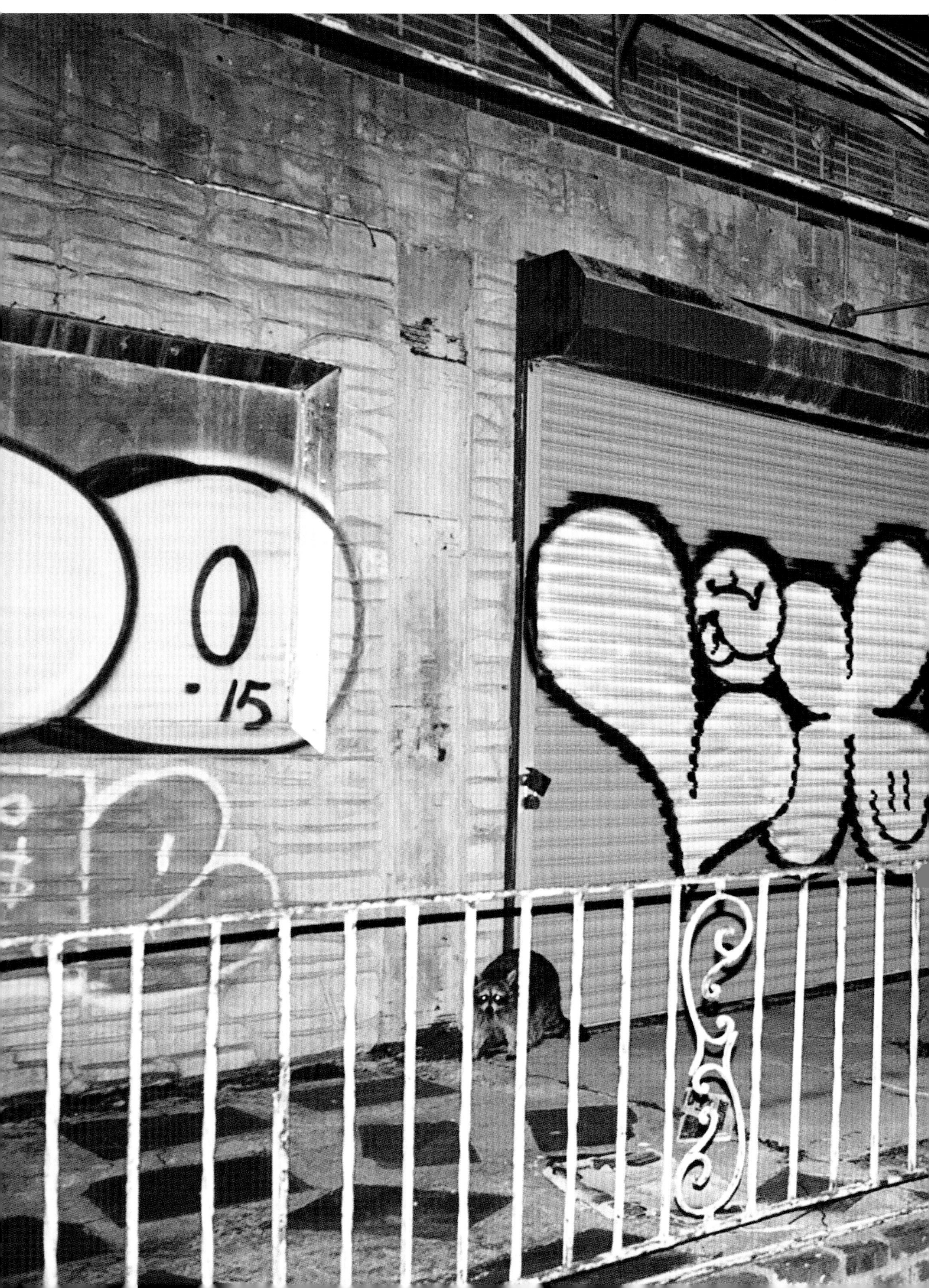

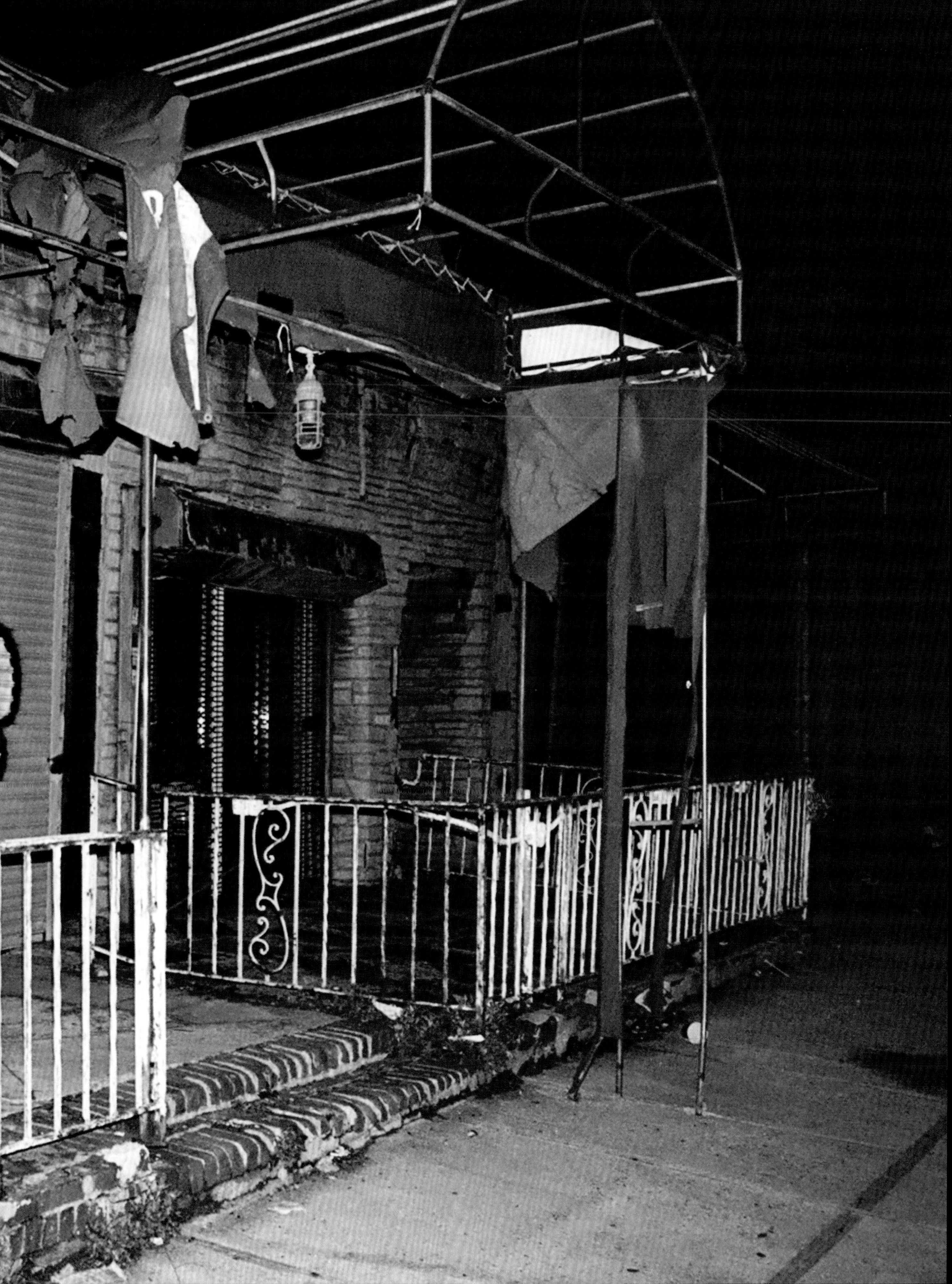

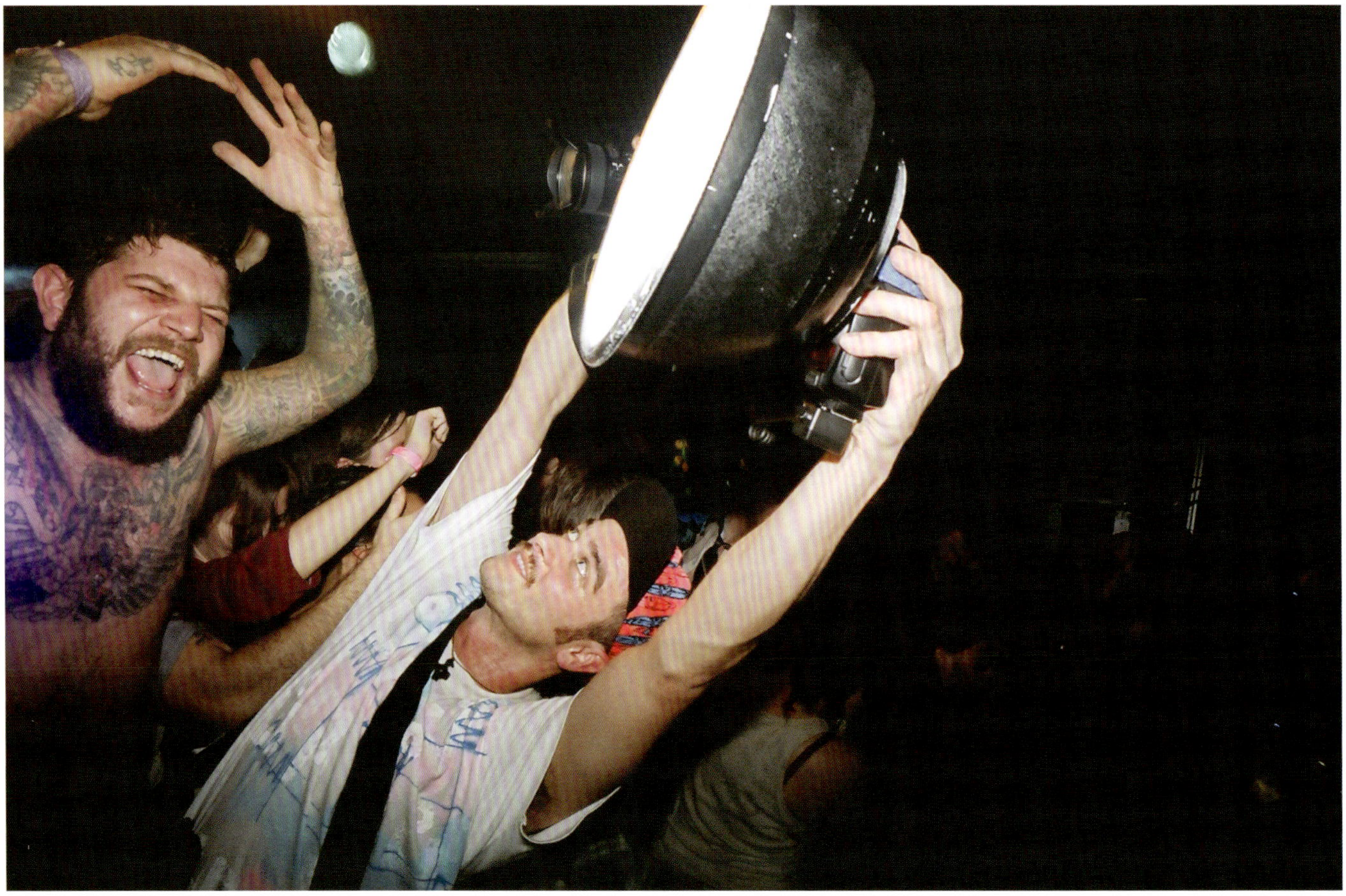

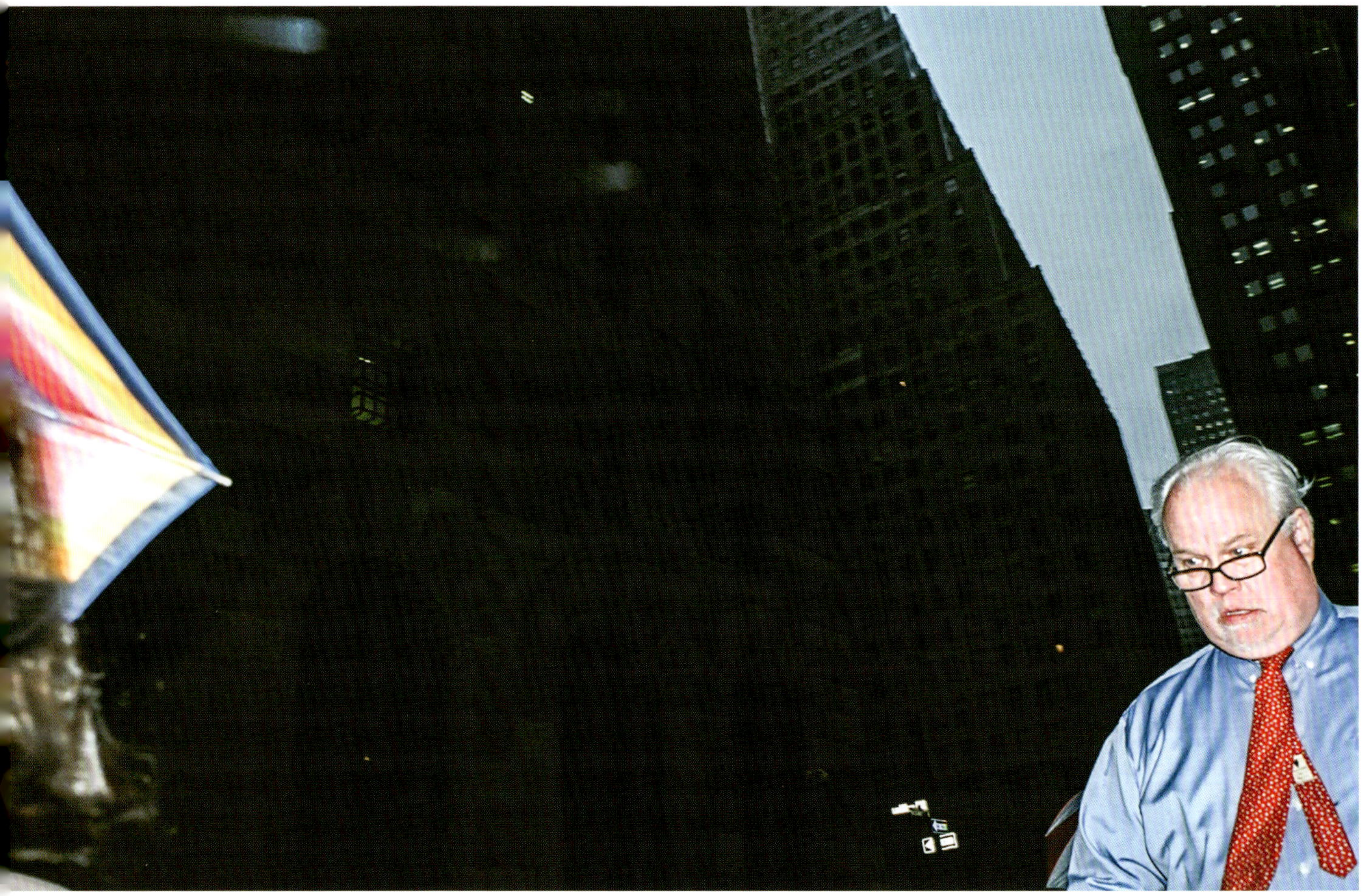

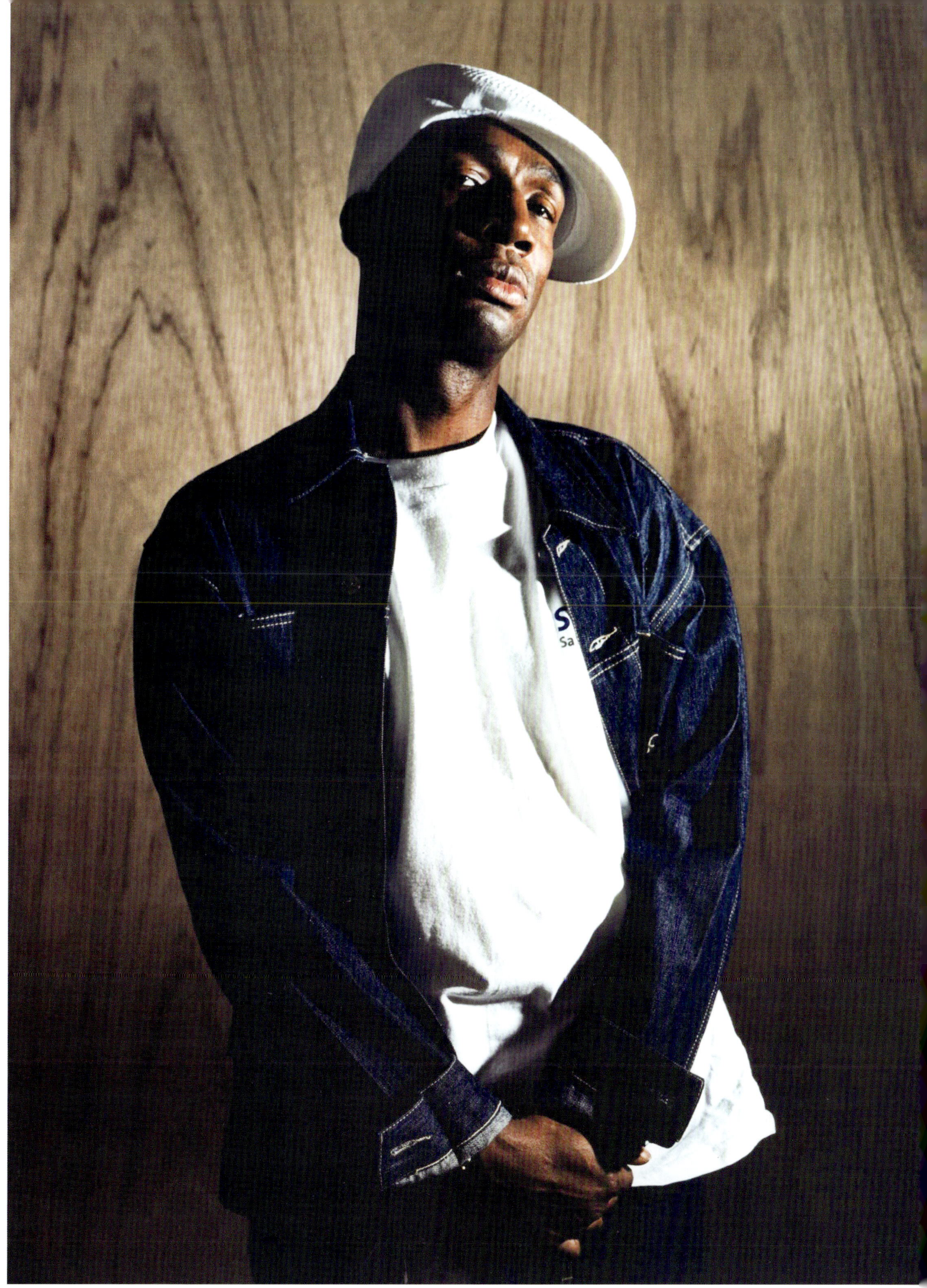

GIRL

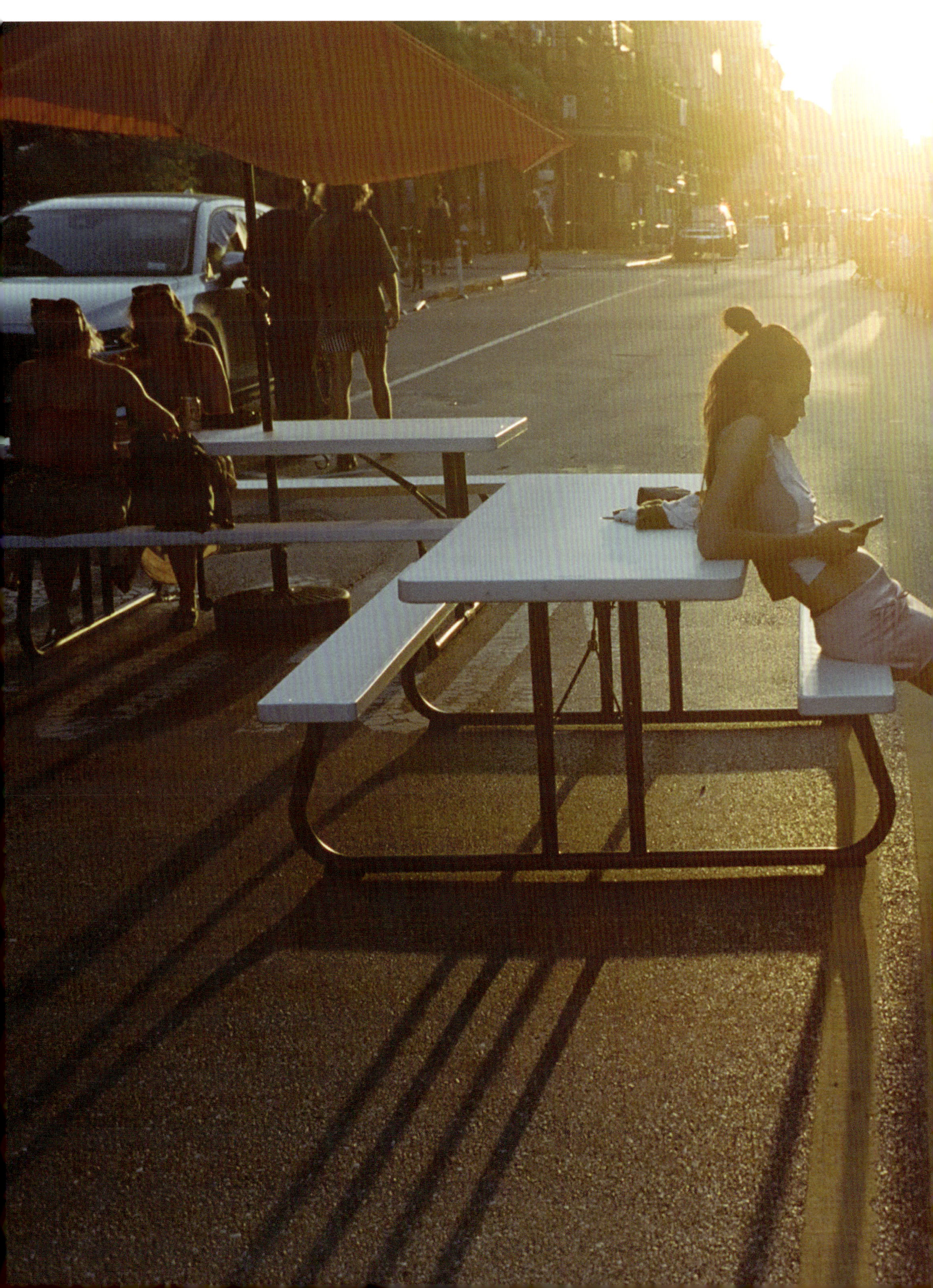

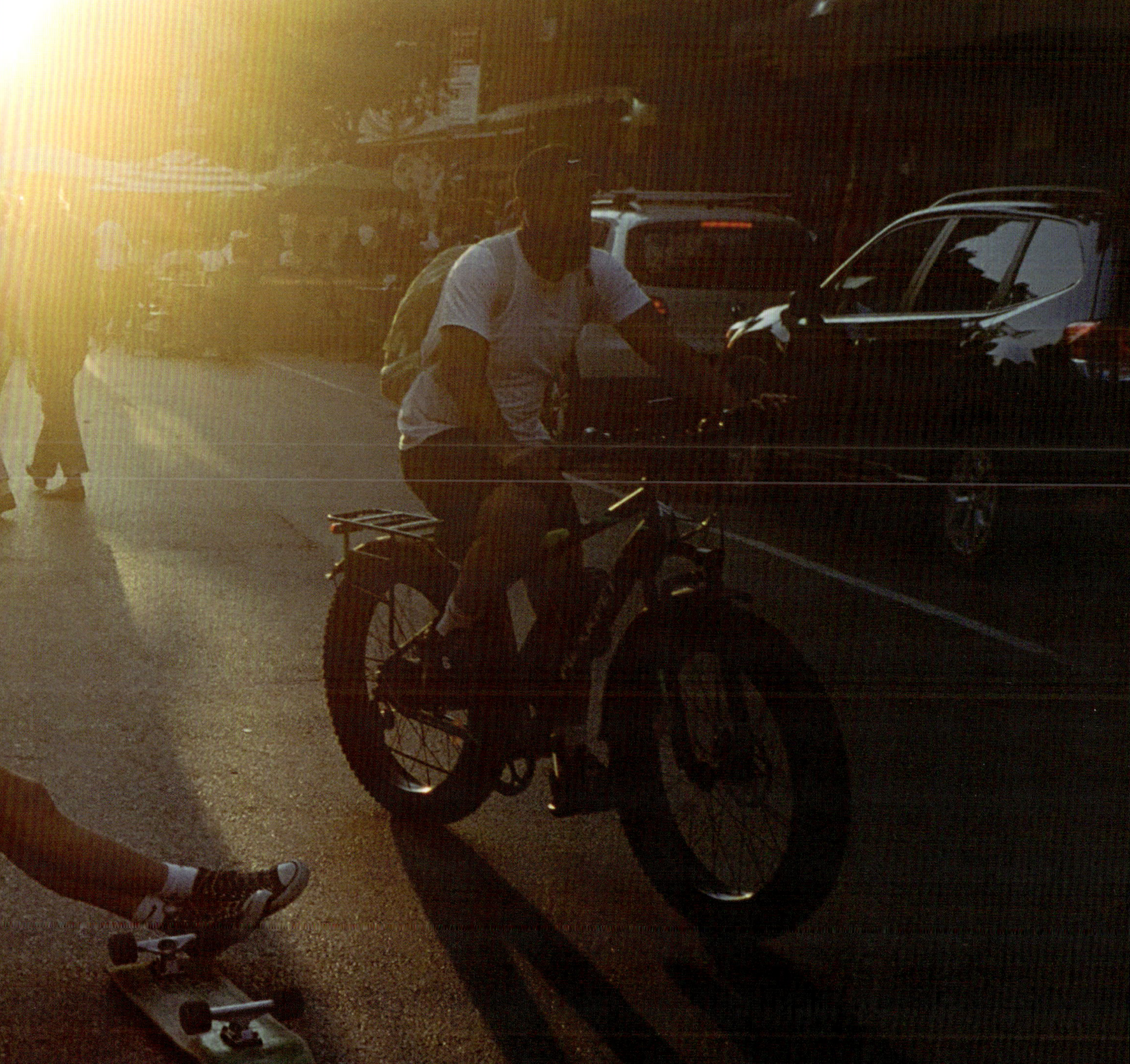

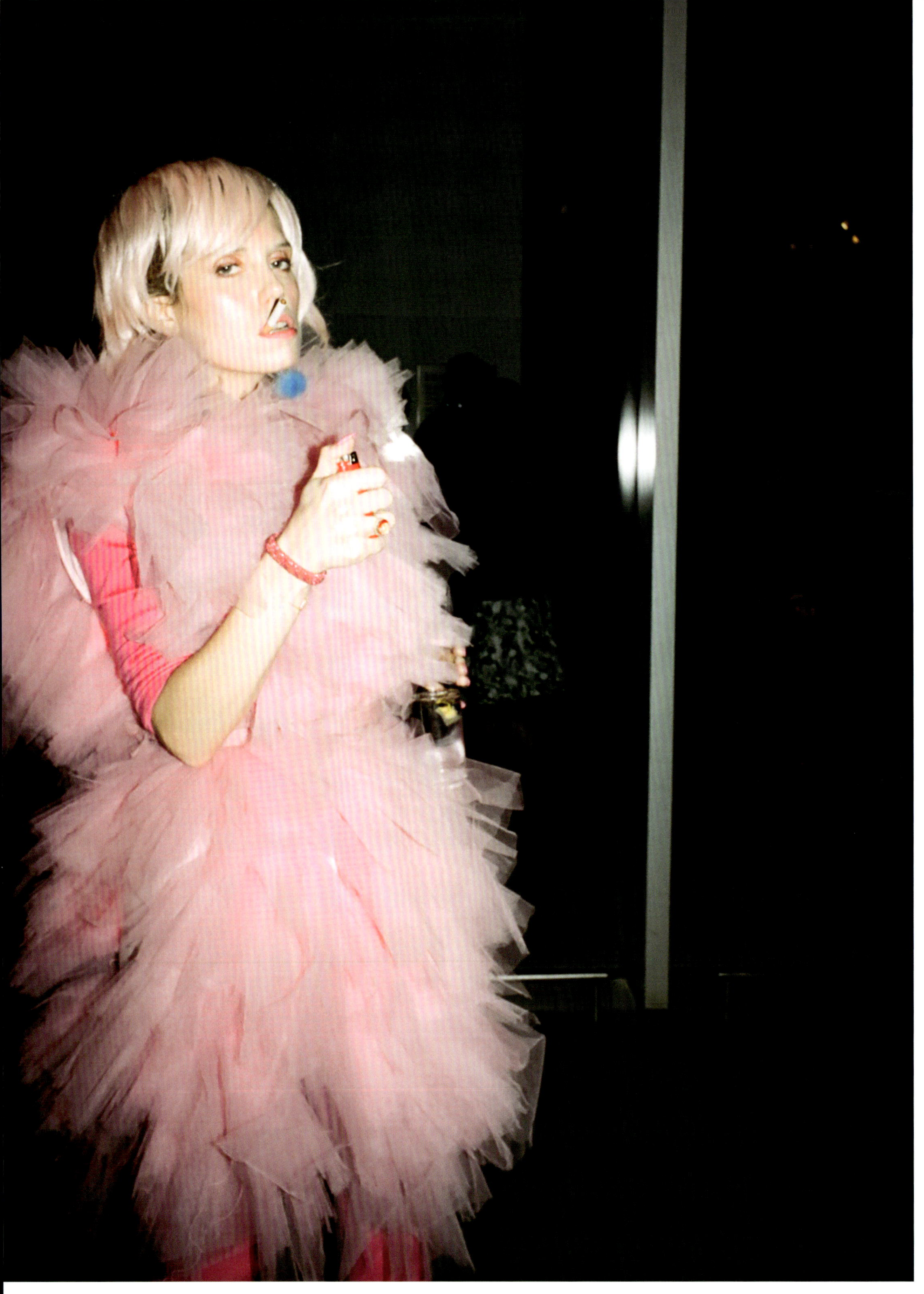

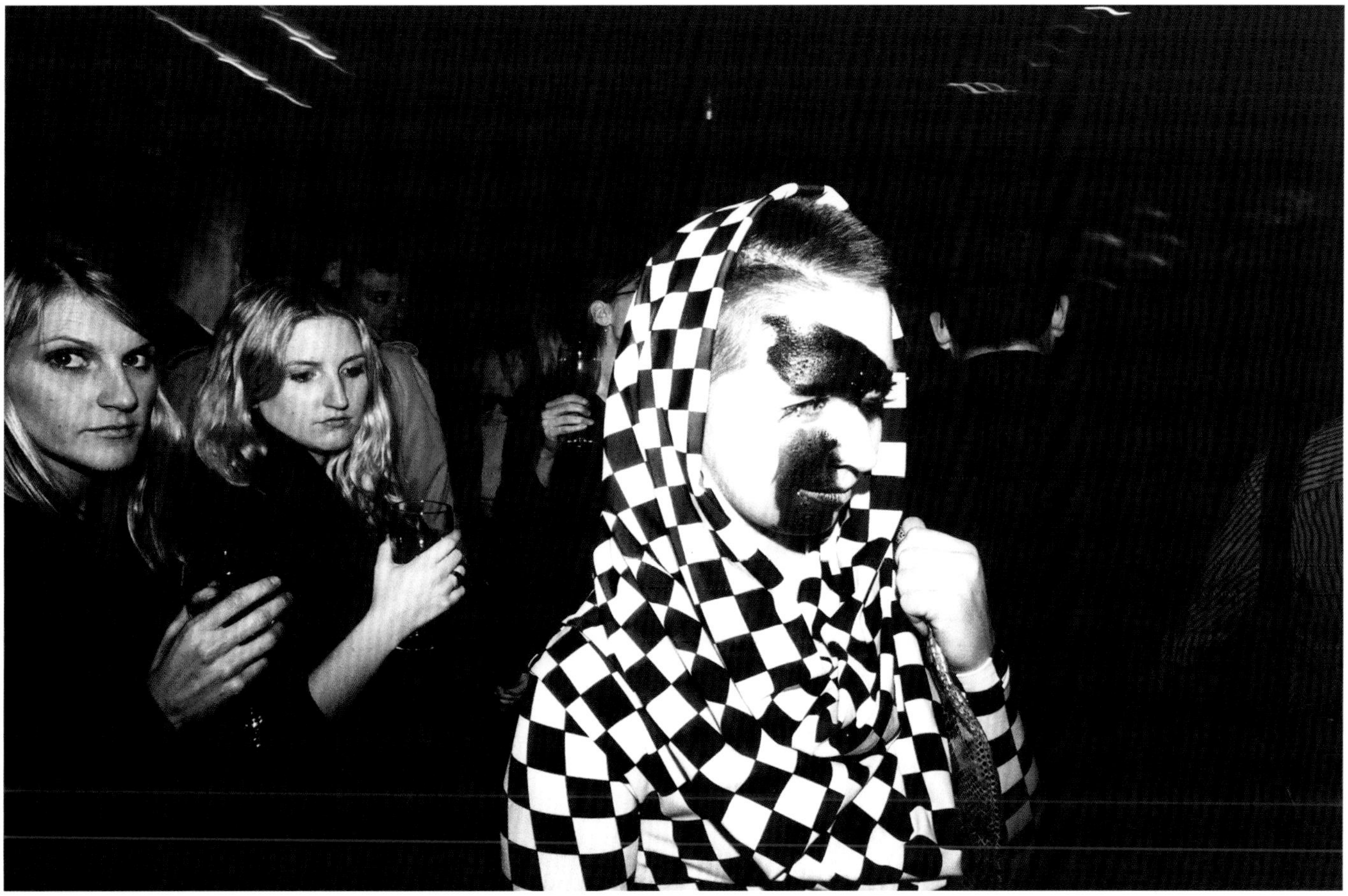

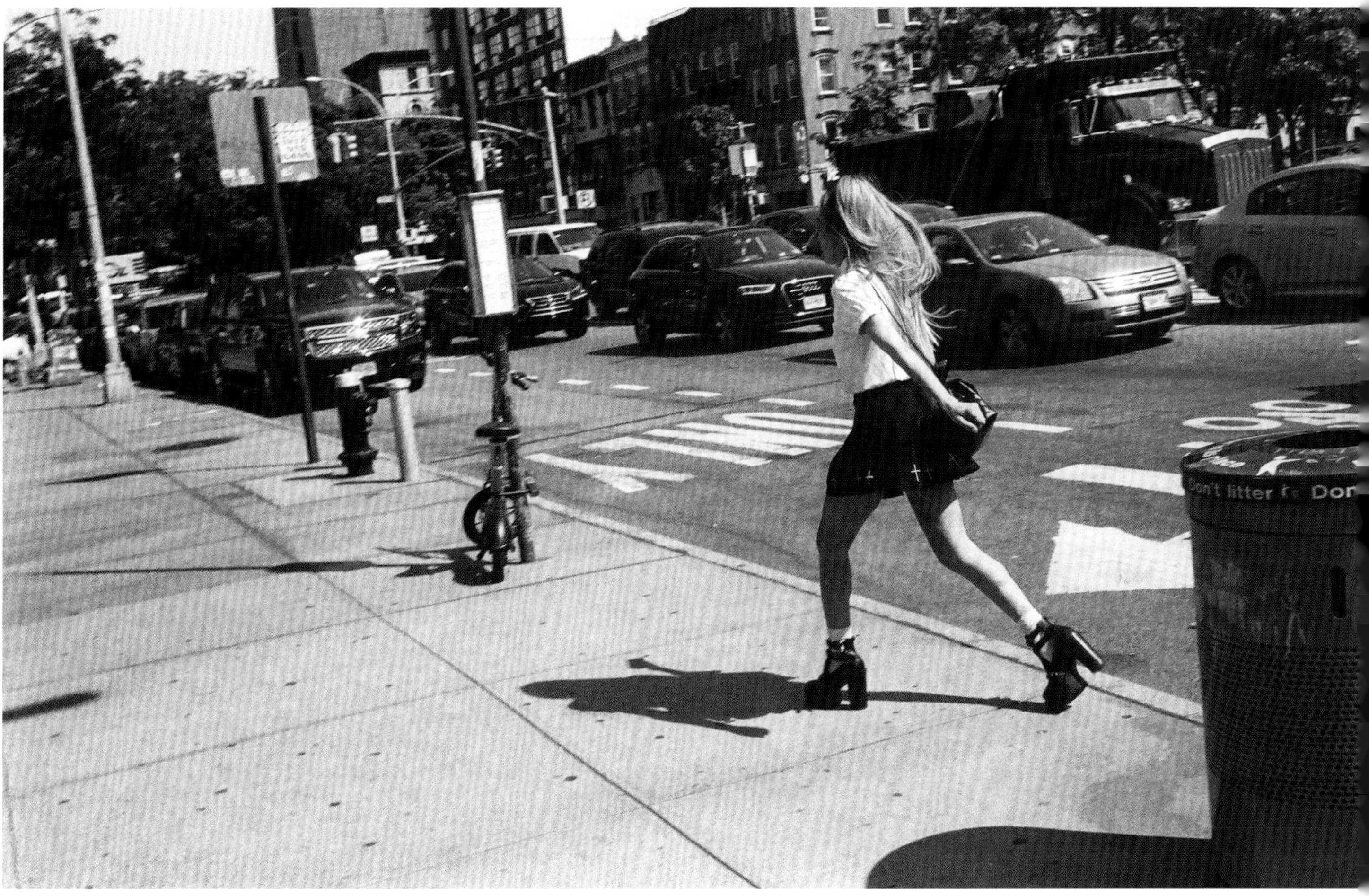

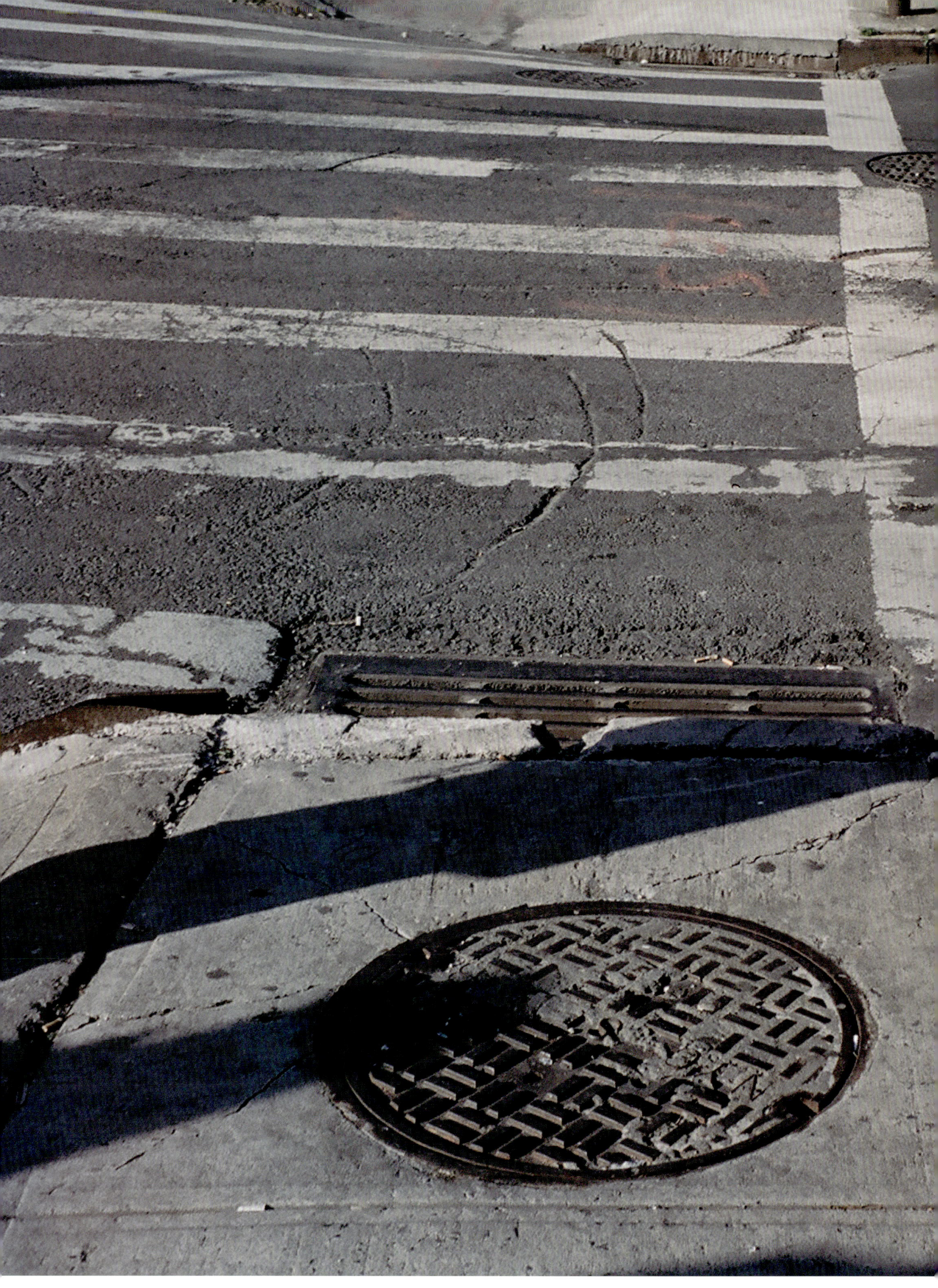

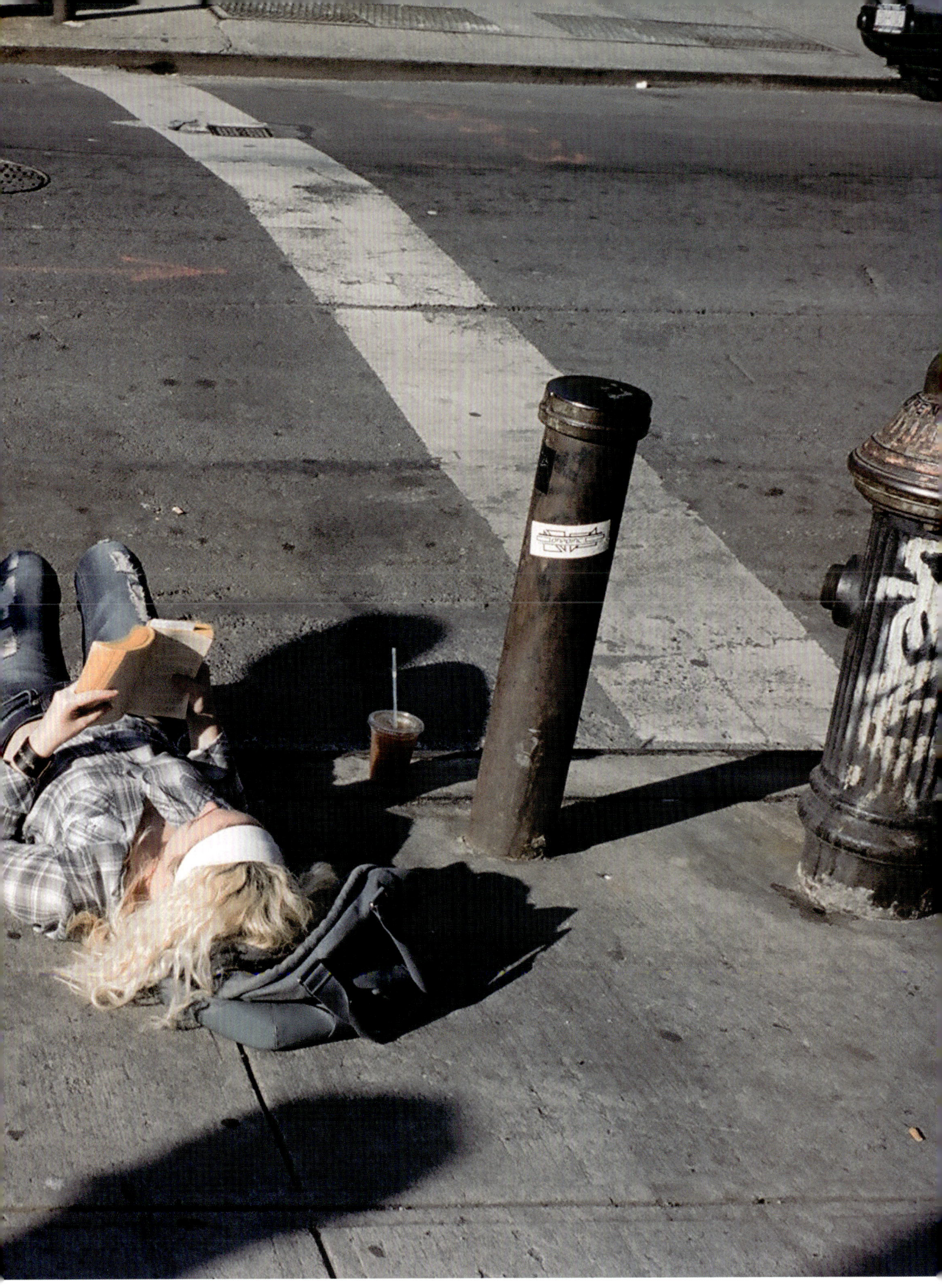

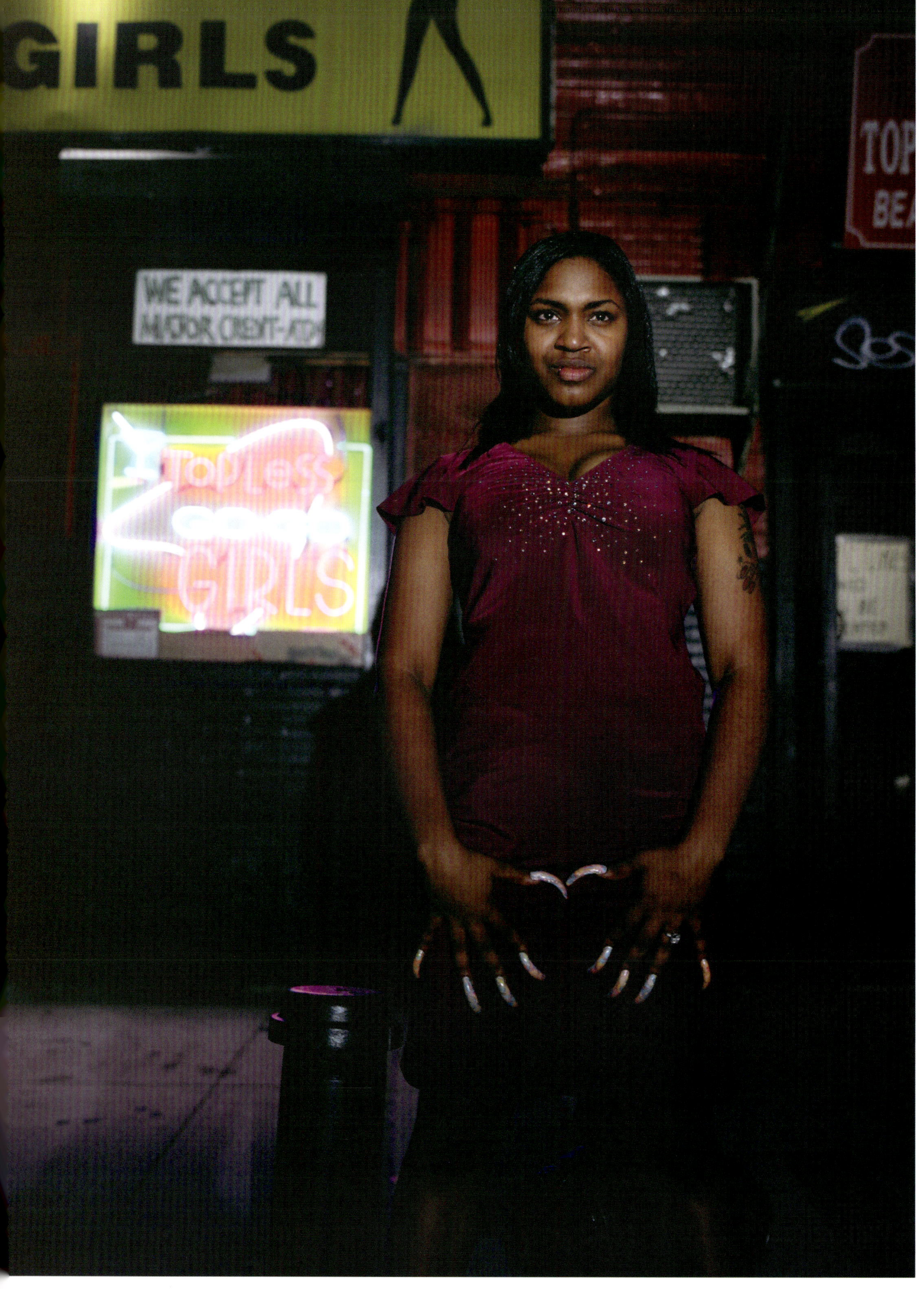
GIRLS
WE ACCEPT ALL
MAJOR CREDIT-ATM
TOPLESS
GIRLS

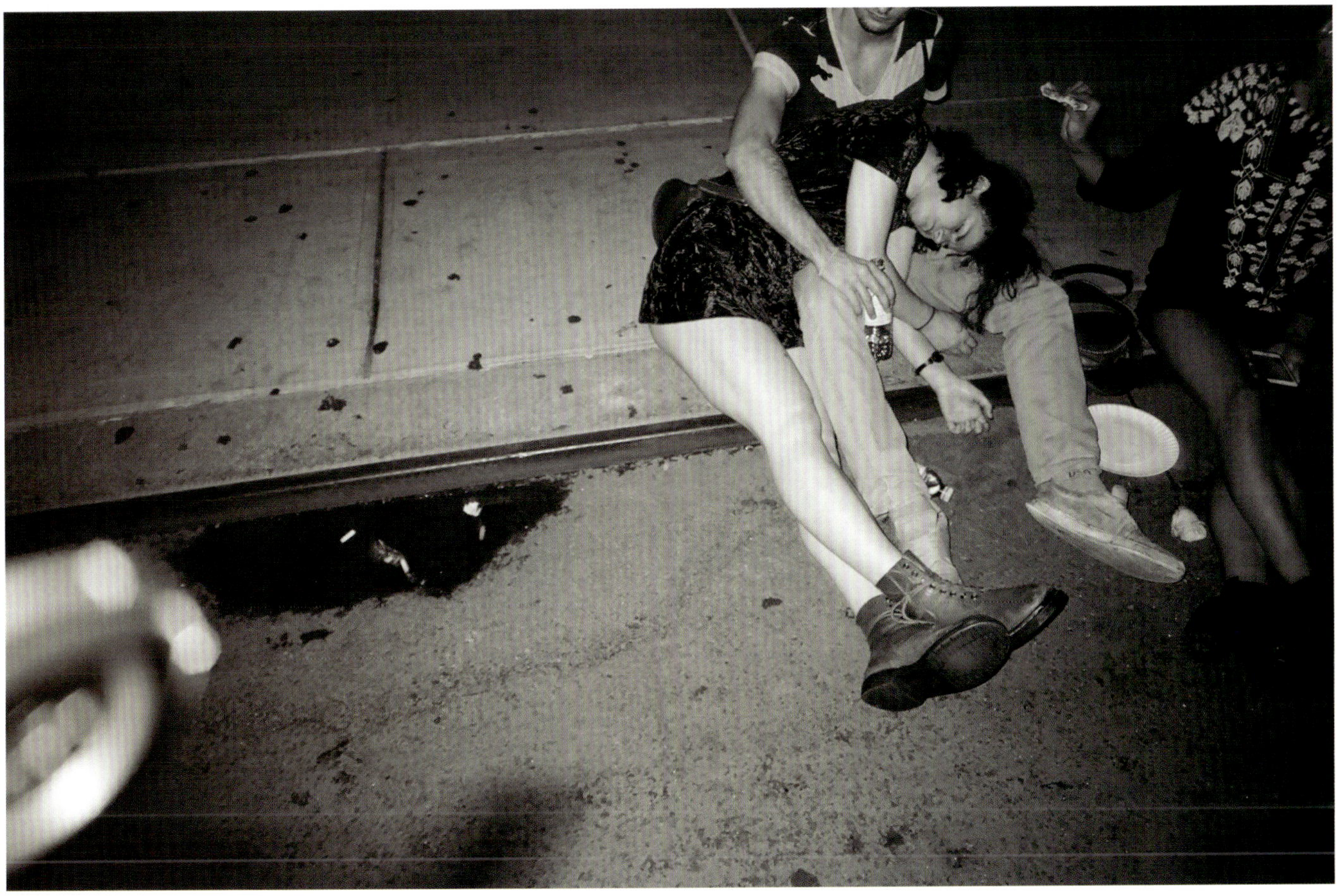

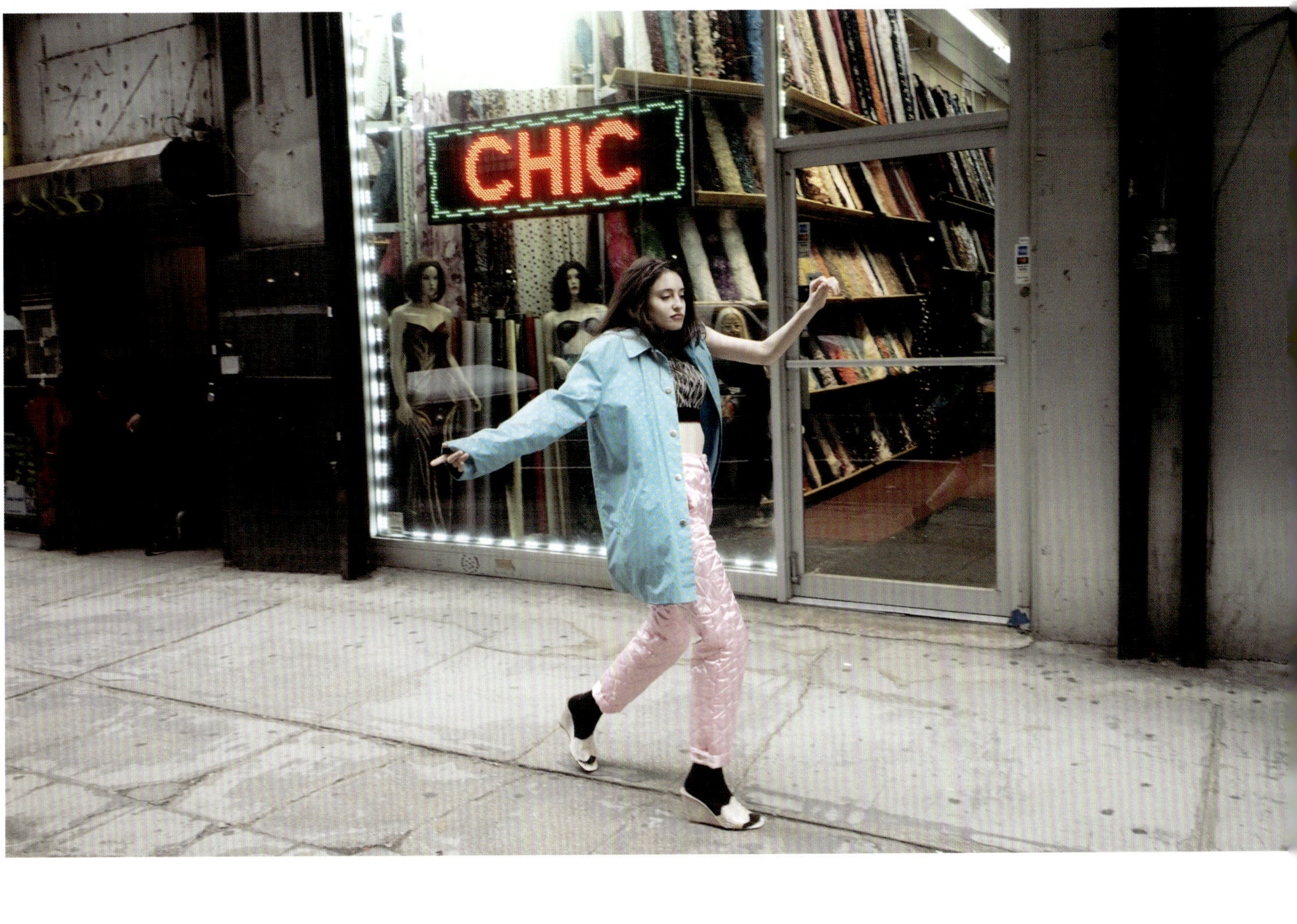

GOD

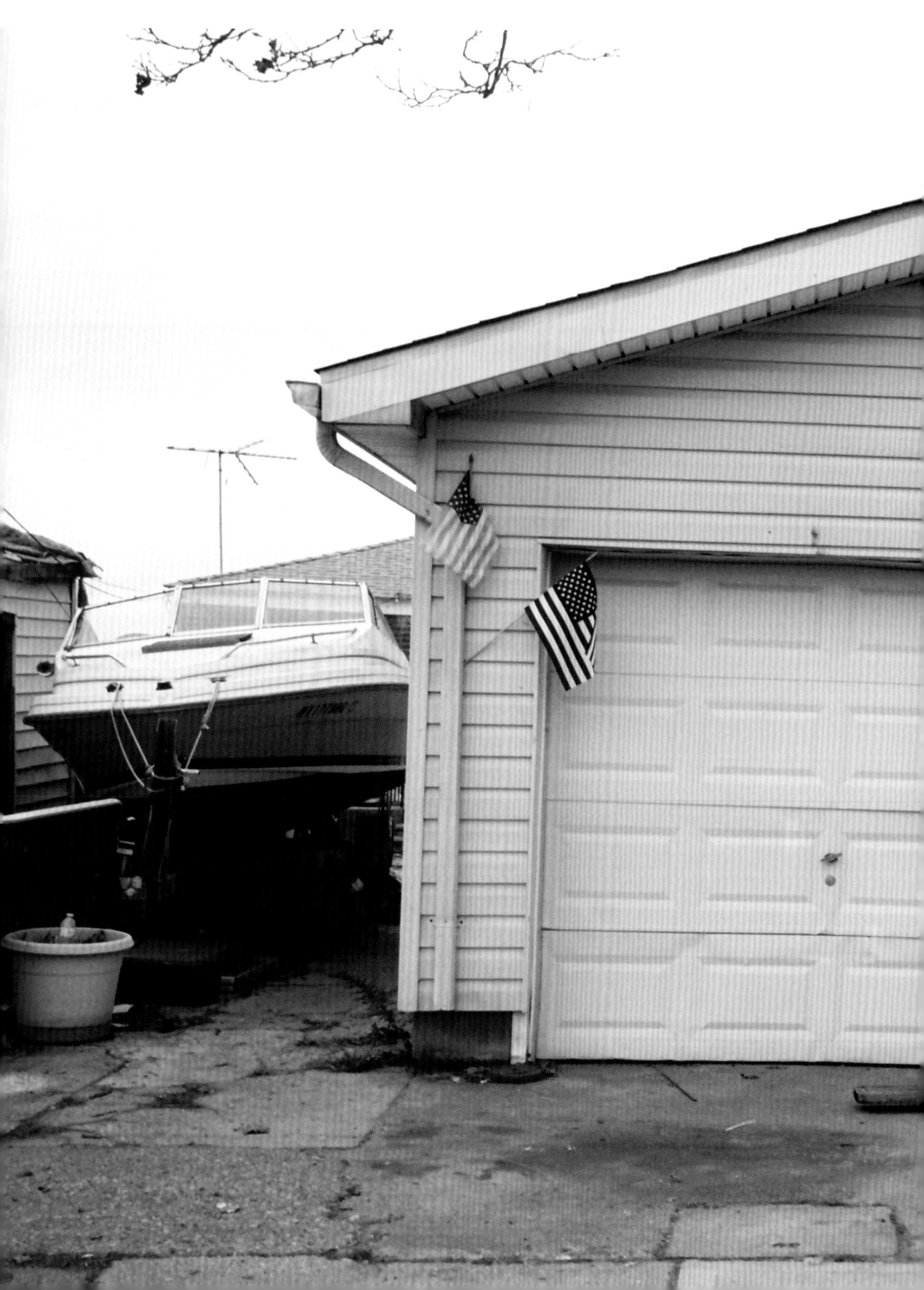

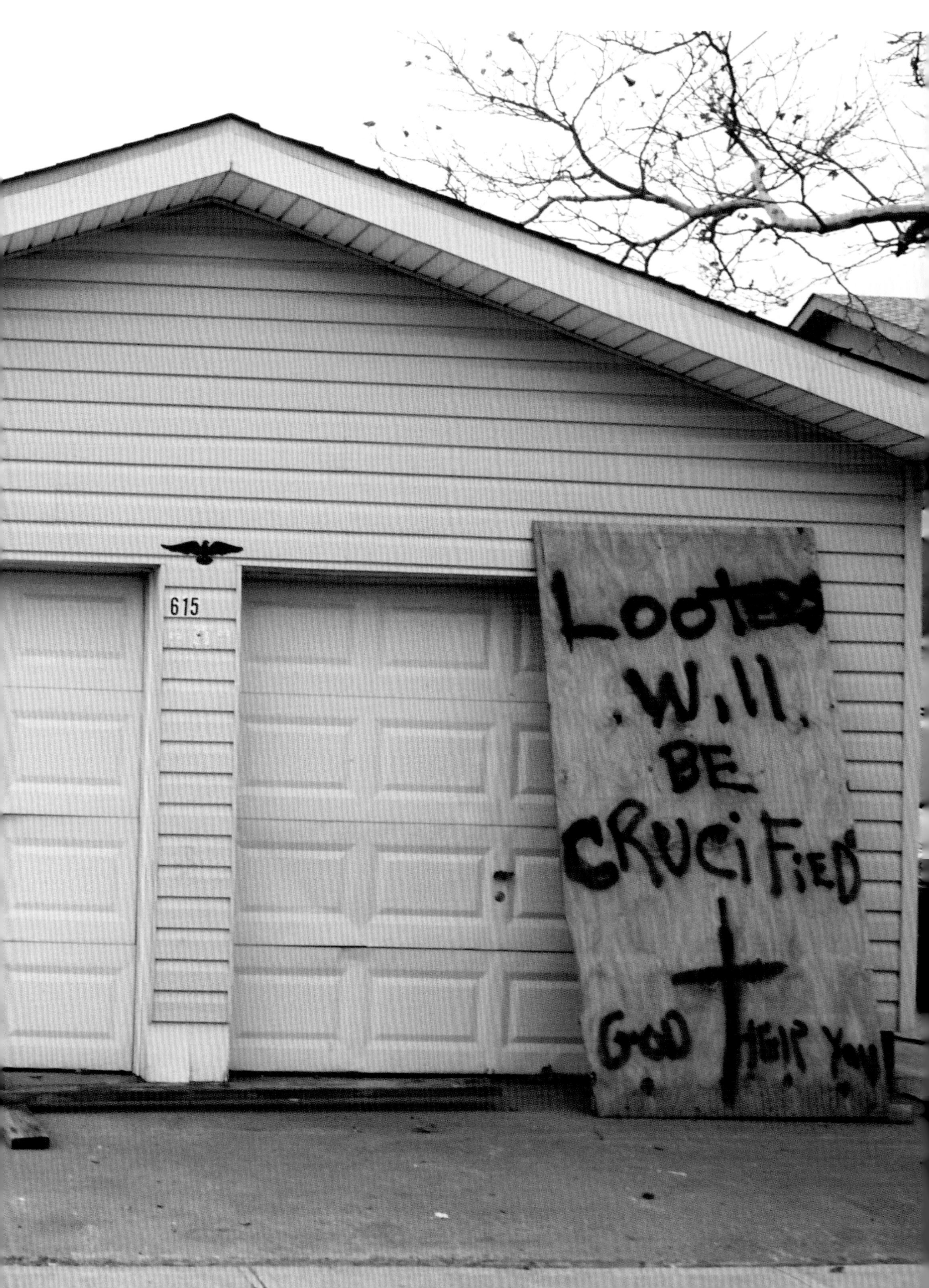
615
Looters
Will
BE
CRUCIFIED
GOD HELP YOU

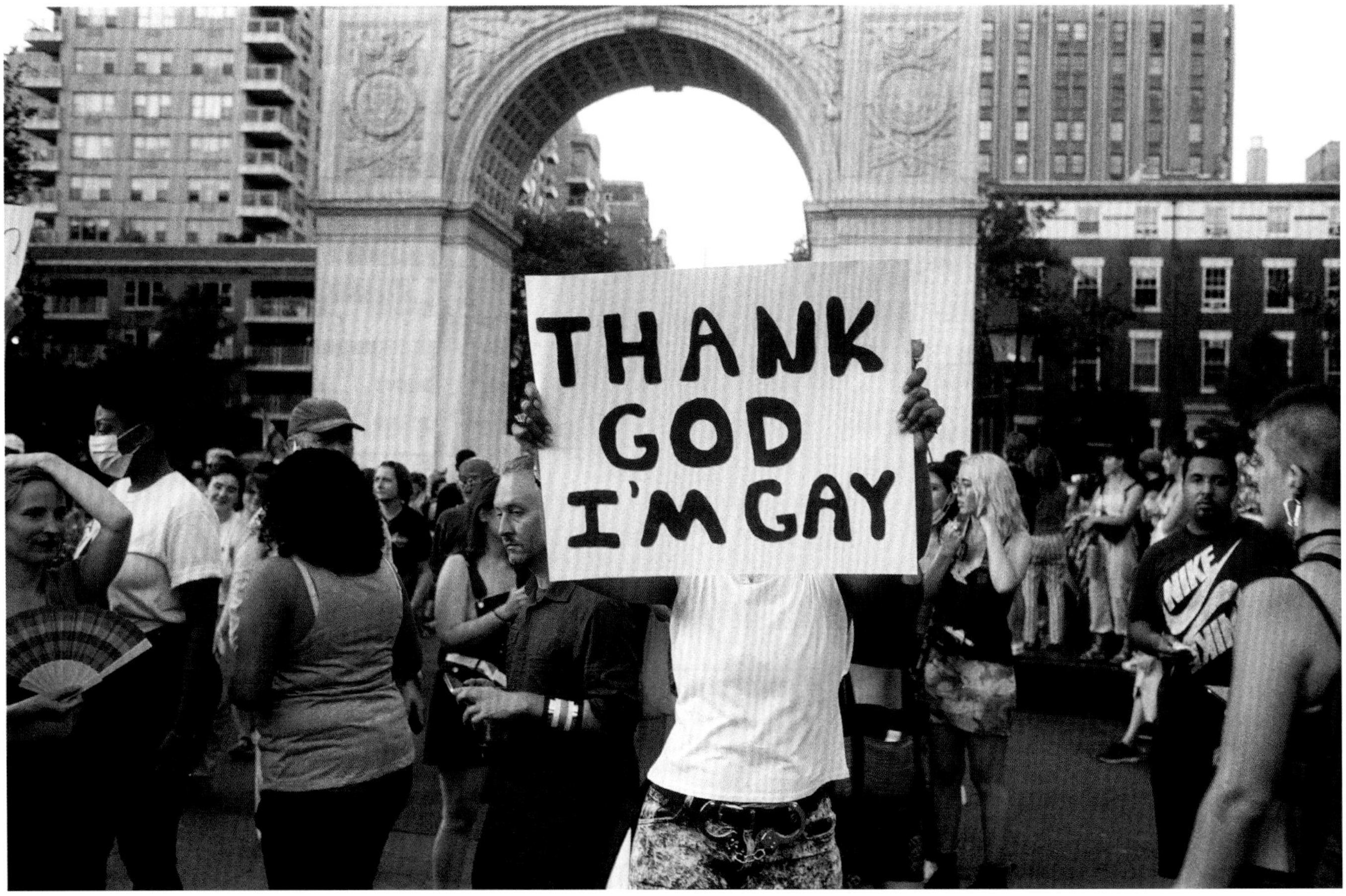
THANK
GOD
I'M GAY

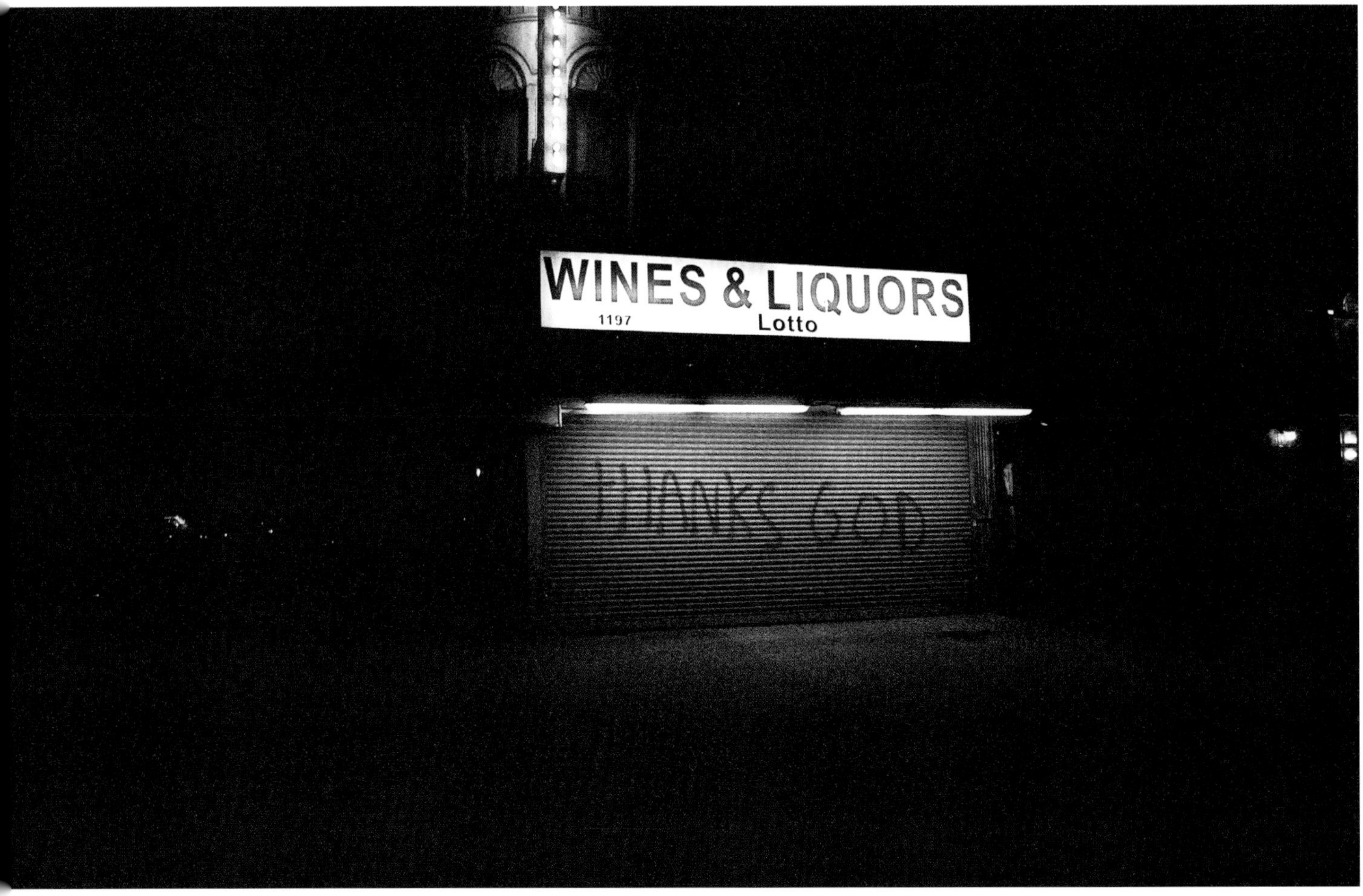
WINES & LIQUORS
1197
Lotto
THANKS GOD

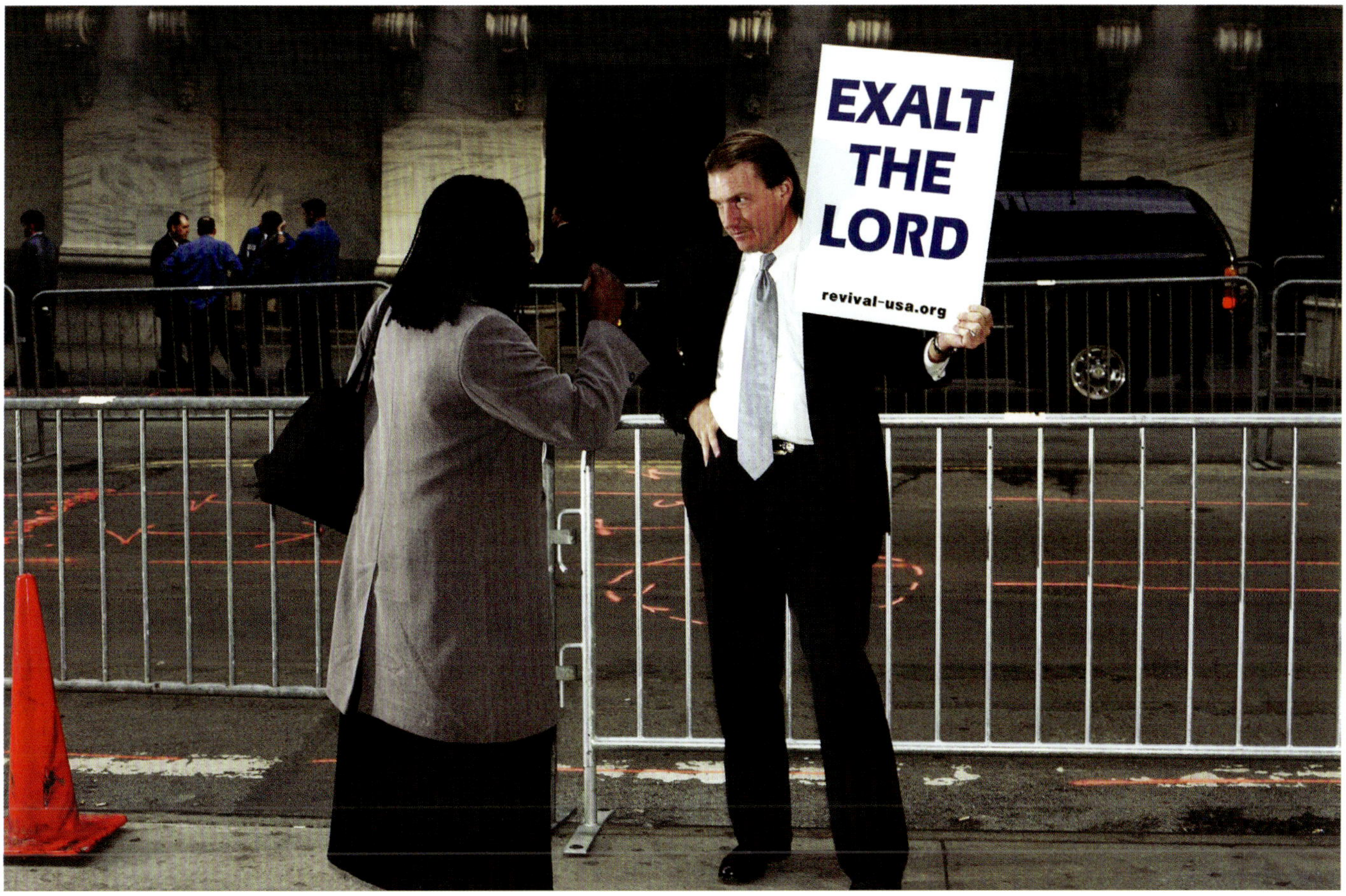
EXALT
THE
LORD
revival-usa.org

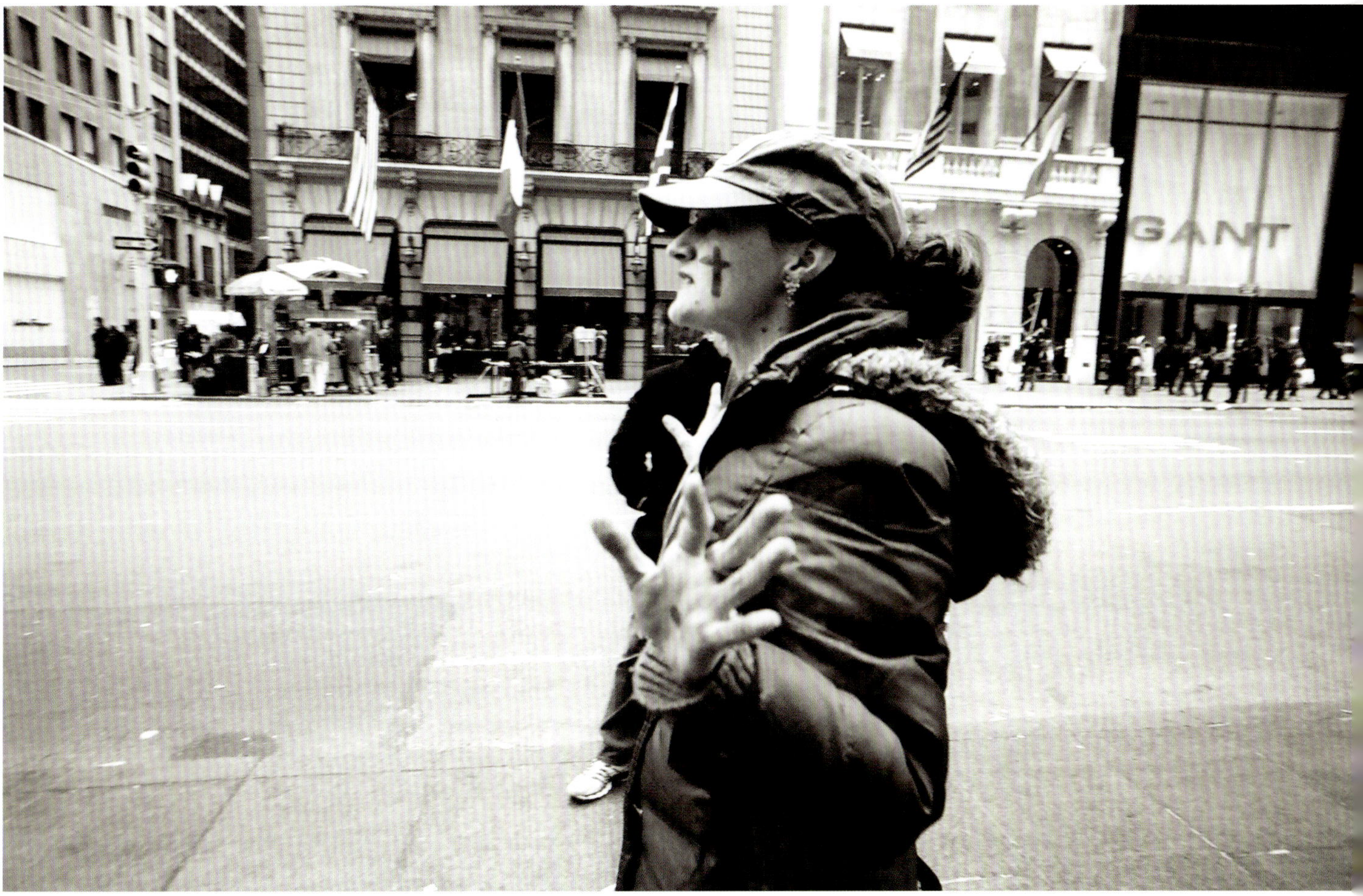
GANT

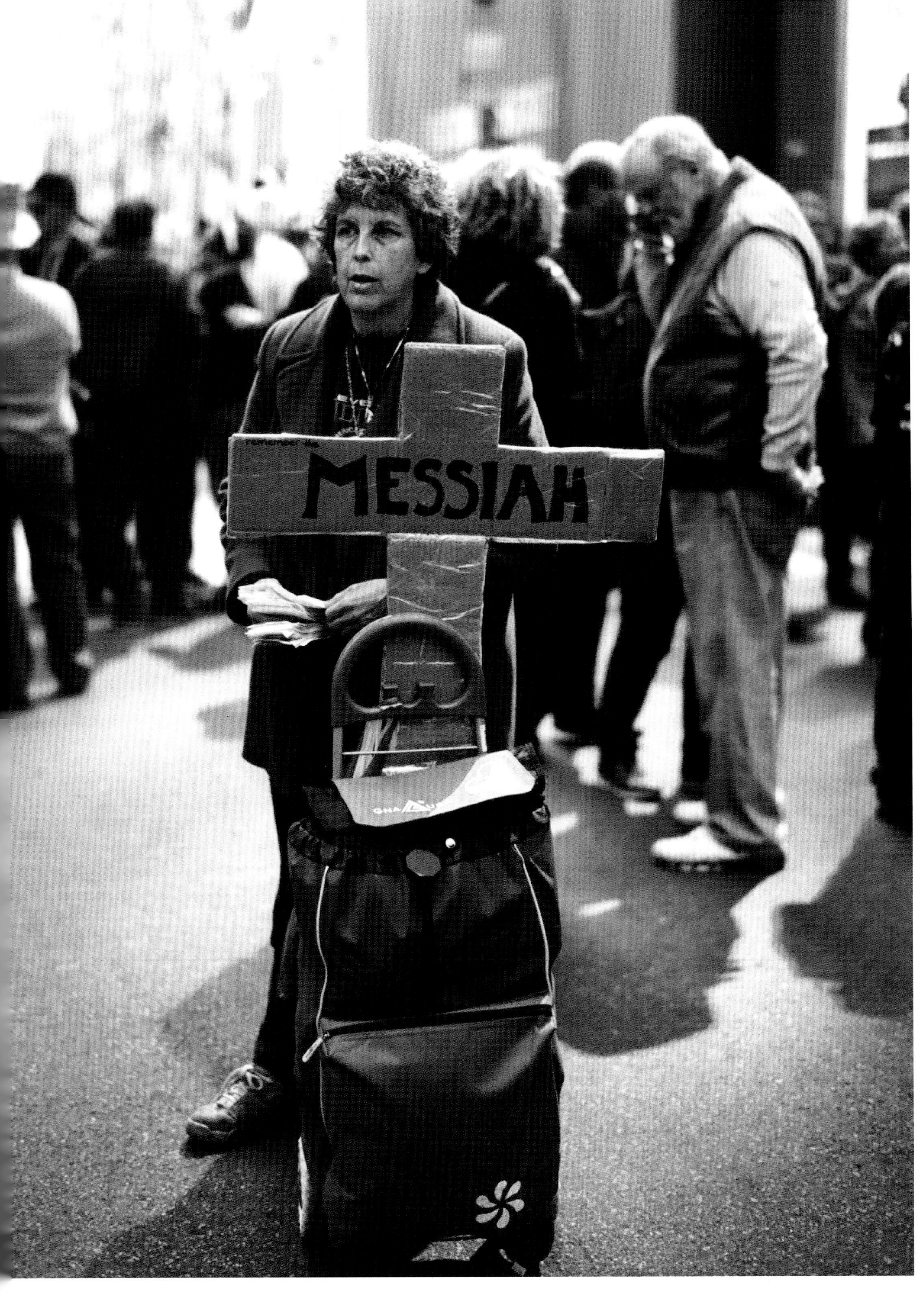
MESSIAH

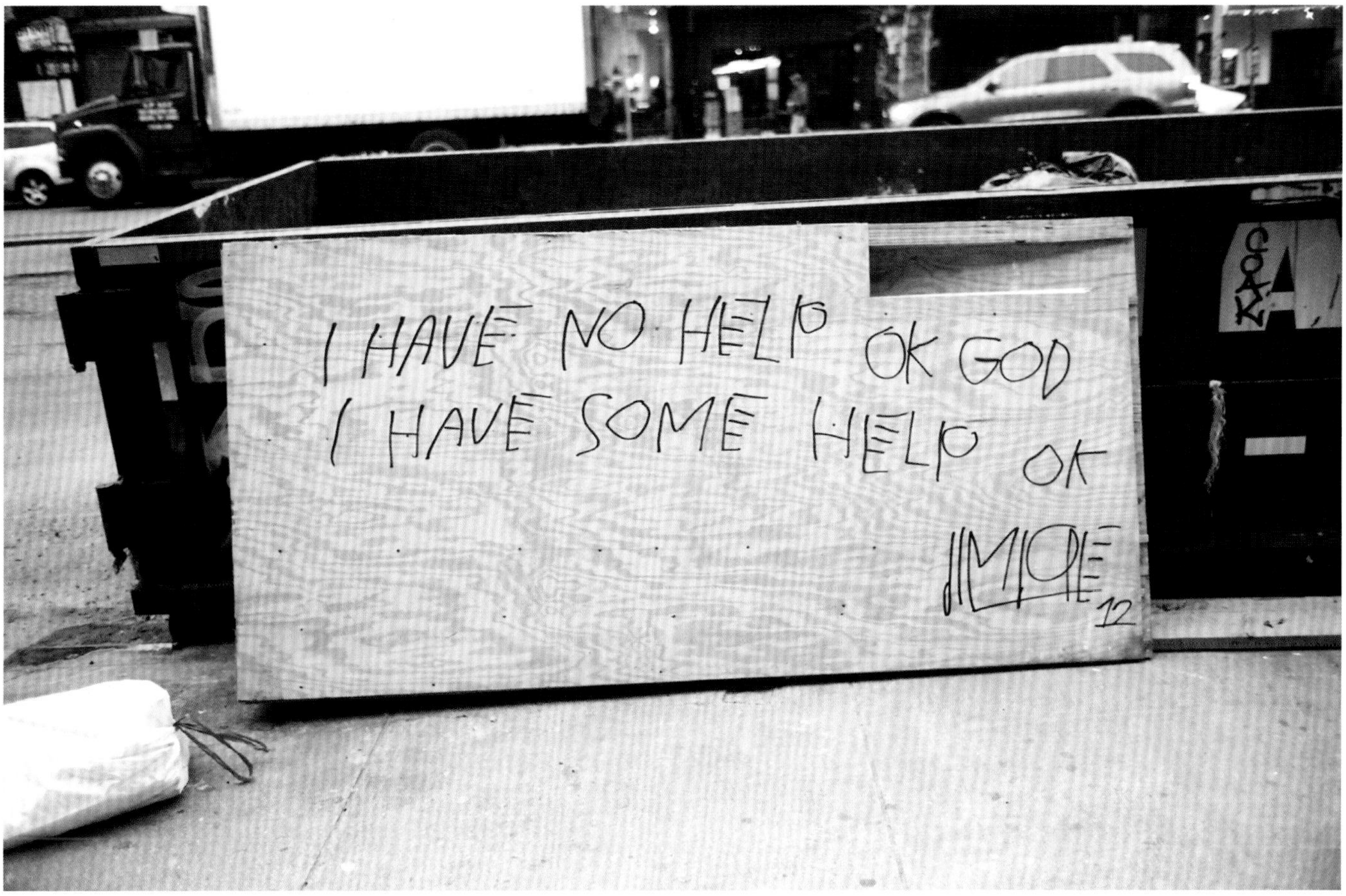
I HAVE NO HELP OK GOD
I HAVE SOME HELP OK
12

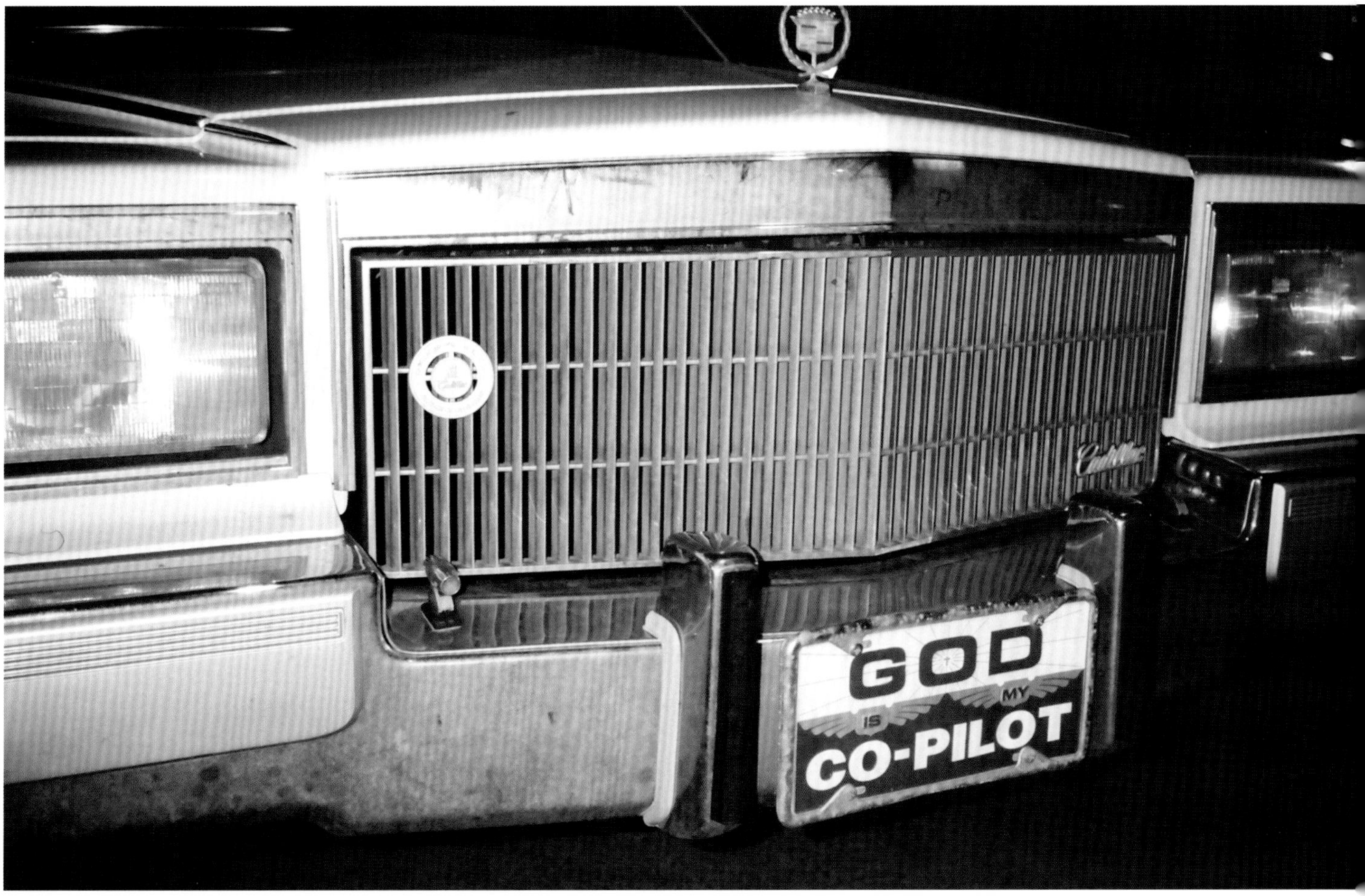
GOD
IS MY
CO-PILOT

HAND

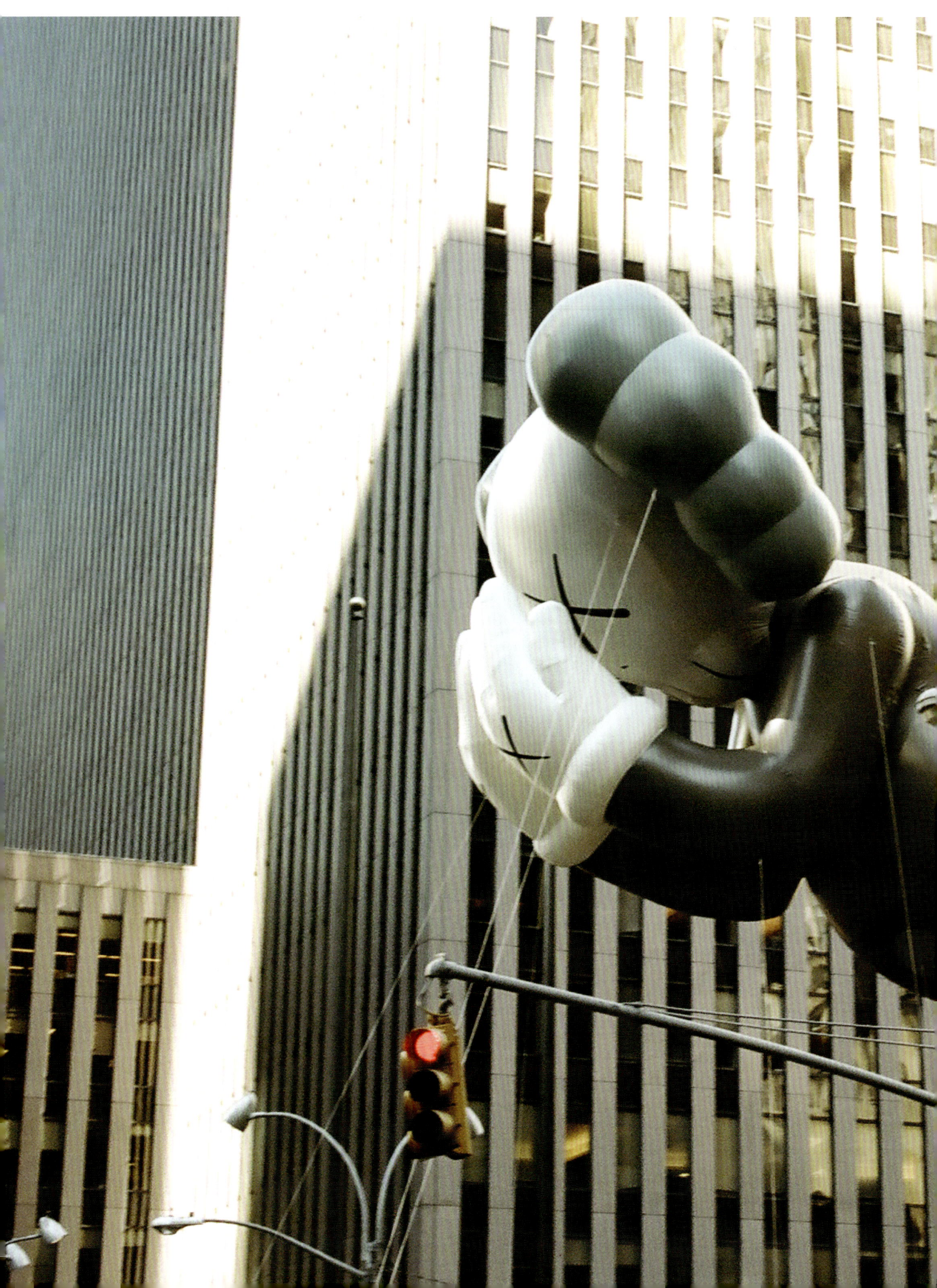

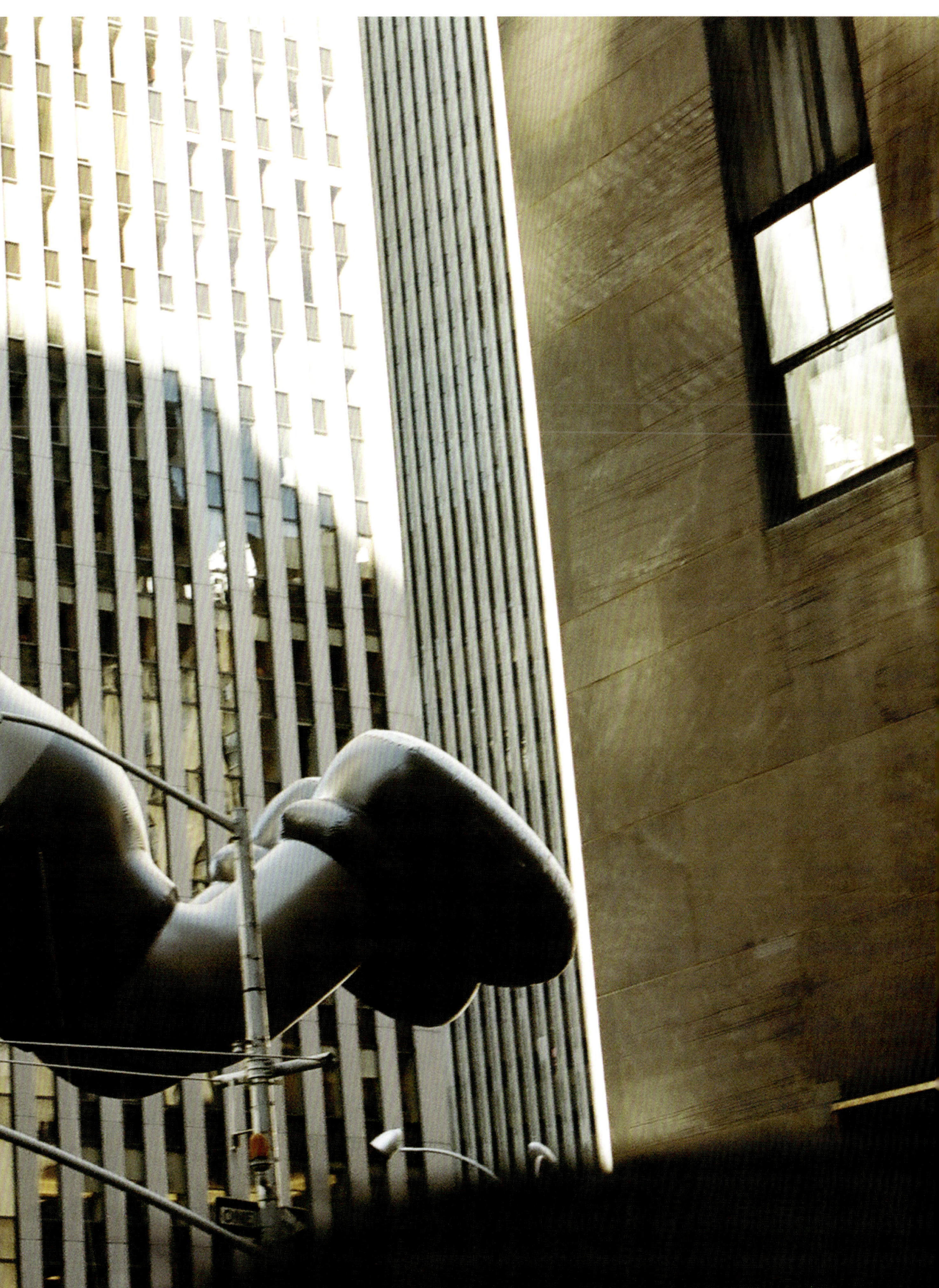

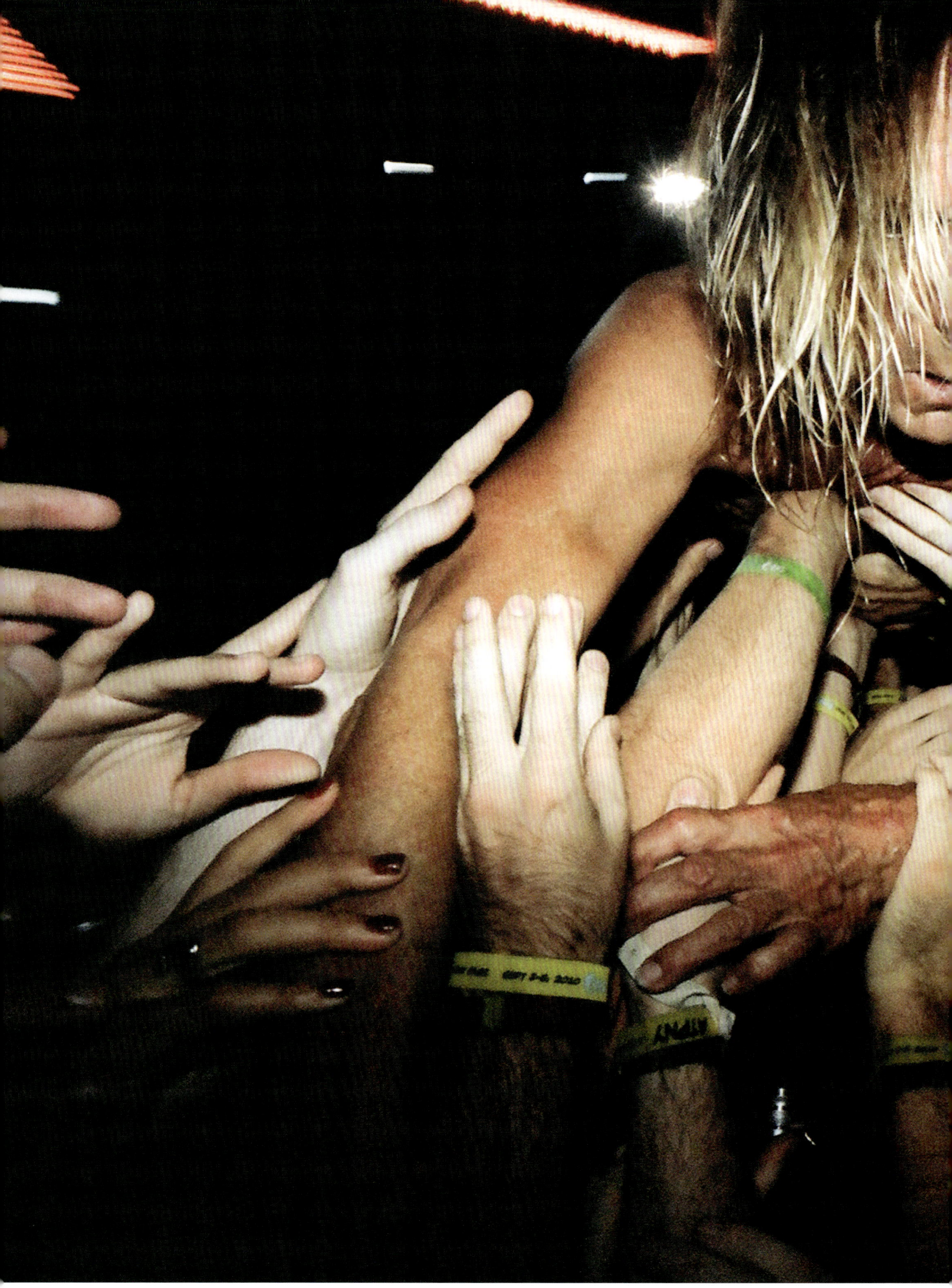

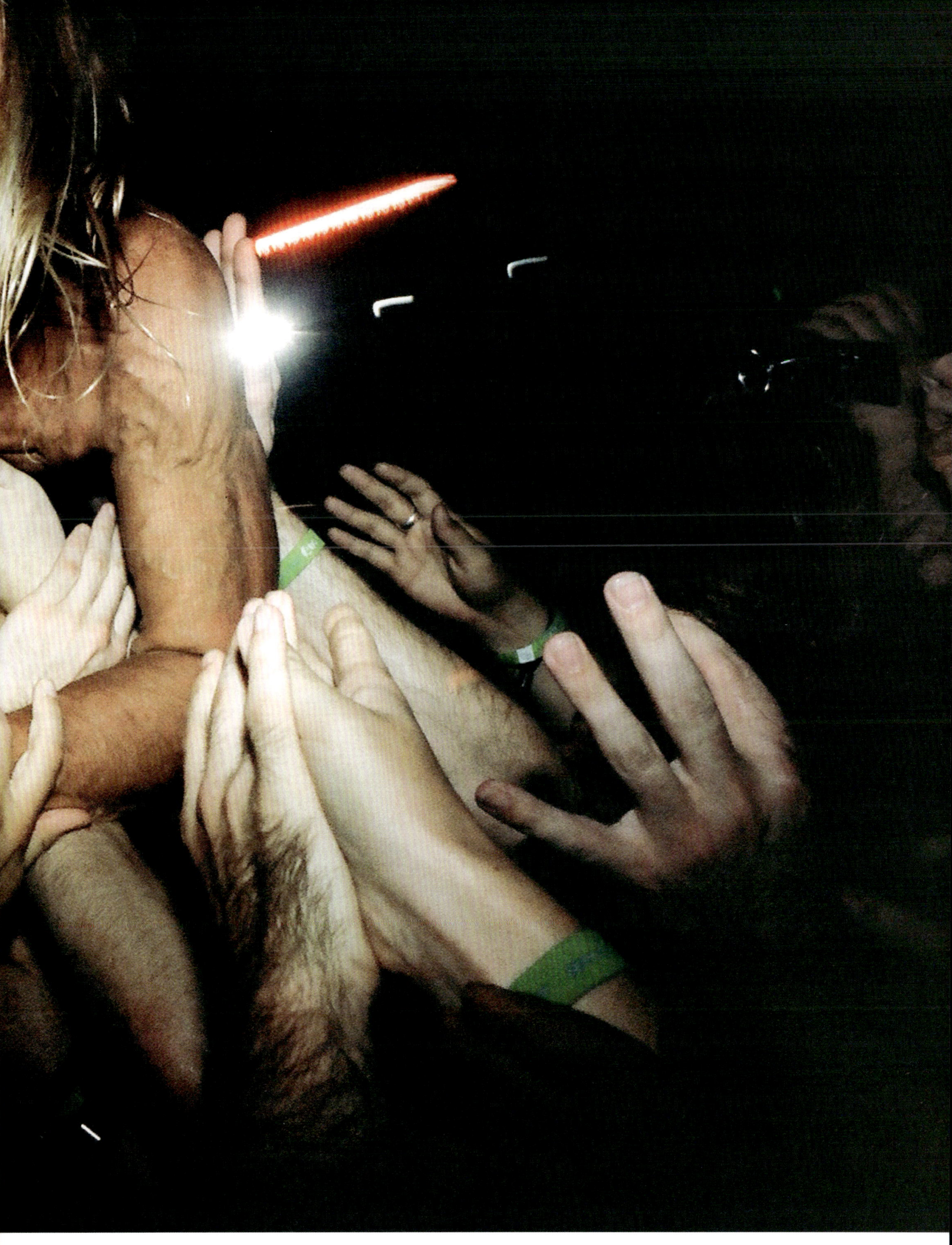

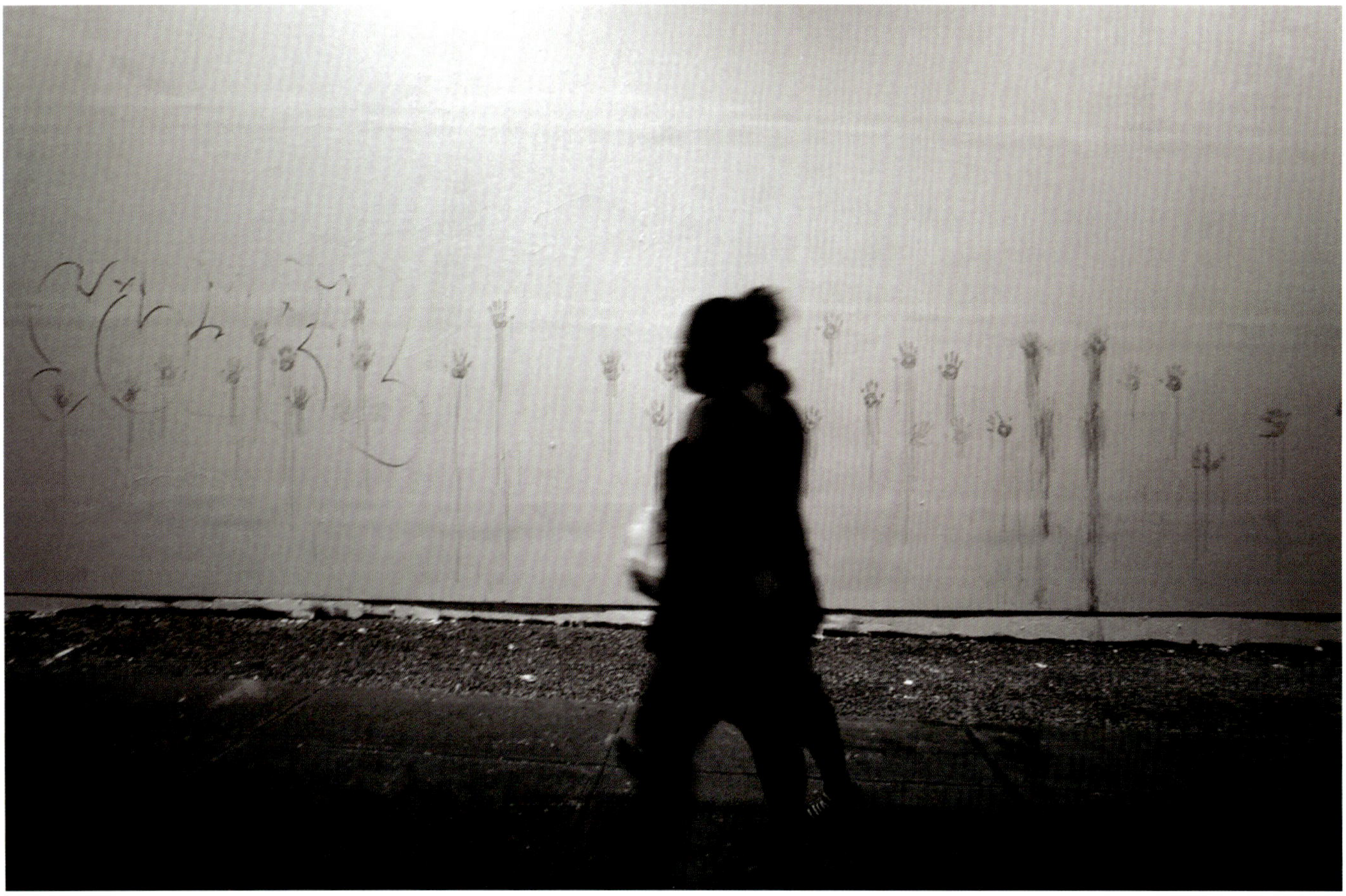

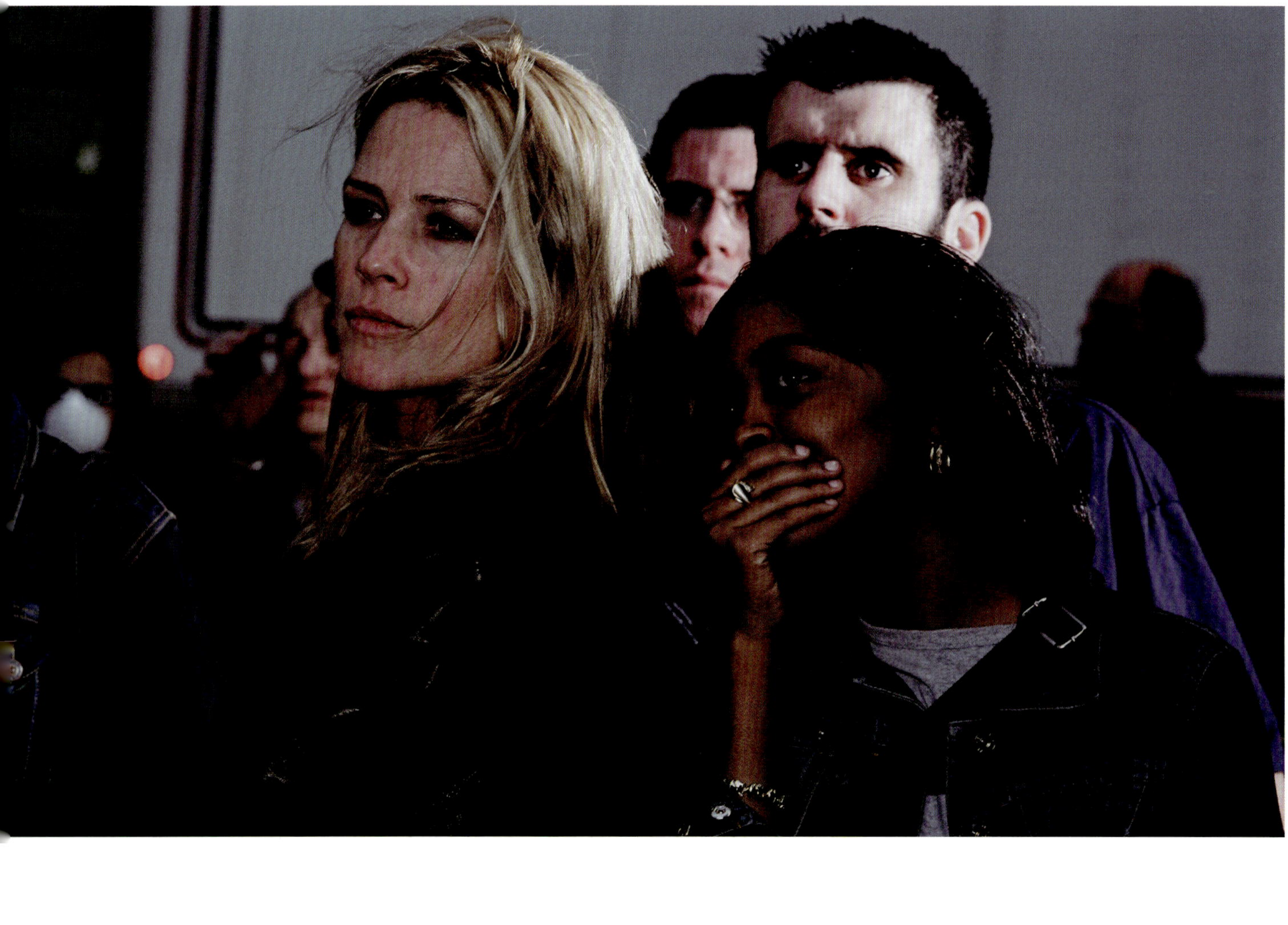

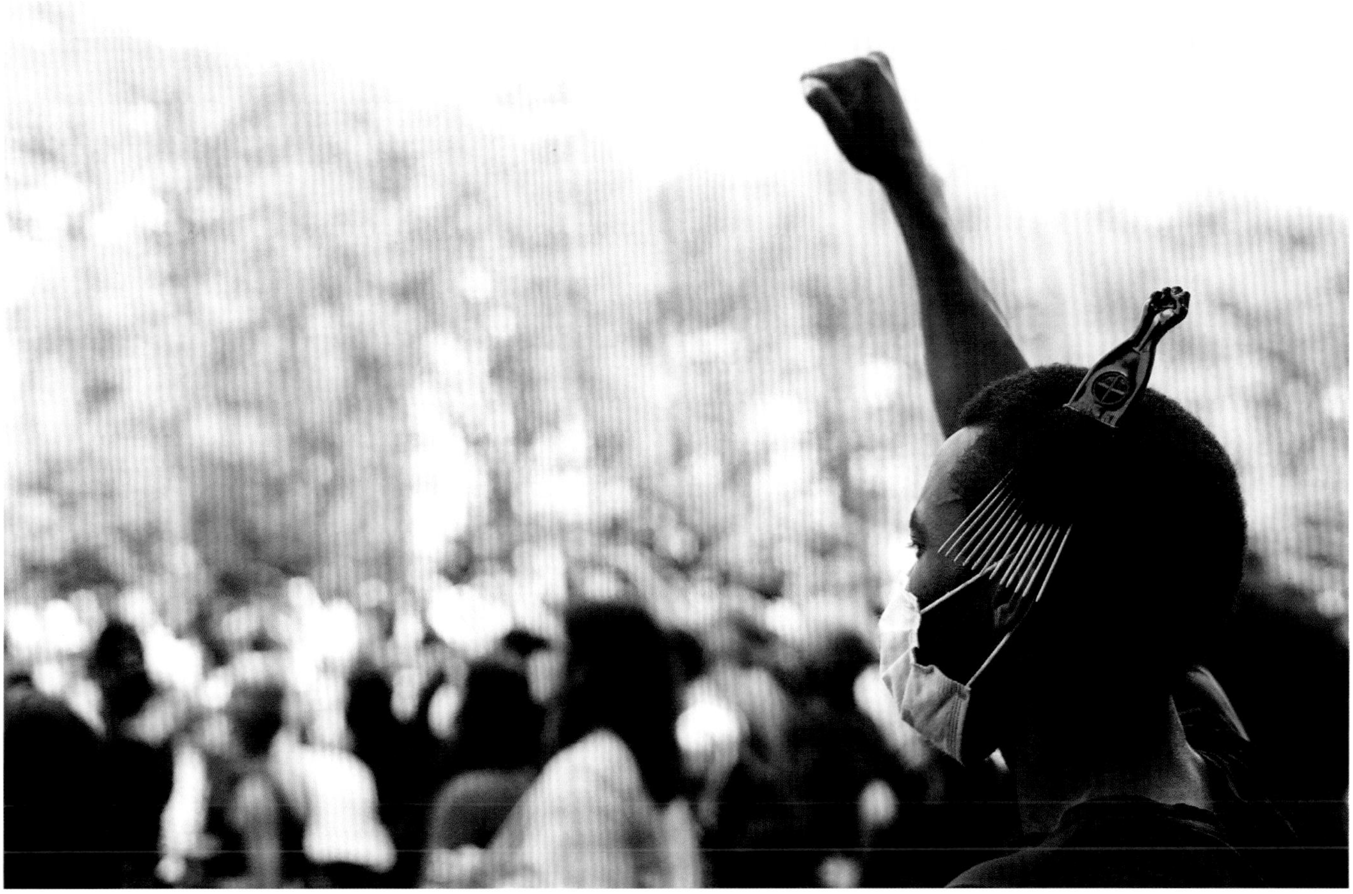

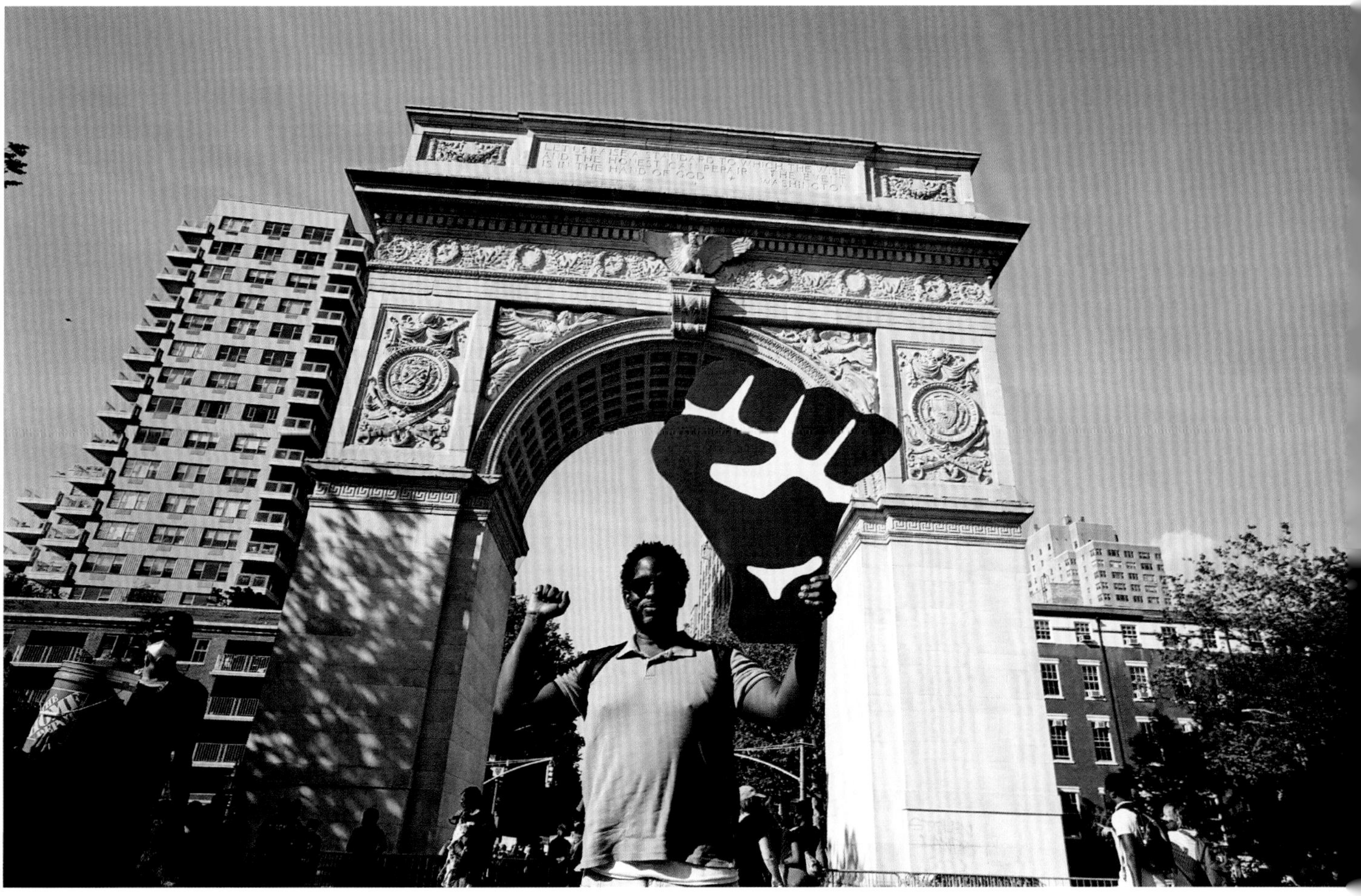

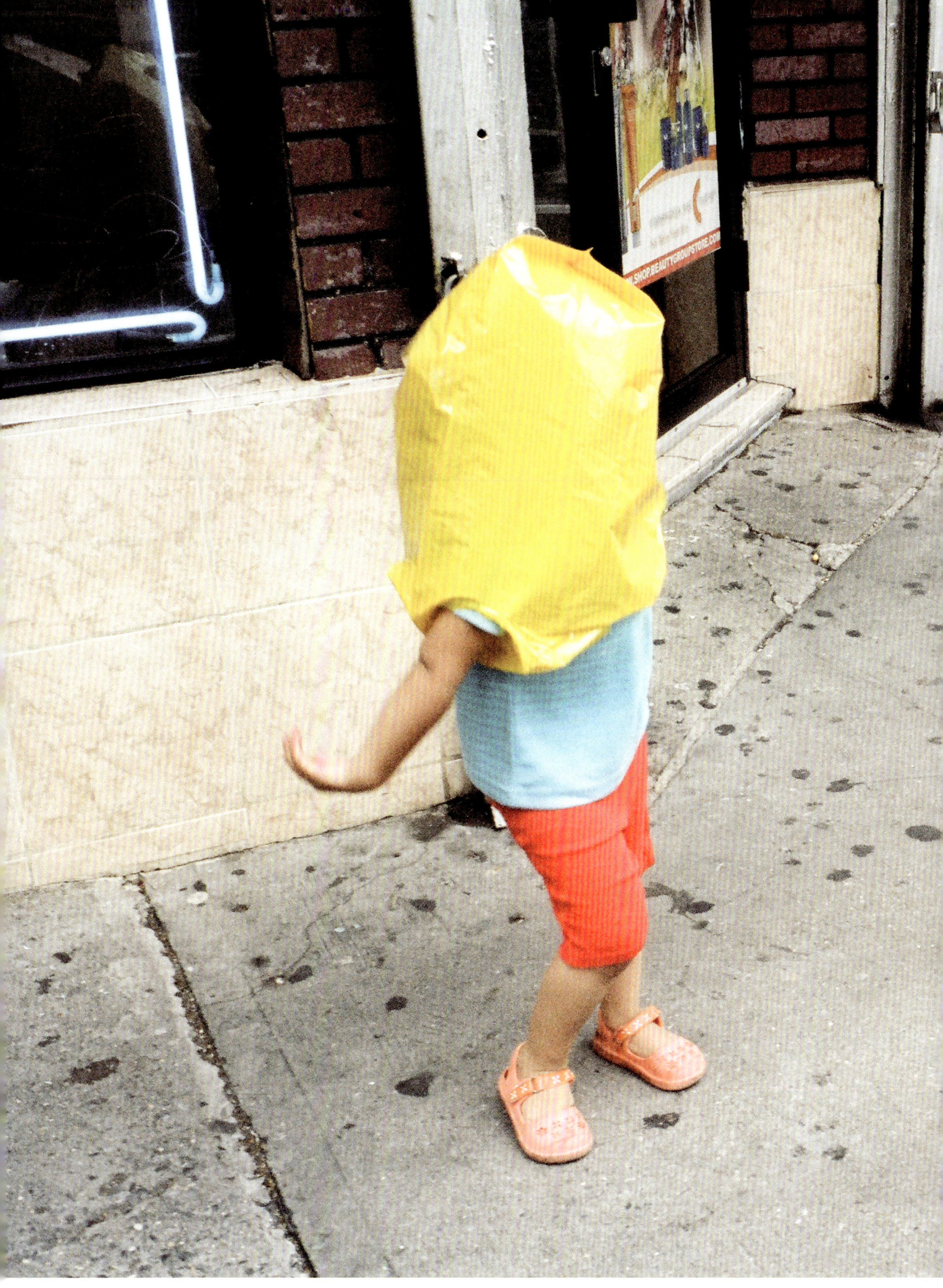

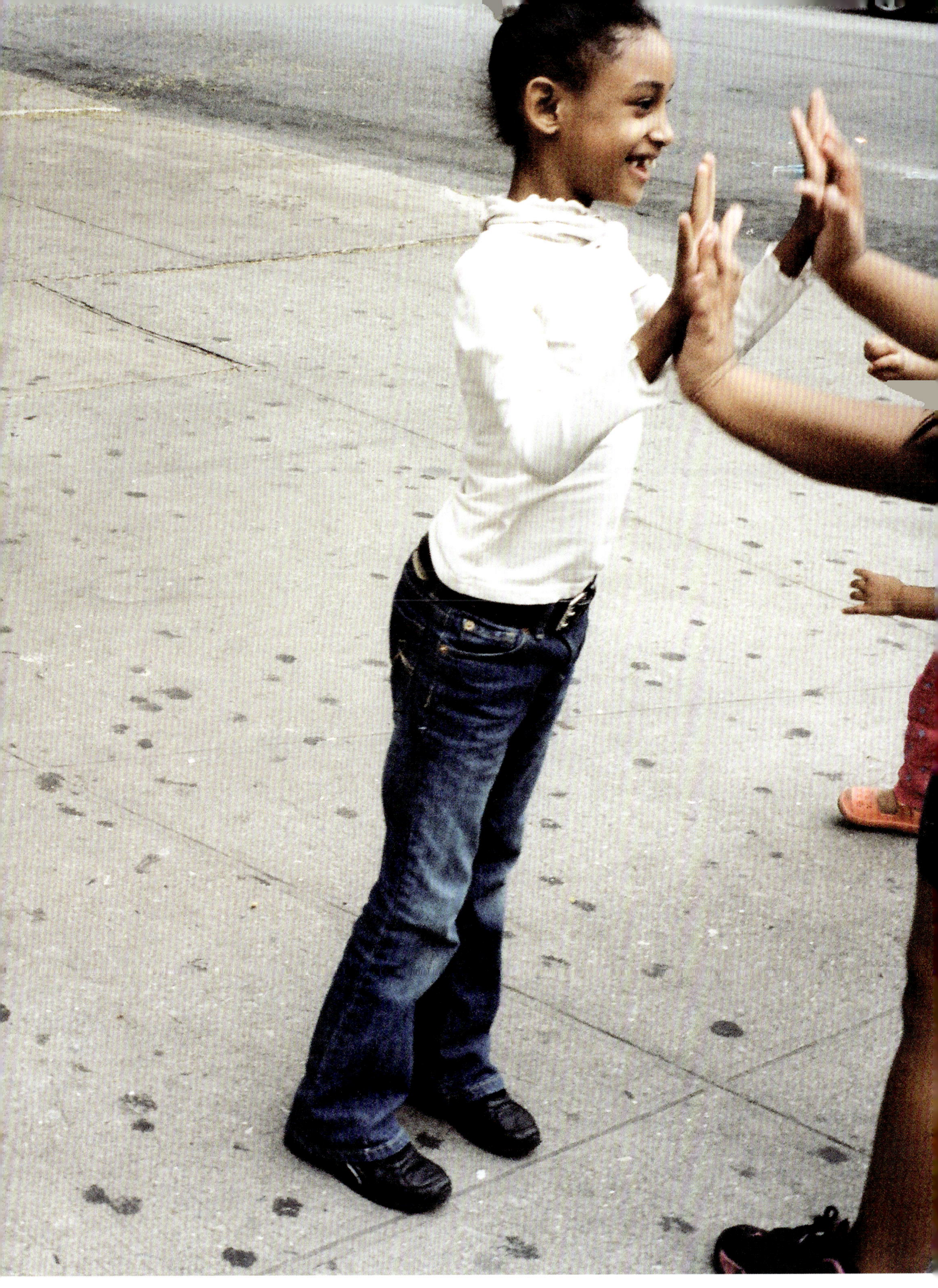

JOE

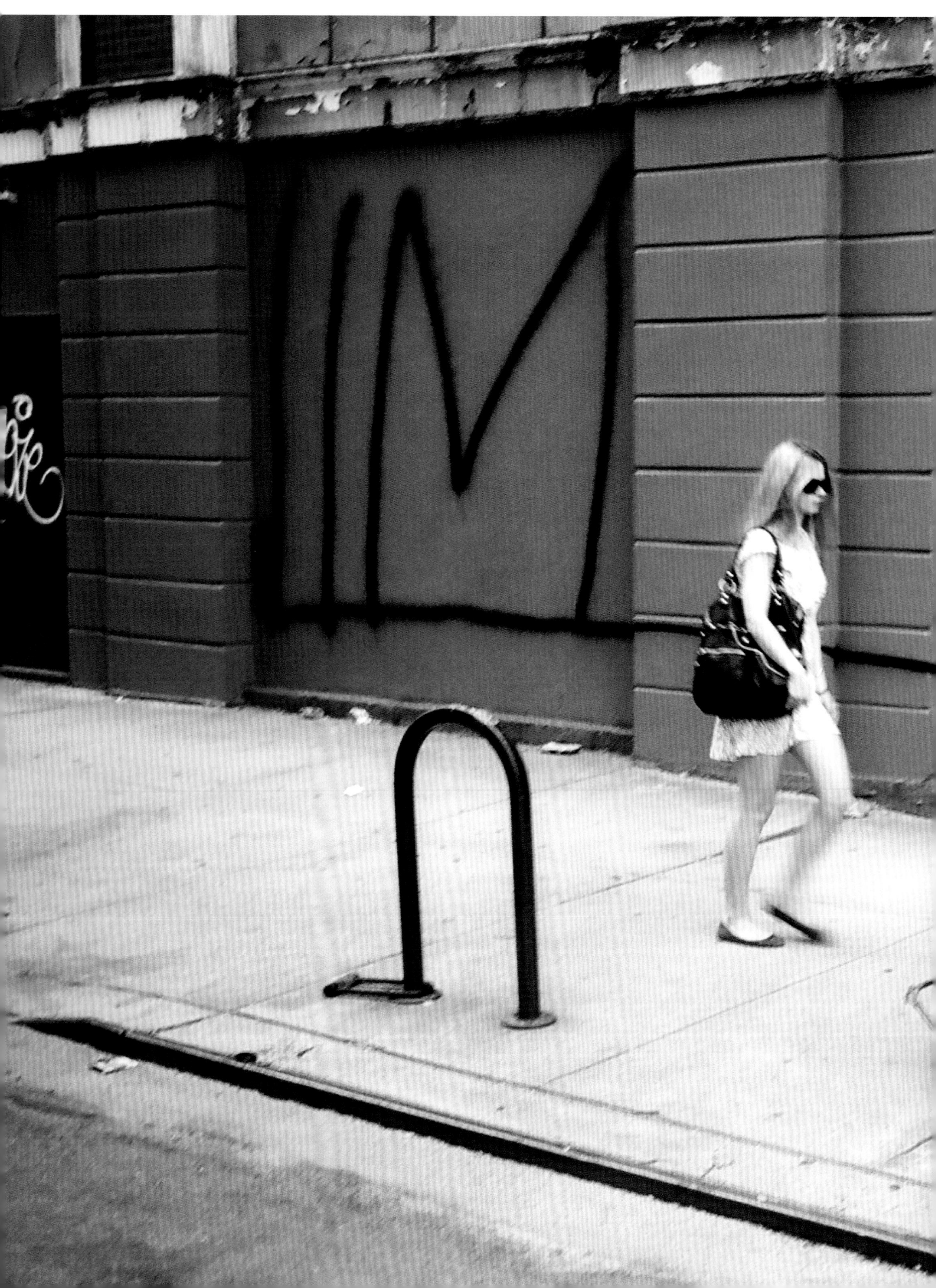

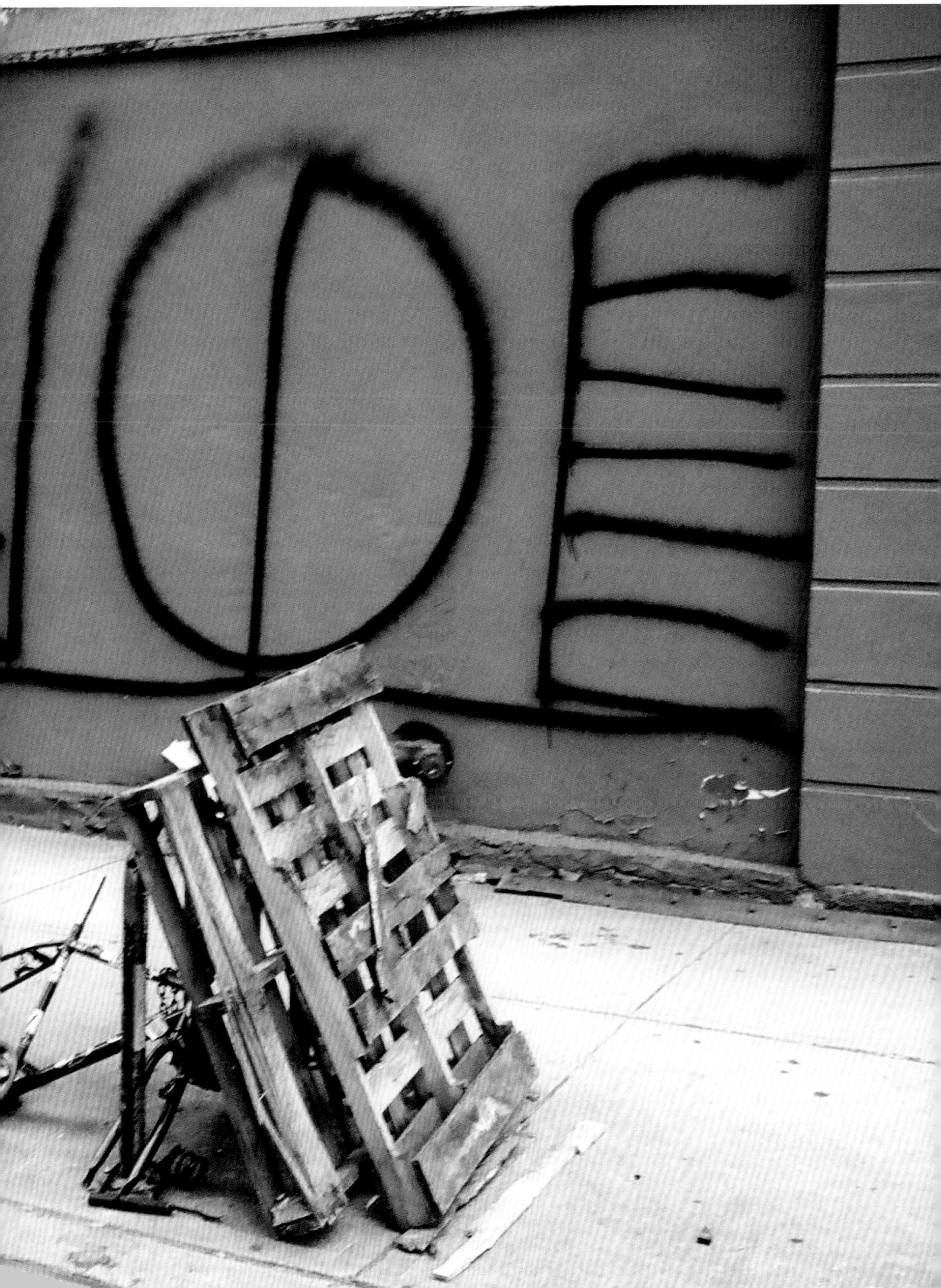

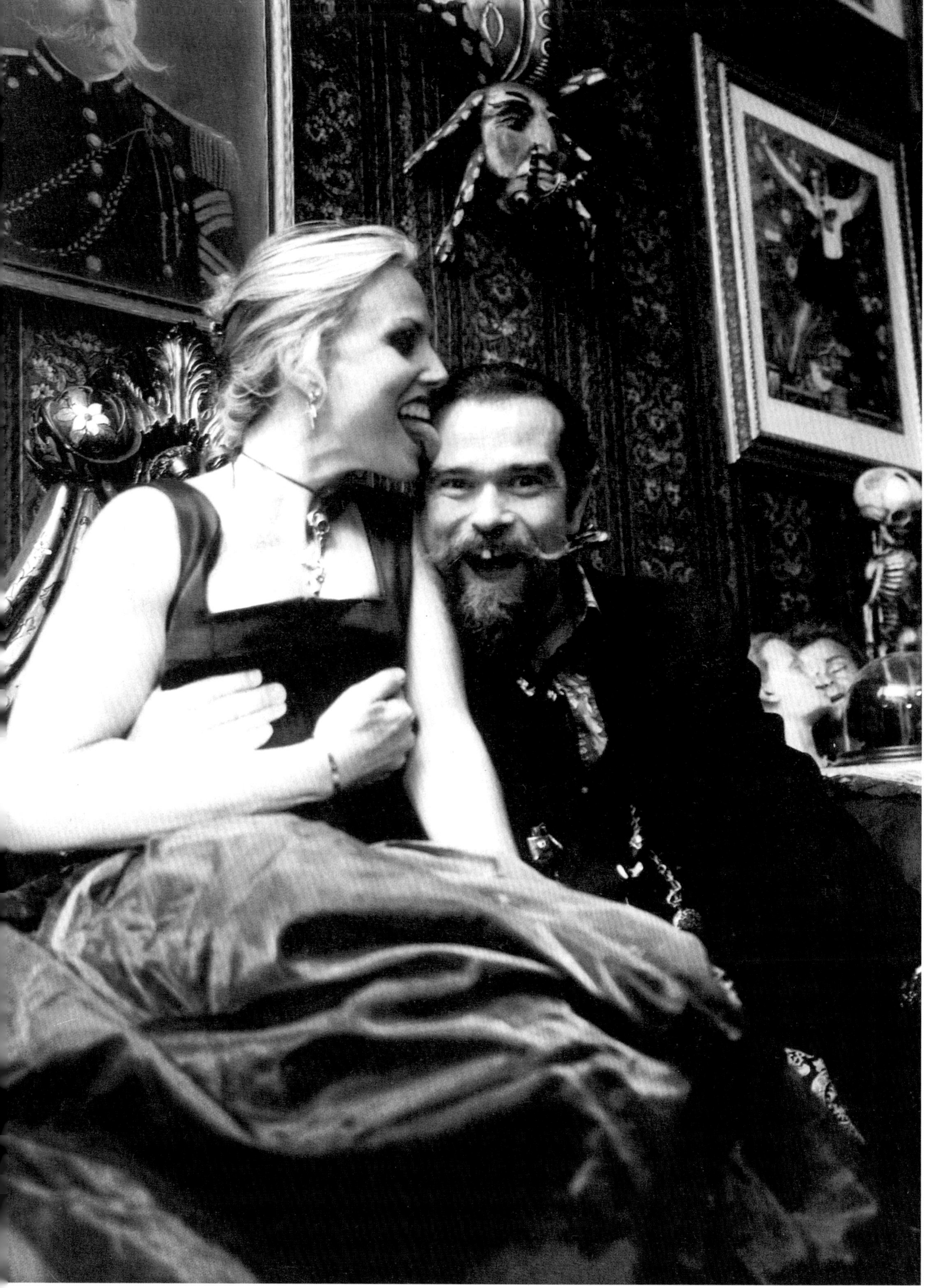

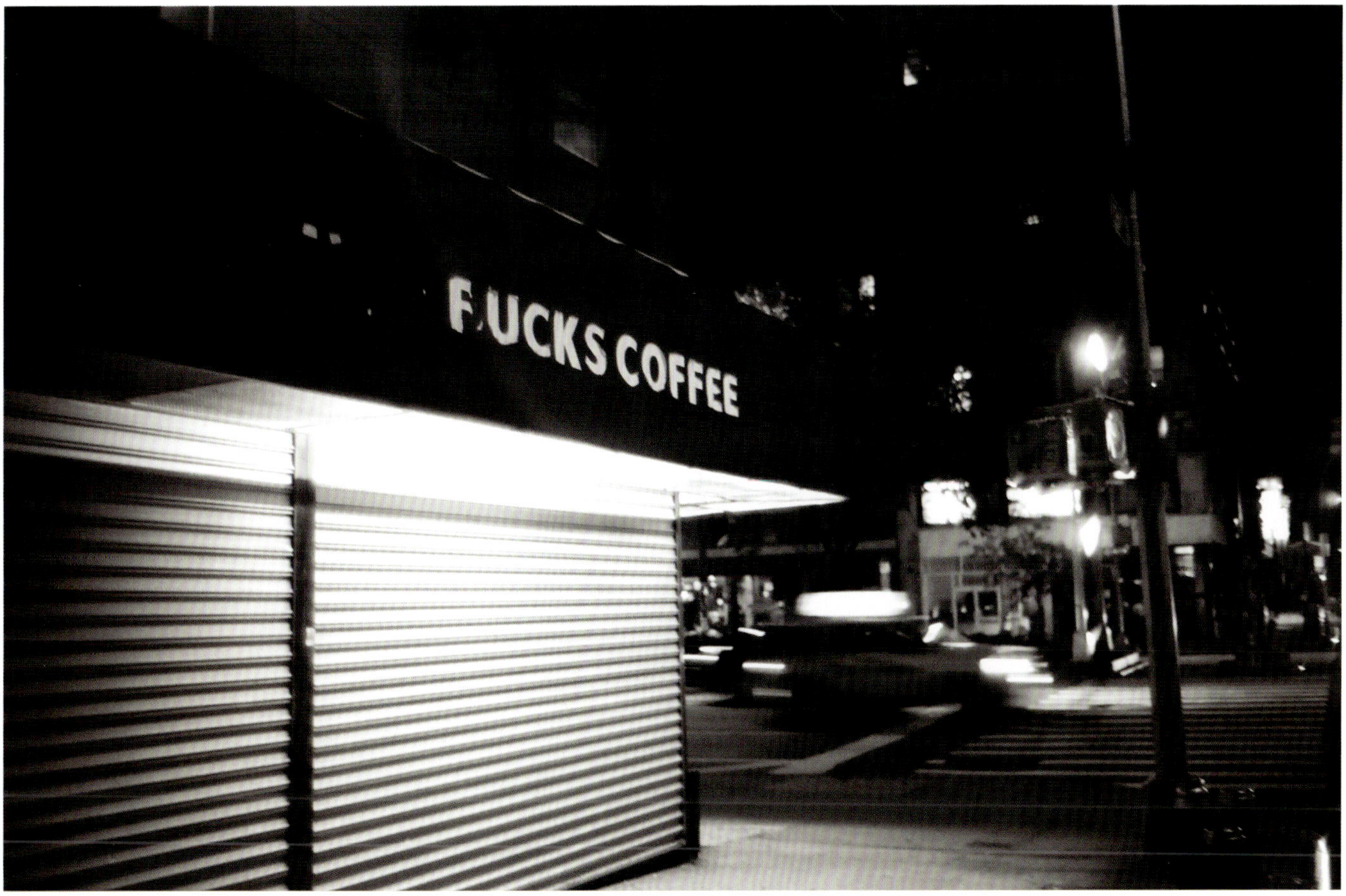

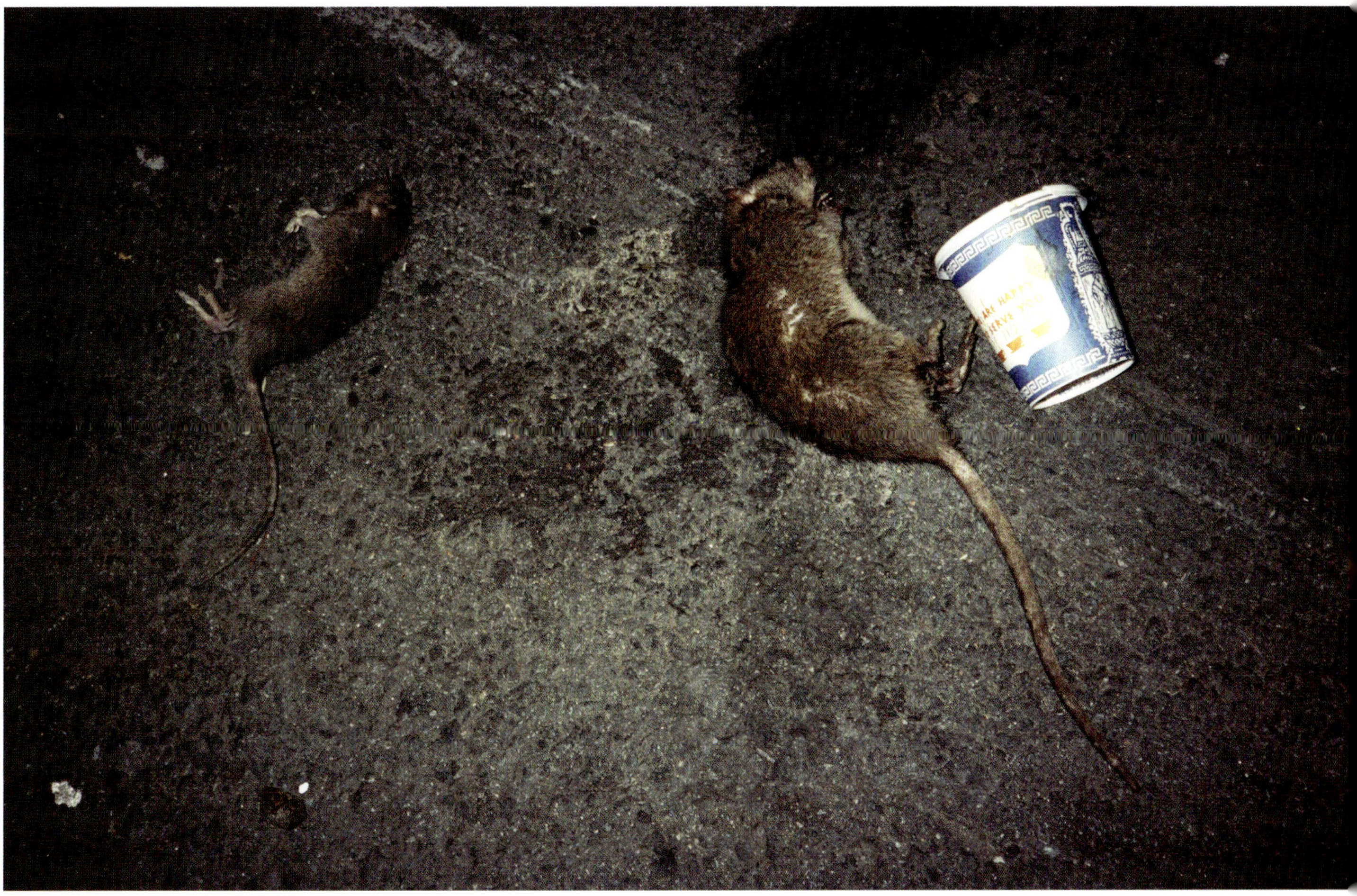

LONELY

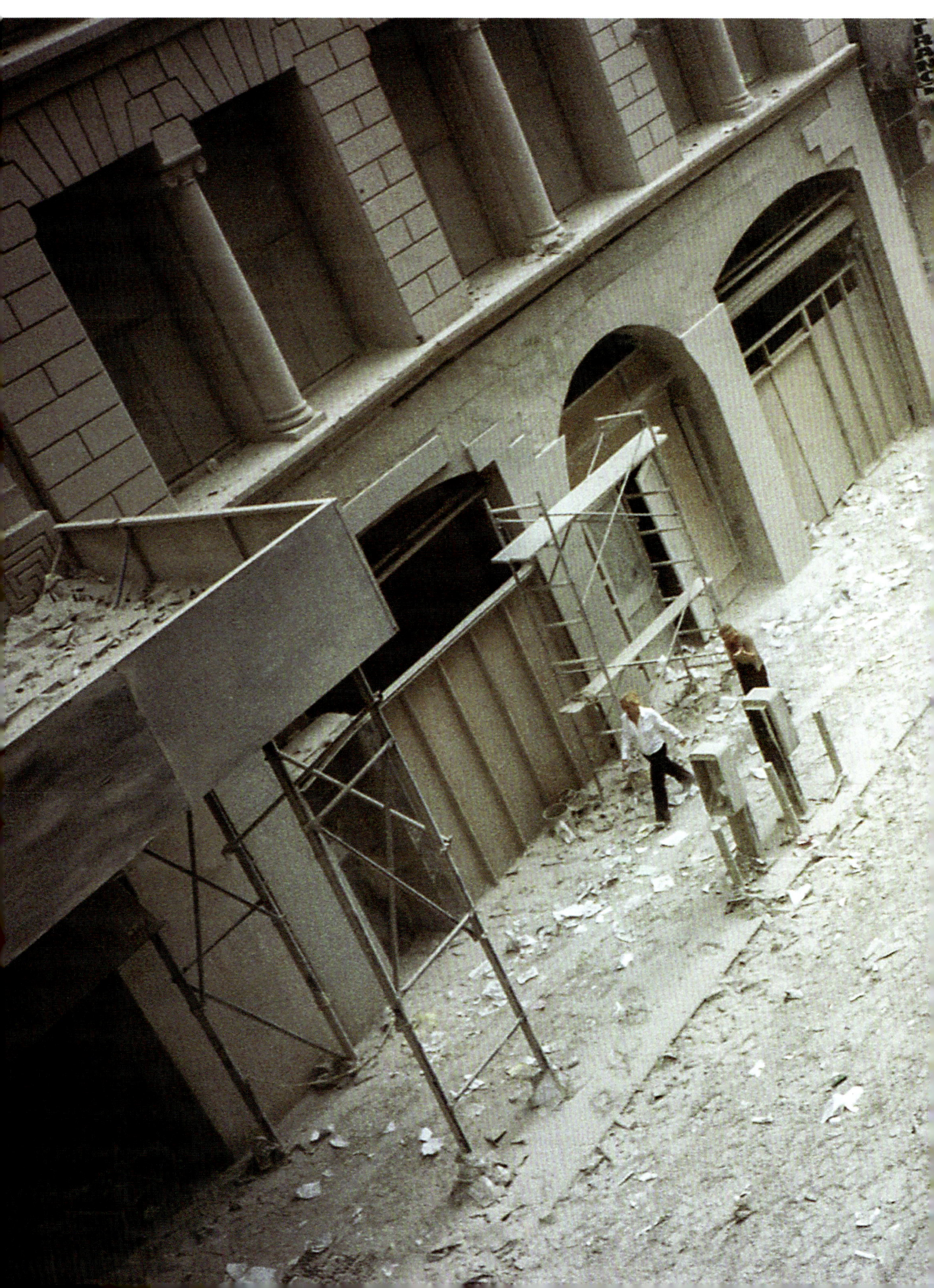

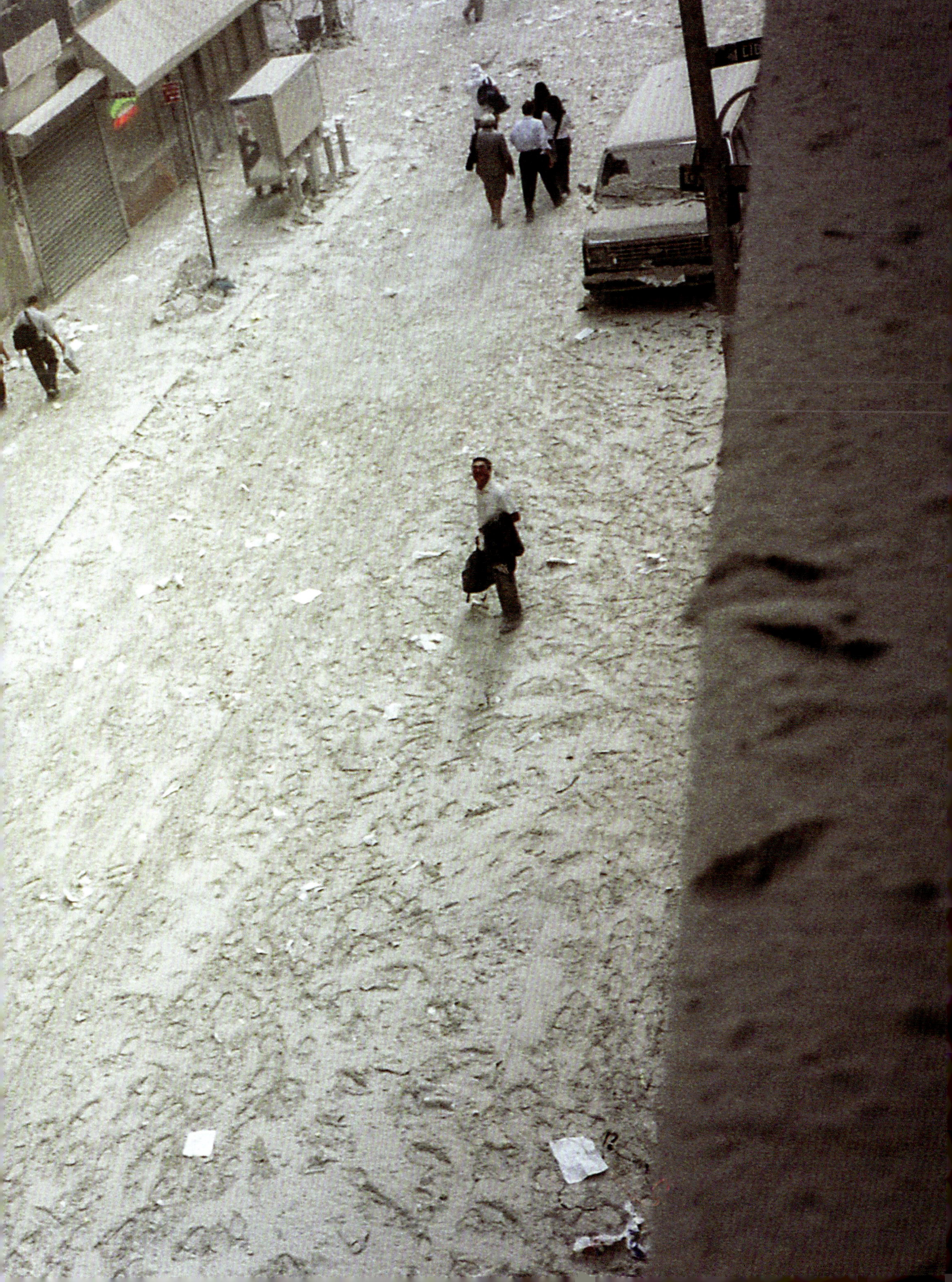

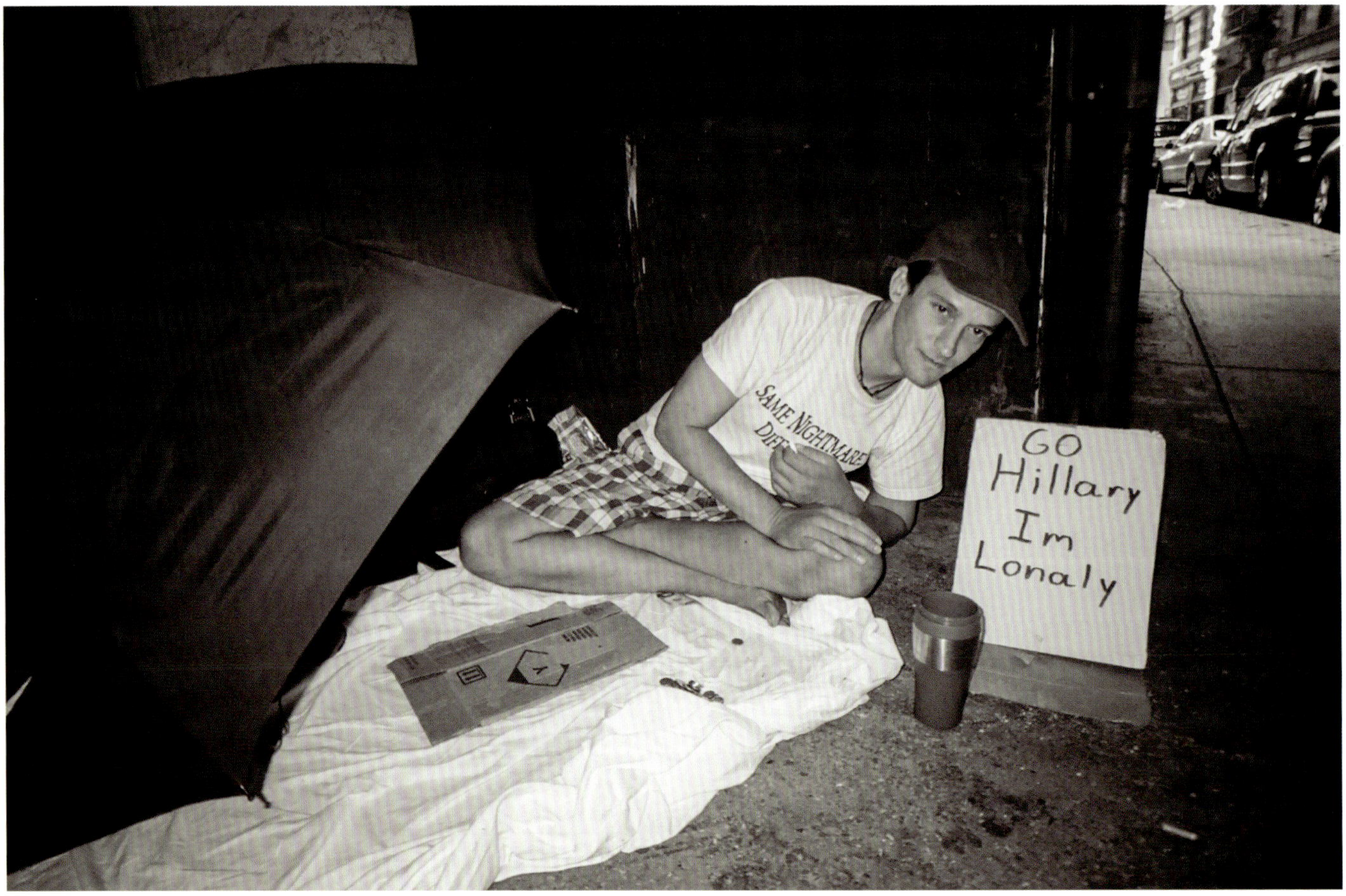

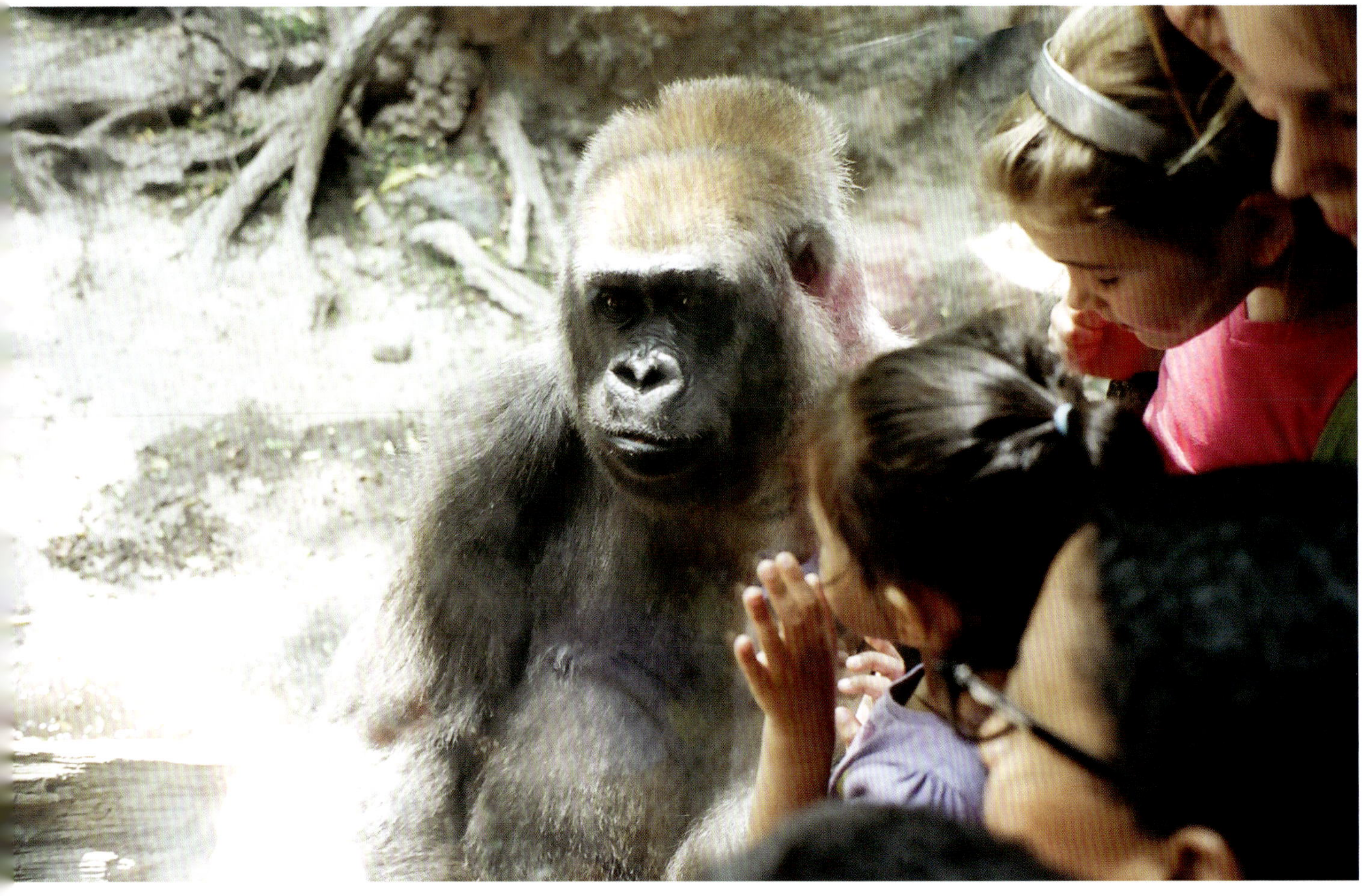

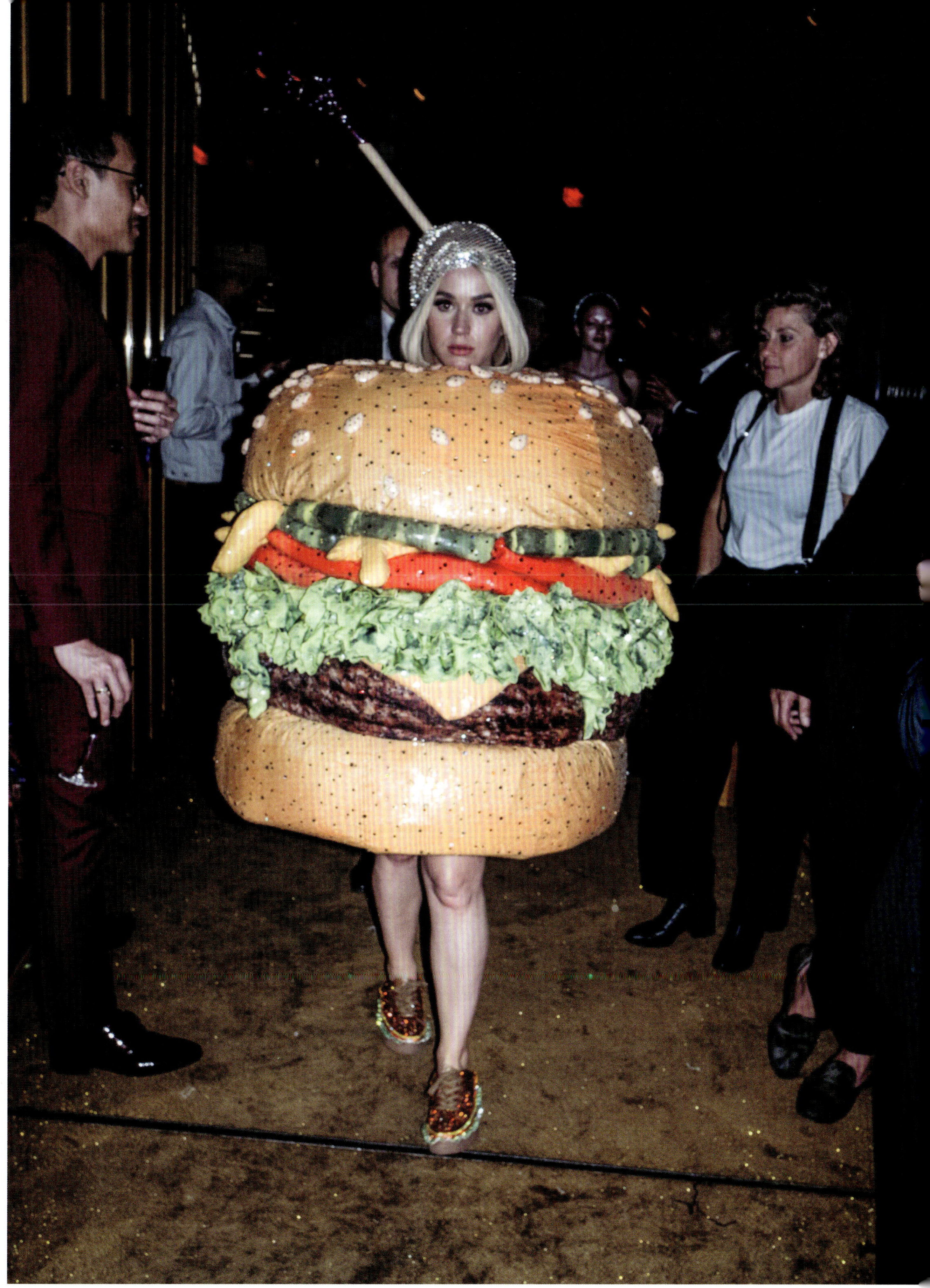

LOVE

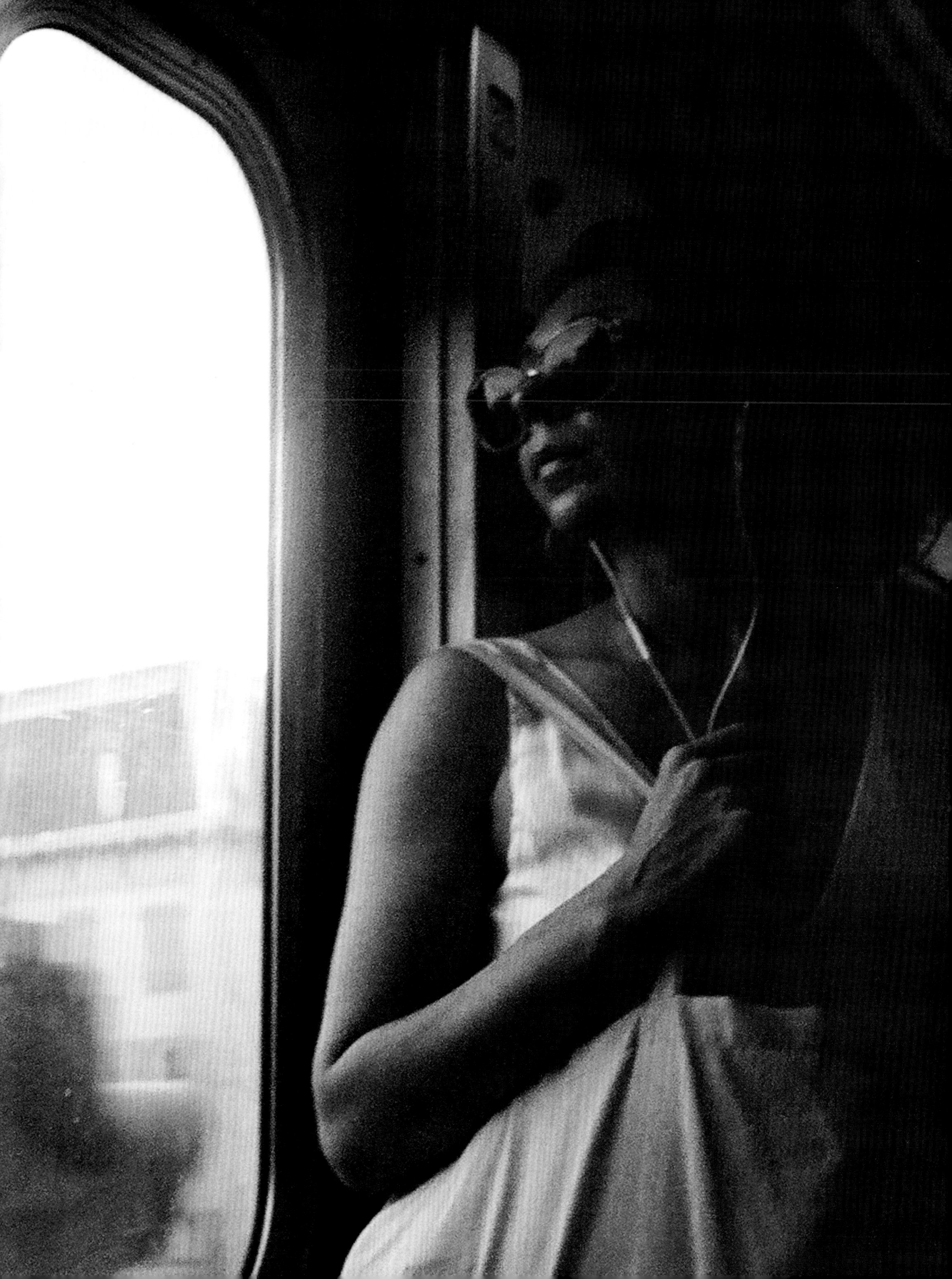

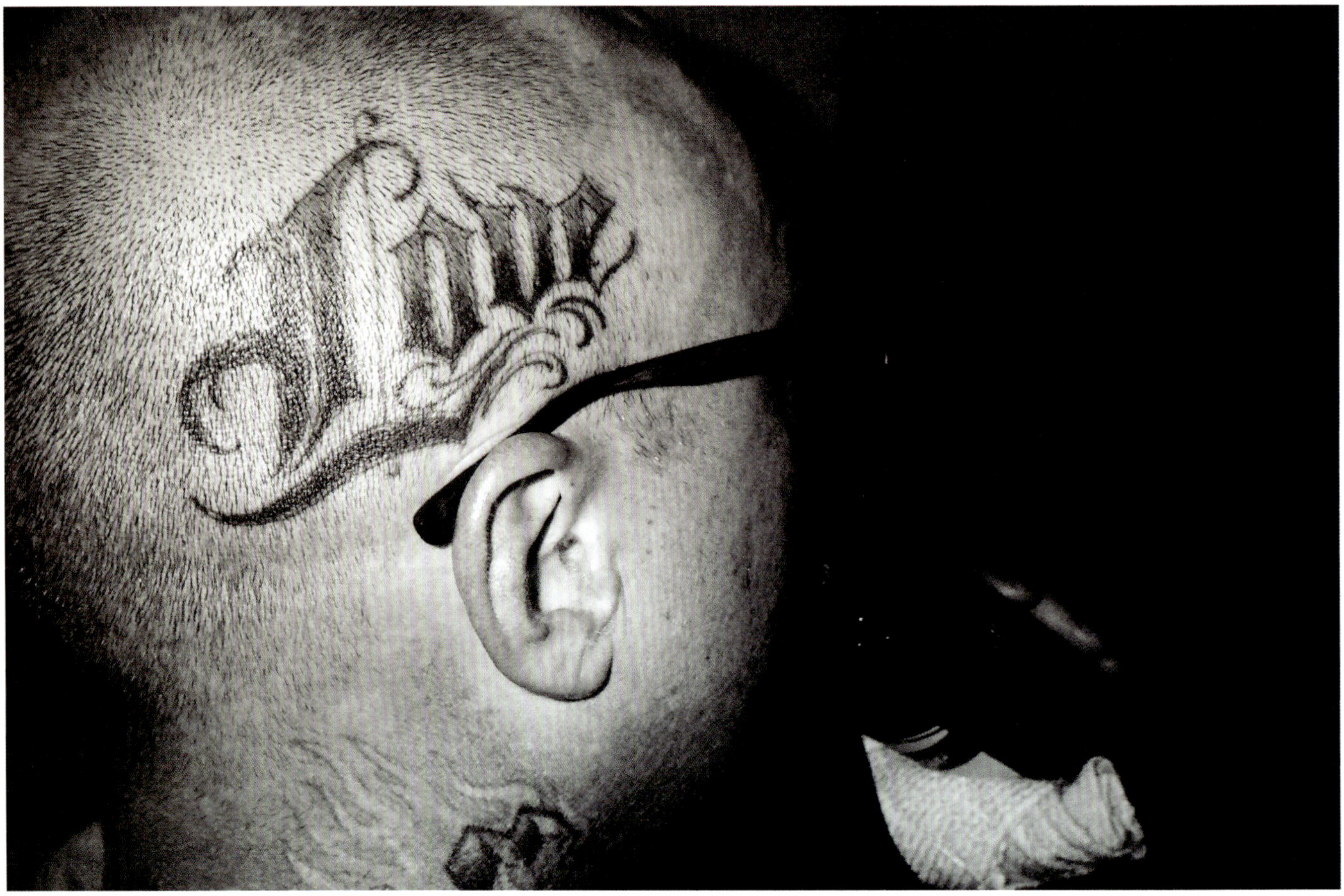

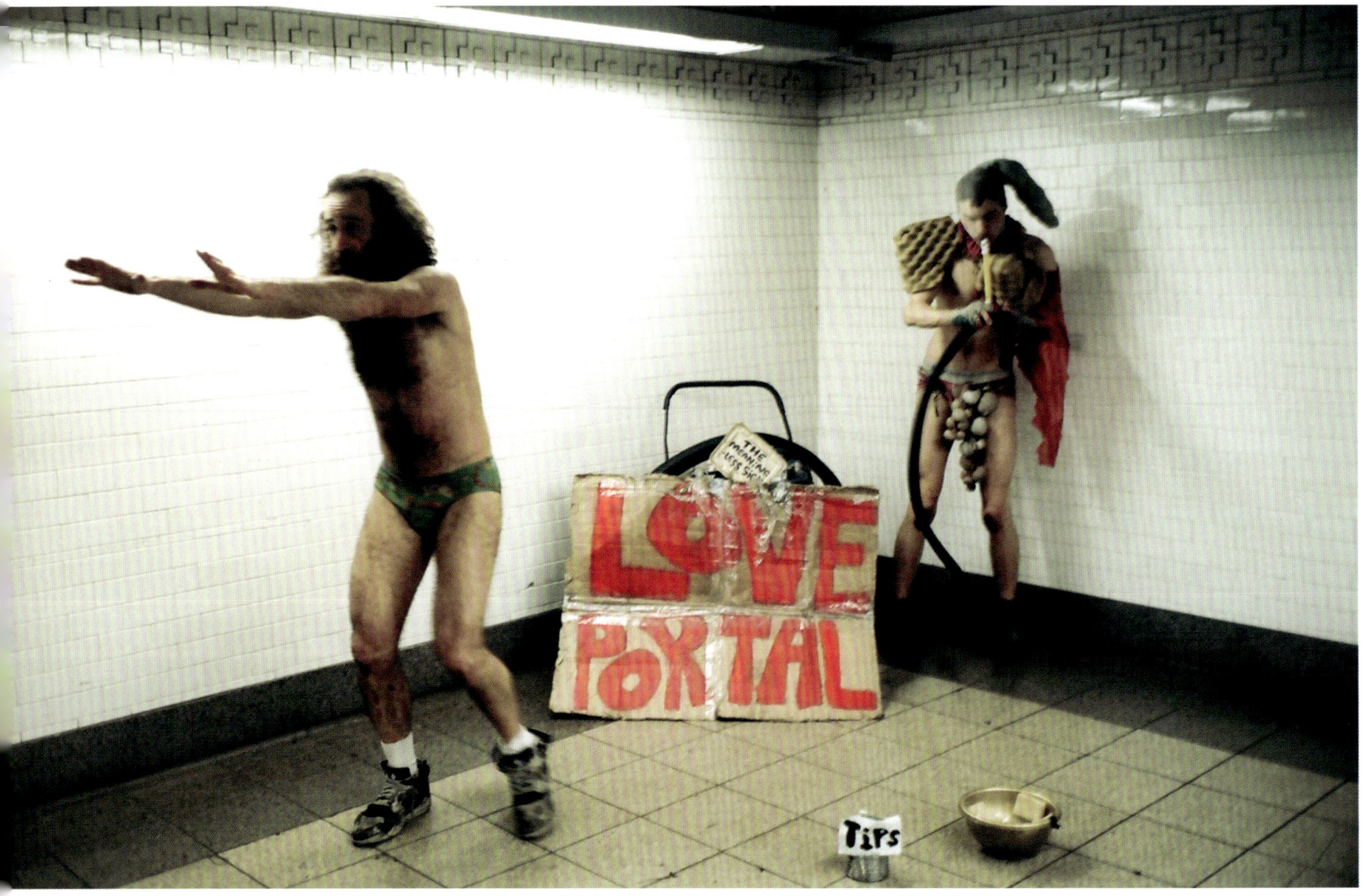

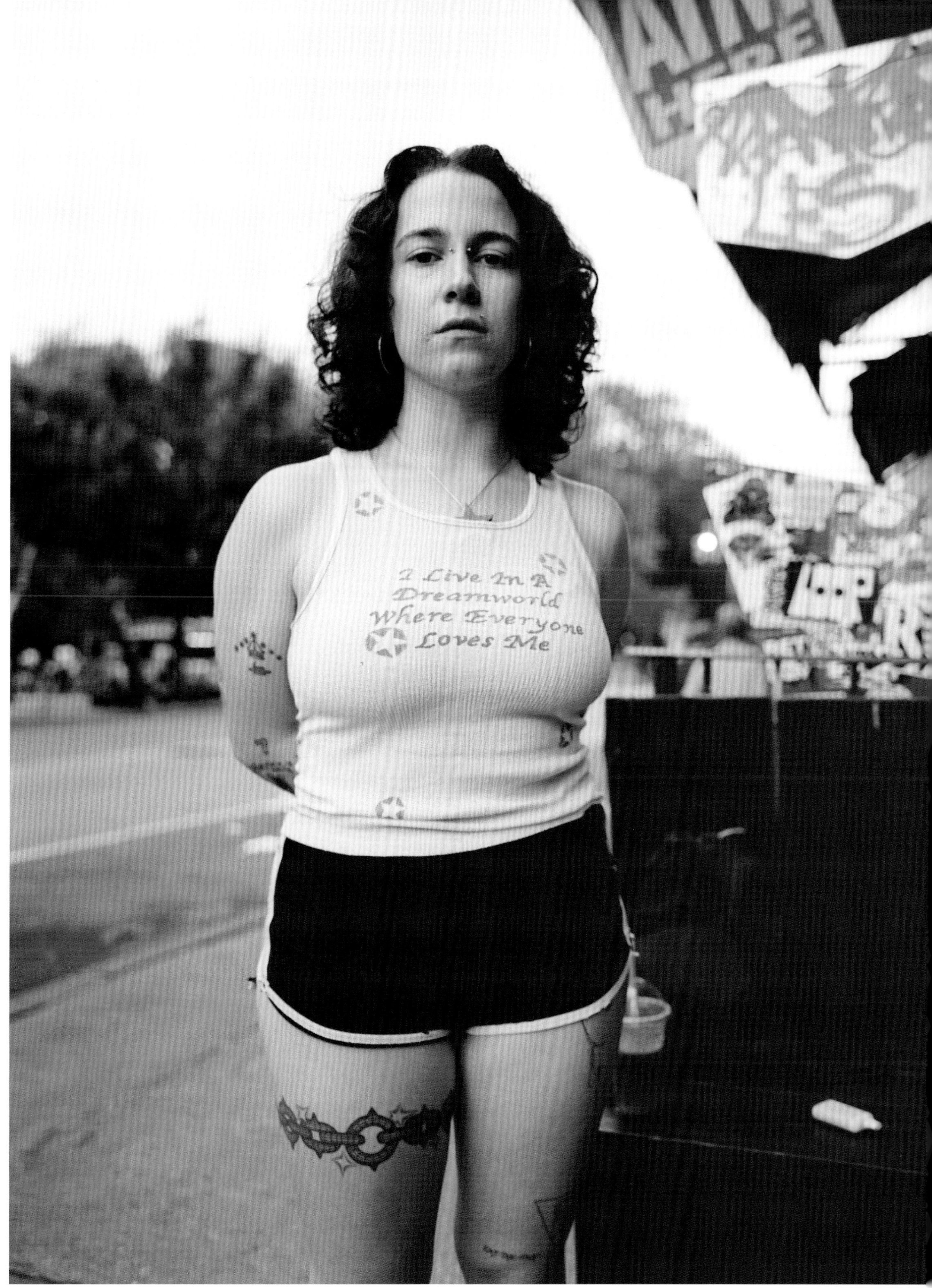
I Live In A
Dreamworld
Where Everyone
Loves Me

MATTRESS

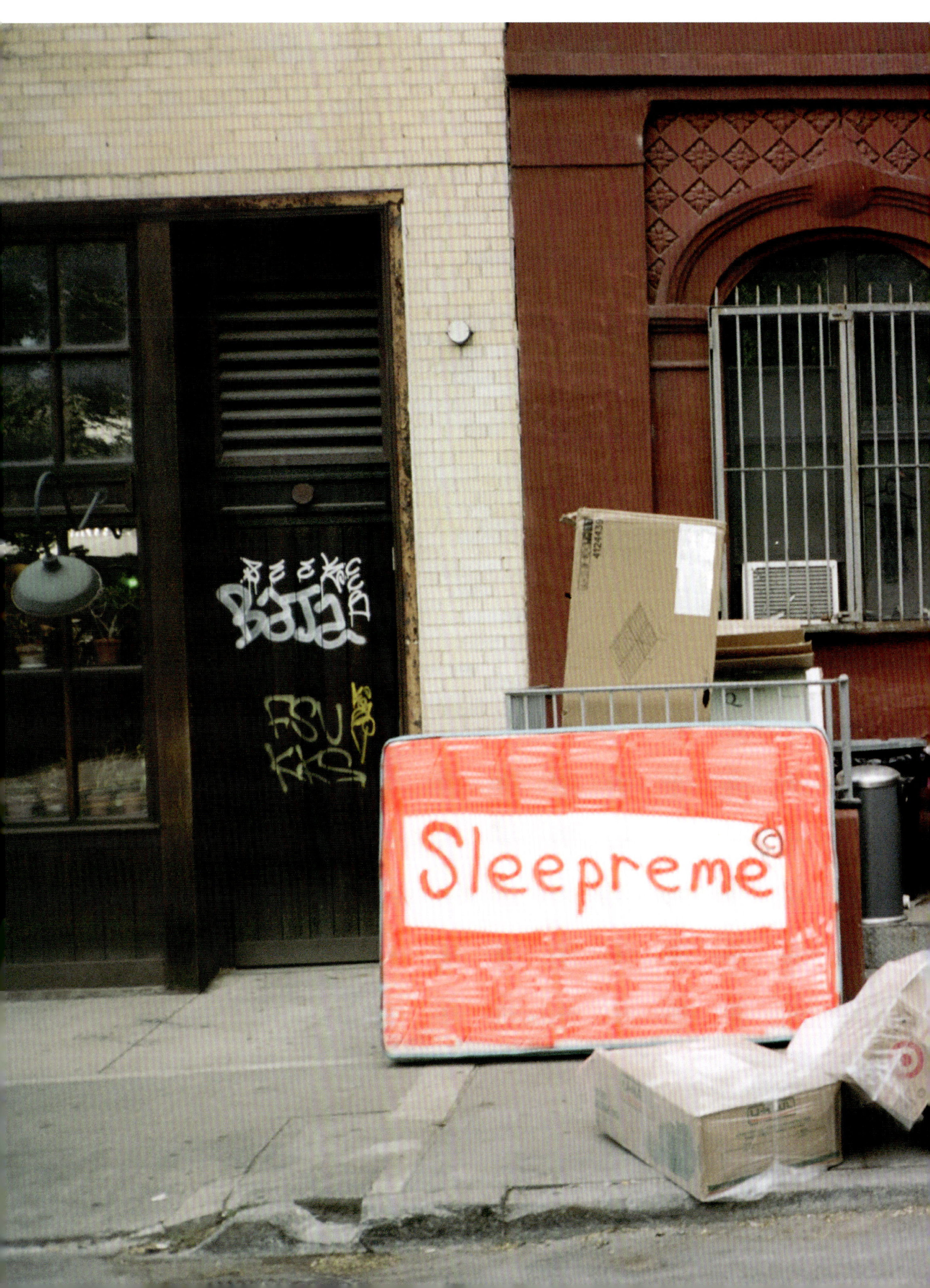

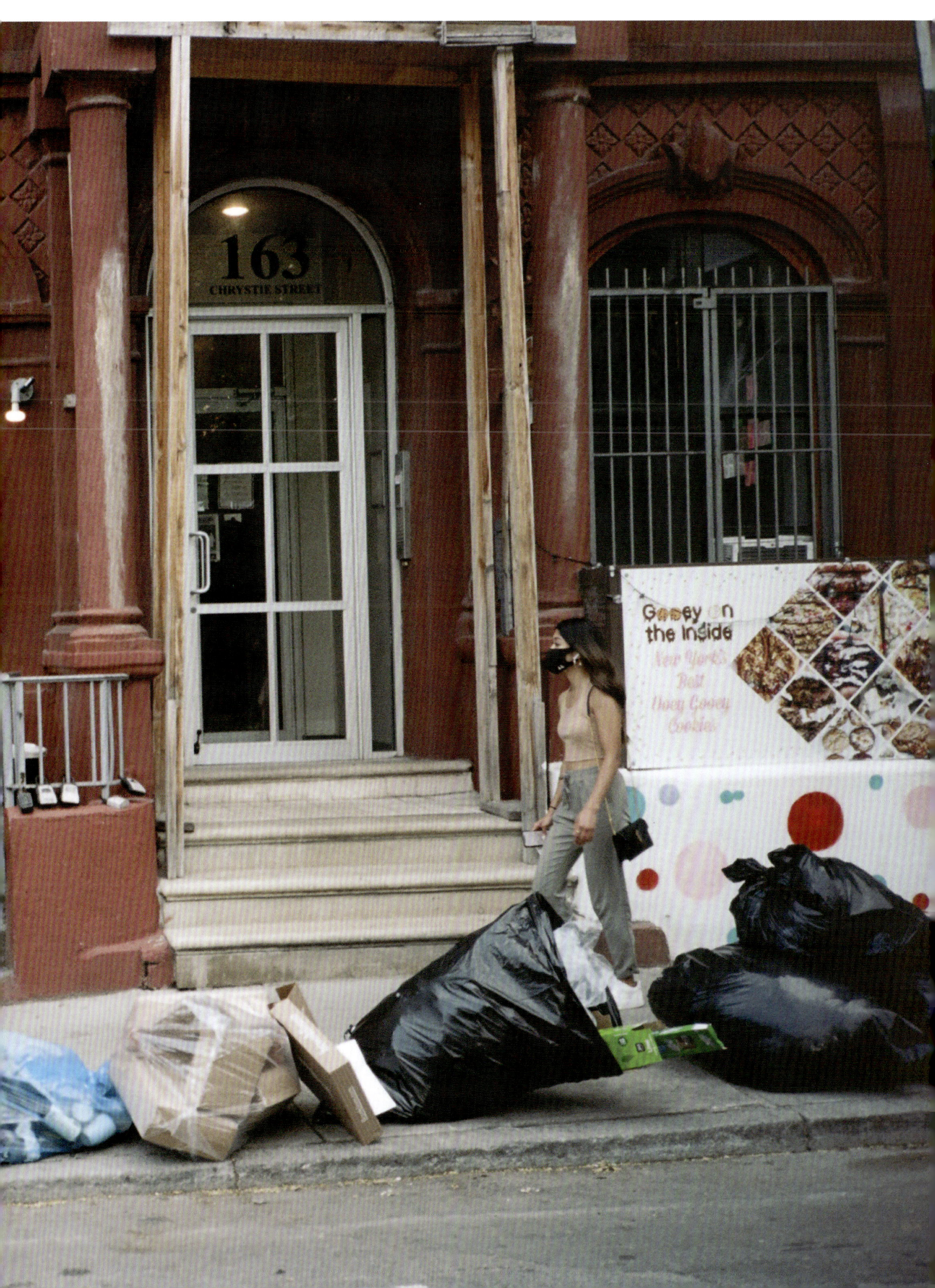
163
CHRYSTIE STREET
Gooey on
the inside

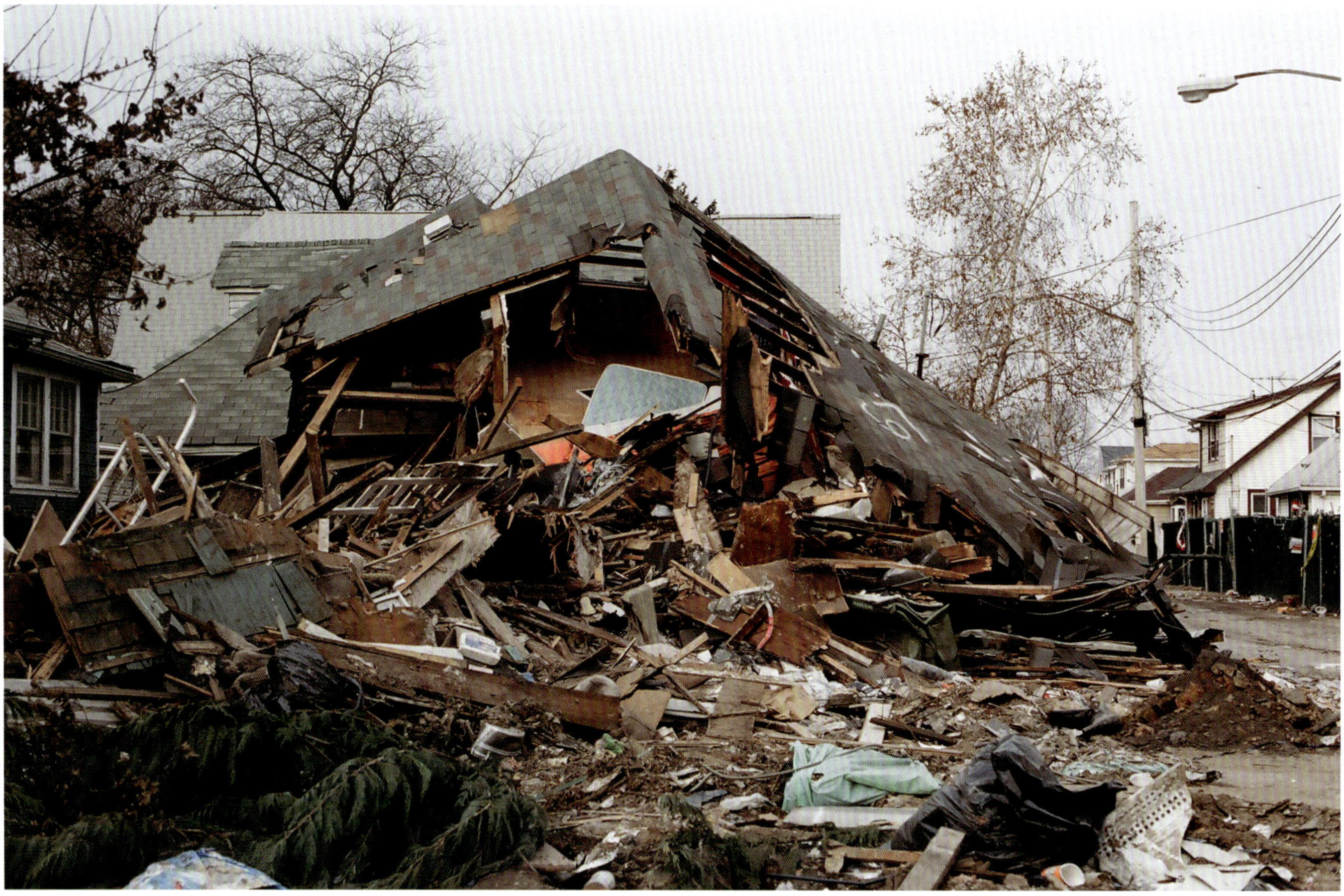

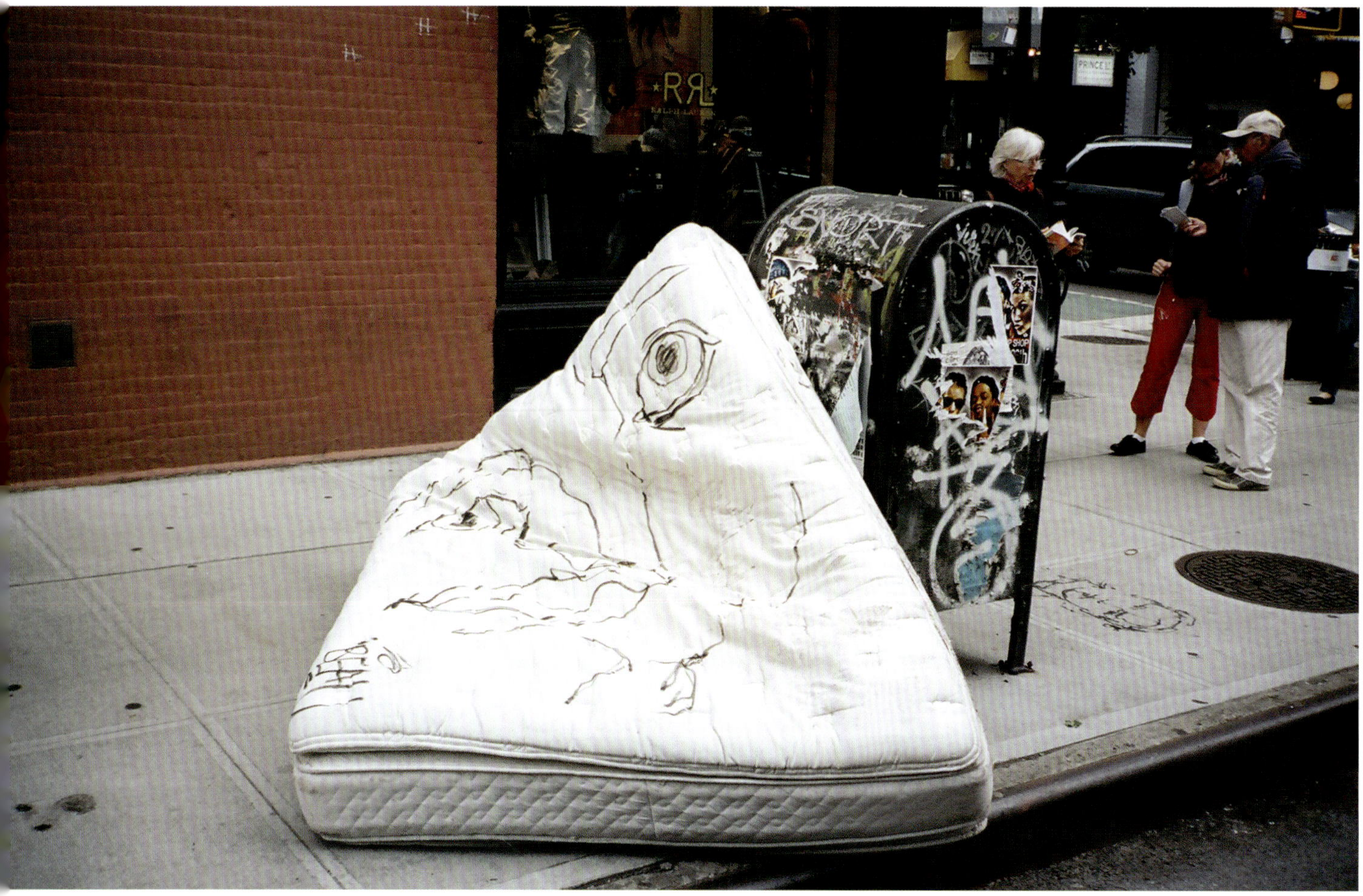

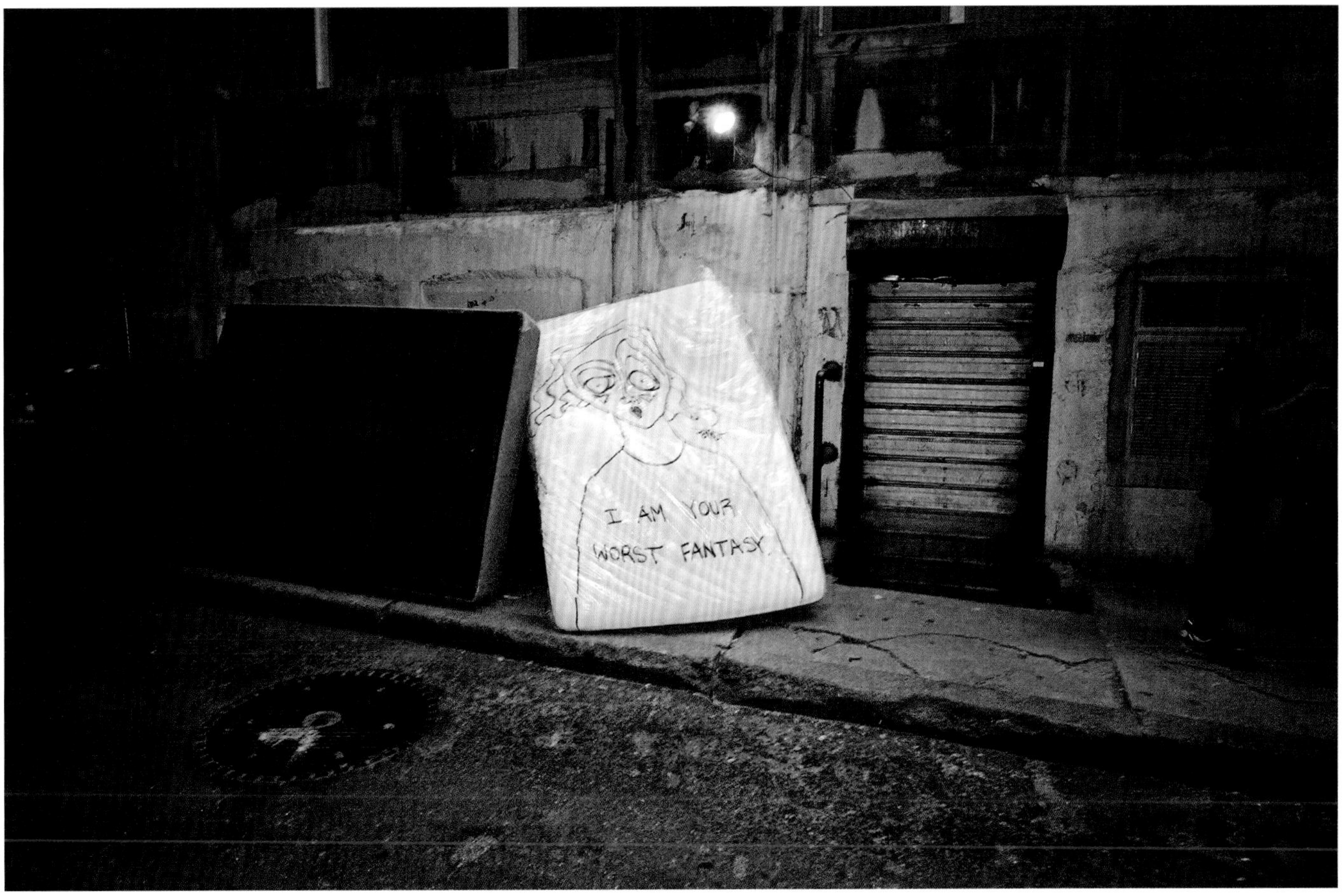

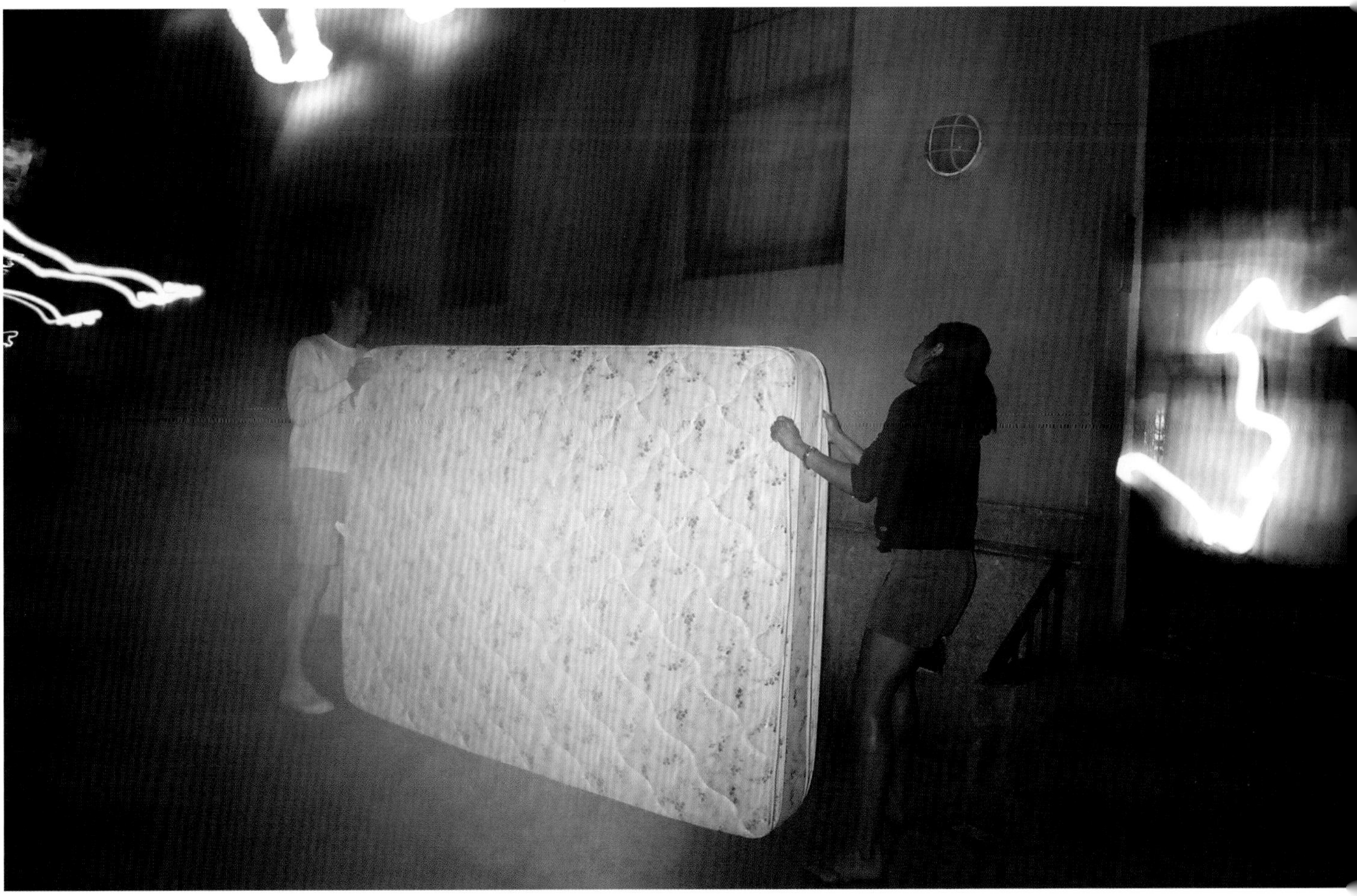

RAT

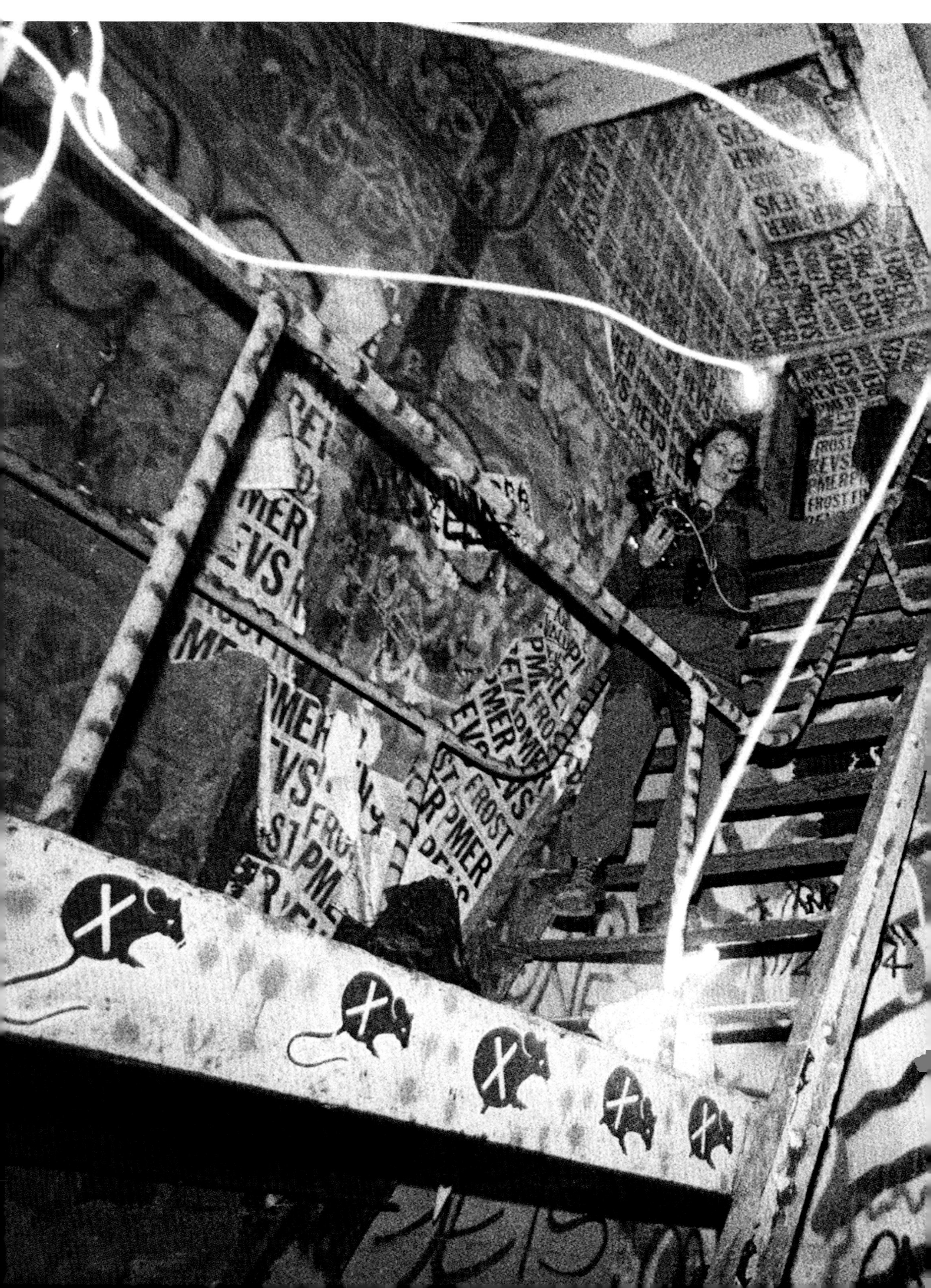

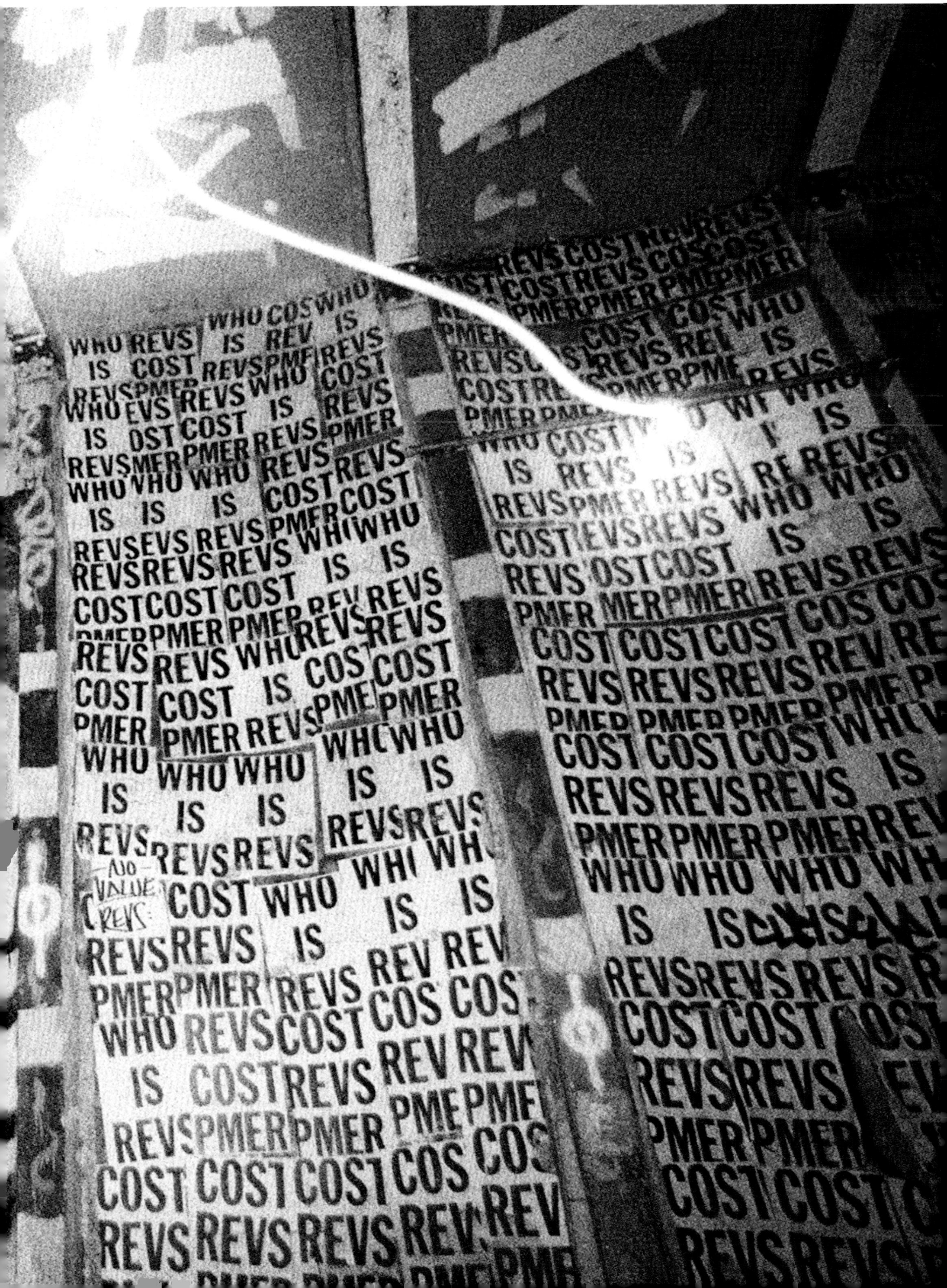

WHO
IS
REVS
COST
PMER
NO VALUE REVS

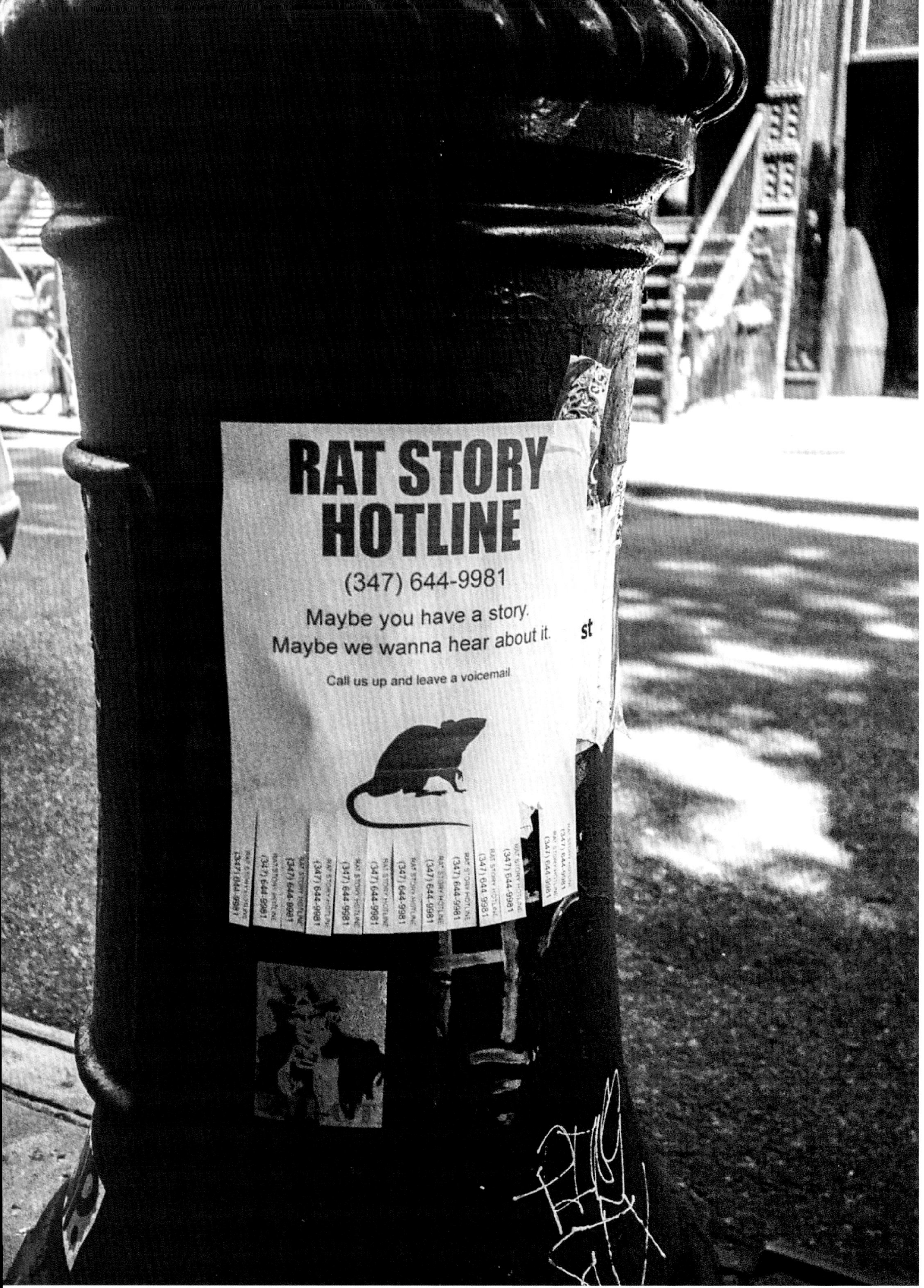
RAT STORY
HOTLINE
(347) 644-9981
Maybe you have a story.
Maybe we wanna hear about it.
Call us up and leave a voicemail

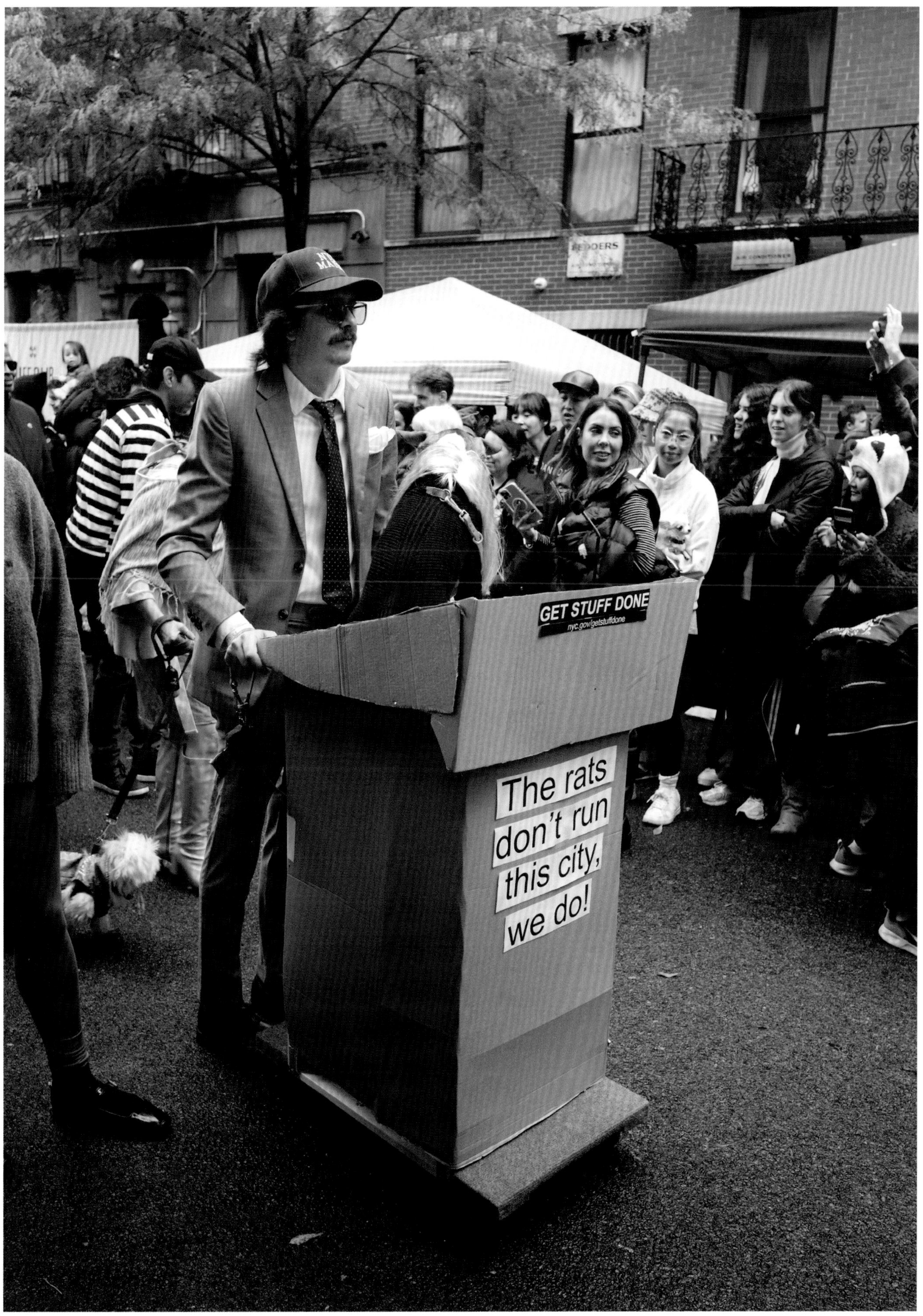
GET STUFF DONE
nyc.gov/getstuffdone
The rats
don't run
this city,
we do!

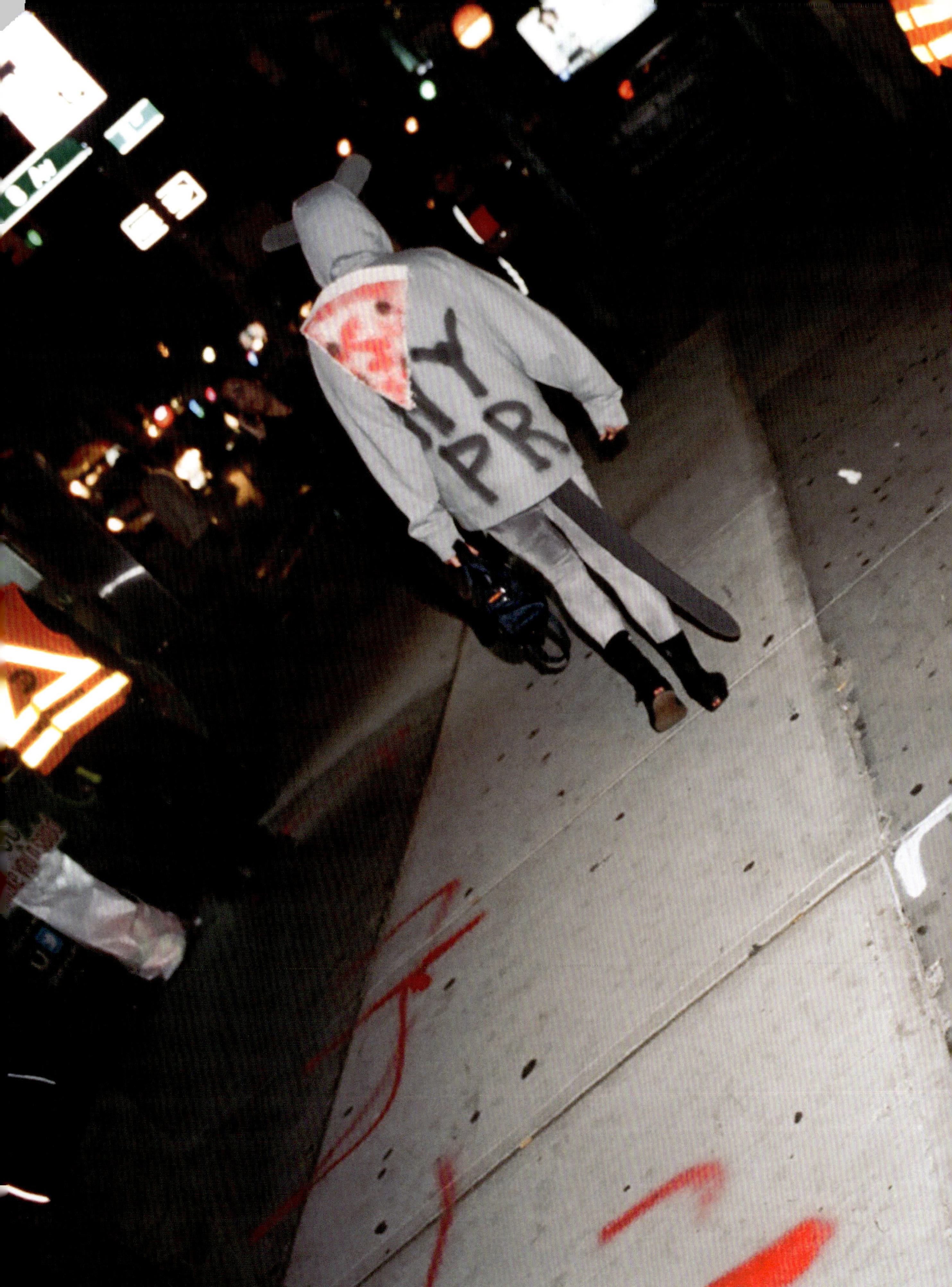

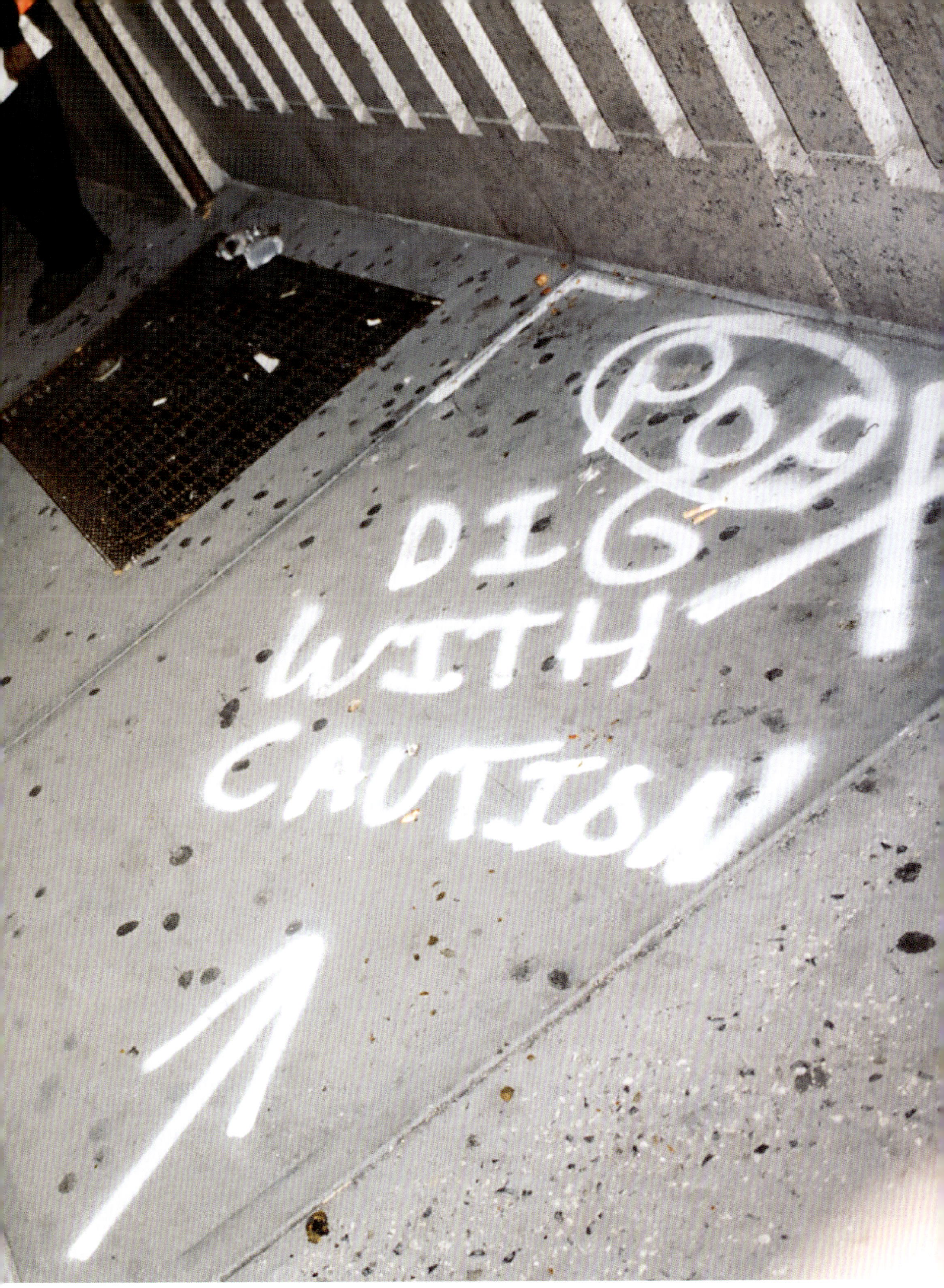
DIG
WITH
CAUTION

ROOFTOP

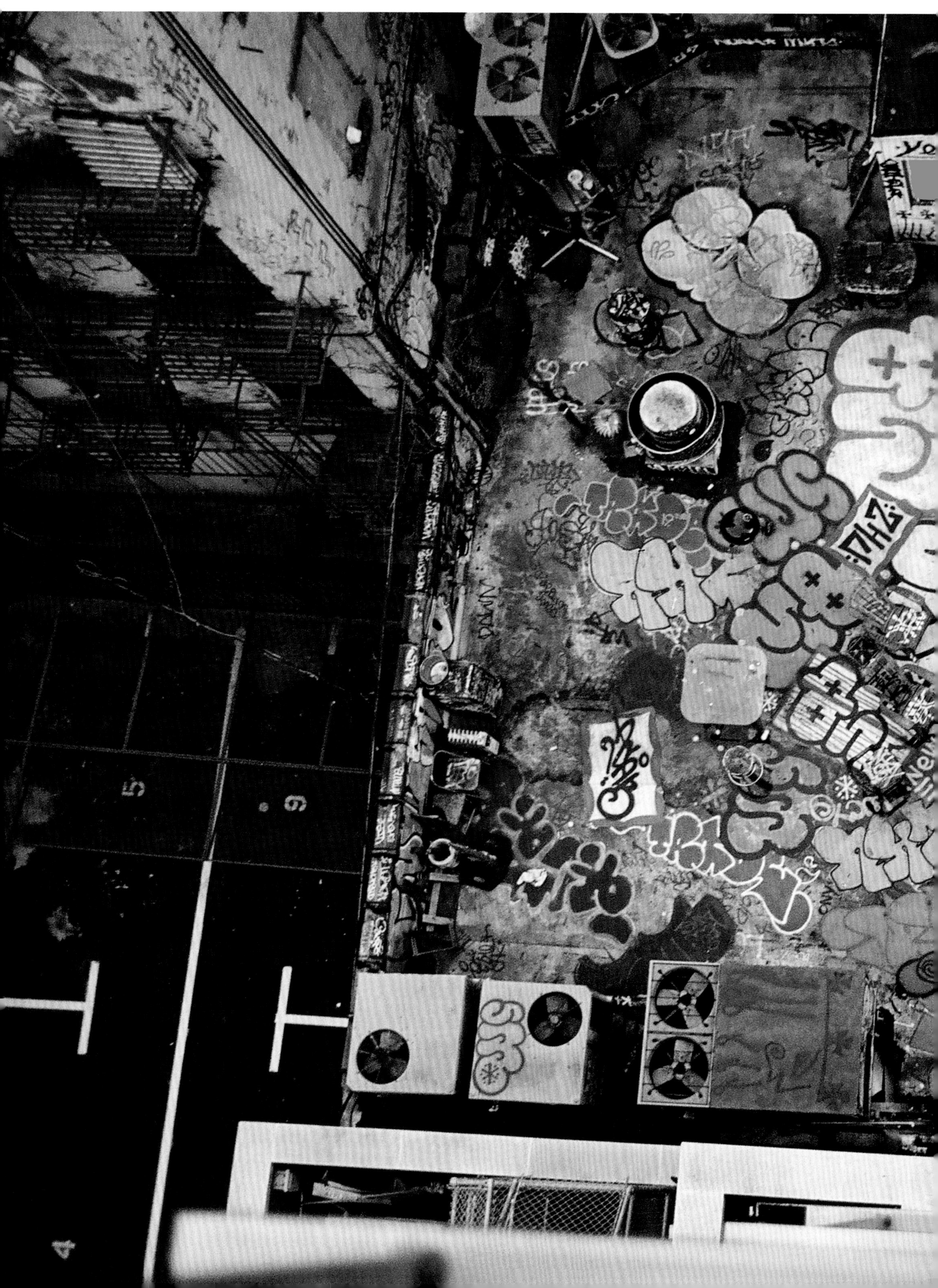

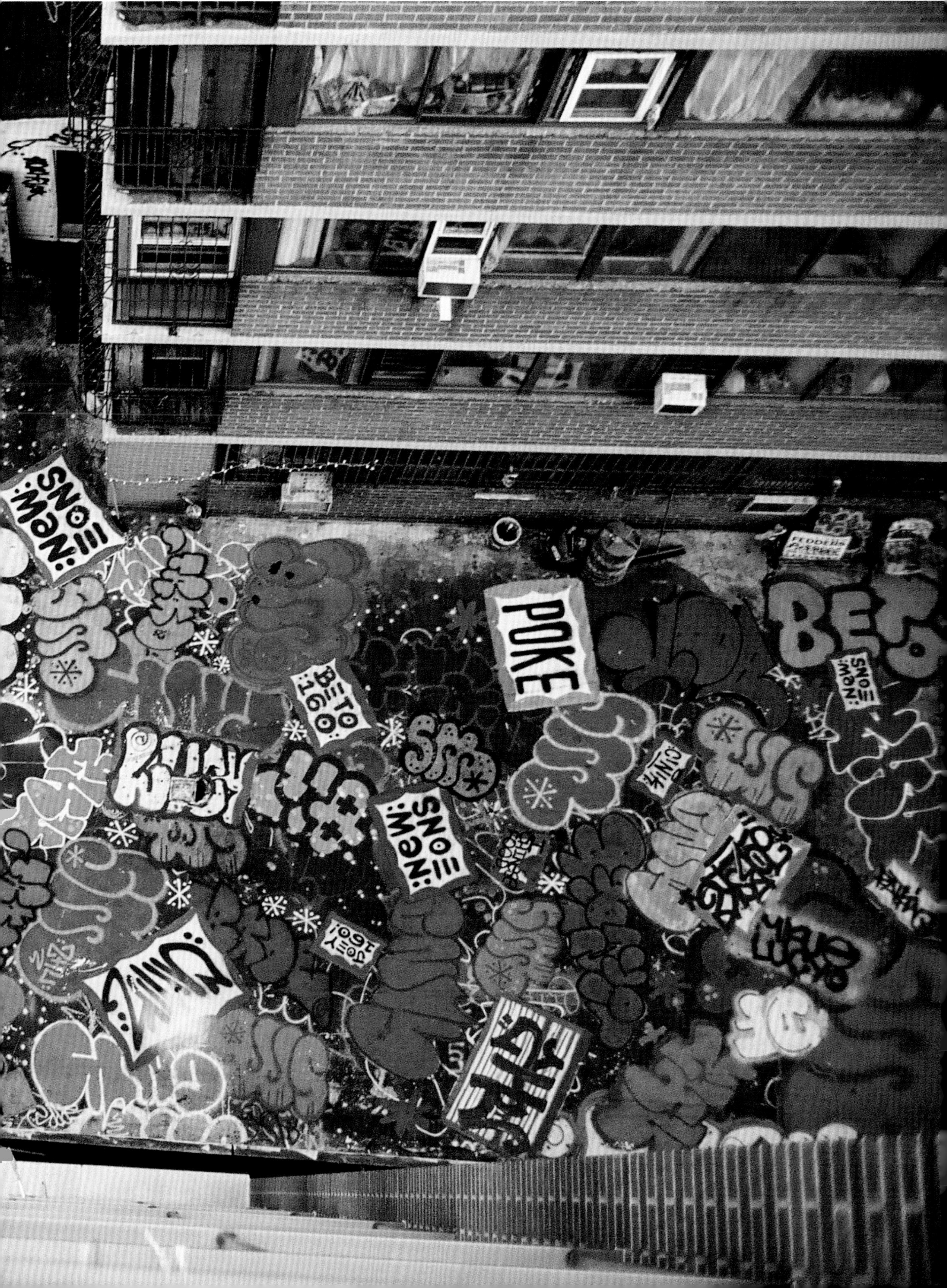
POKE

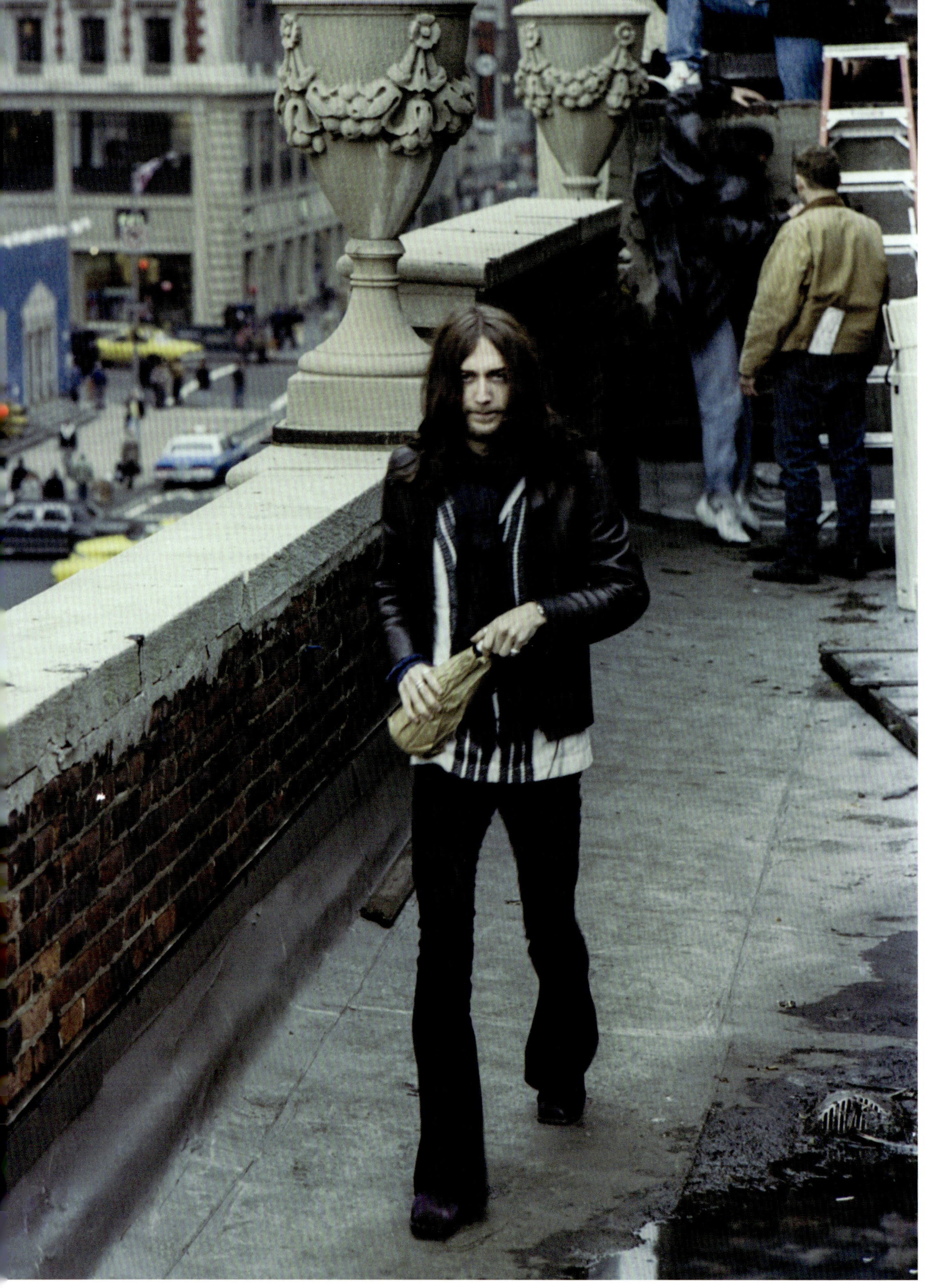

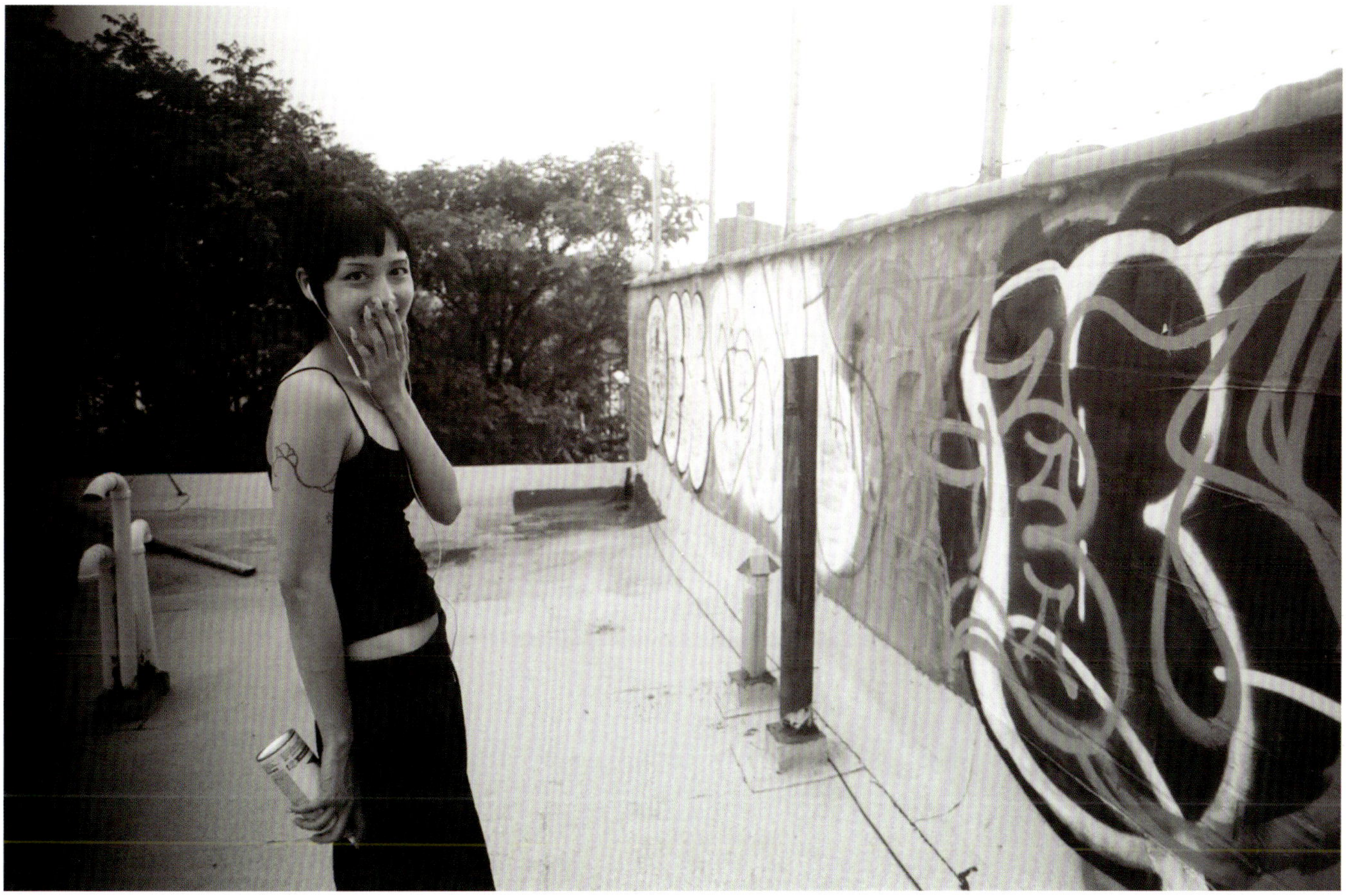

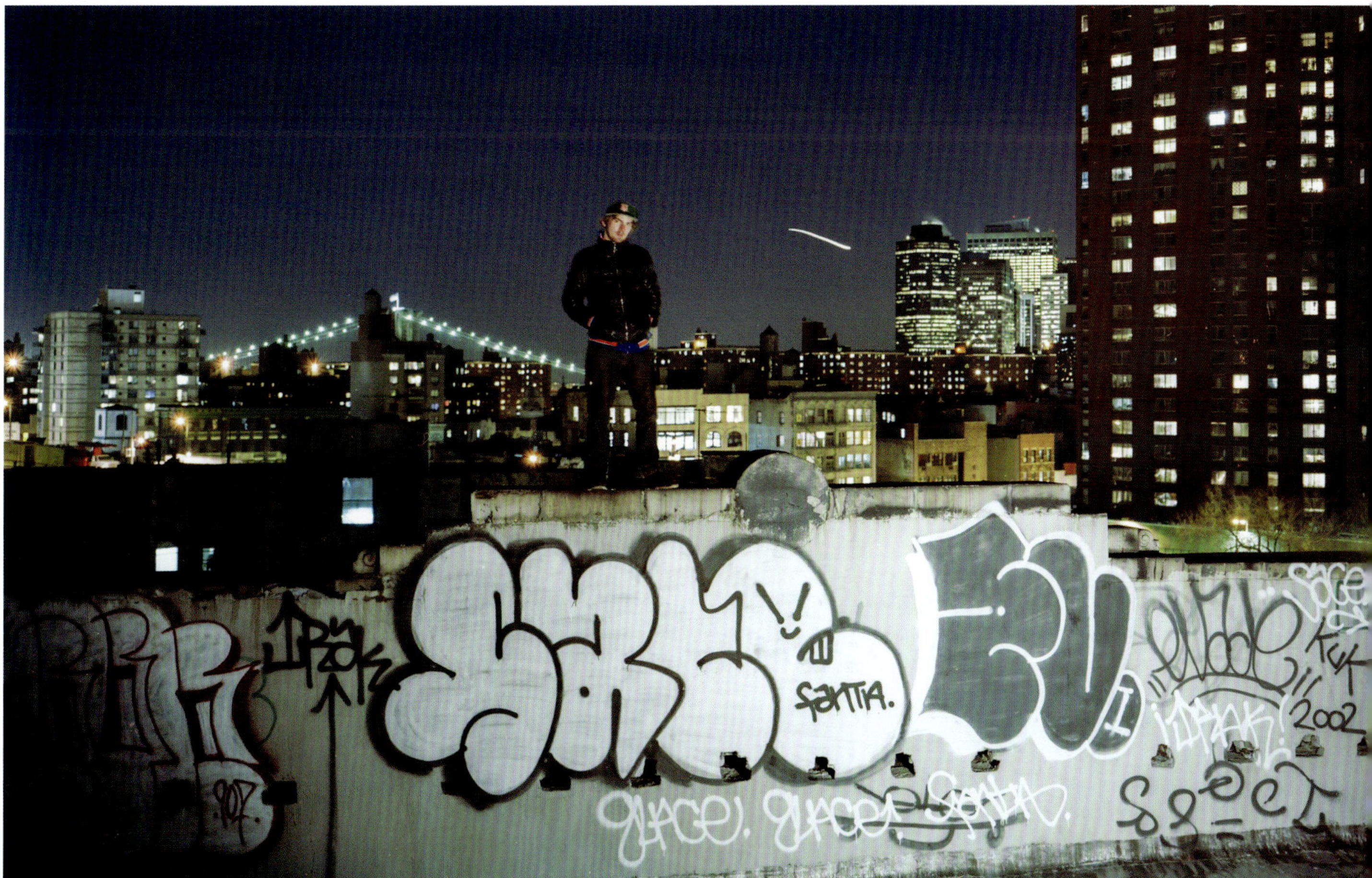

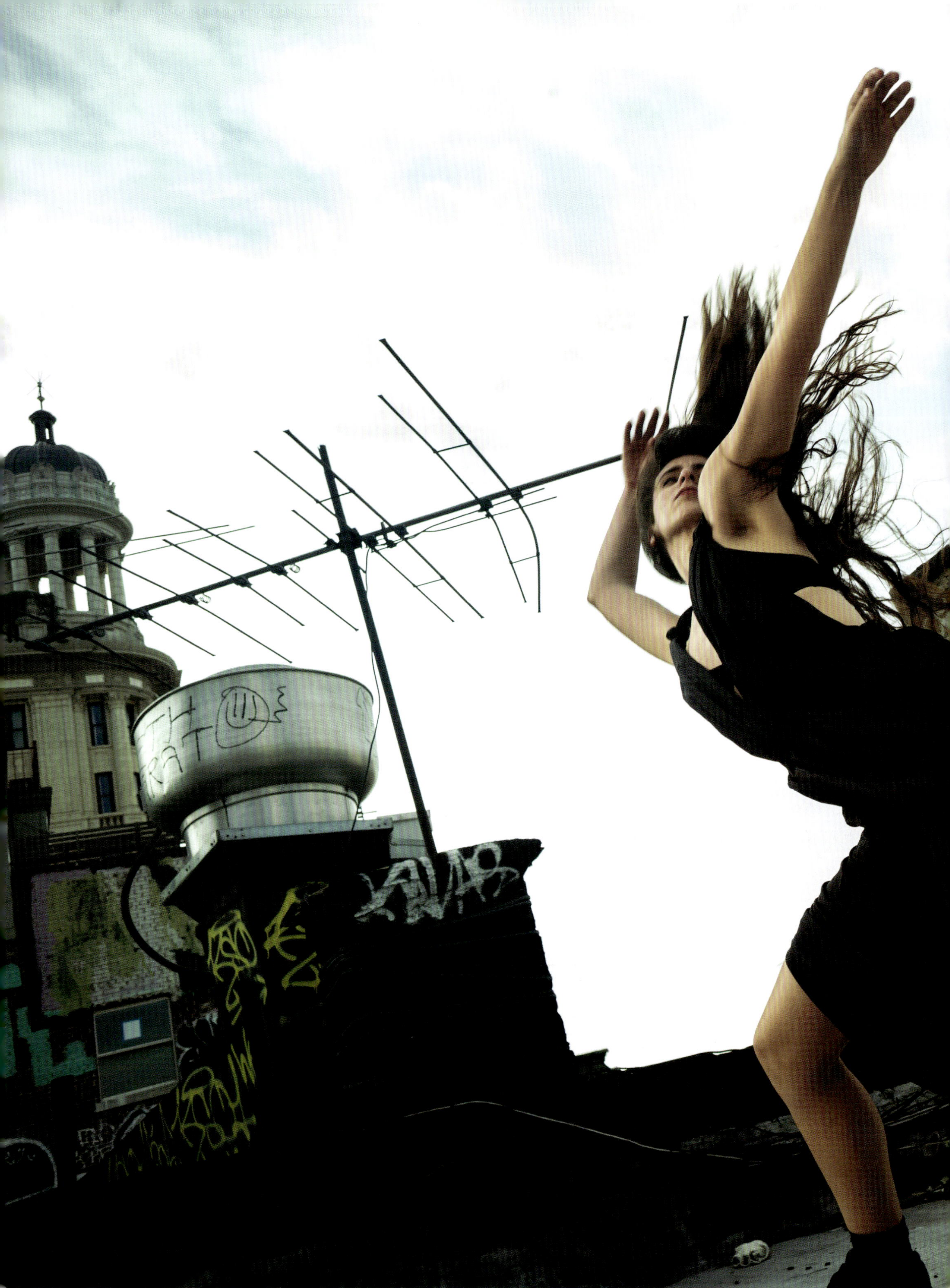

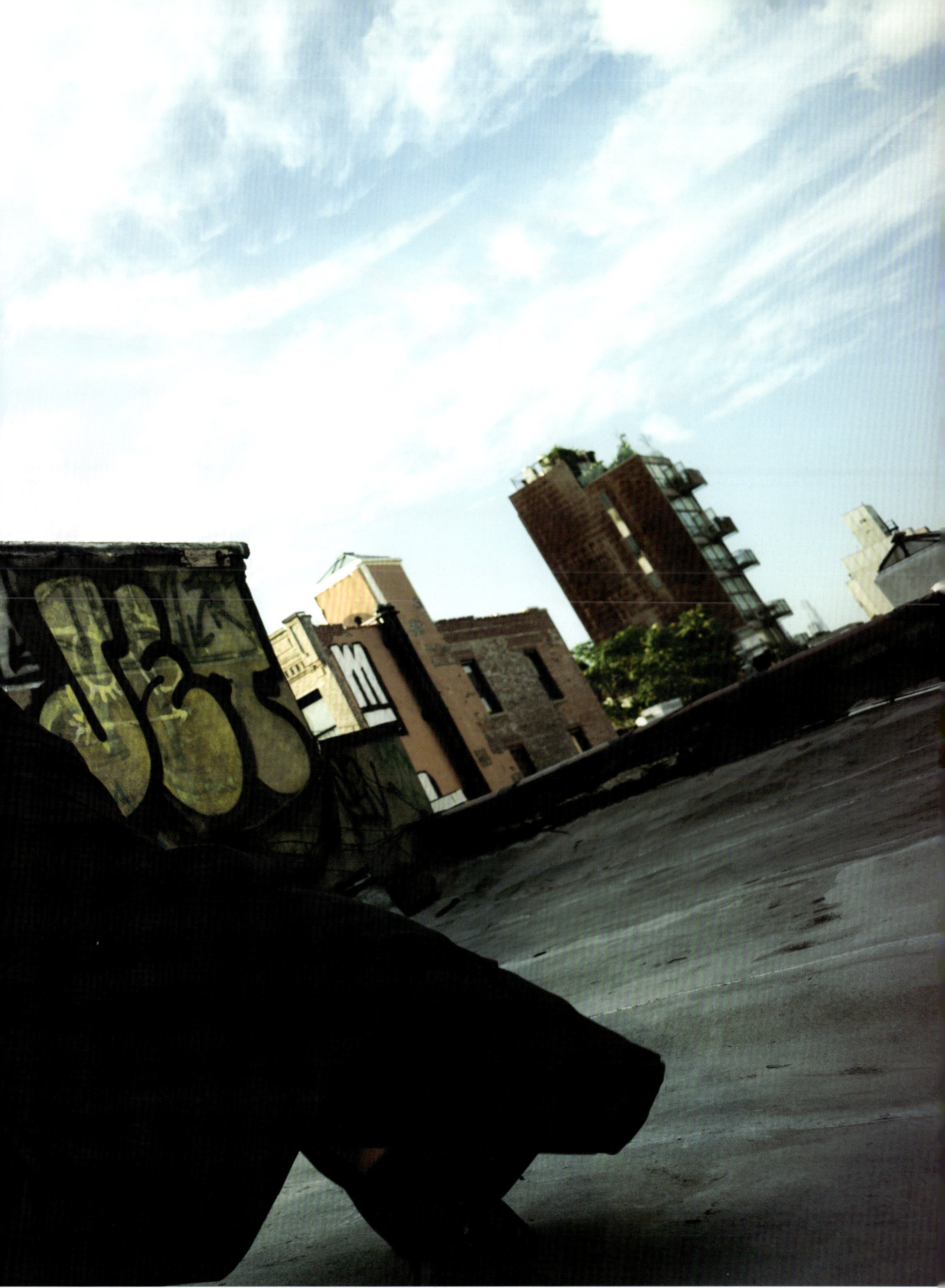

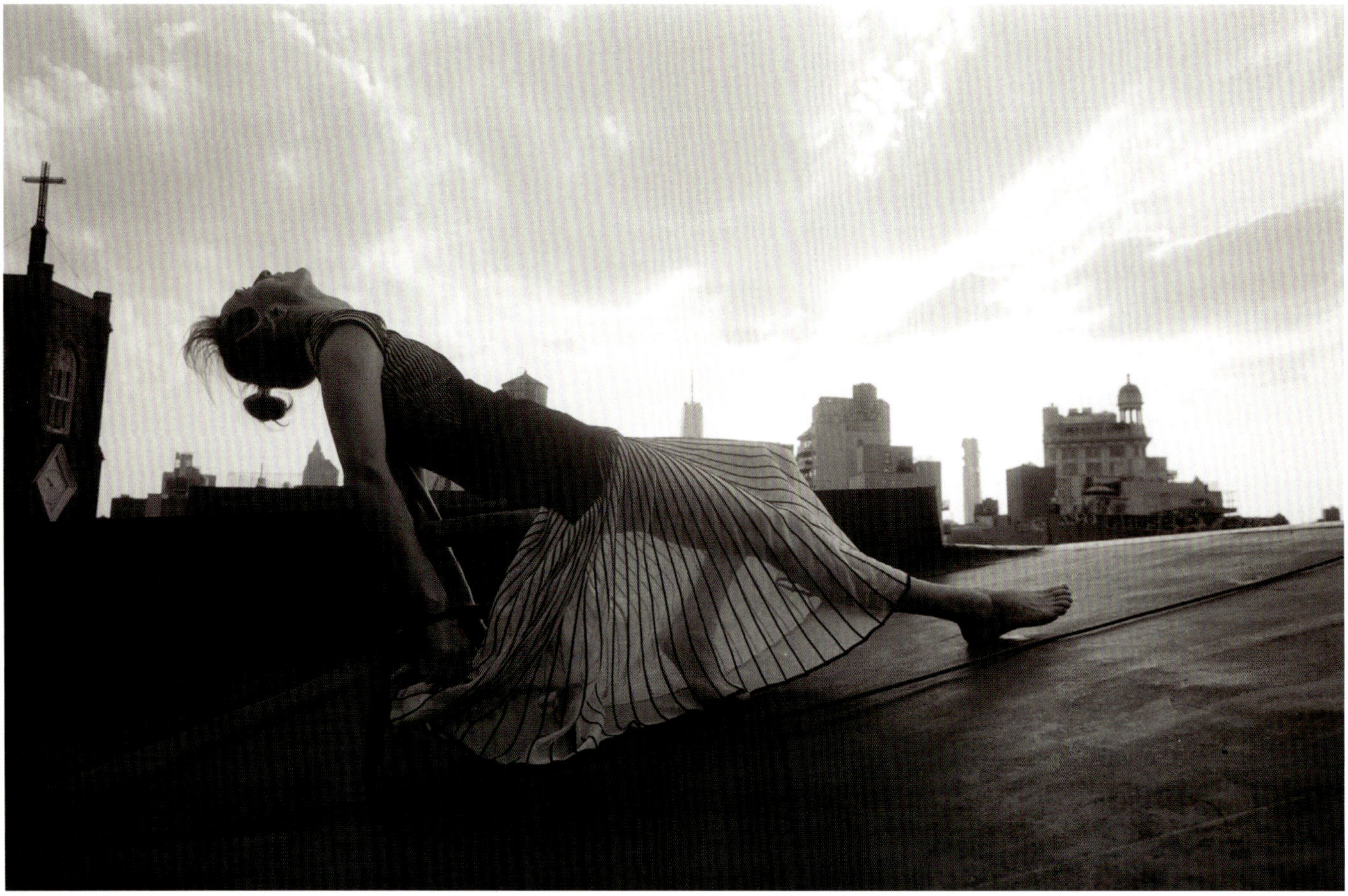

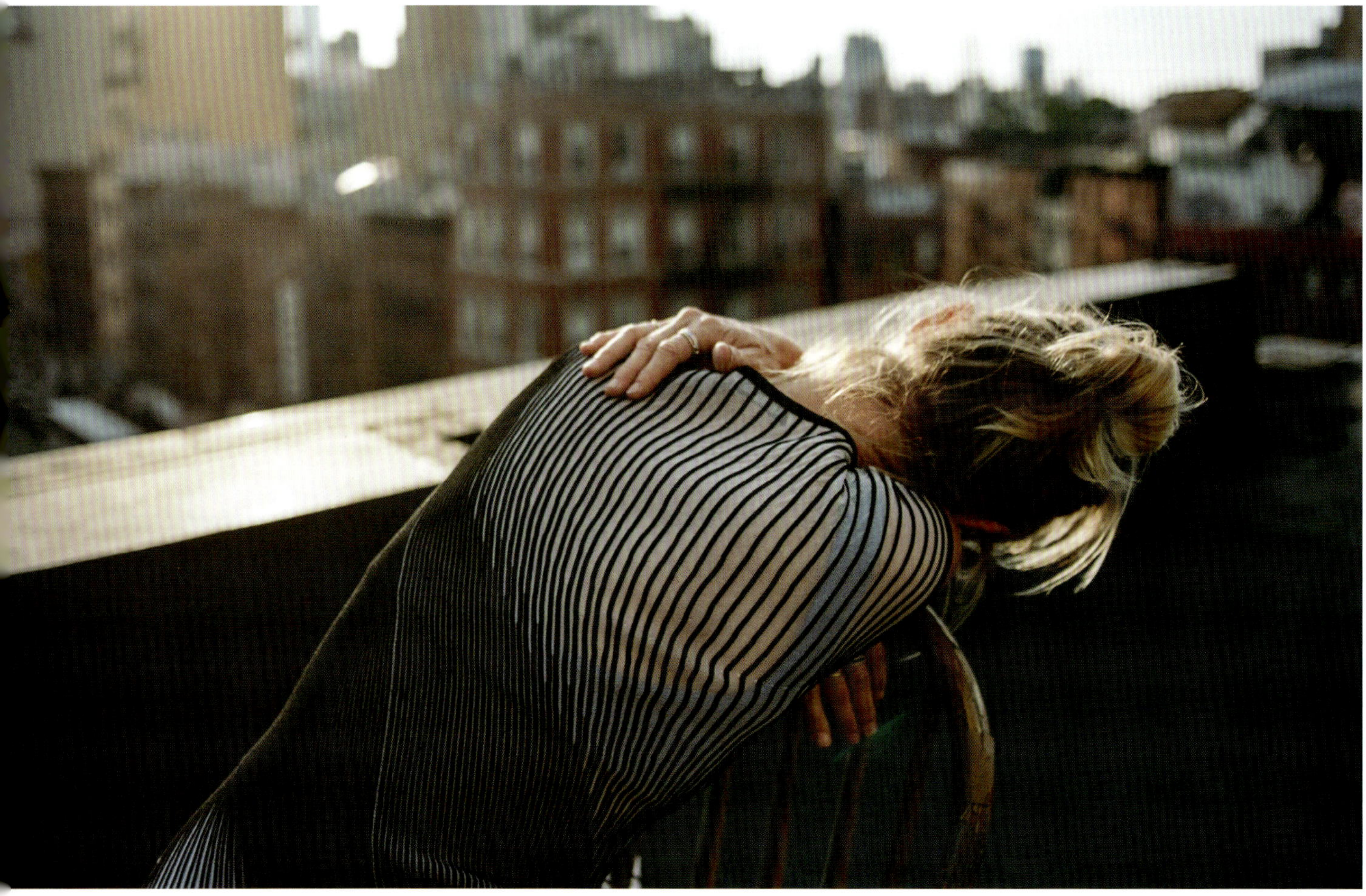

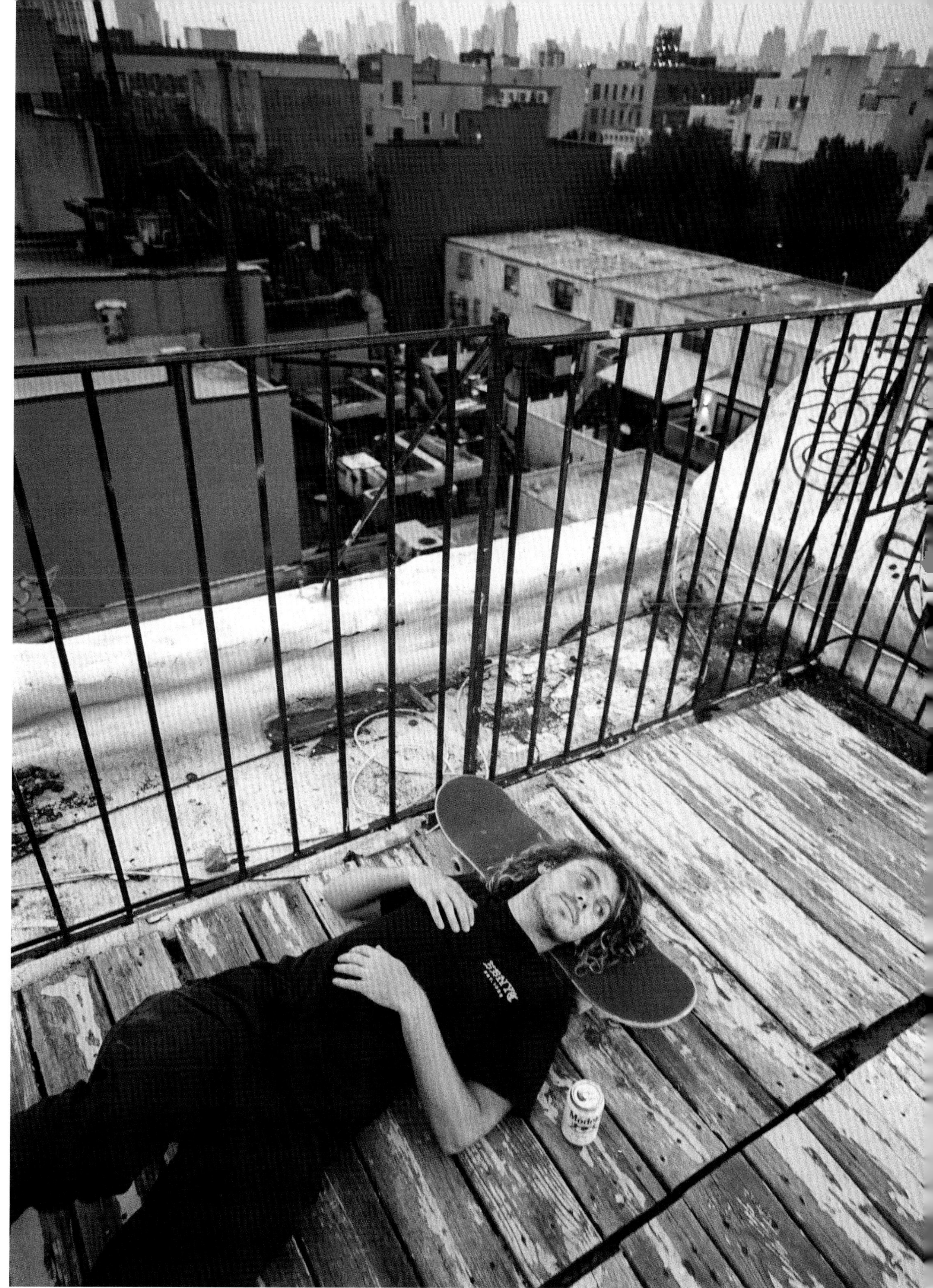

SIGN

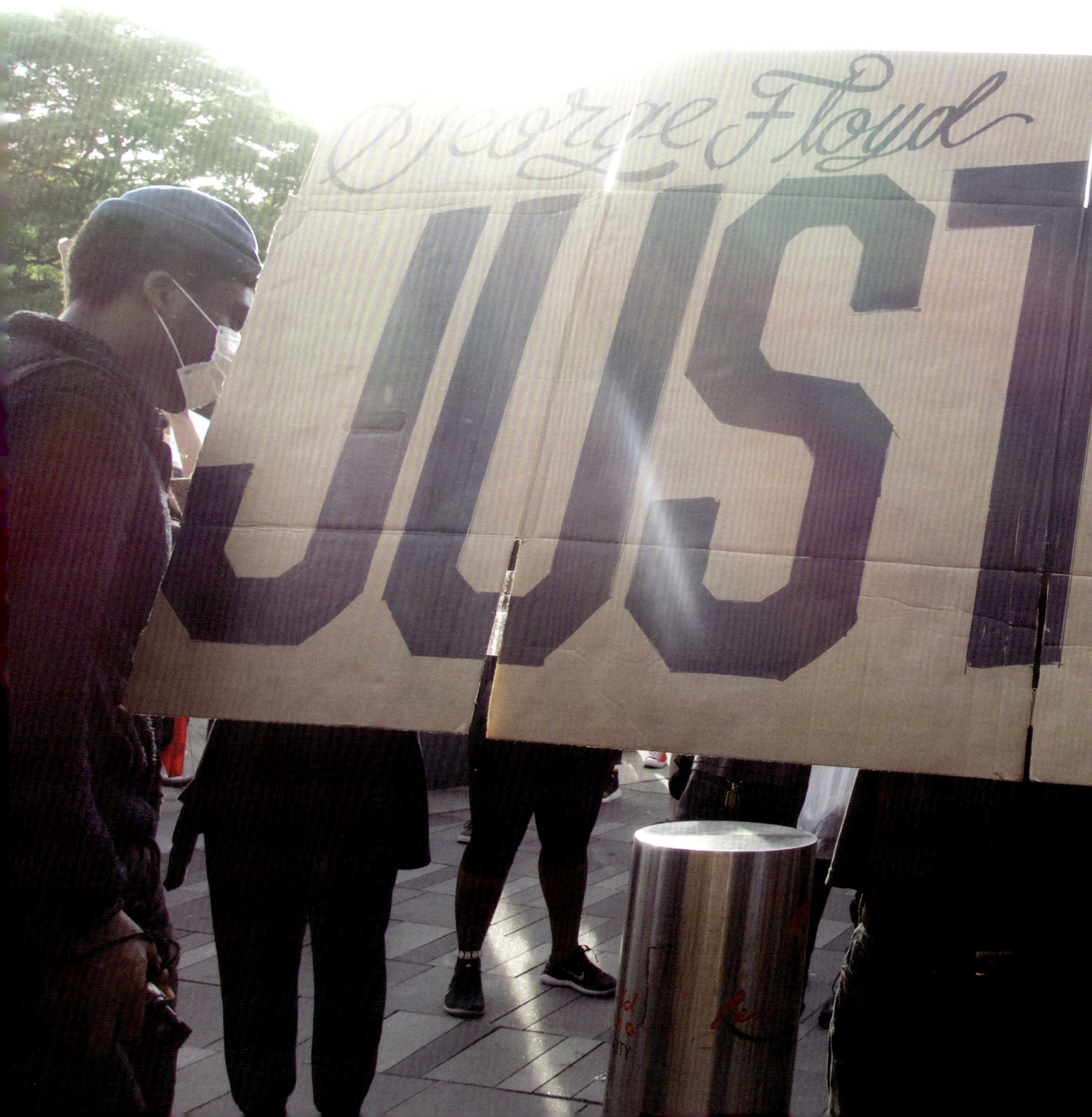

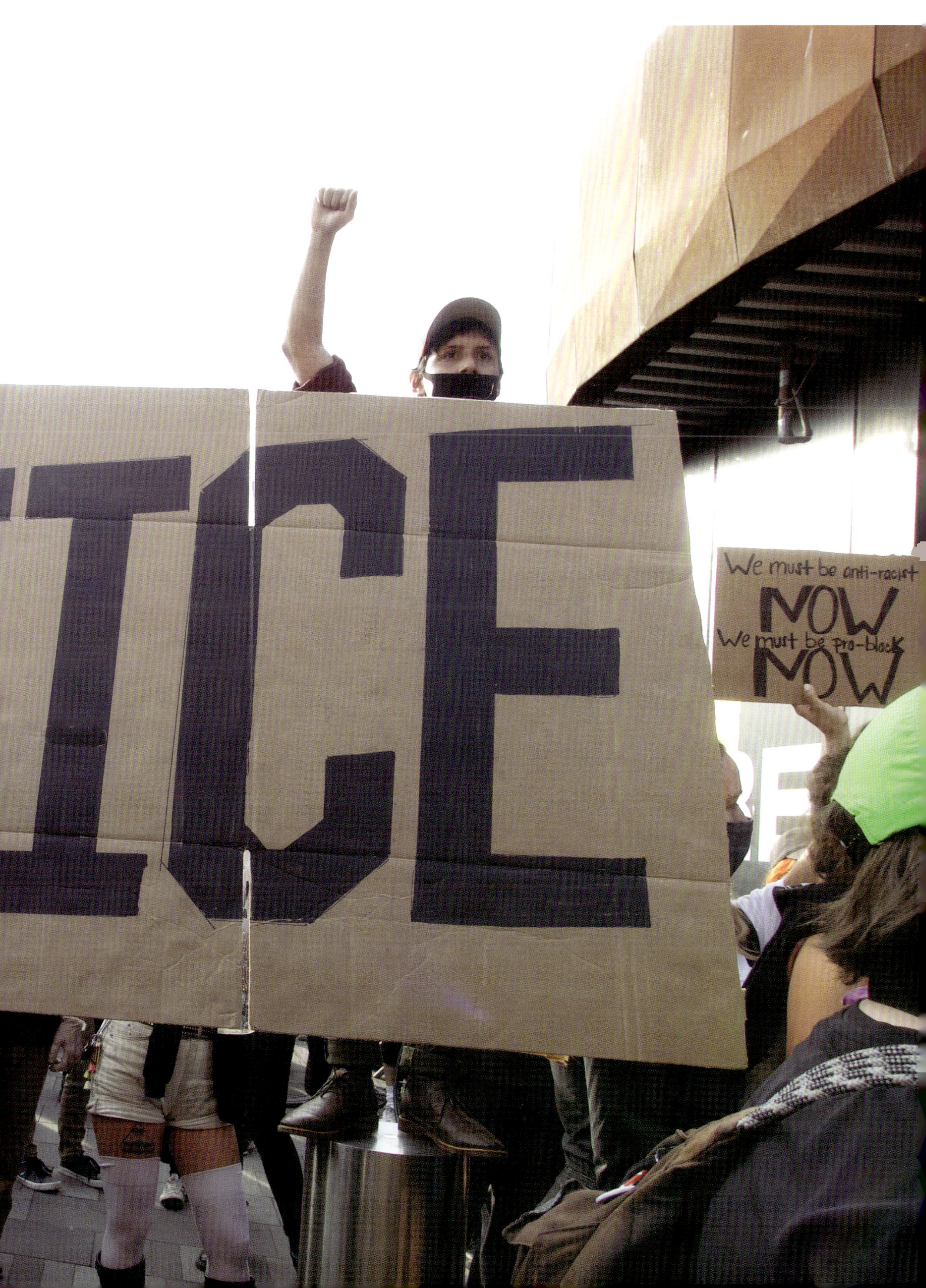
ICE
We must be anti-racist
NOW
We must be pro-black
NOW

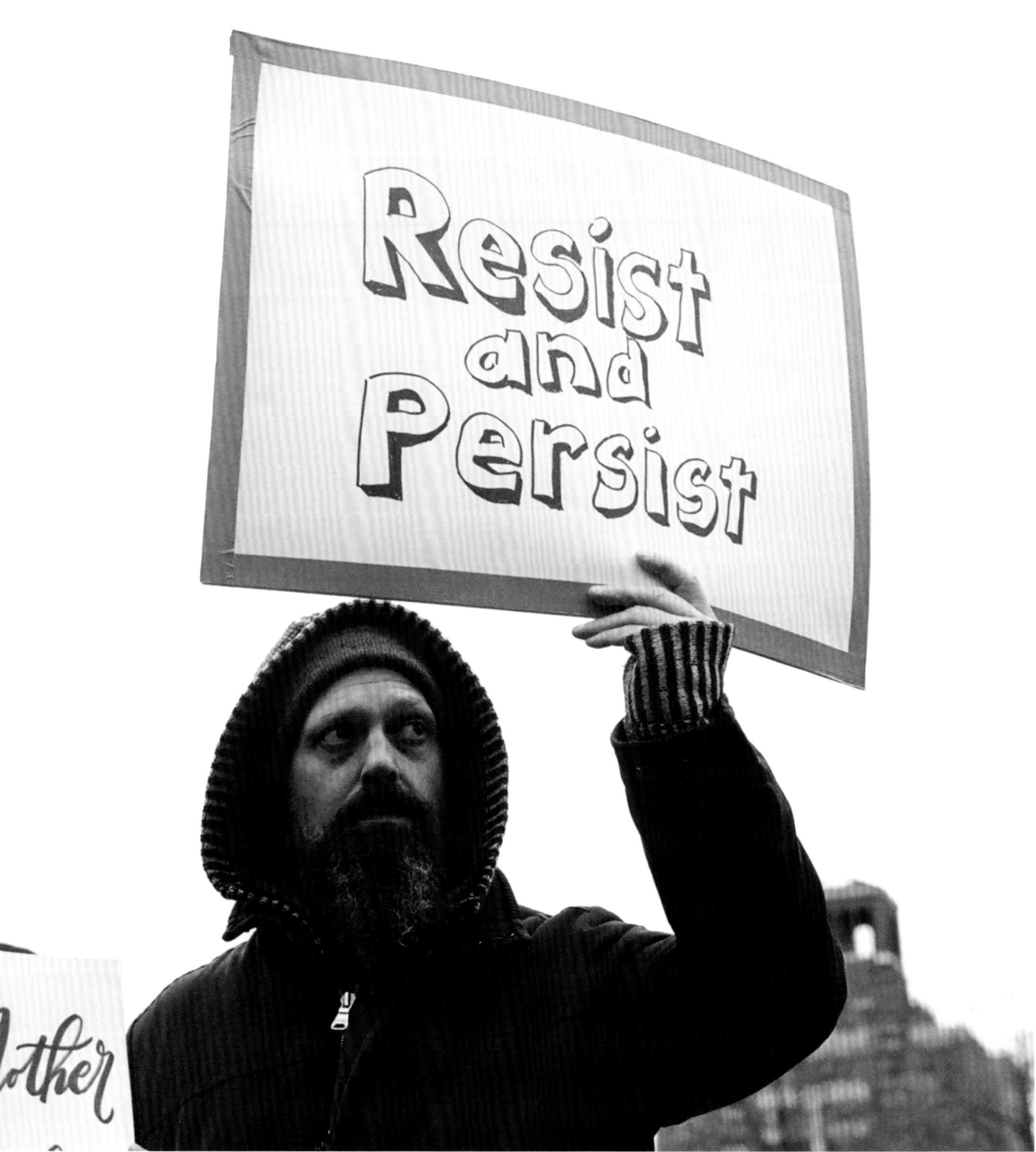
Resist
and
Persist

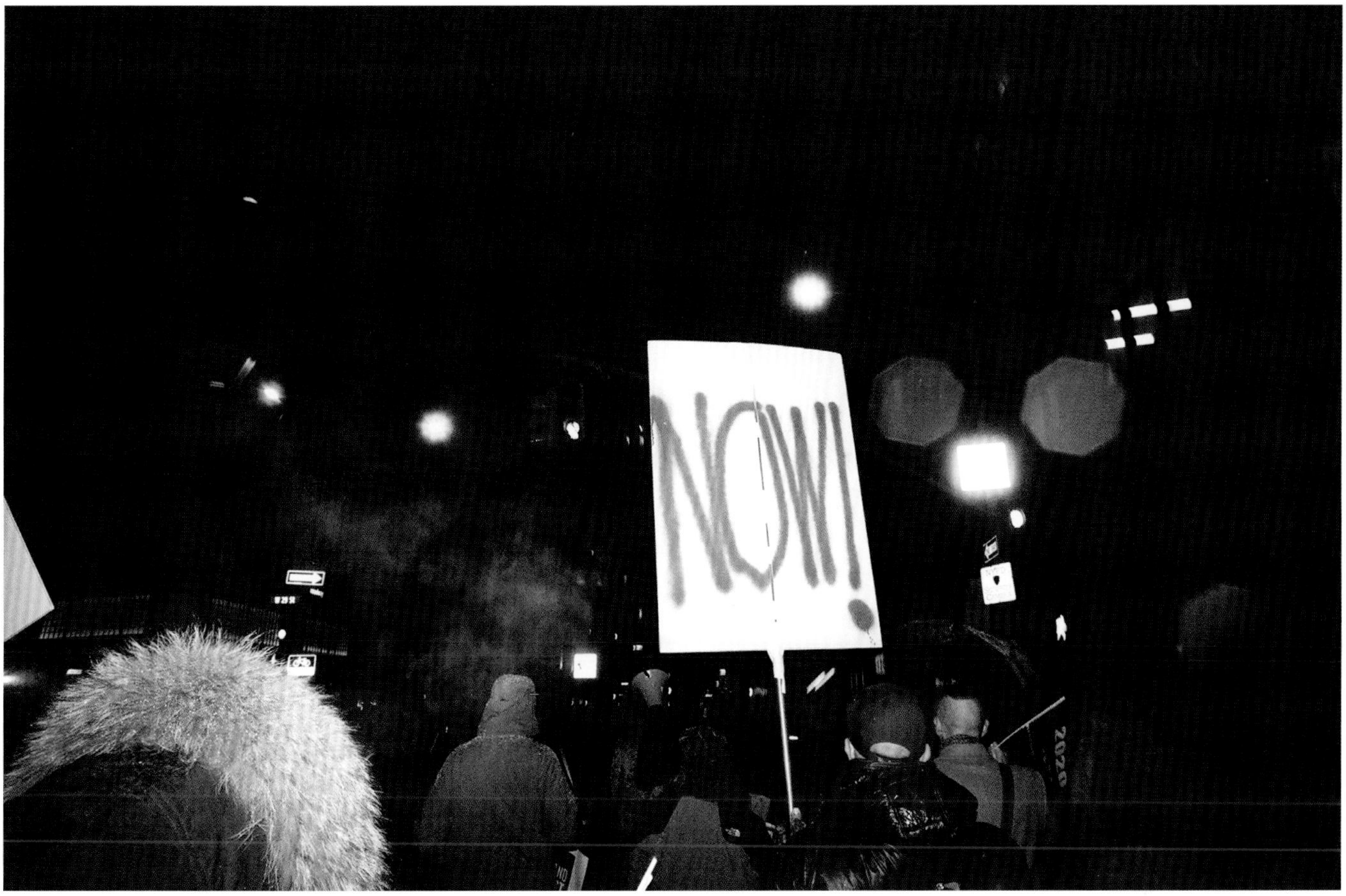

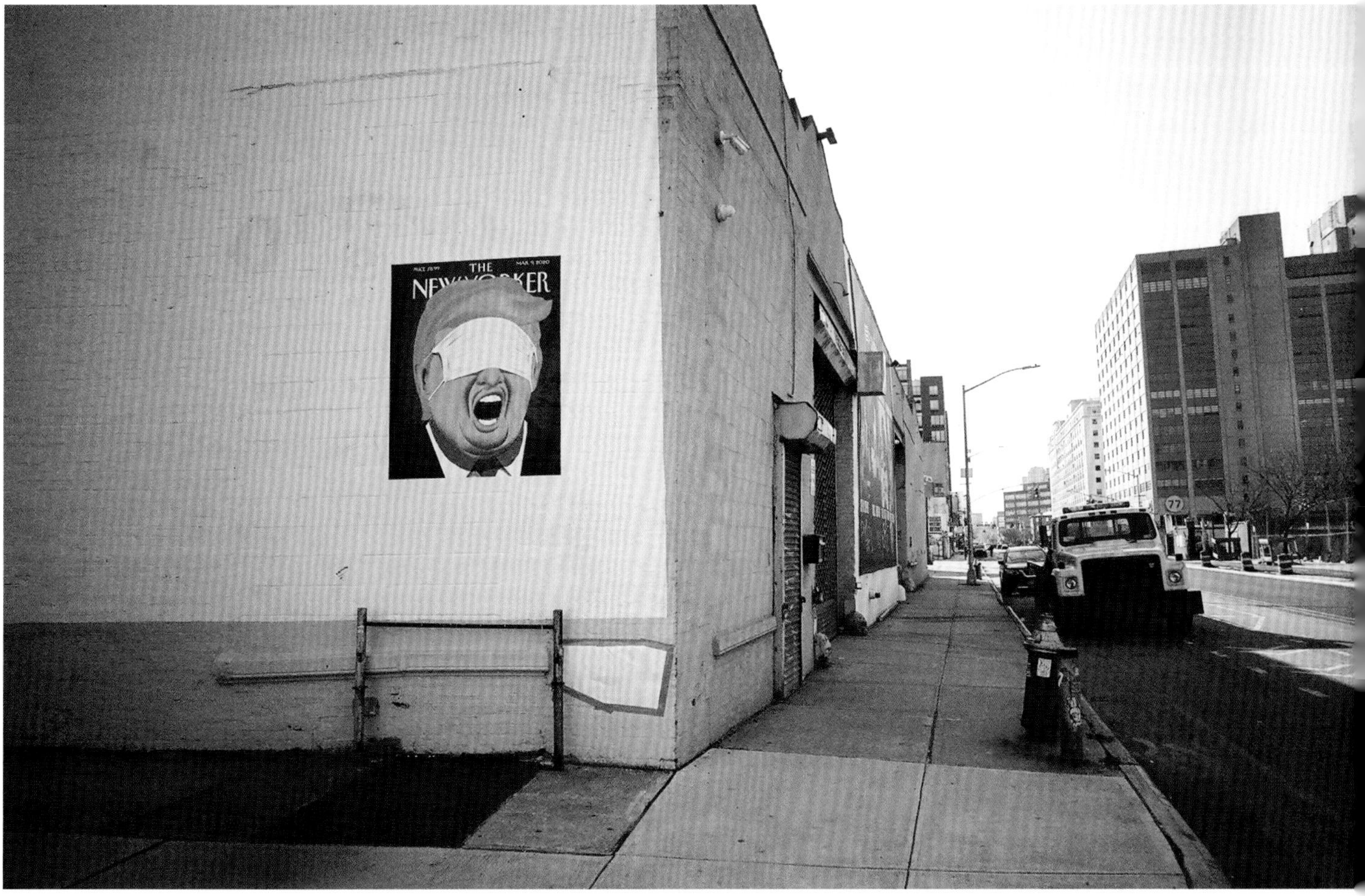

SLEEPING MEN

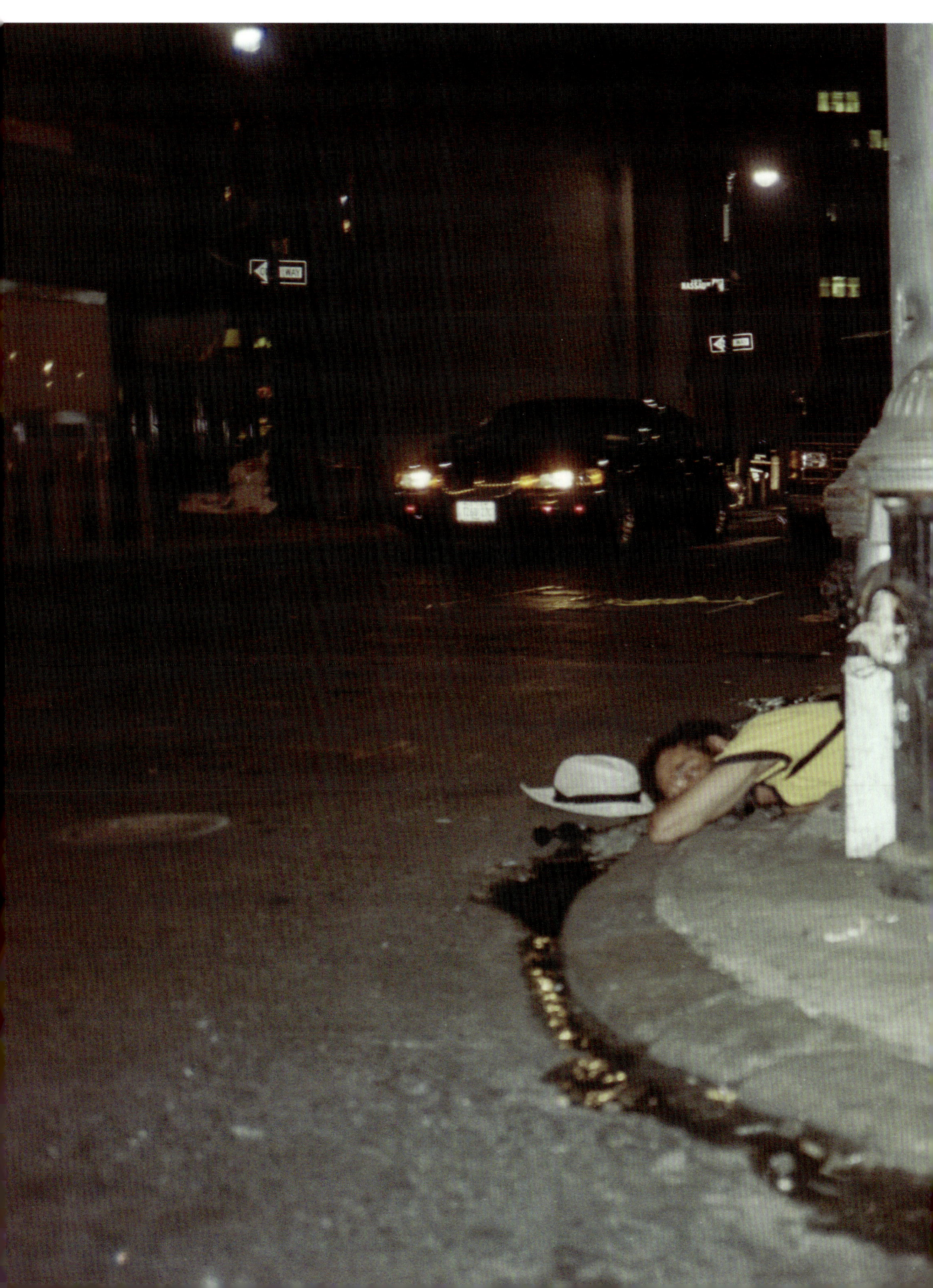

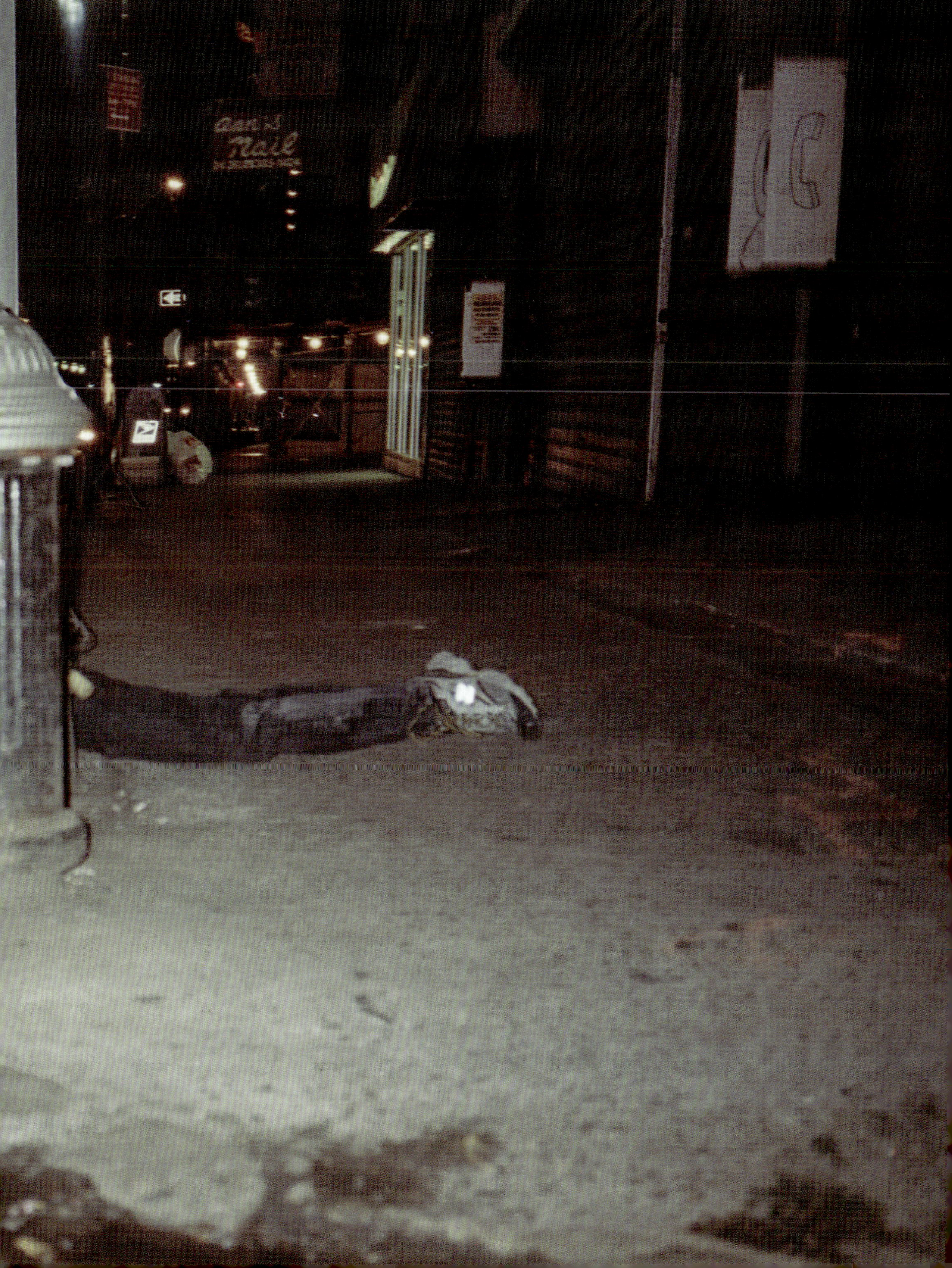
Nail

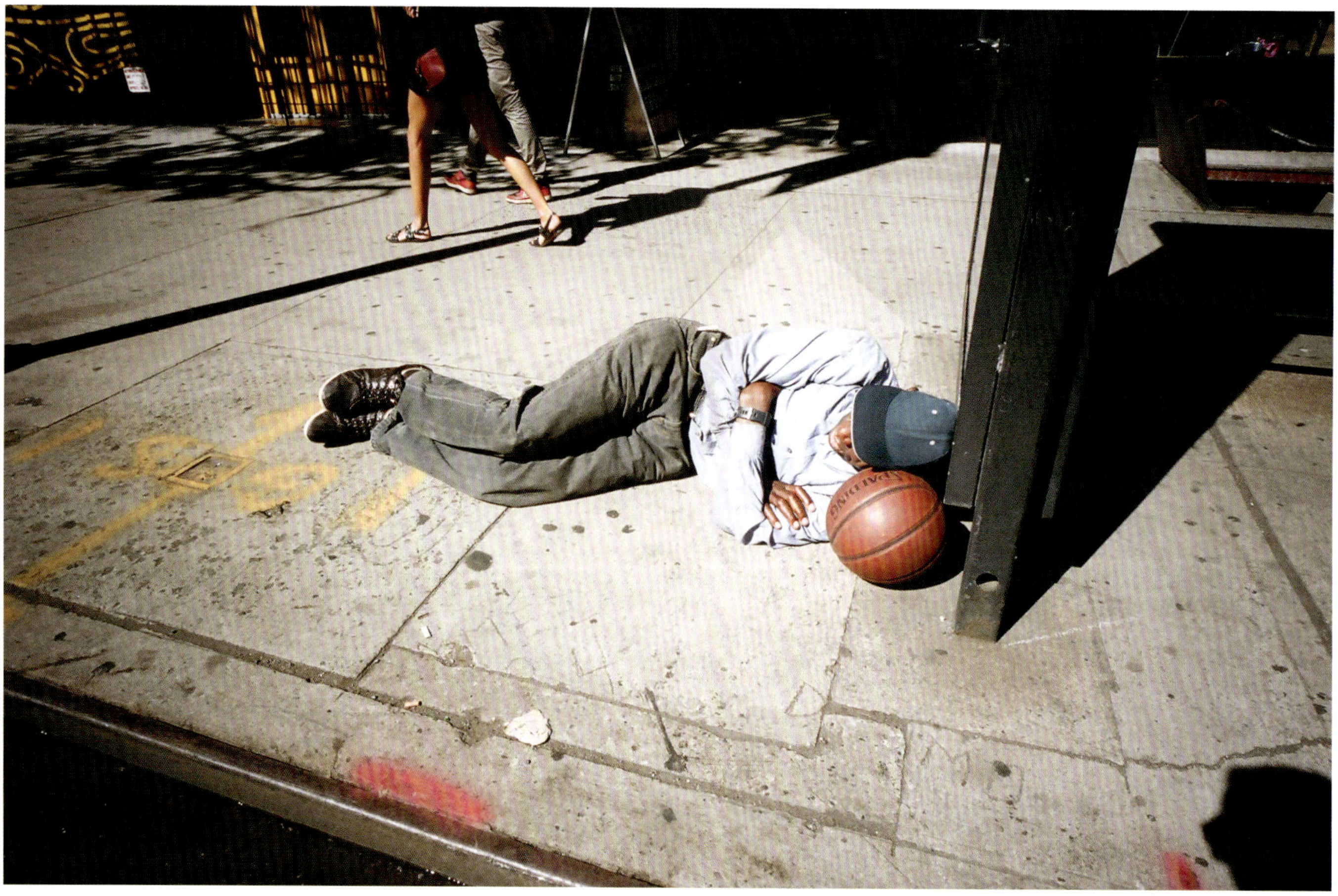

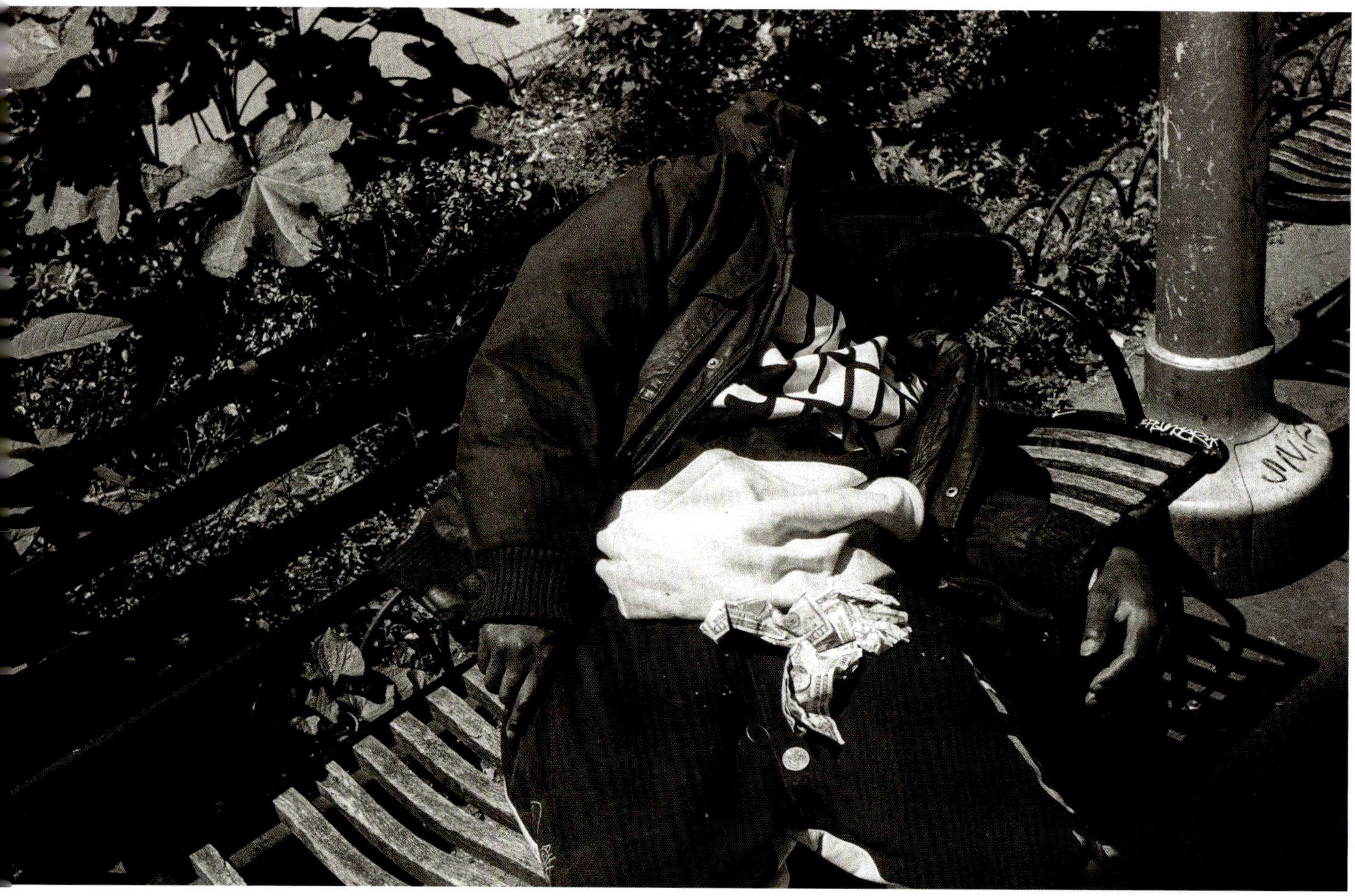

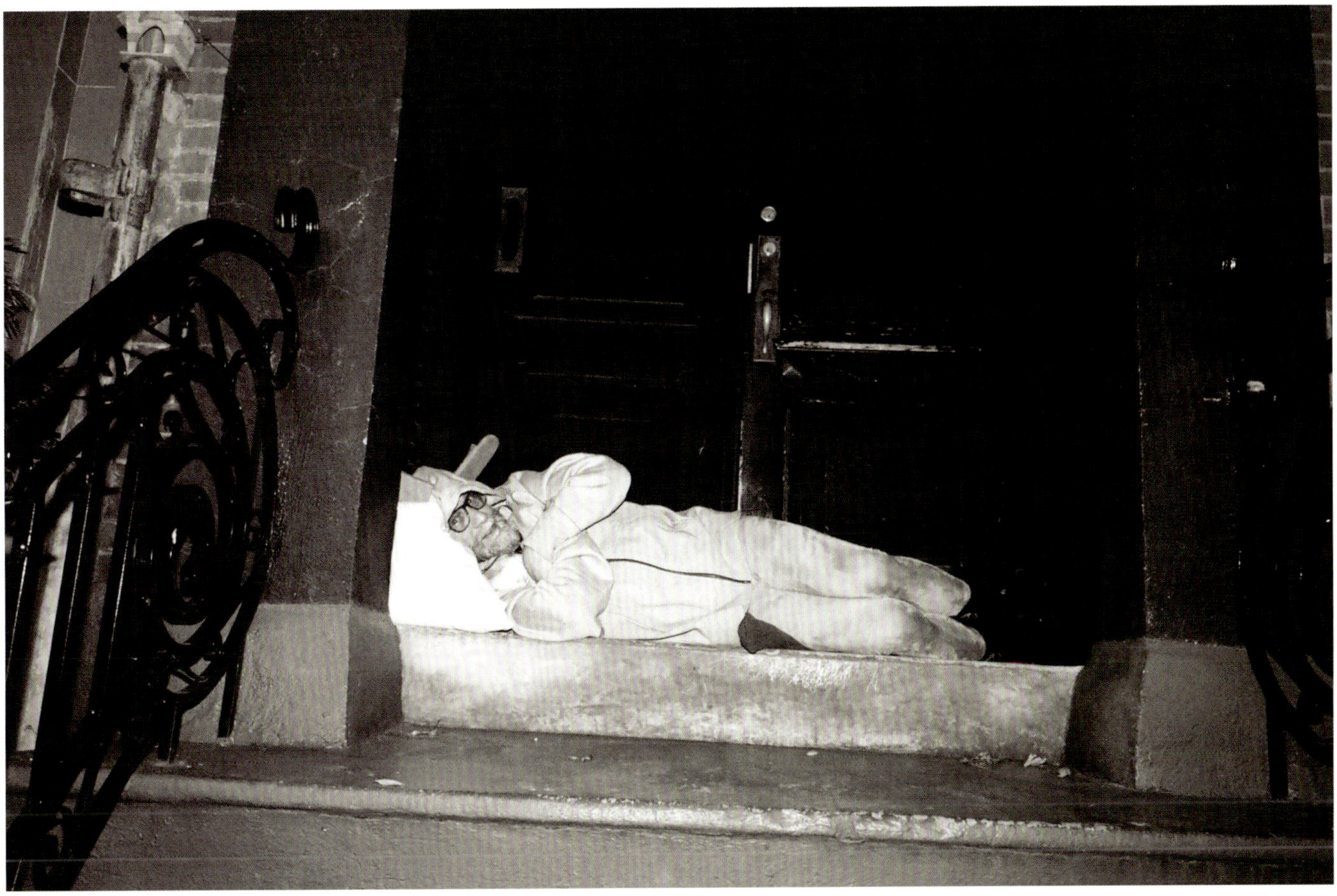

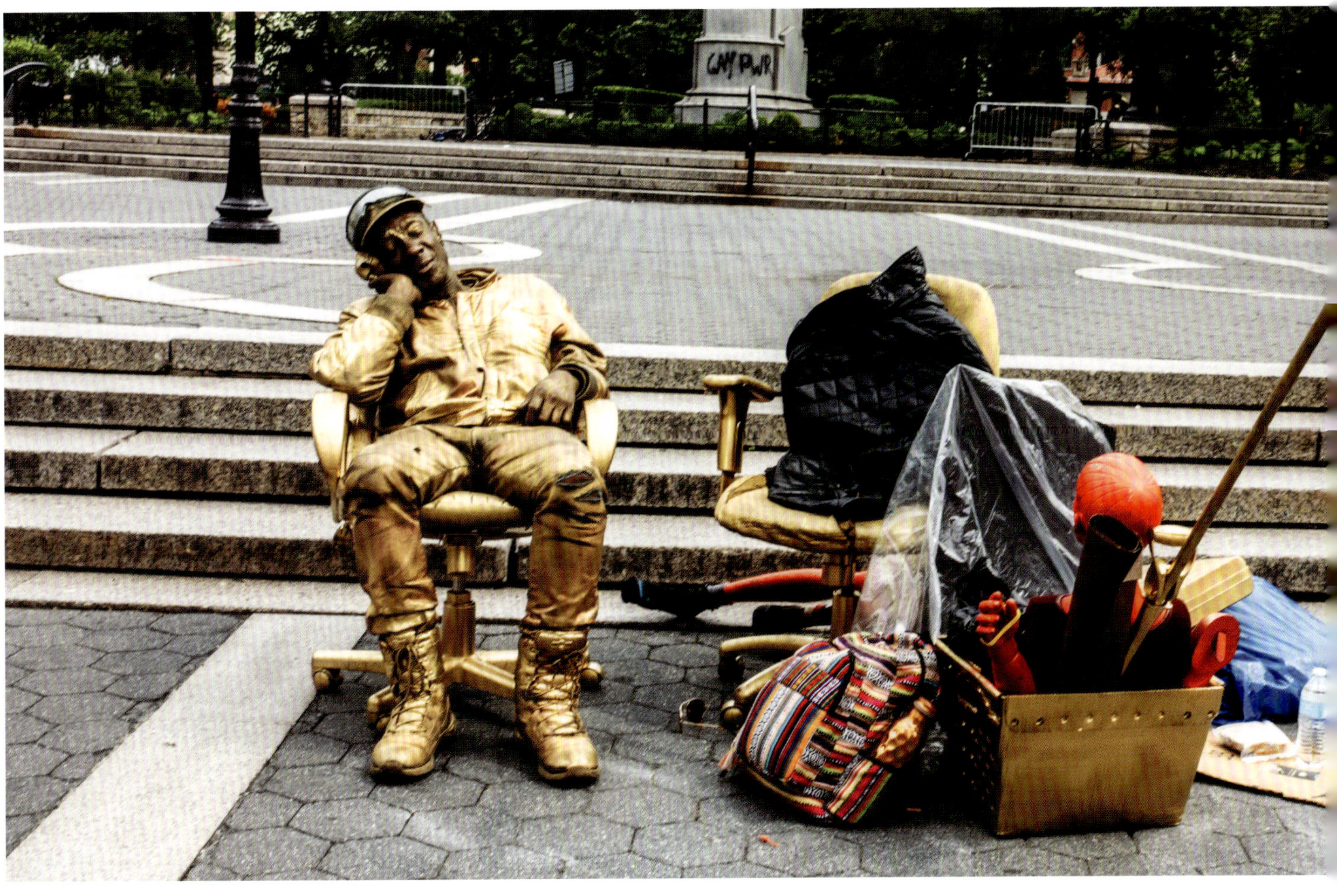

SMILE

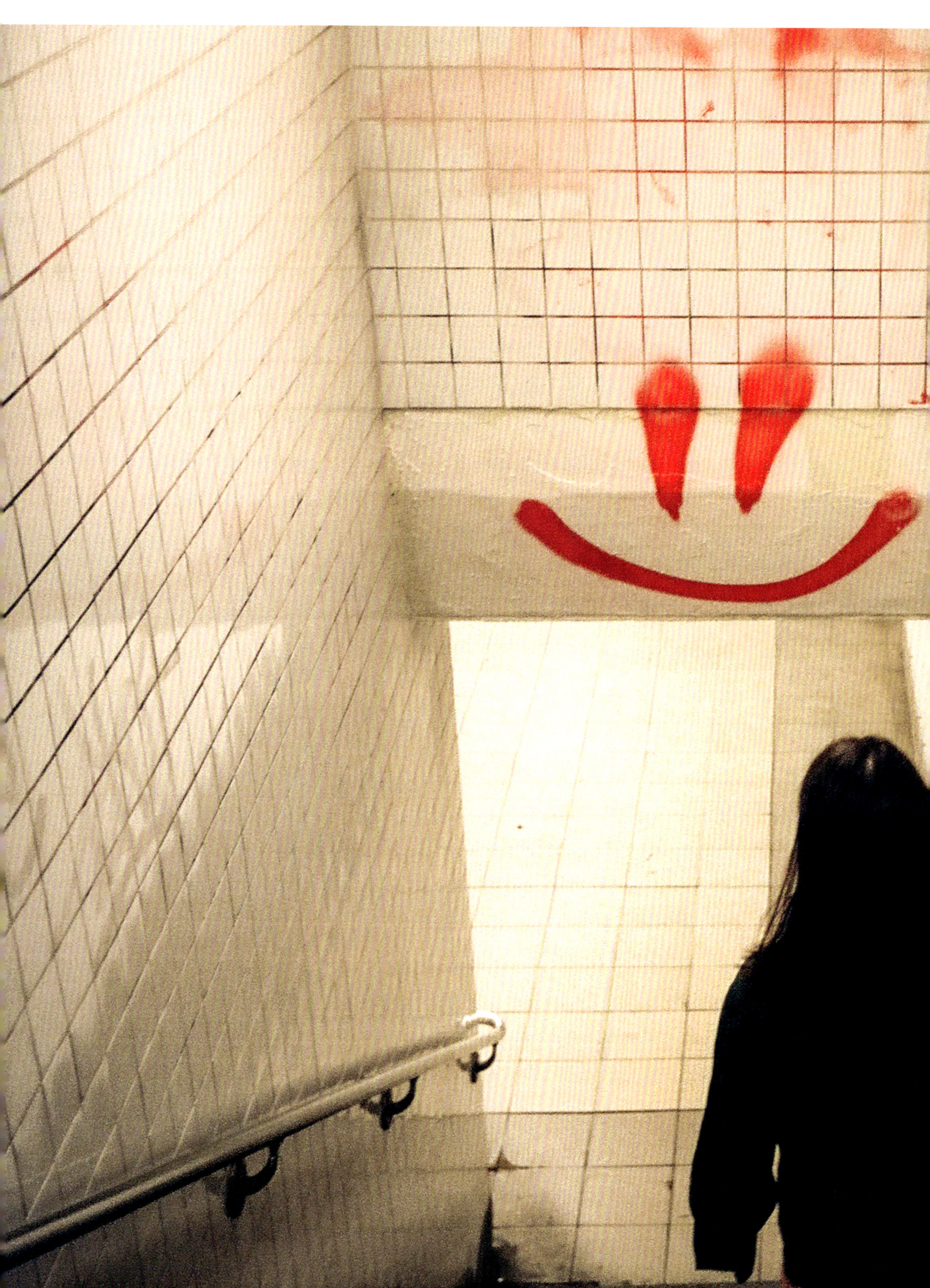

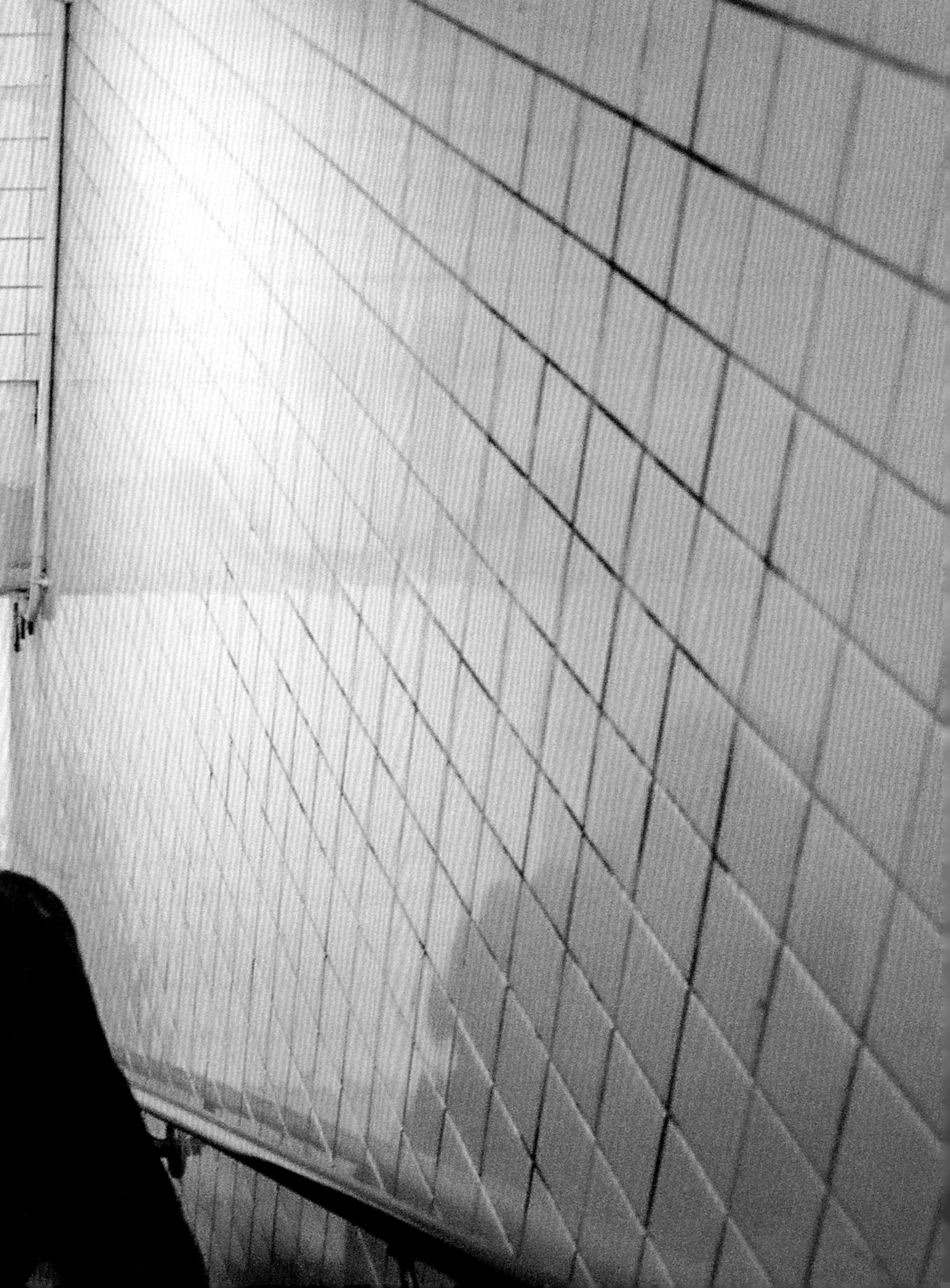

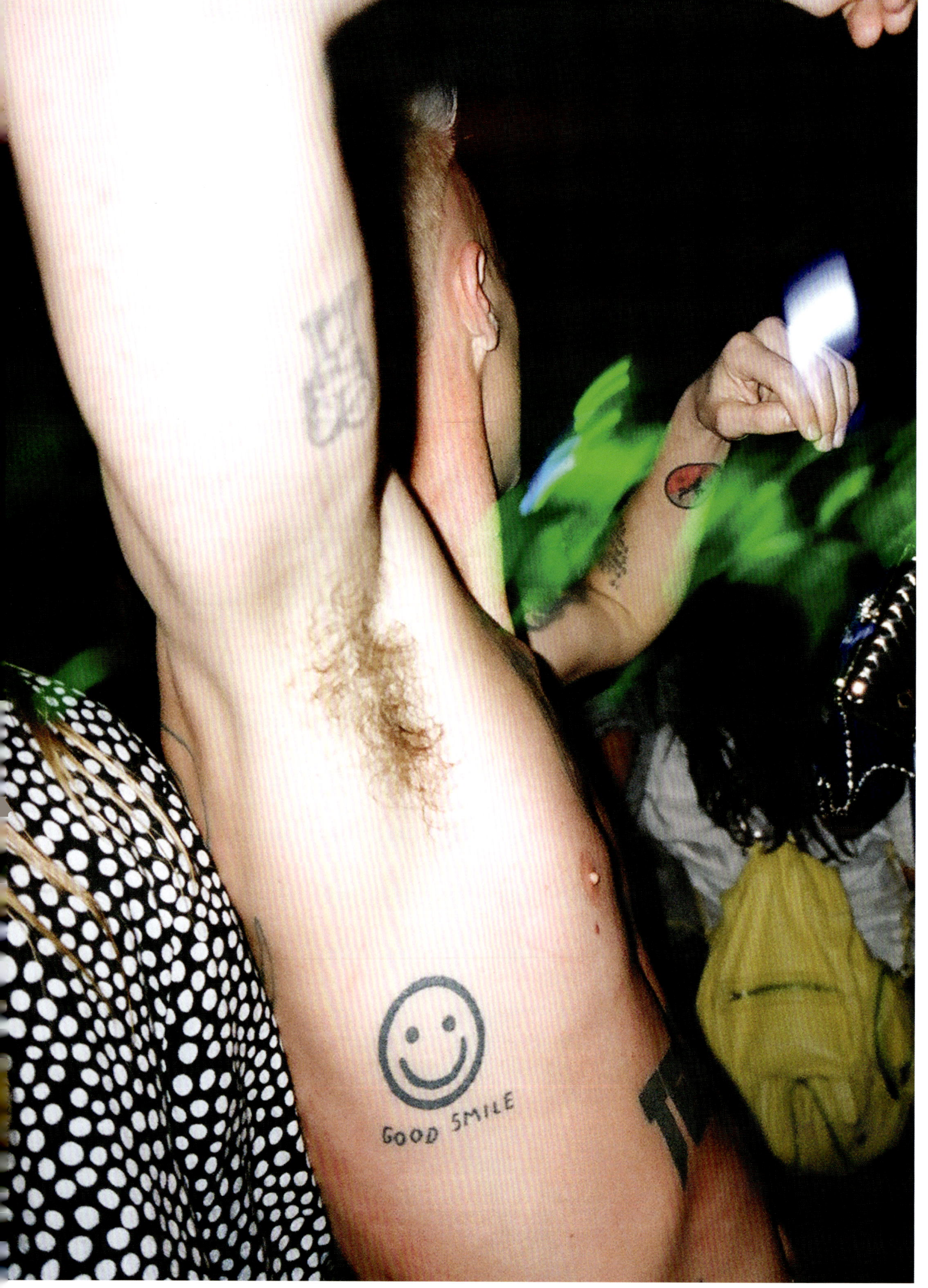
GOOD SMILE

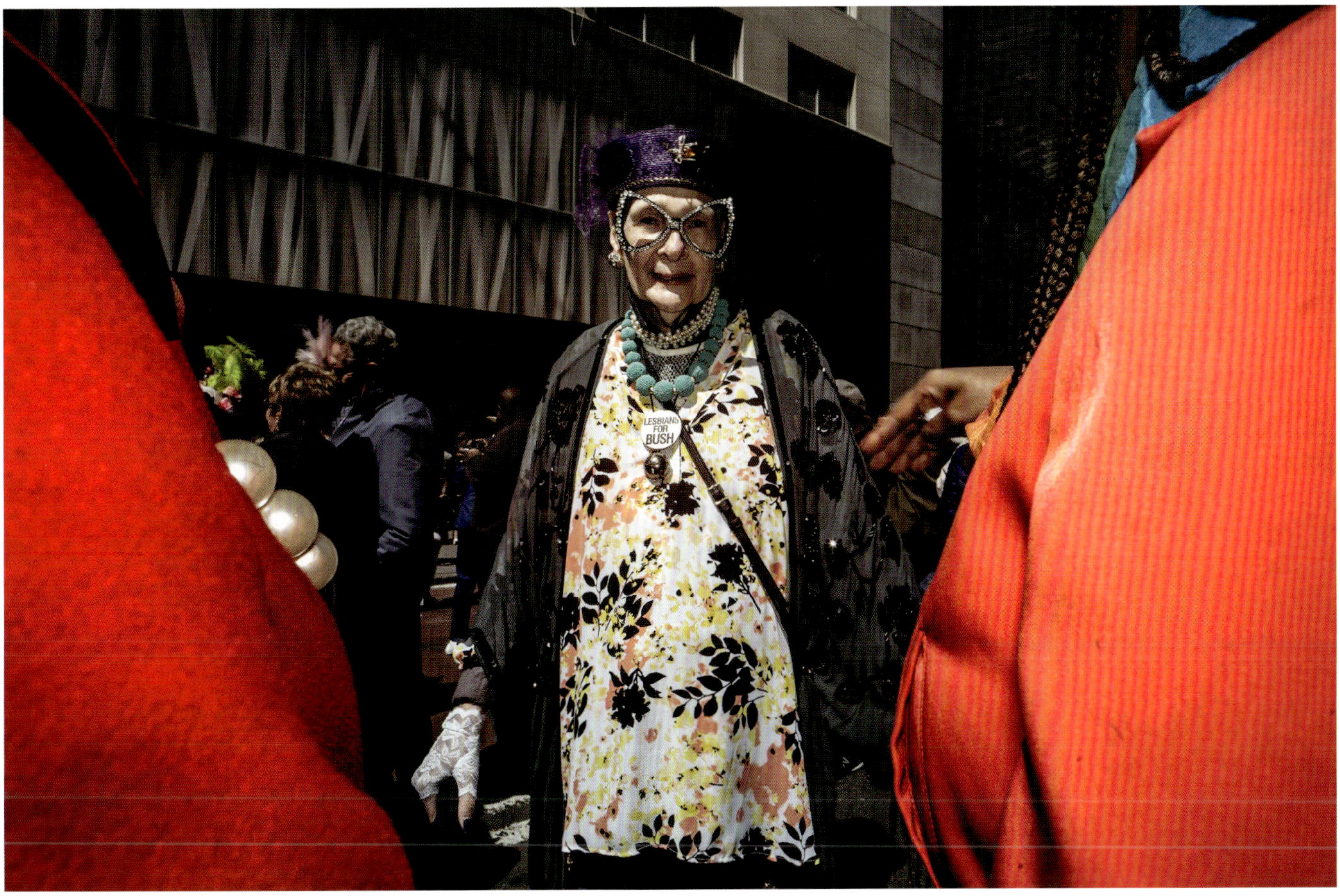
LESBIANS FOR BUSH

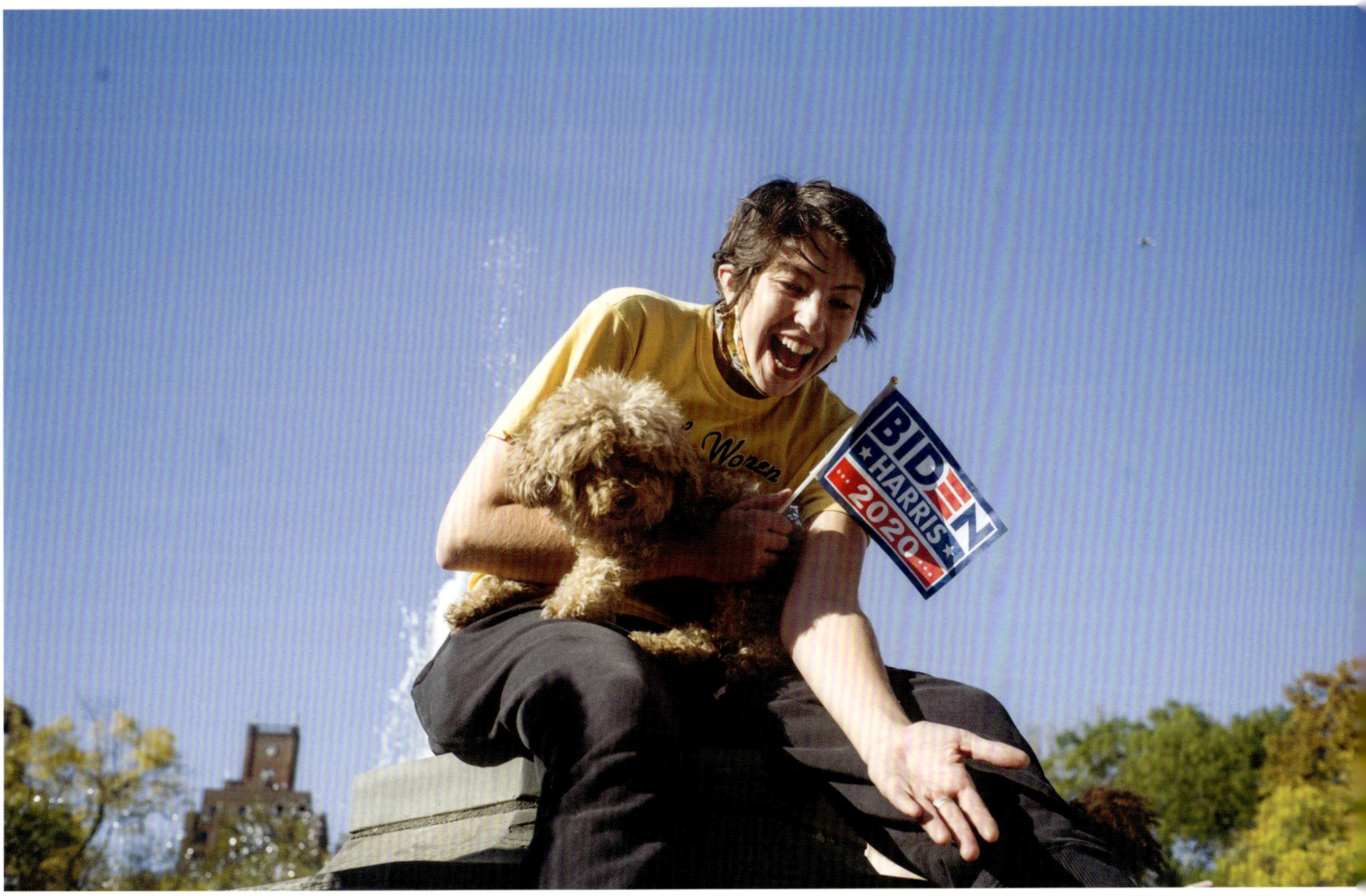
BIDEN
HARRIS
2020

SMOKE

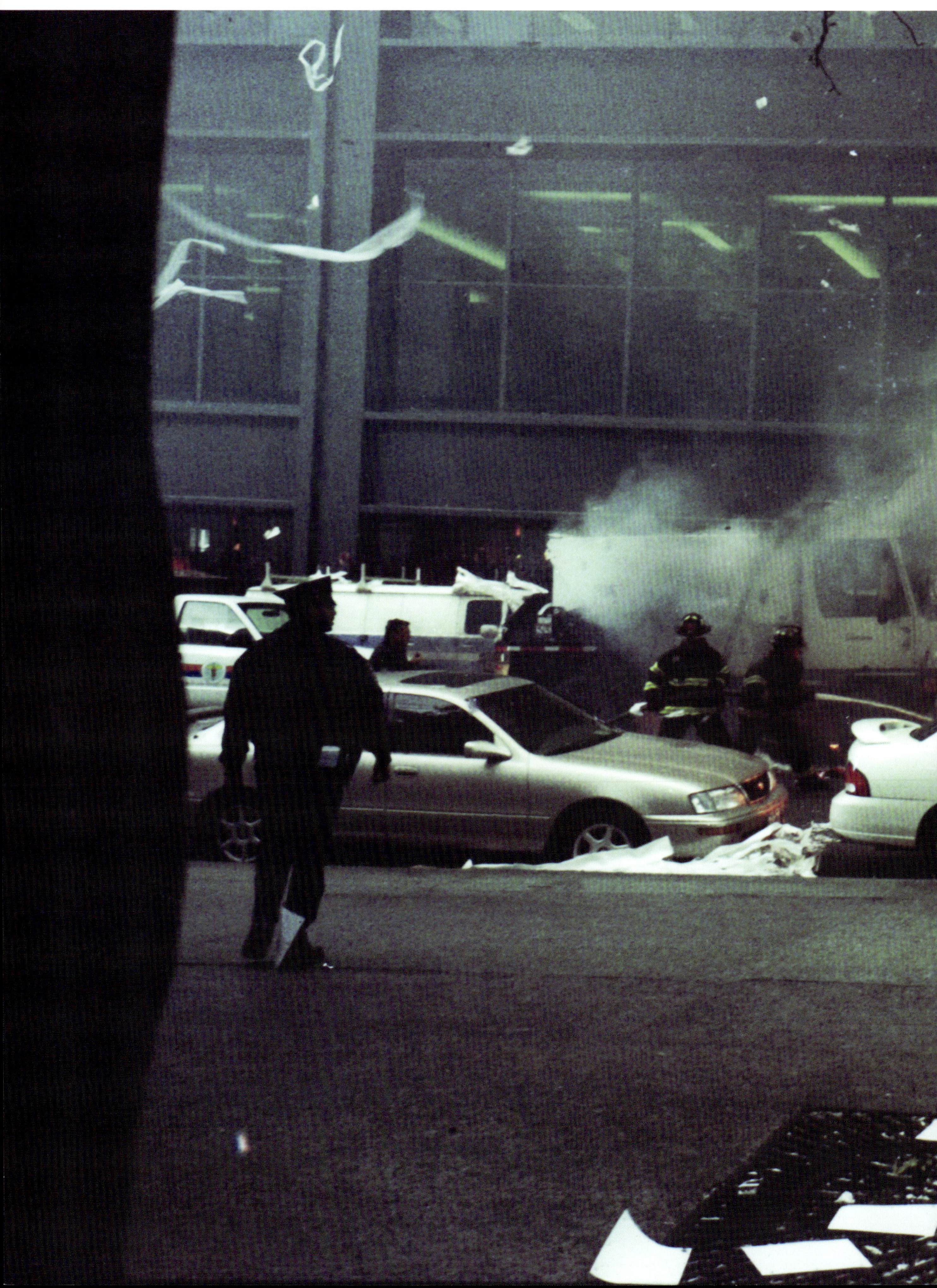

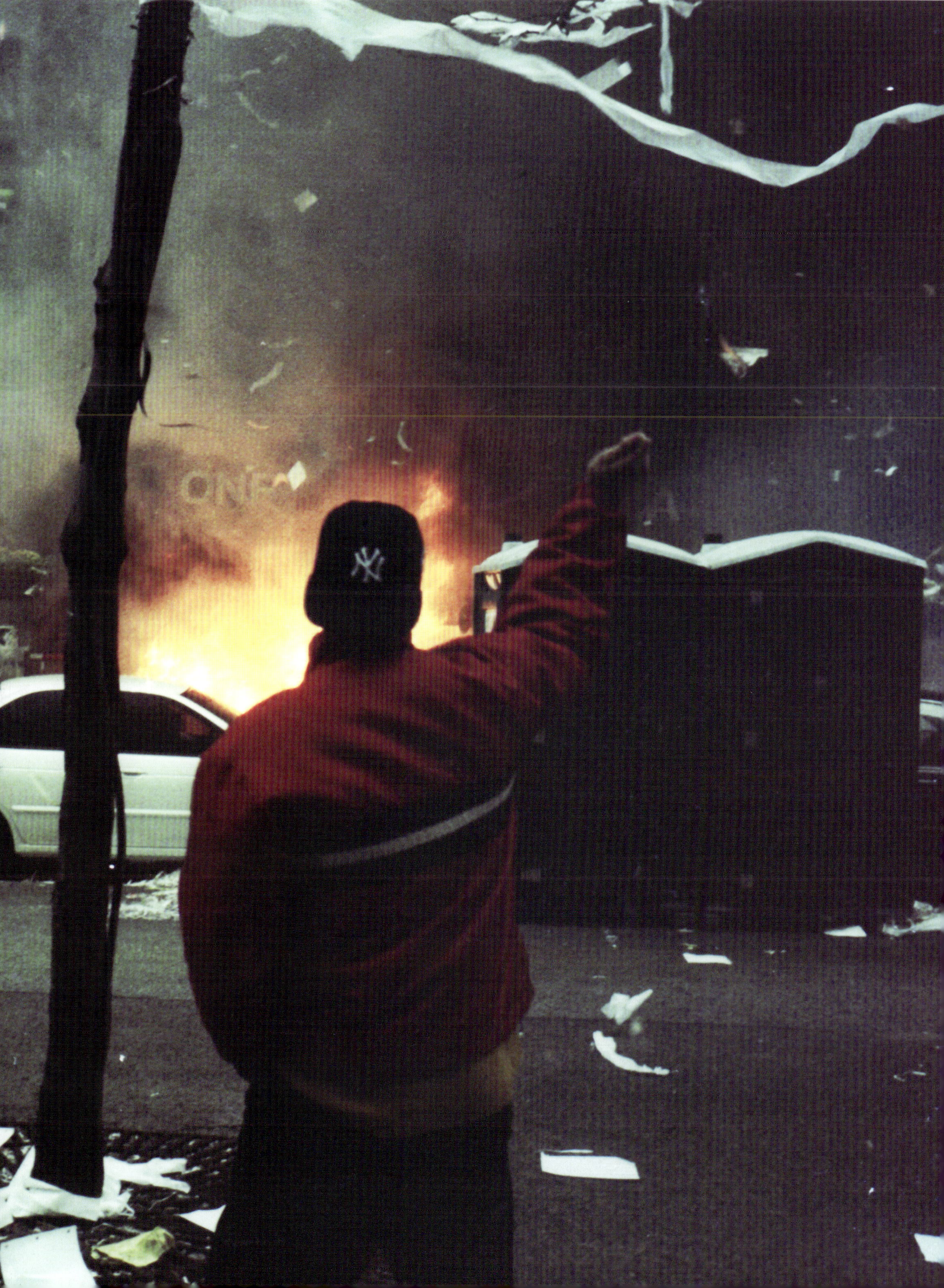

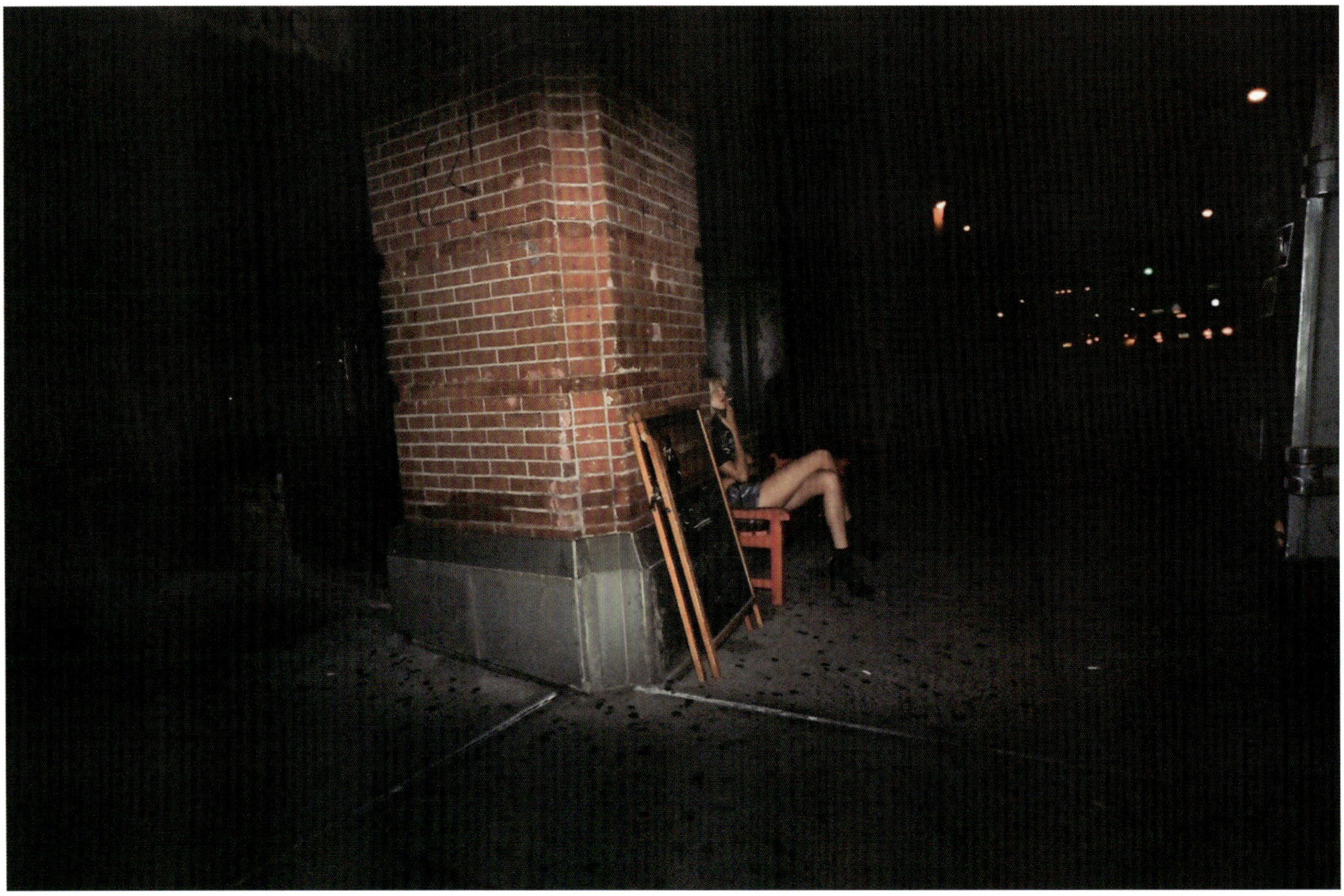

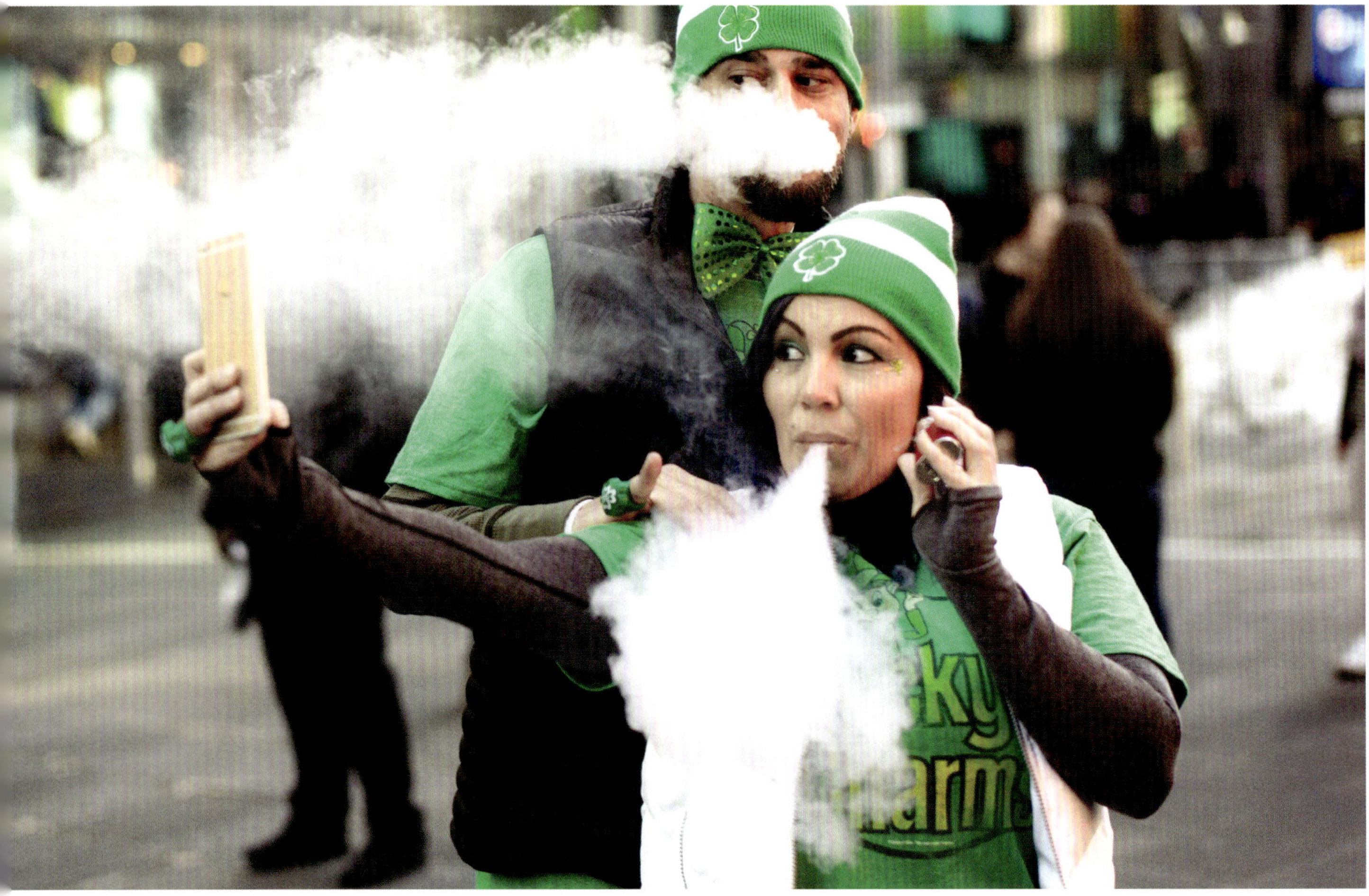

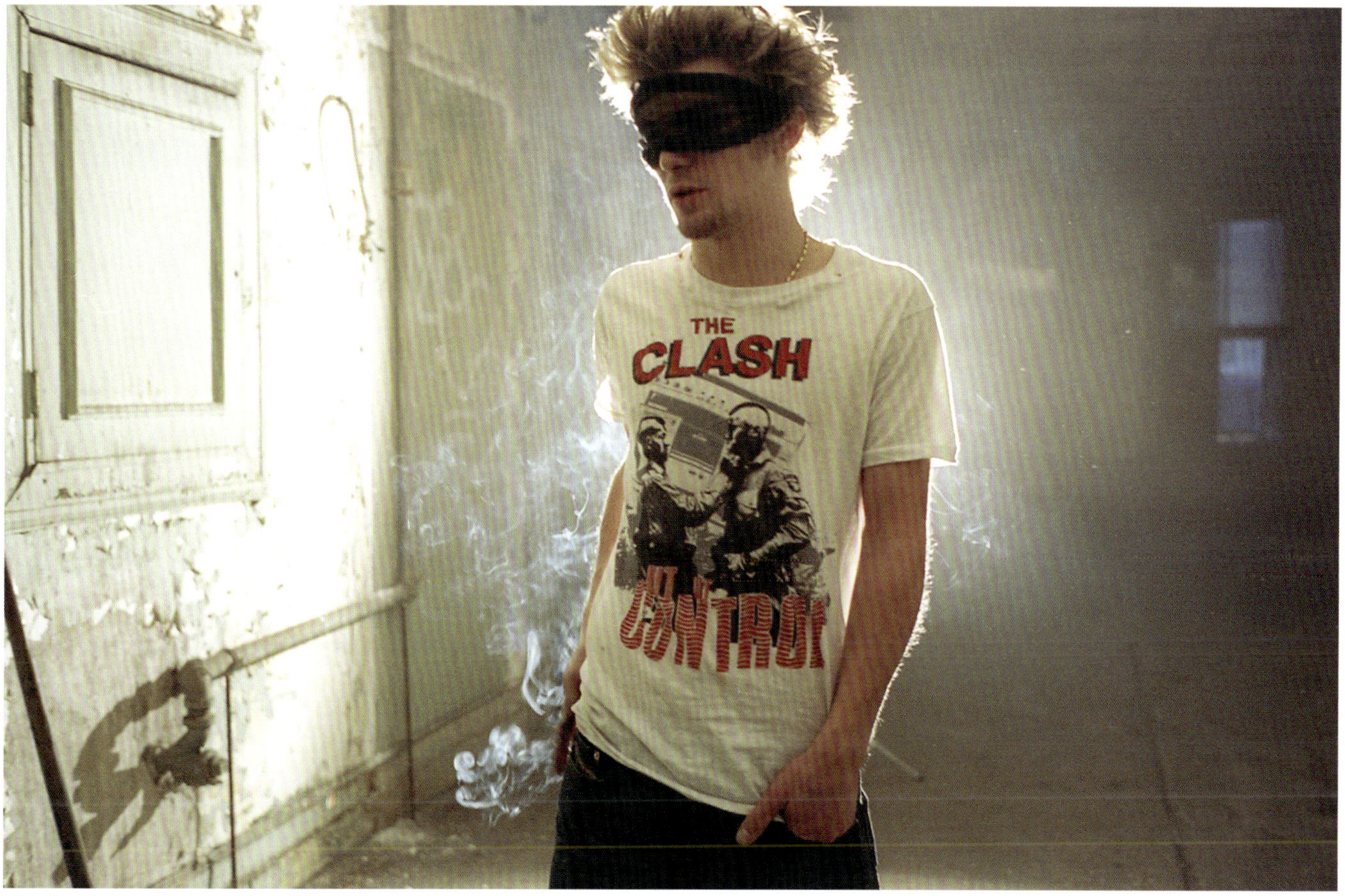

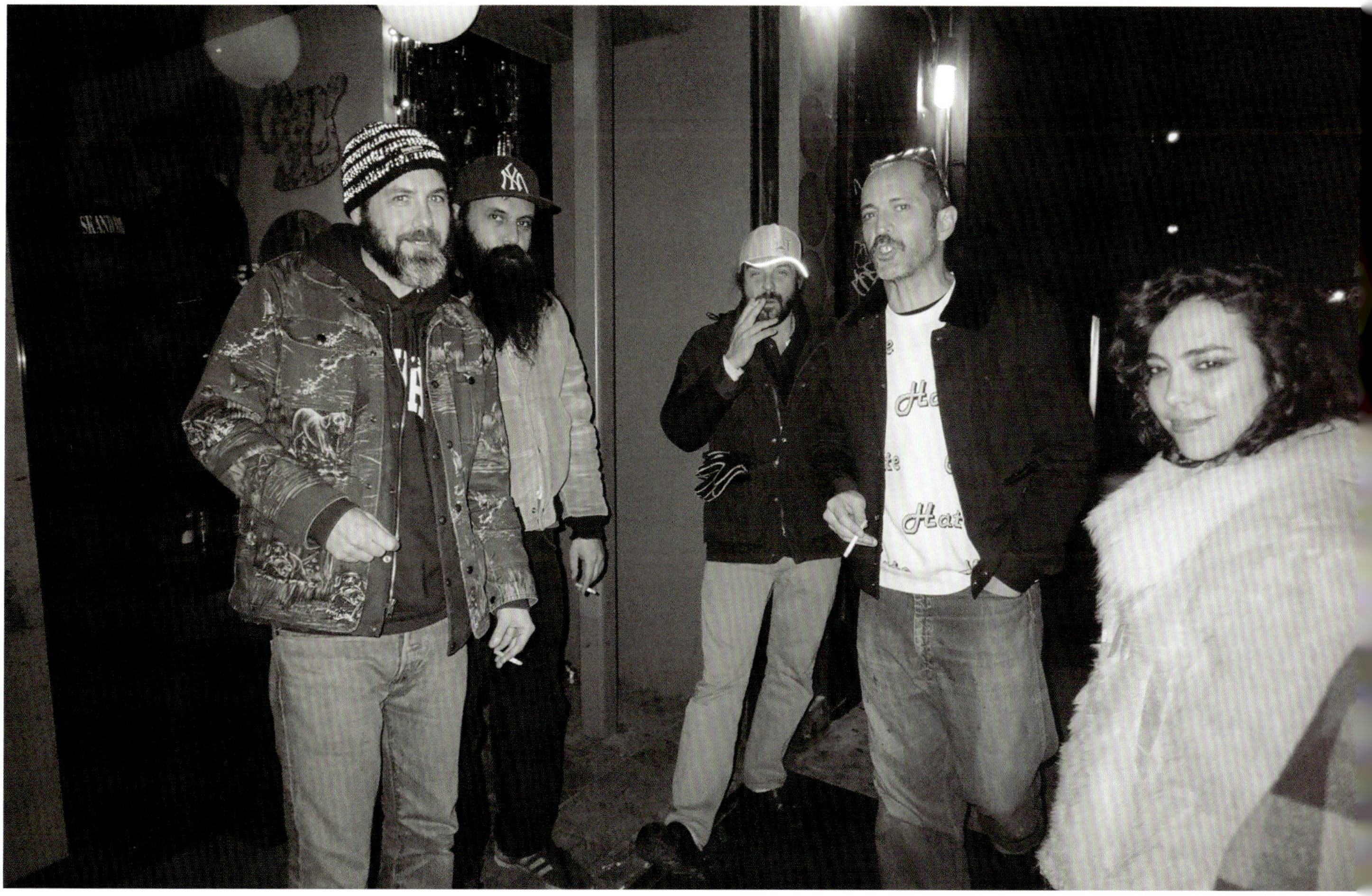

SPILL

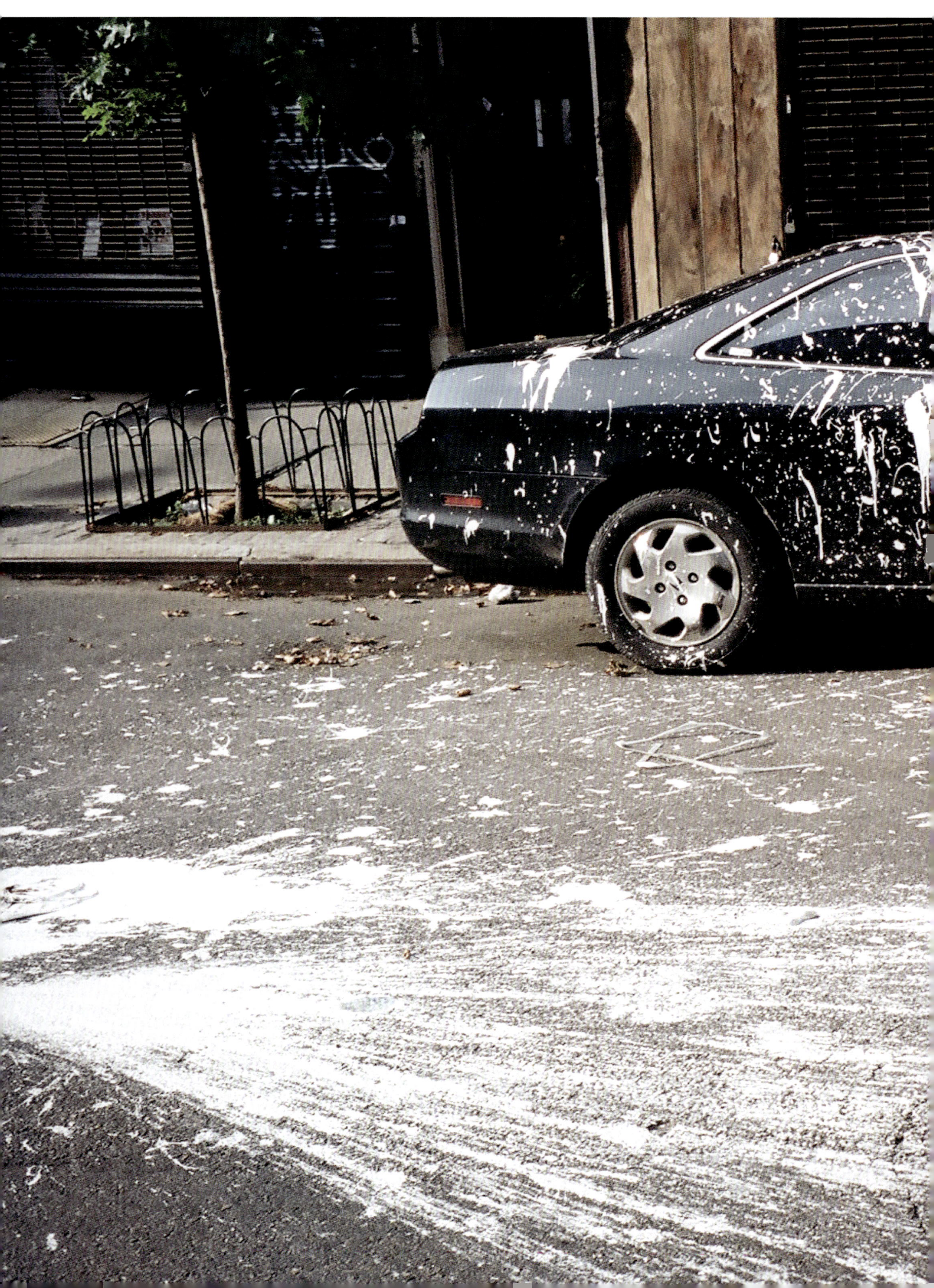

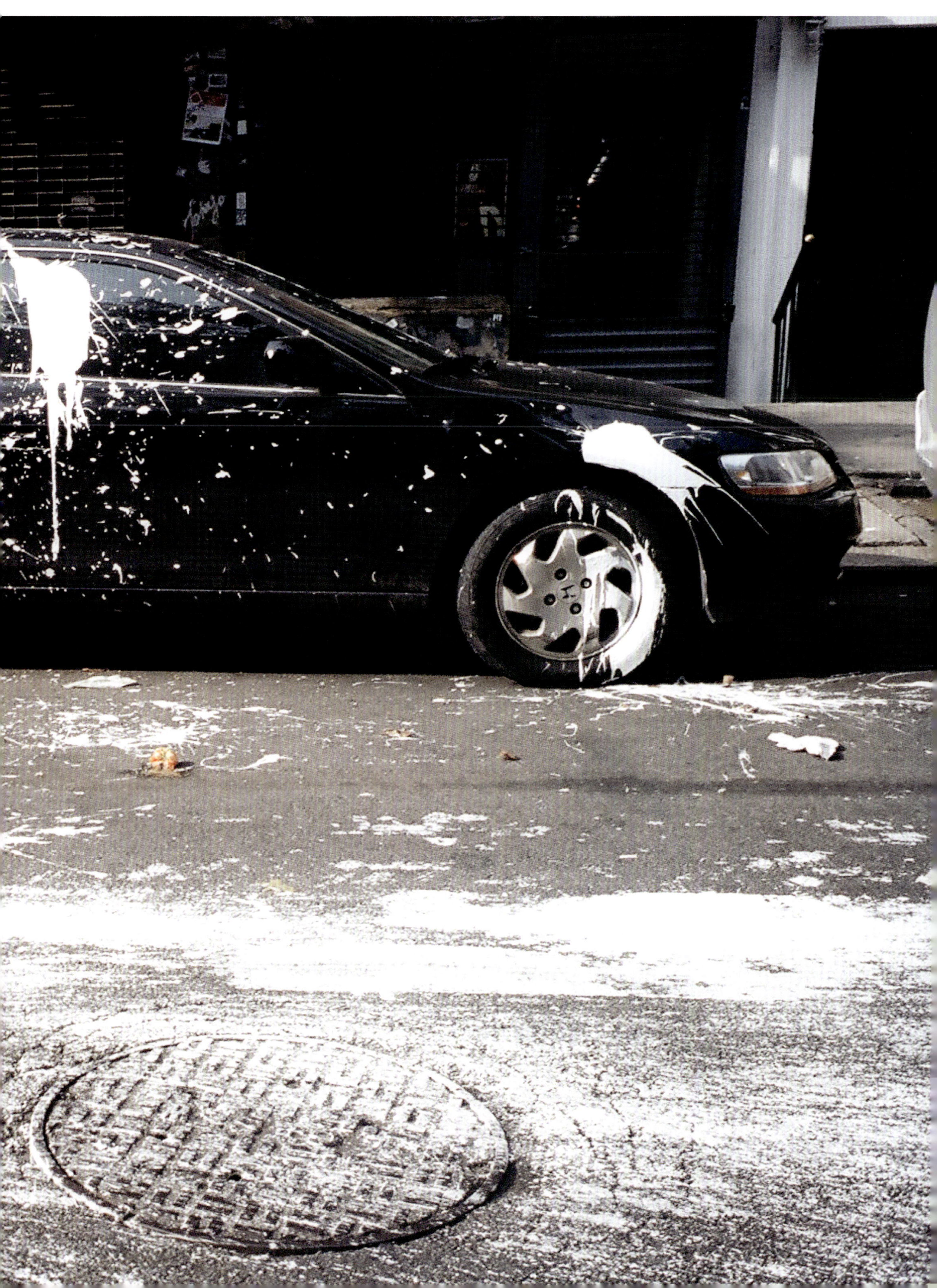

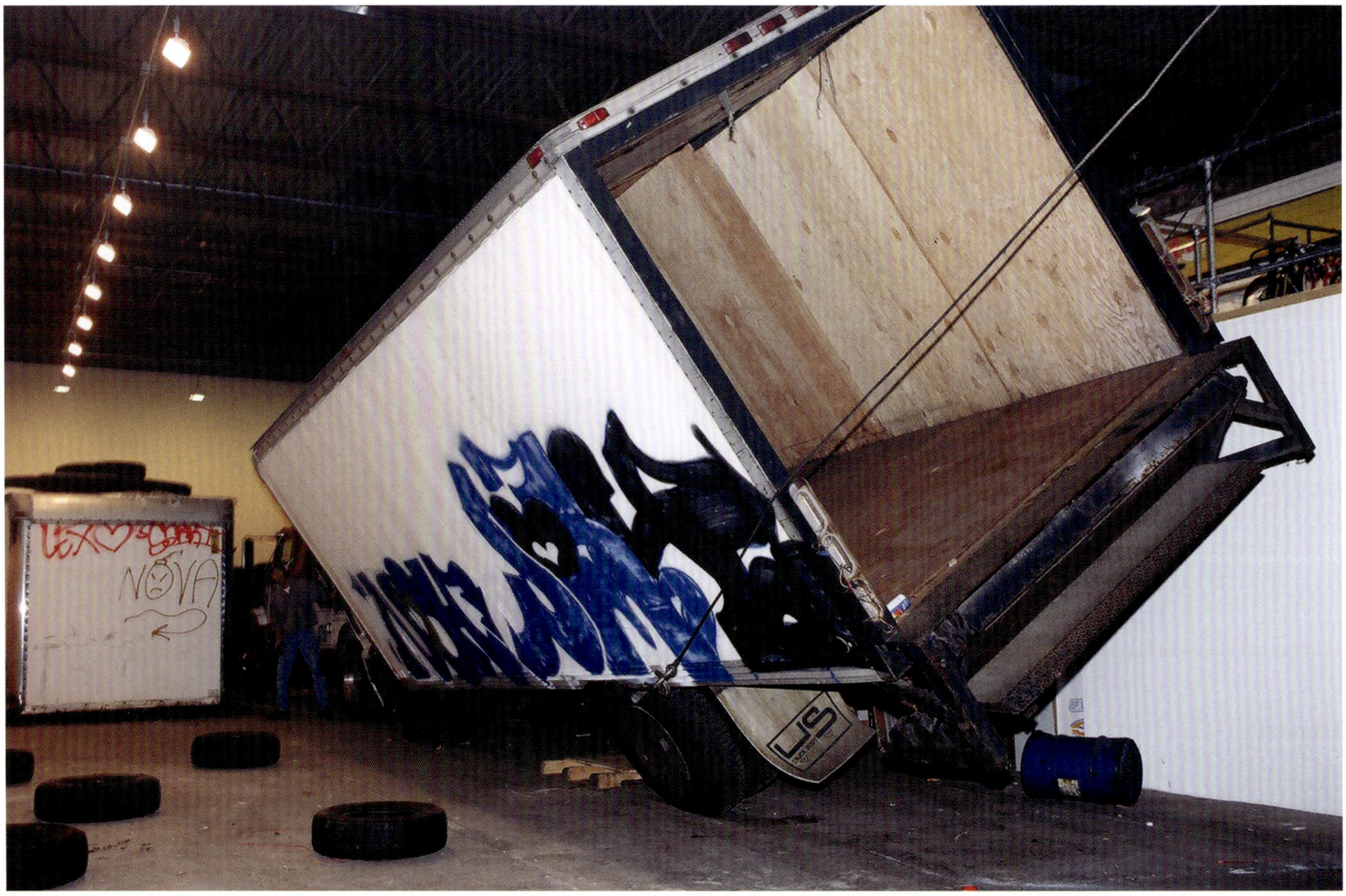

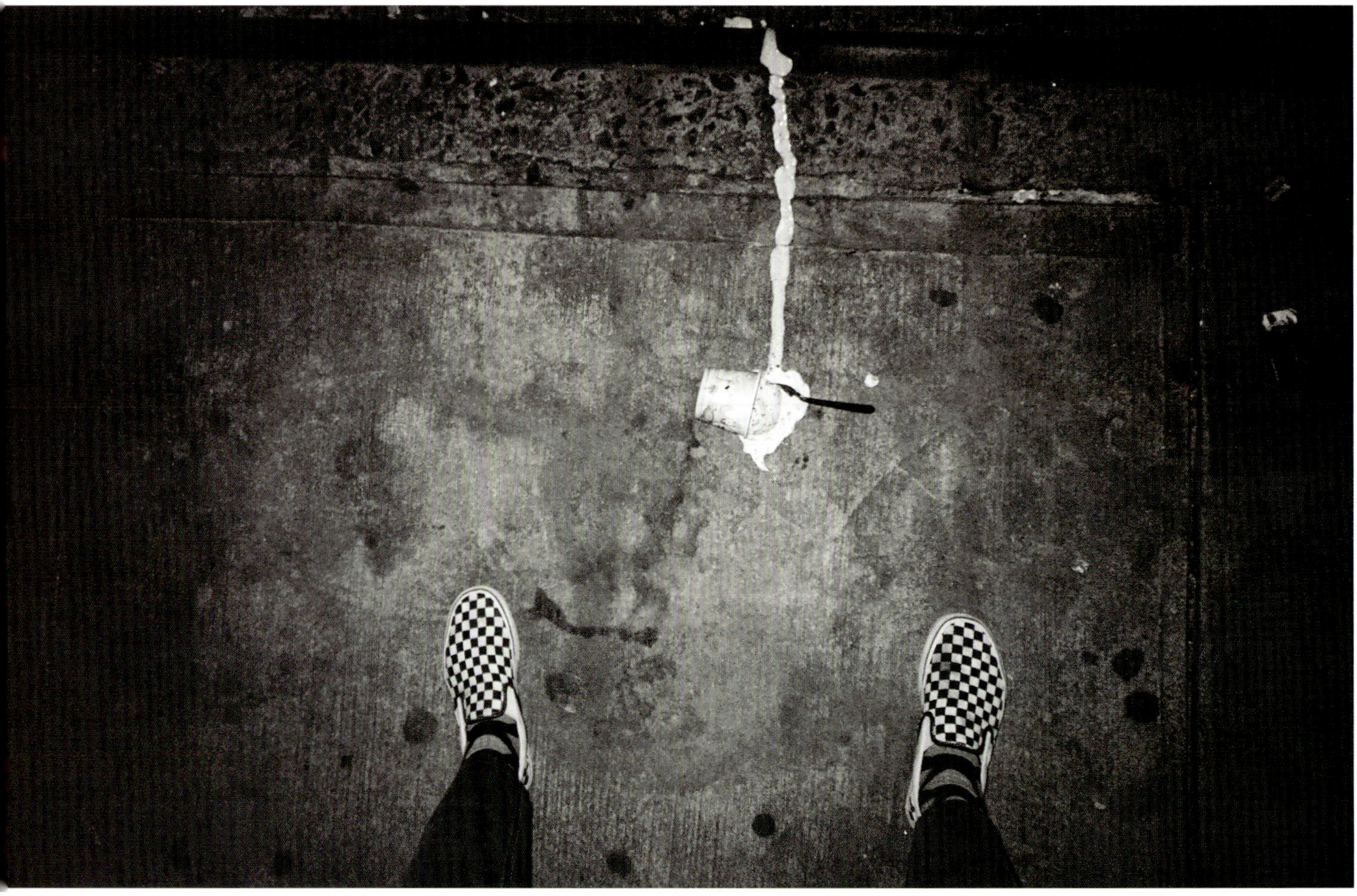

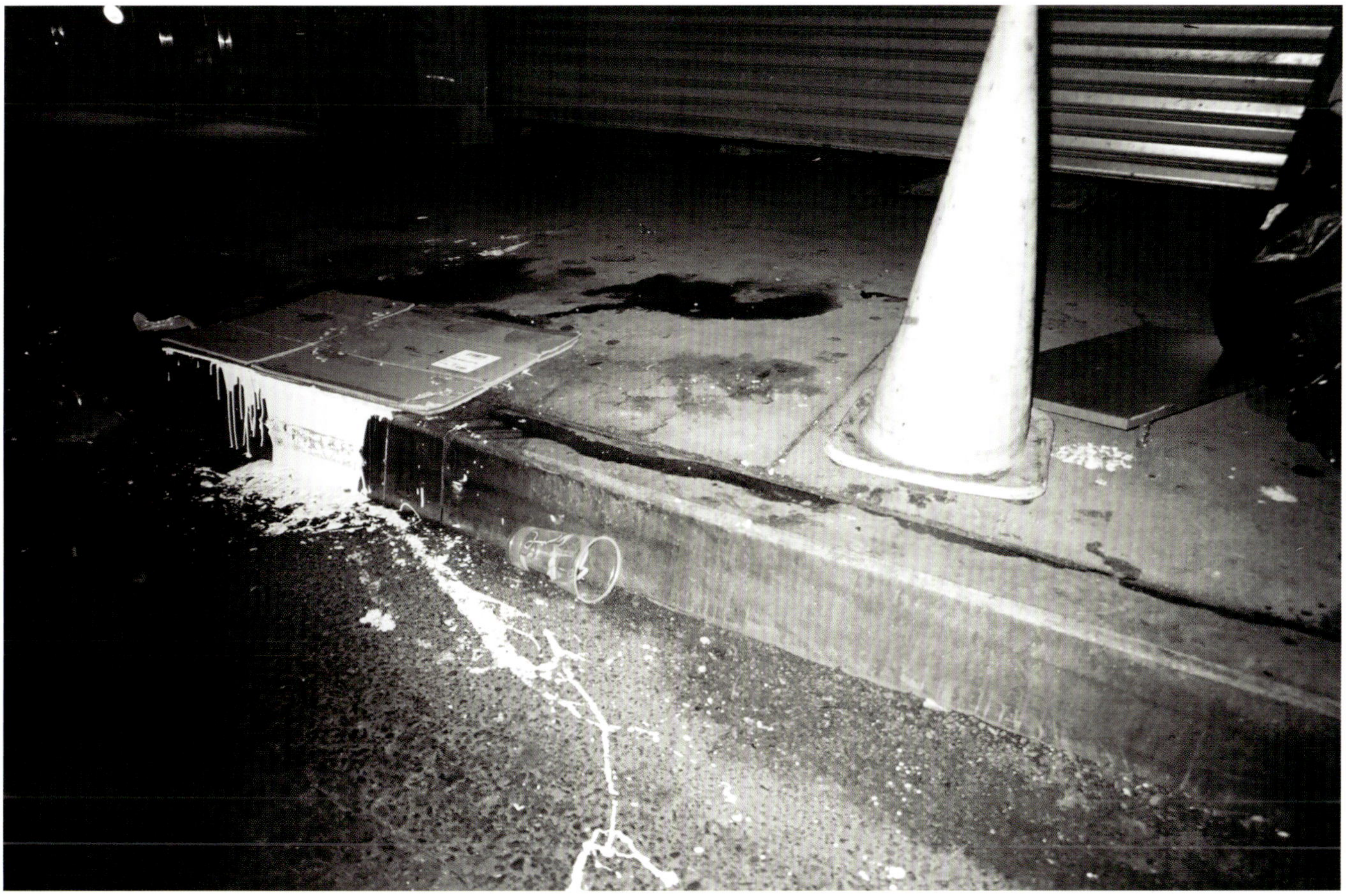

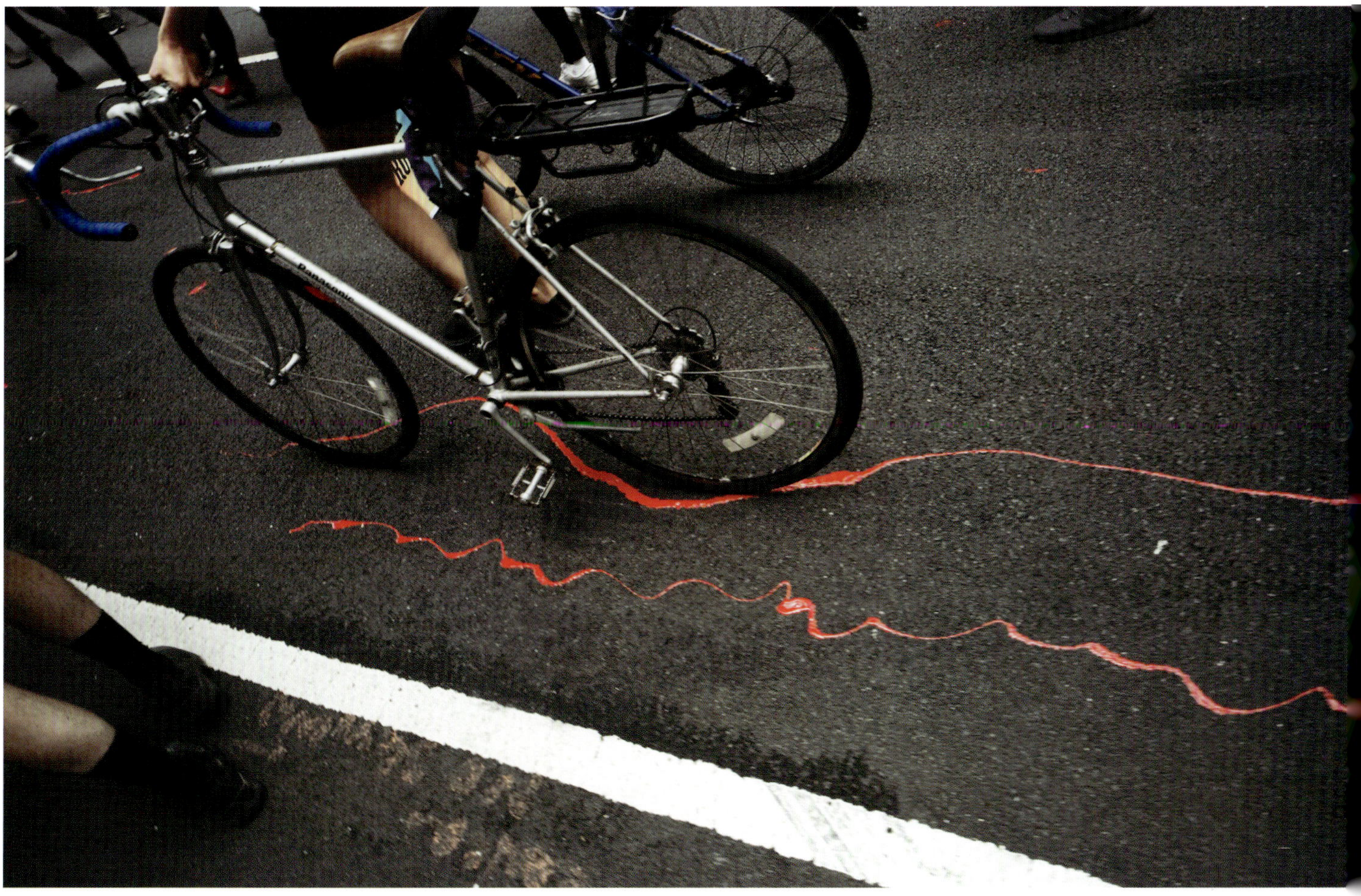

TIRE

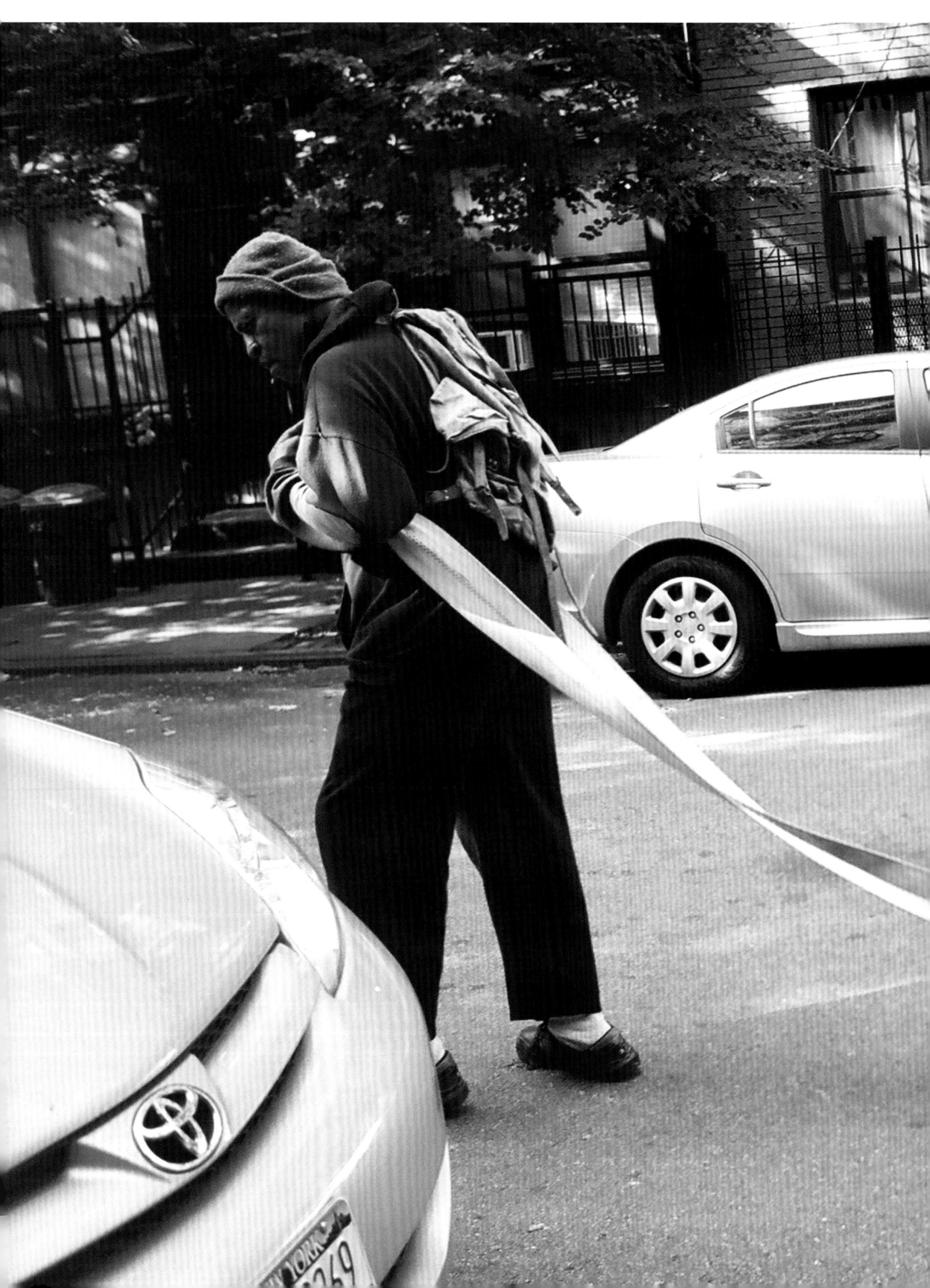

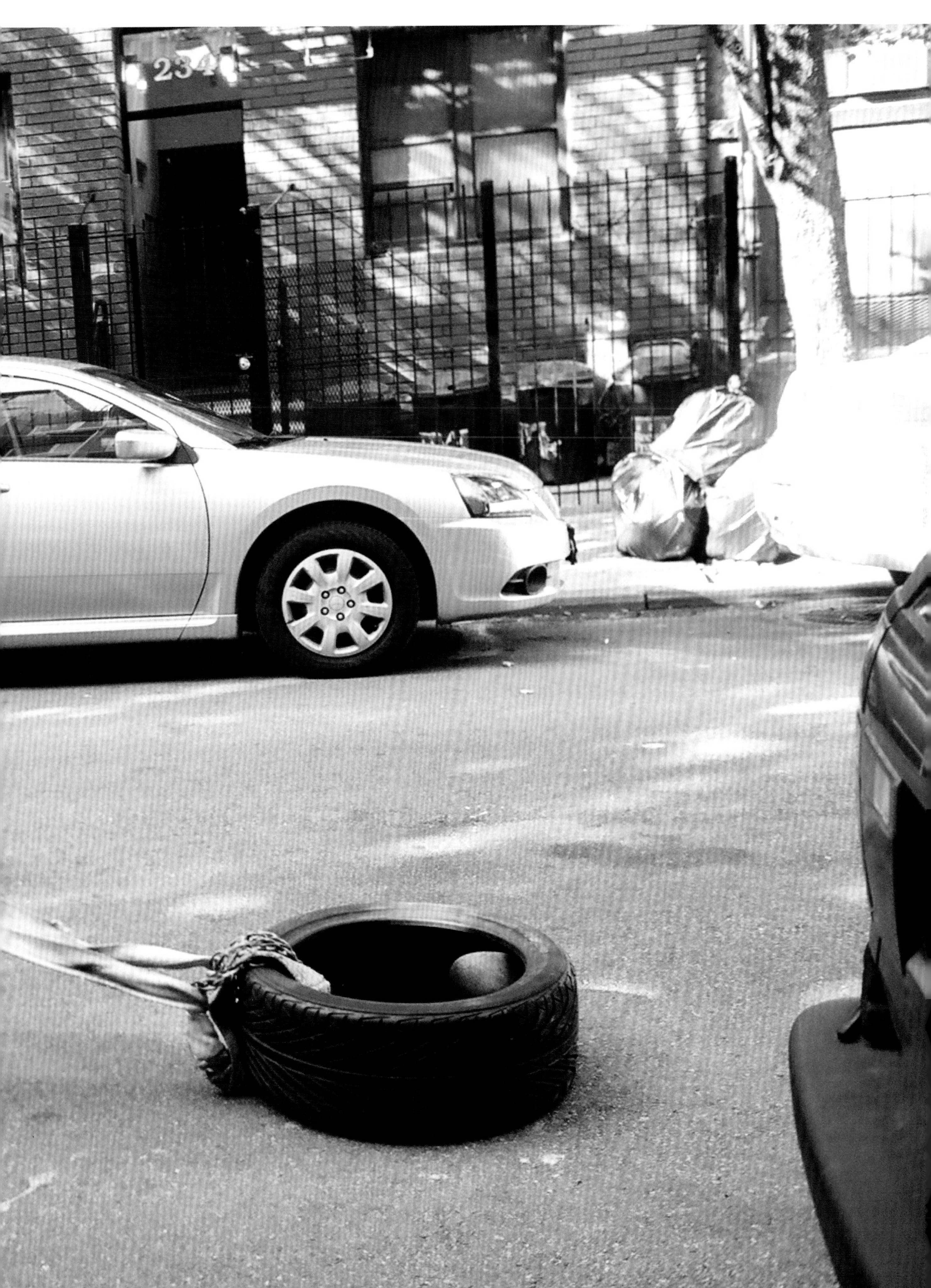
234

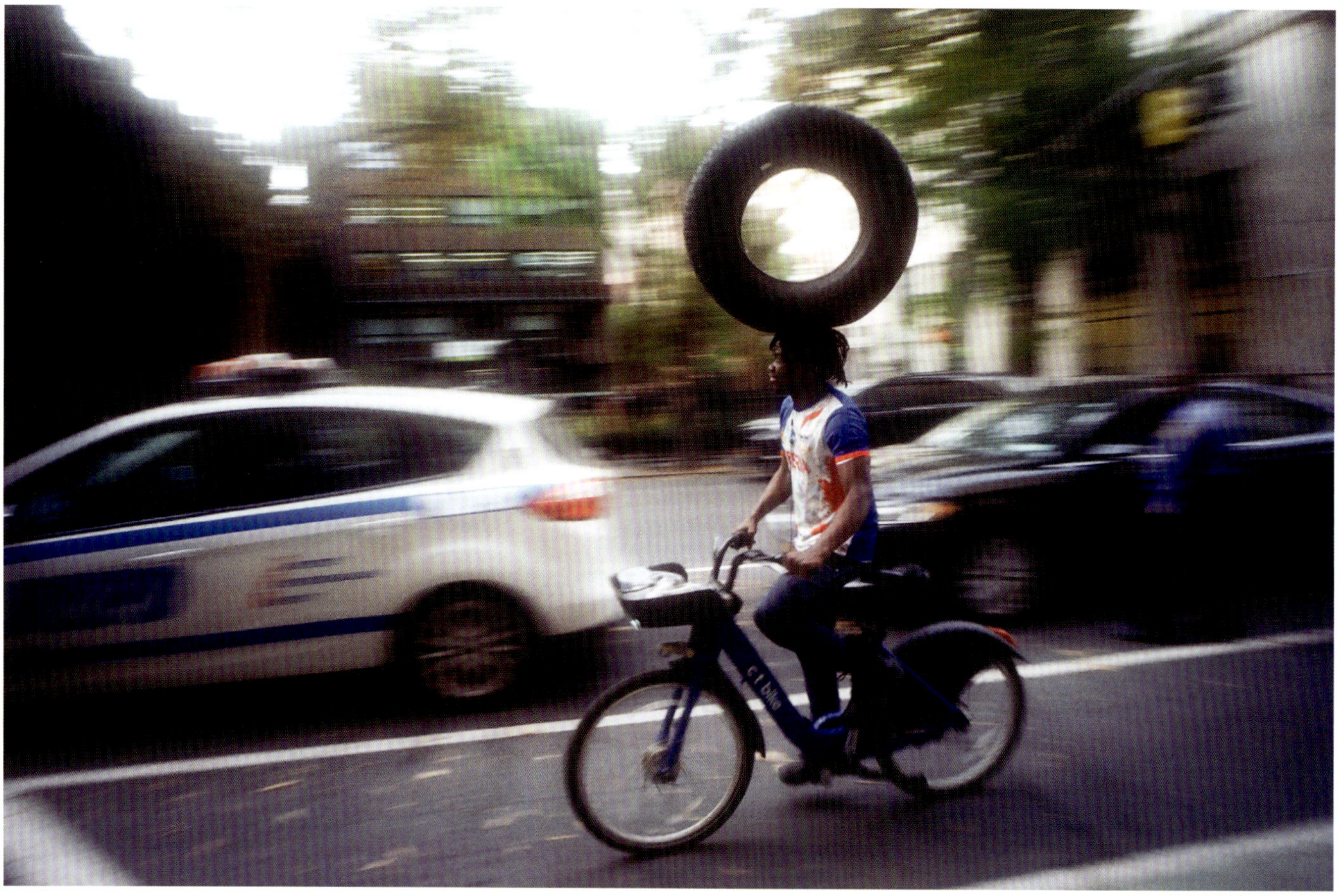

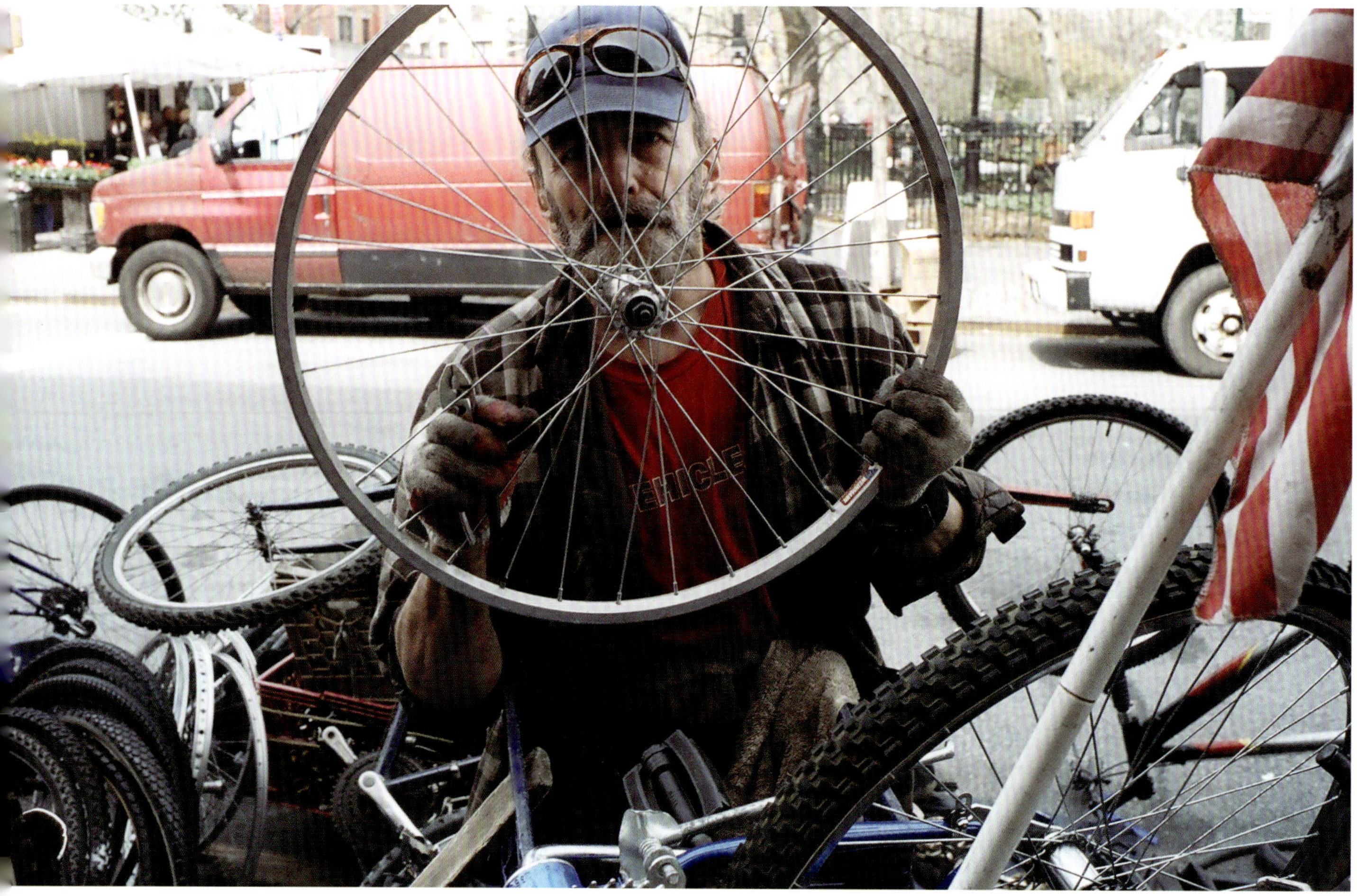

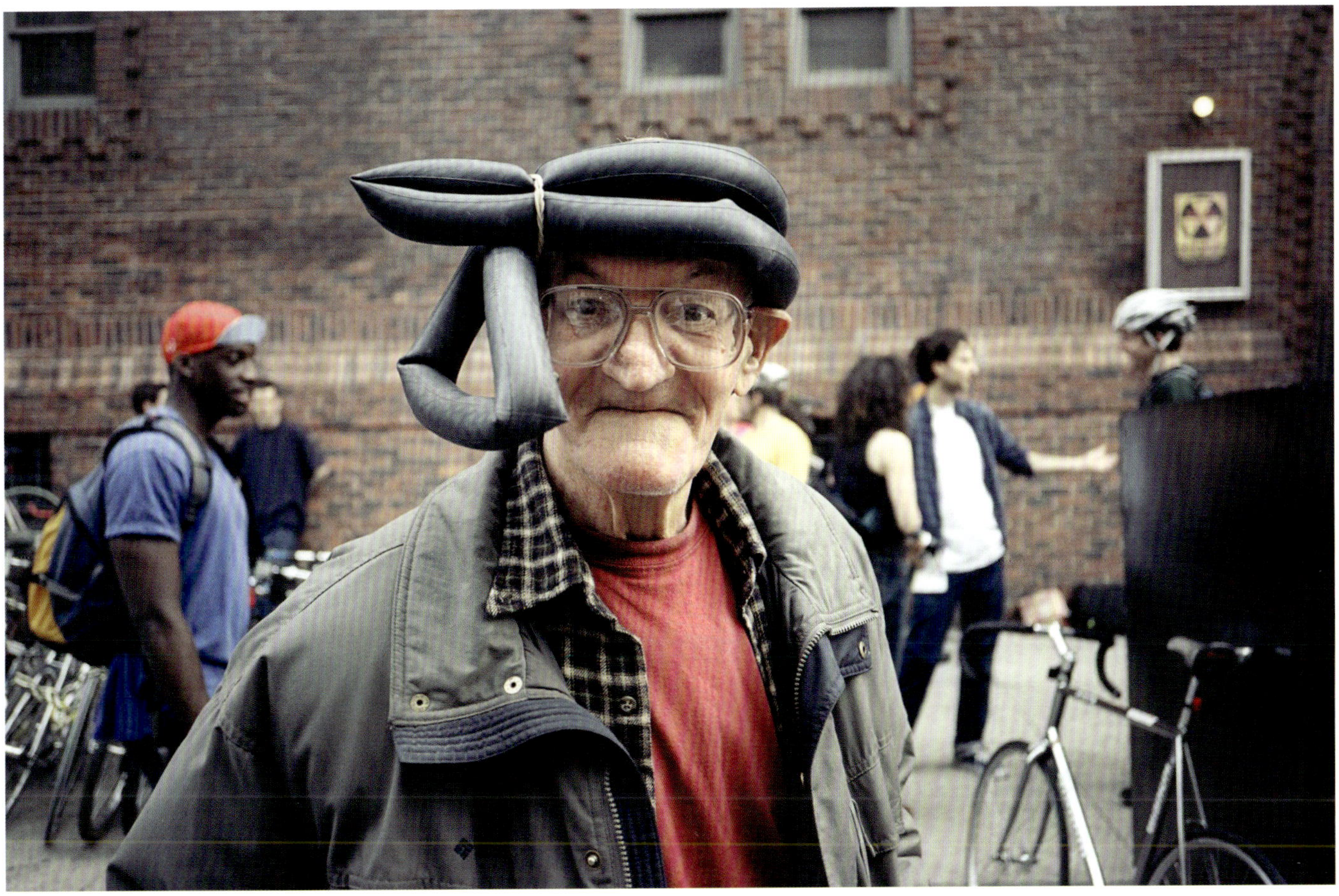

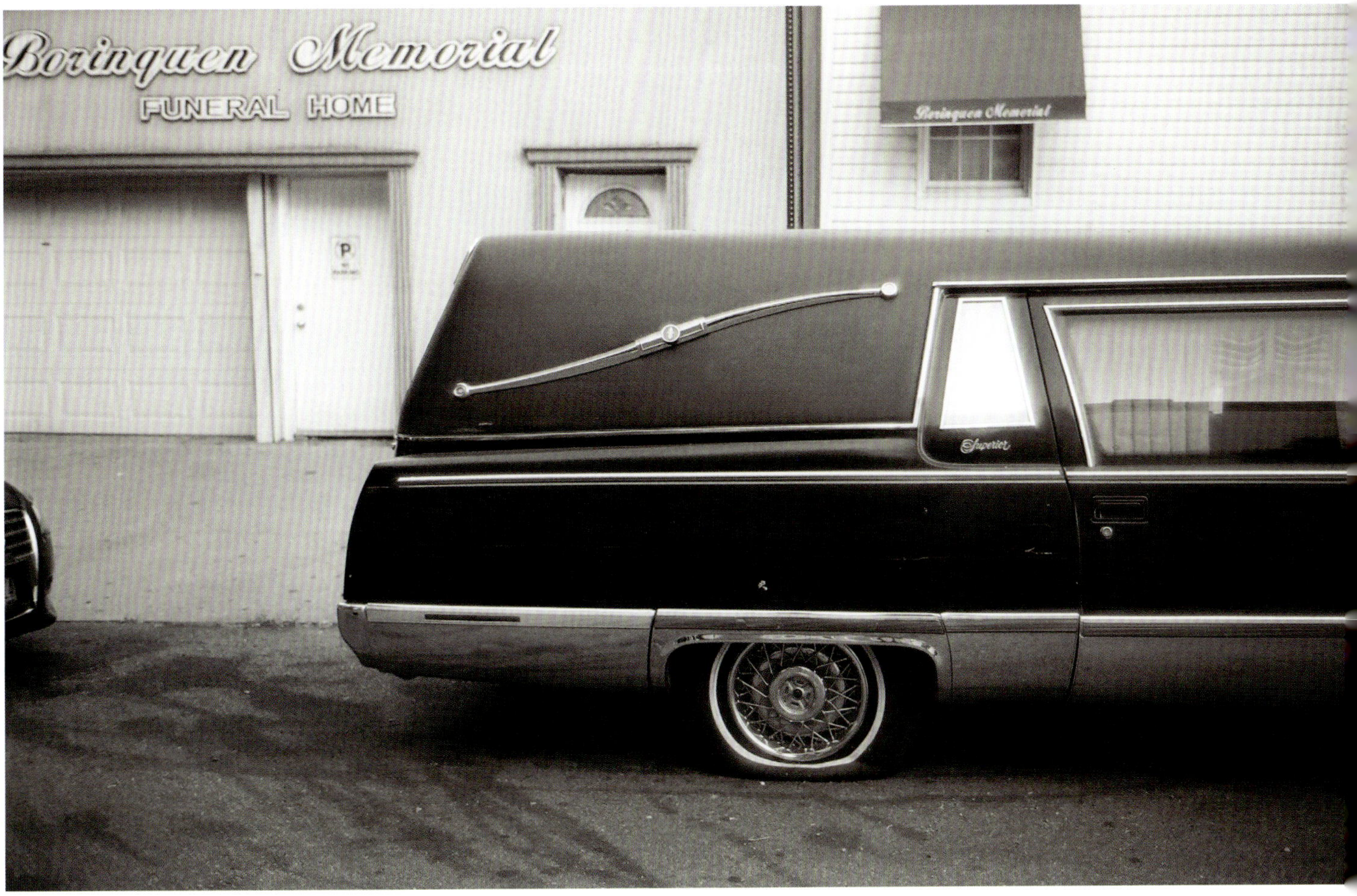

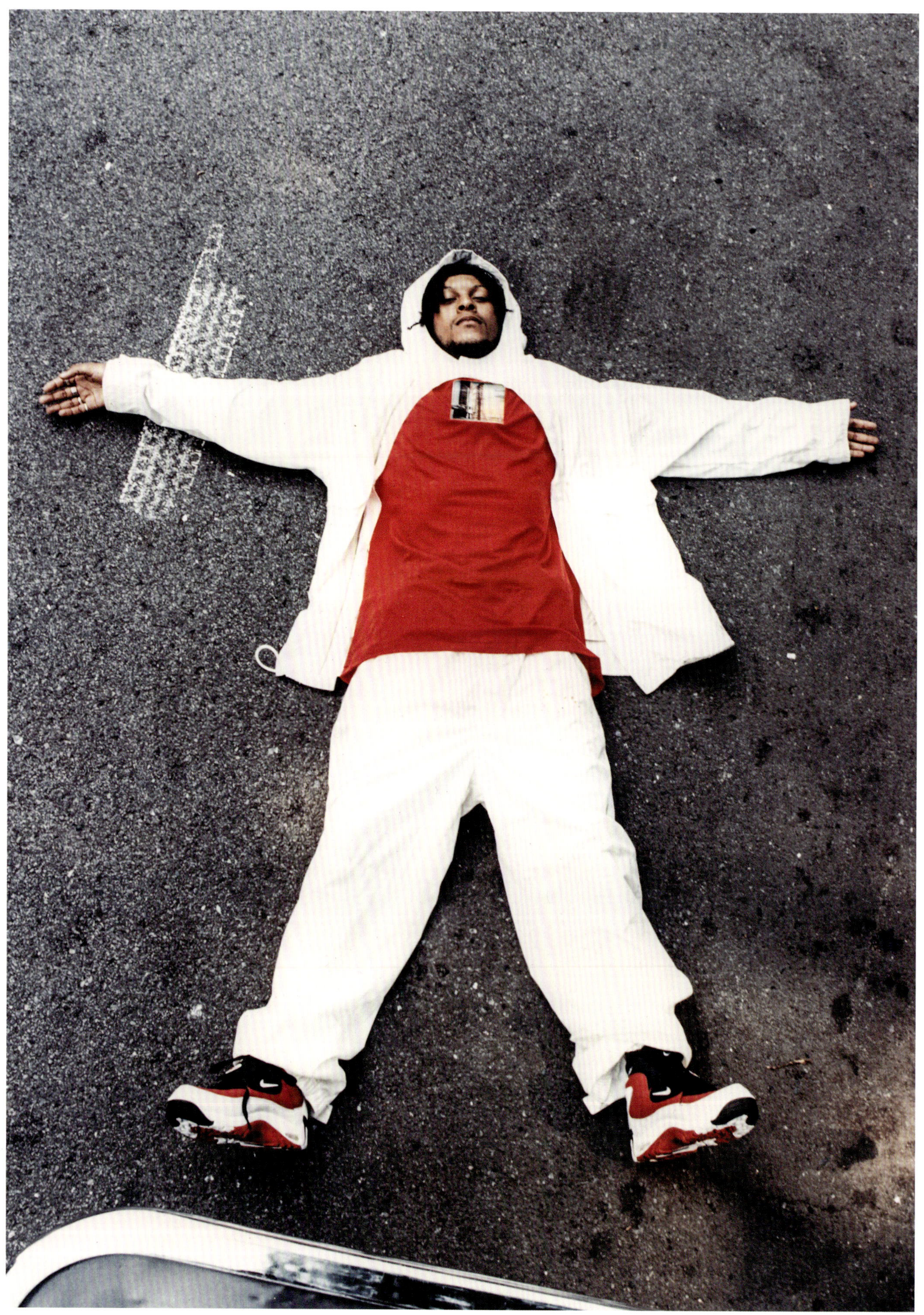

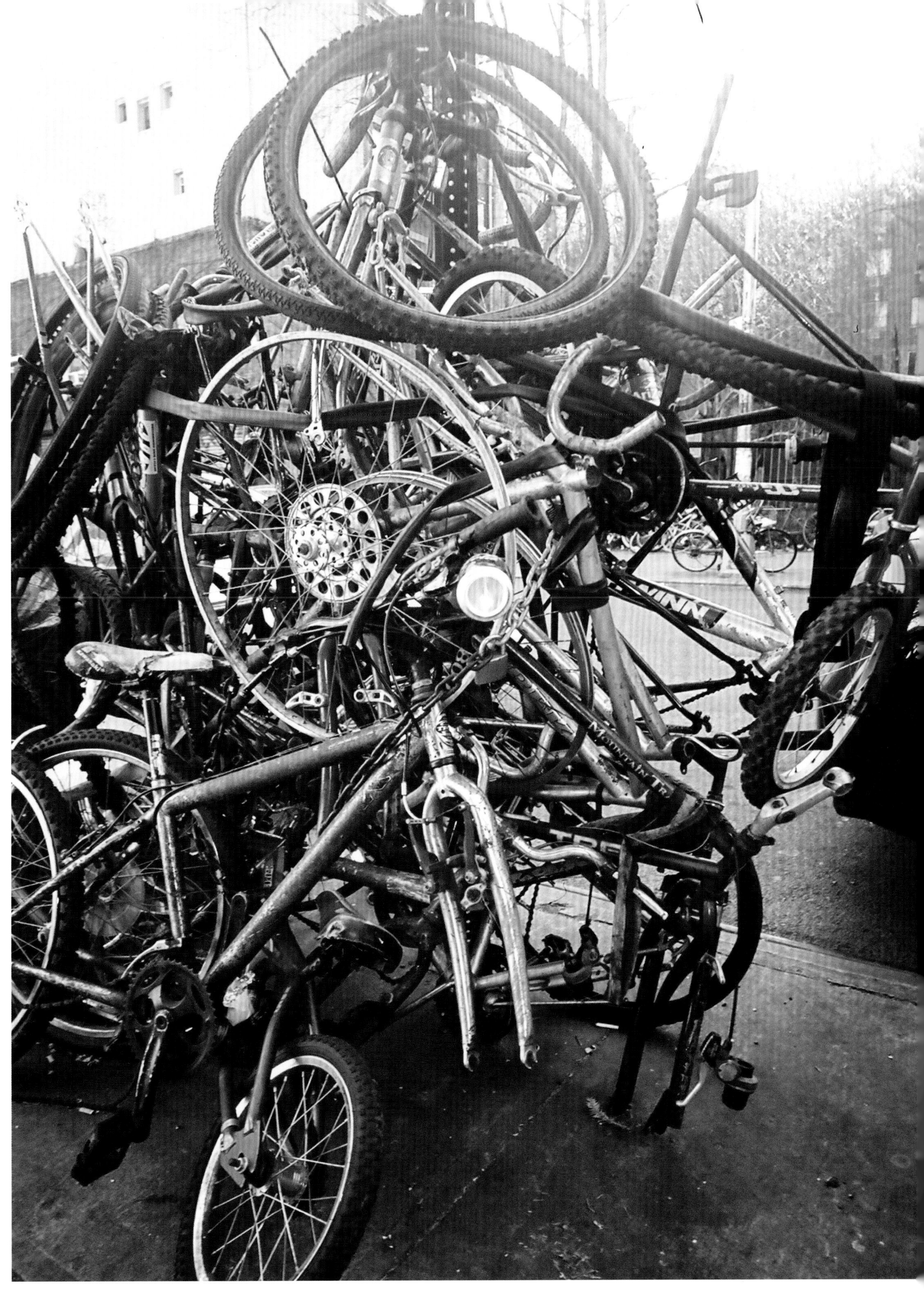

TRAIL

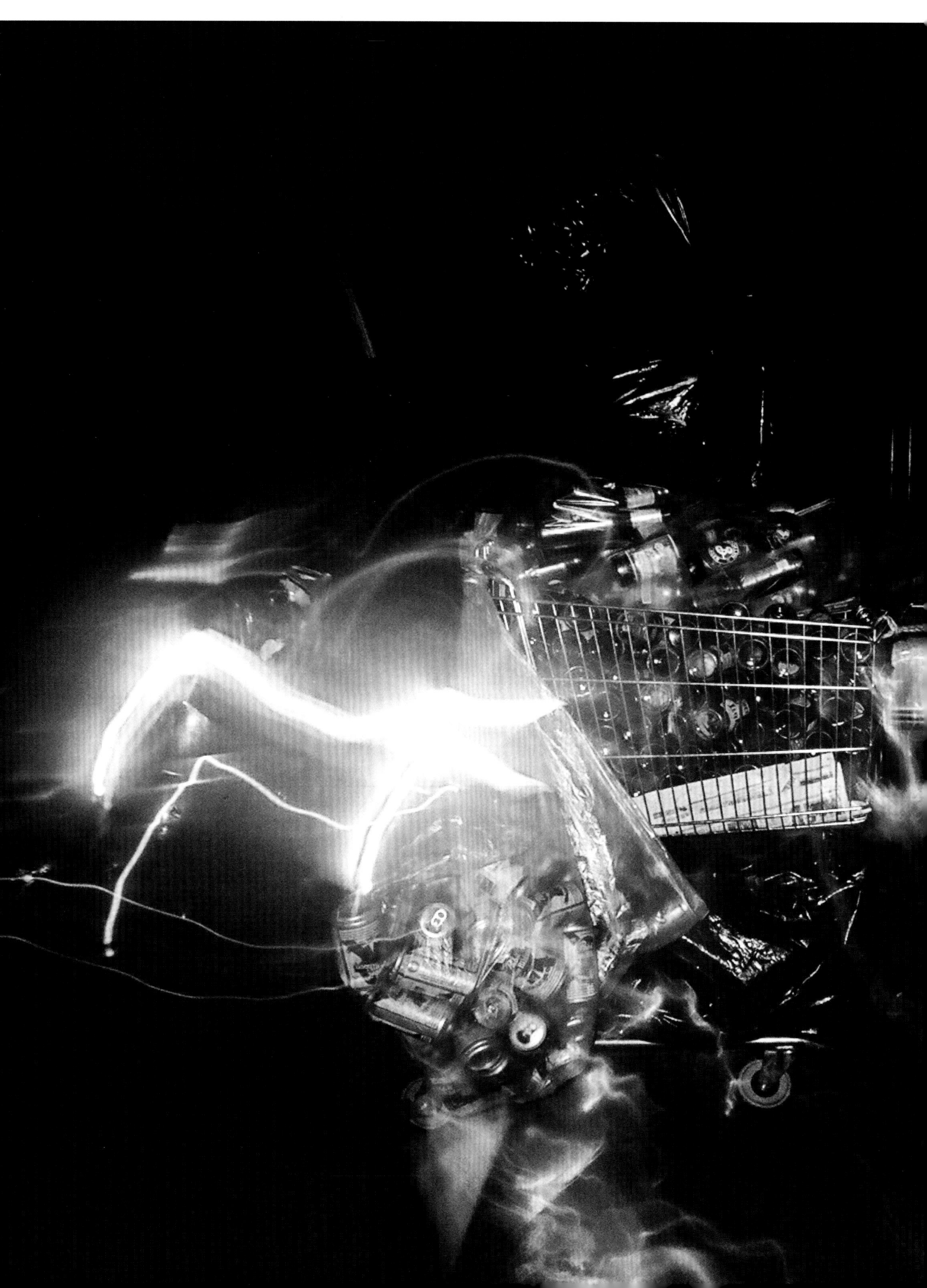

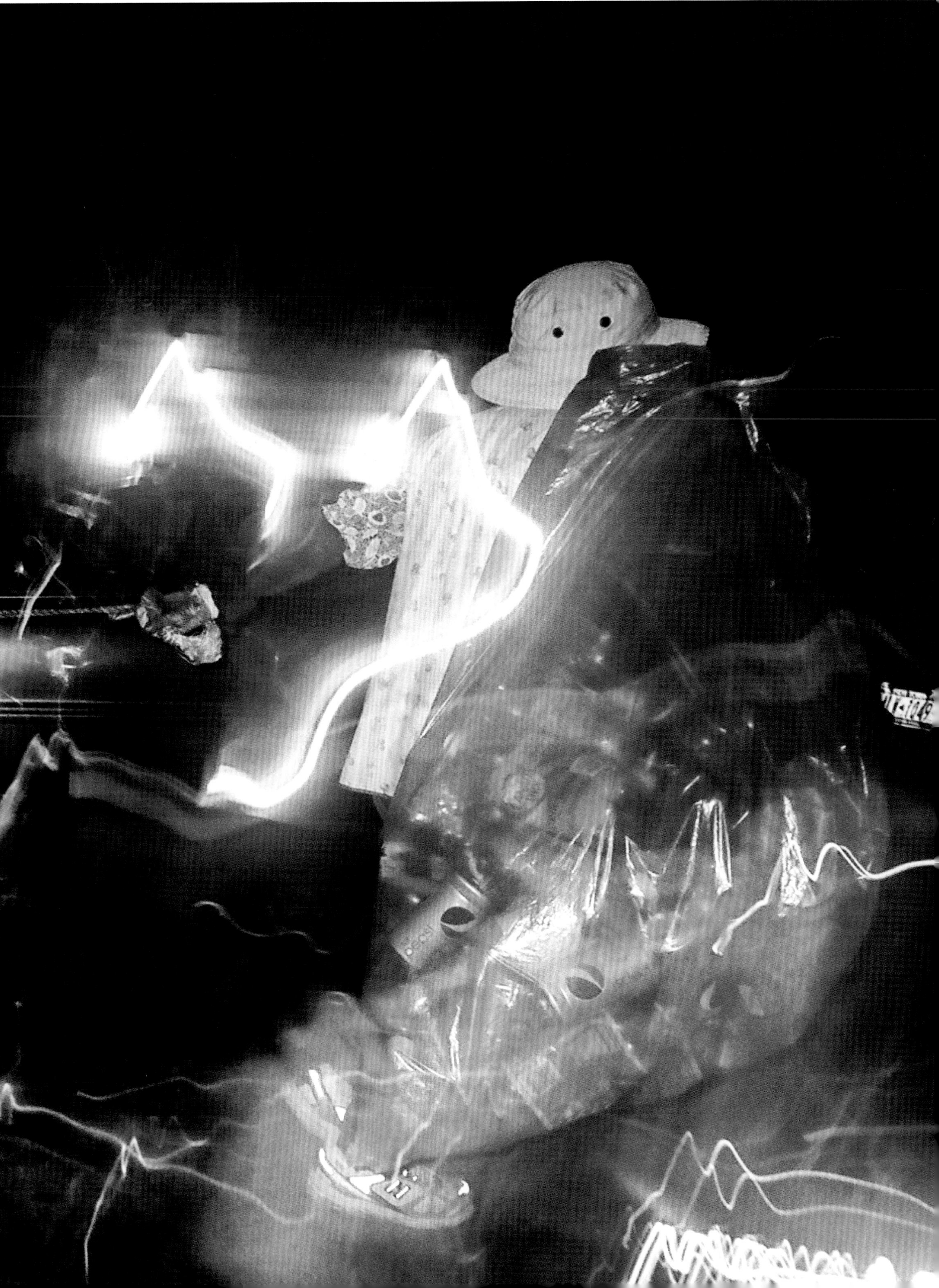

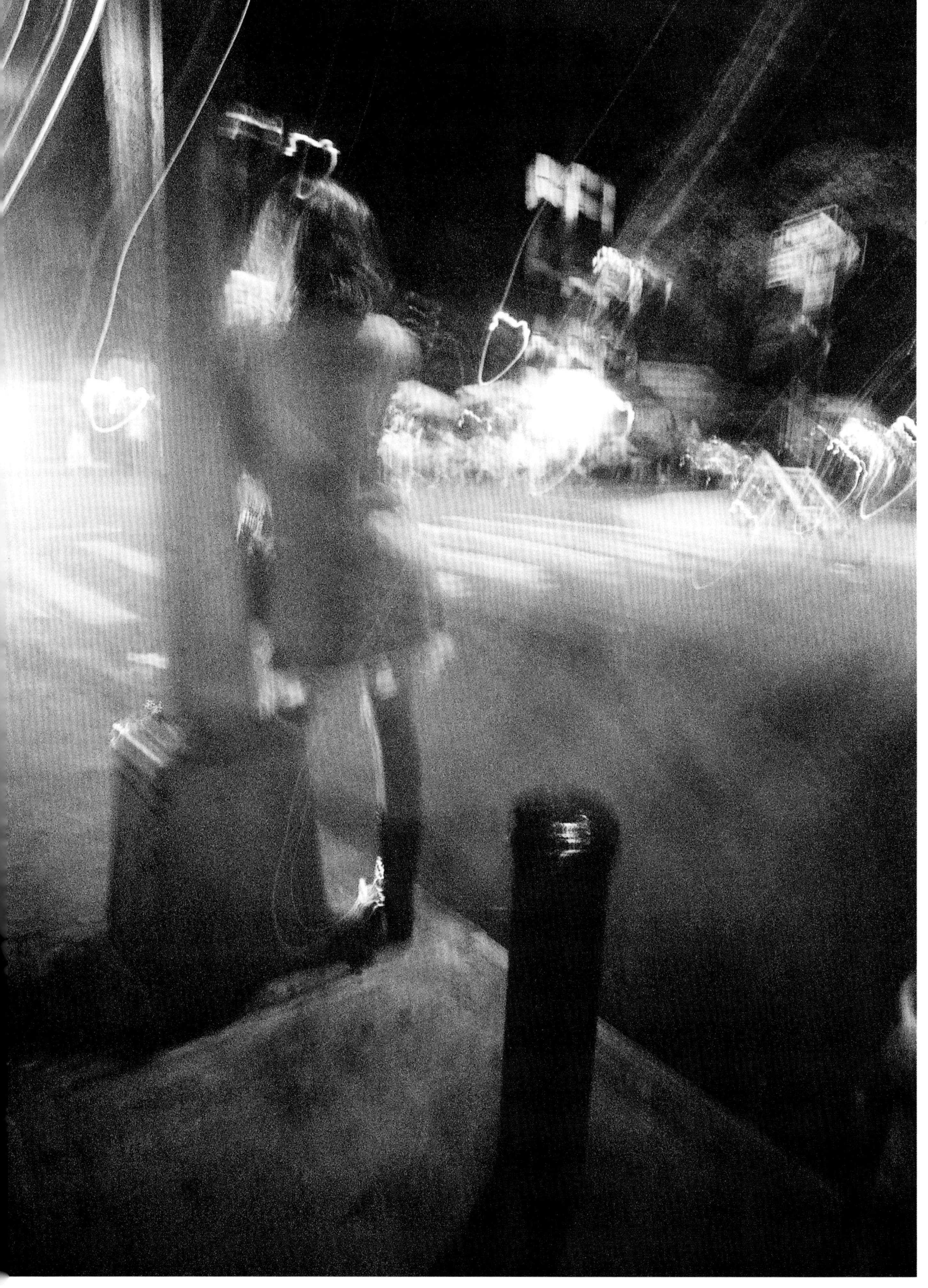

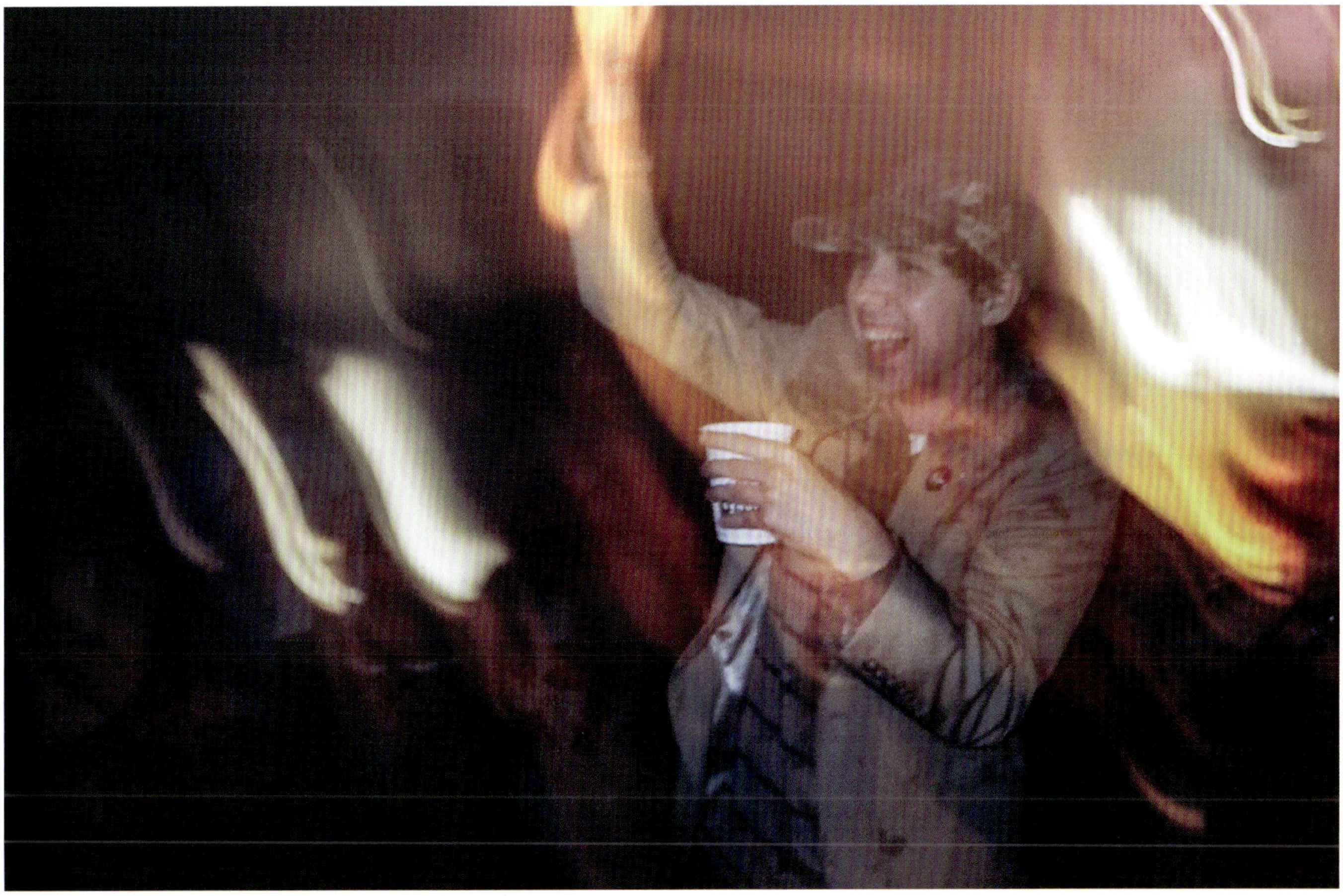

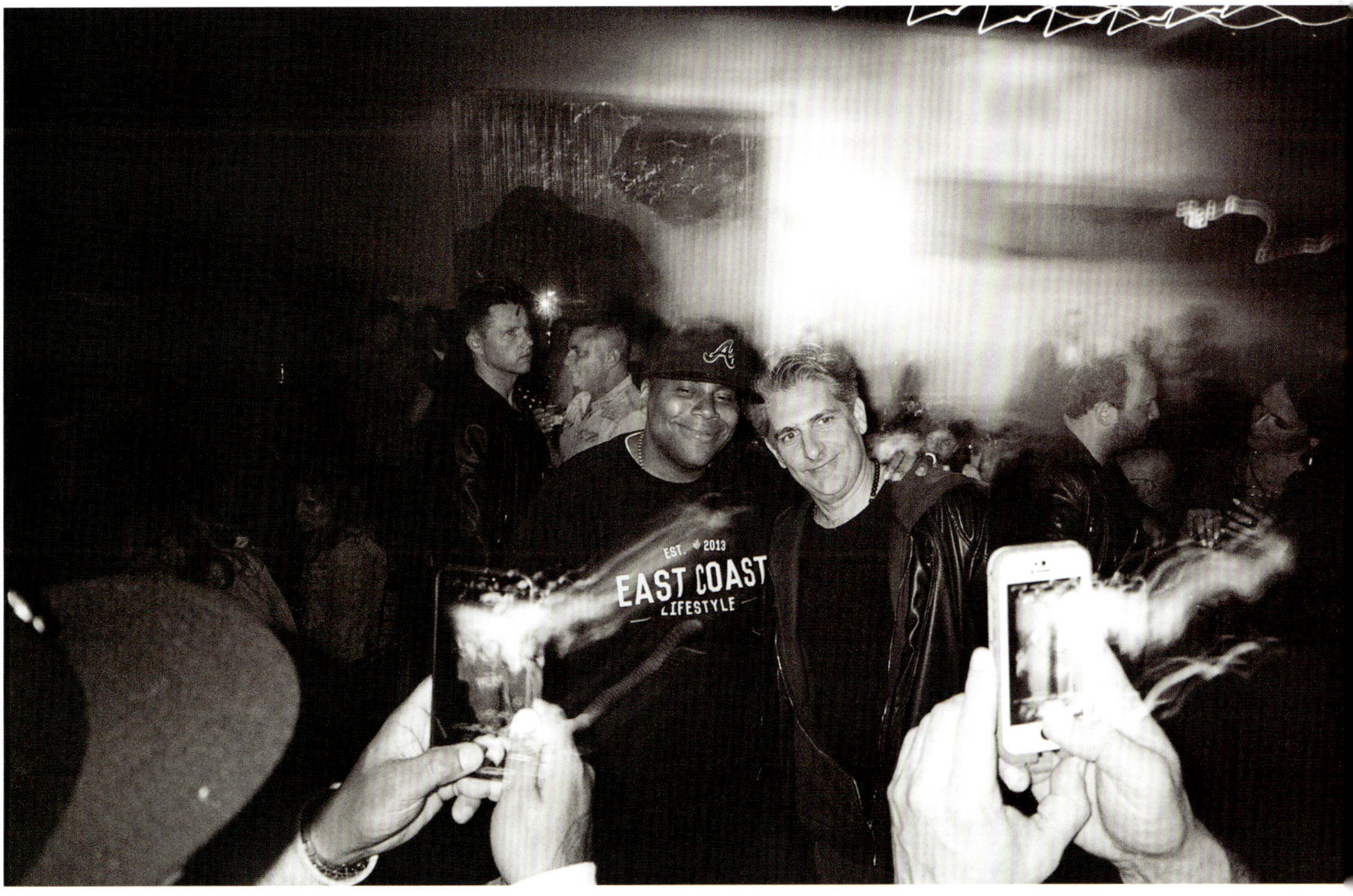

TV

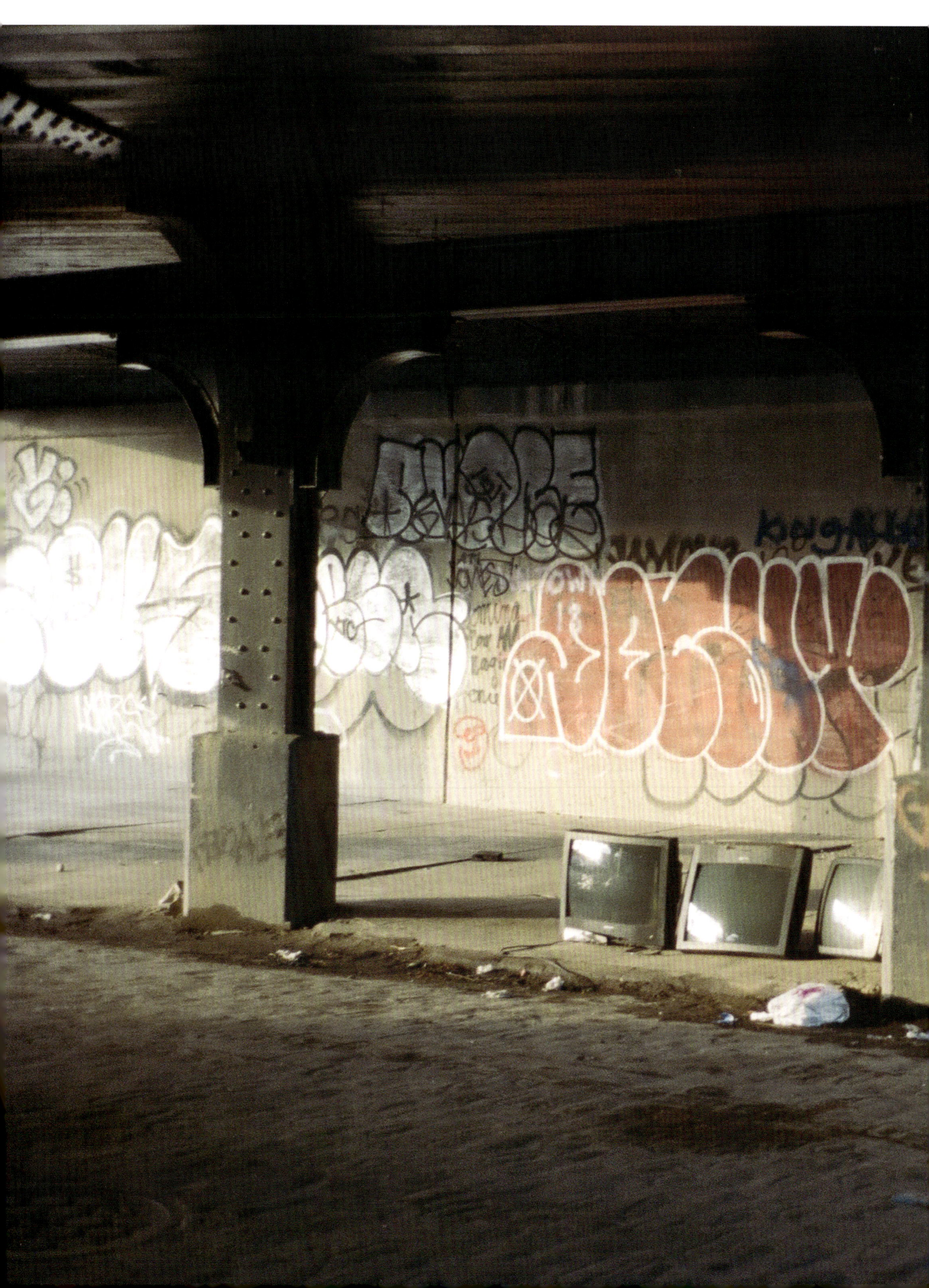

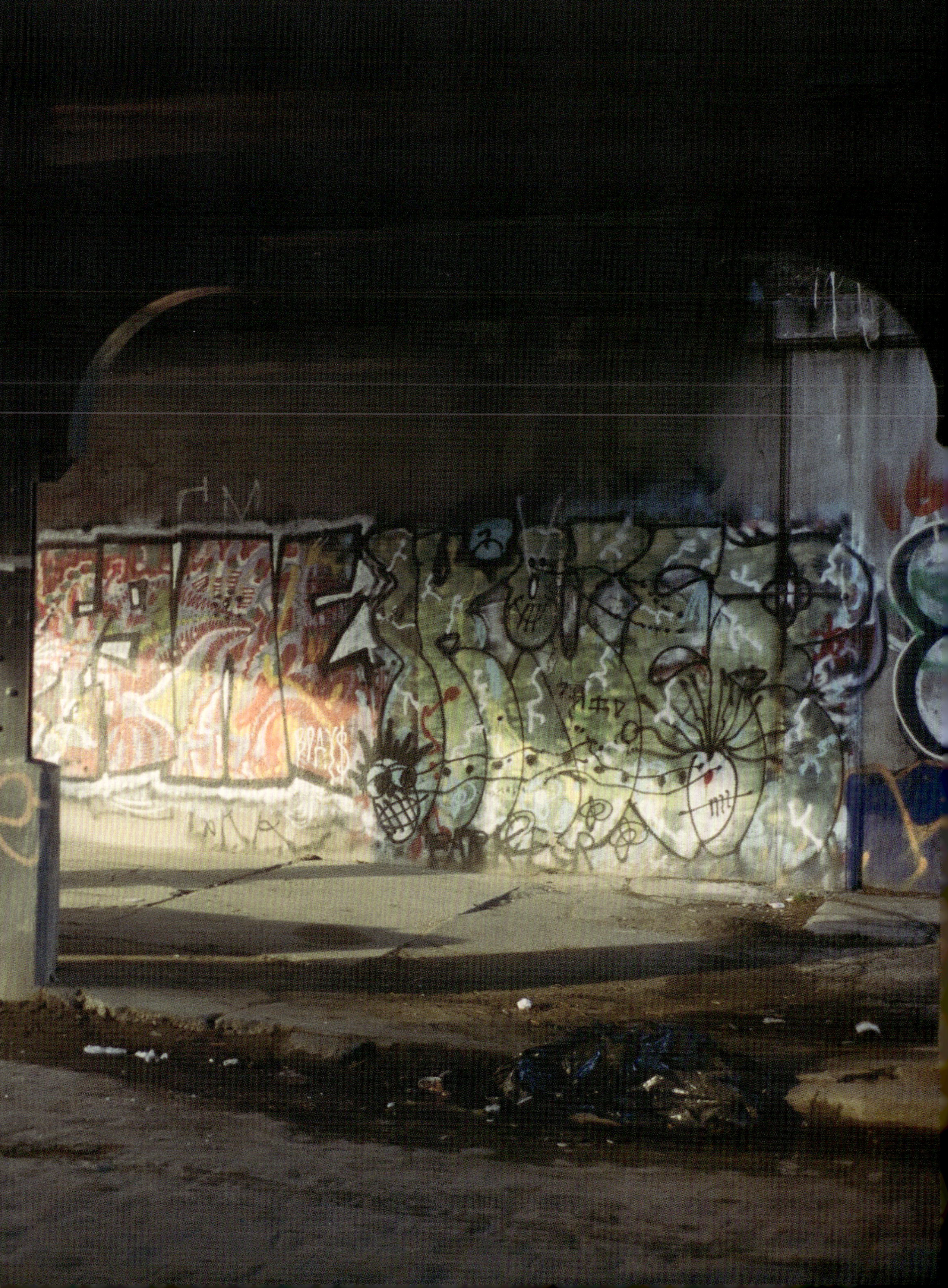

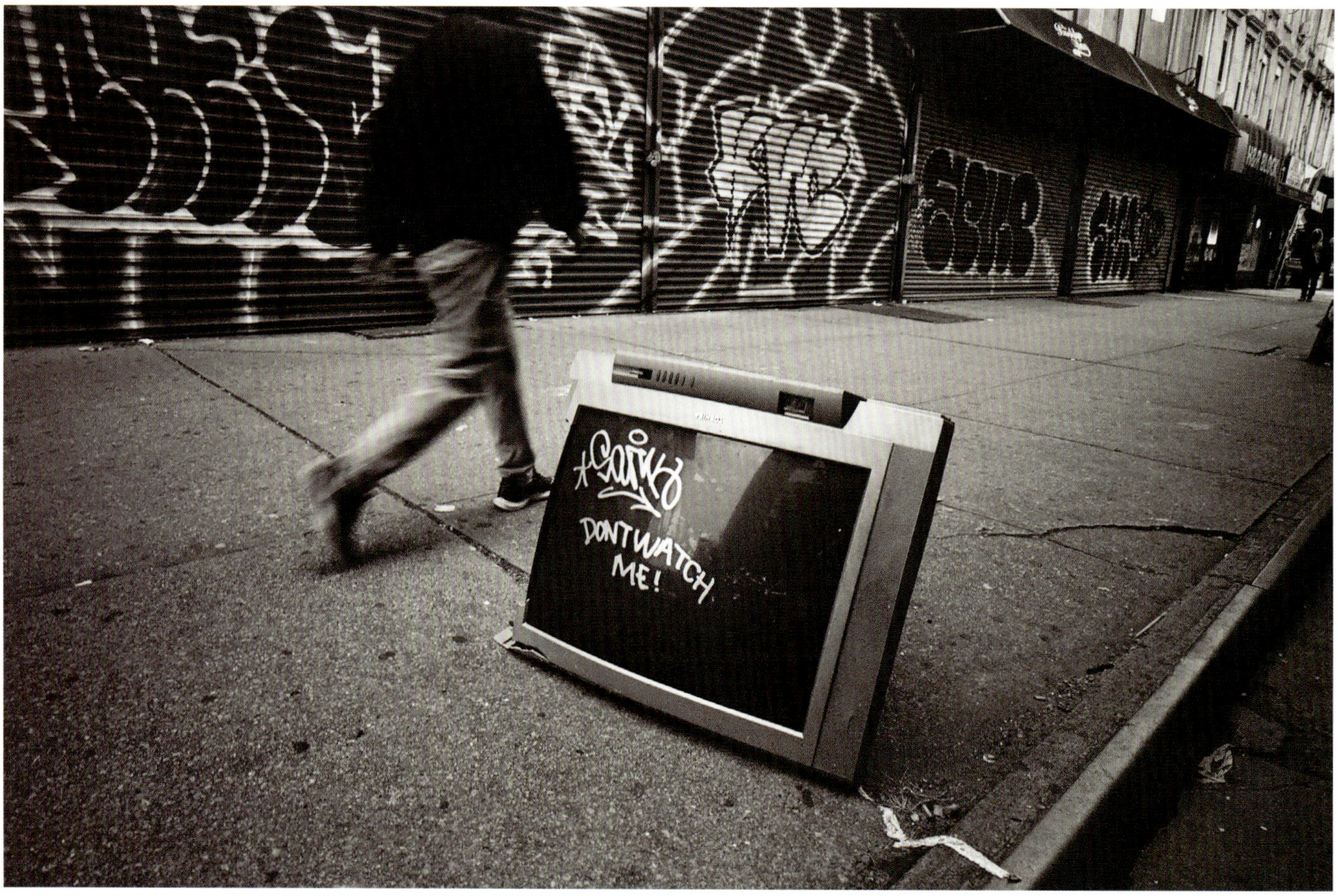

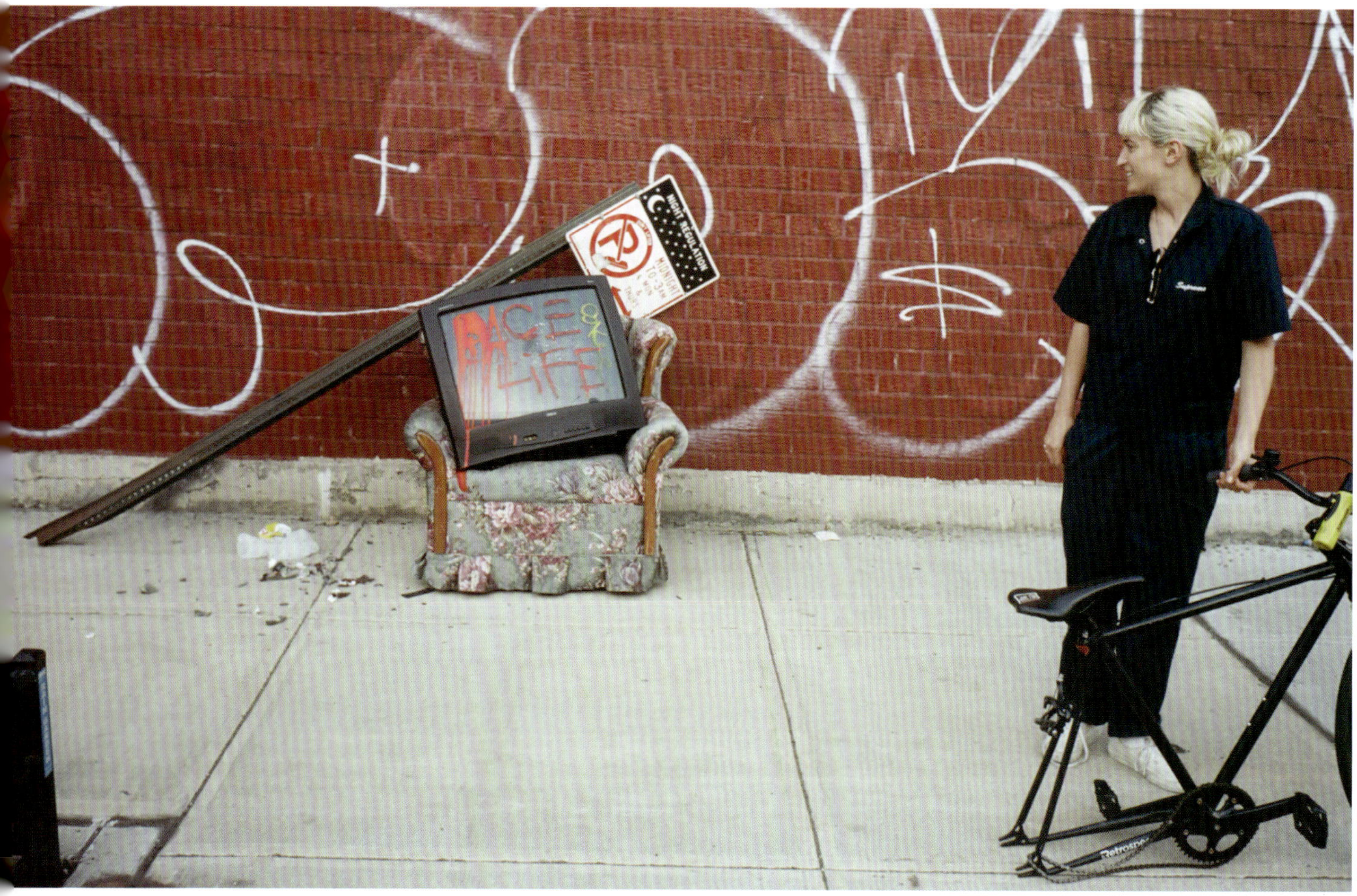

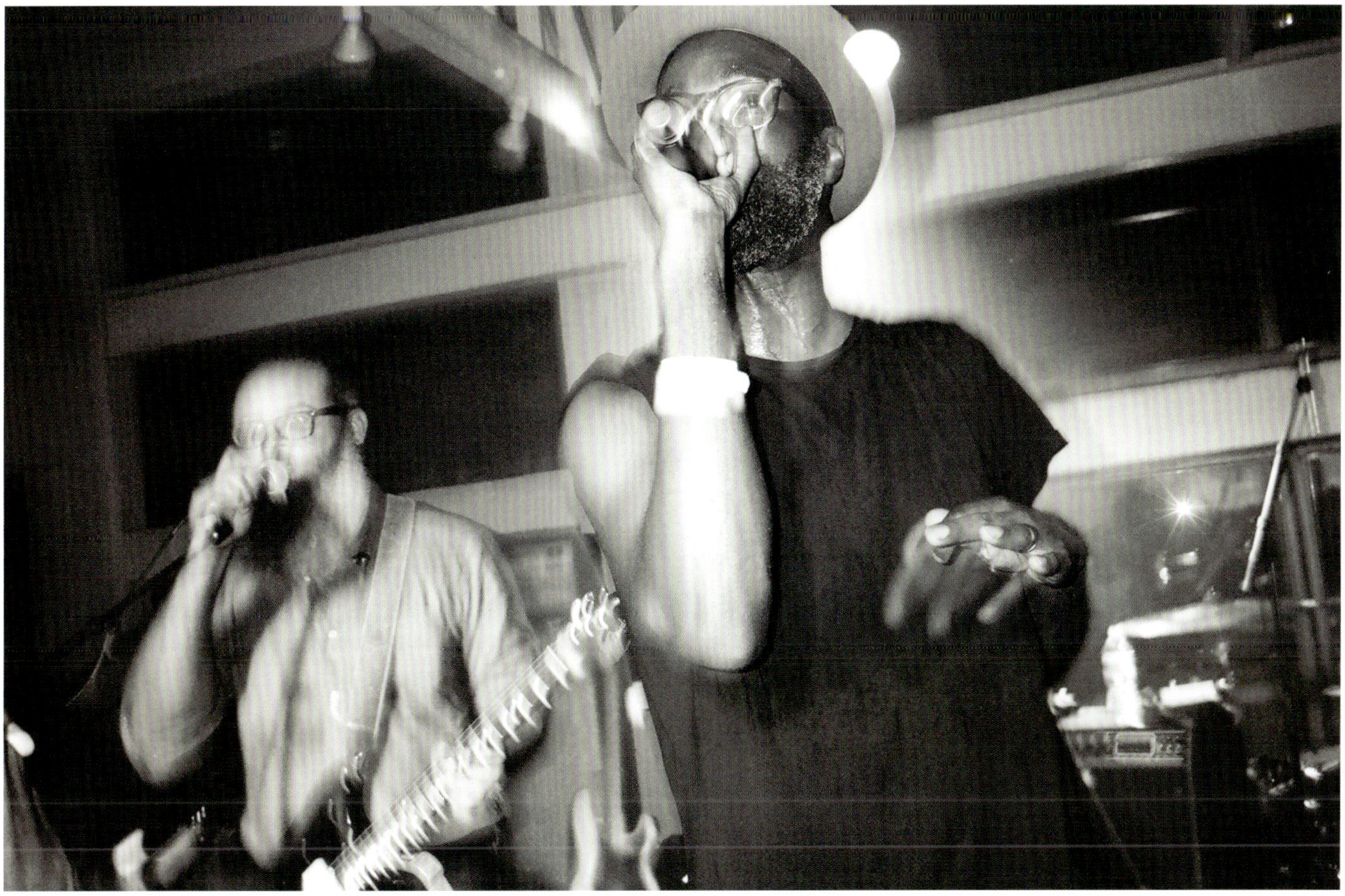

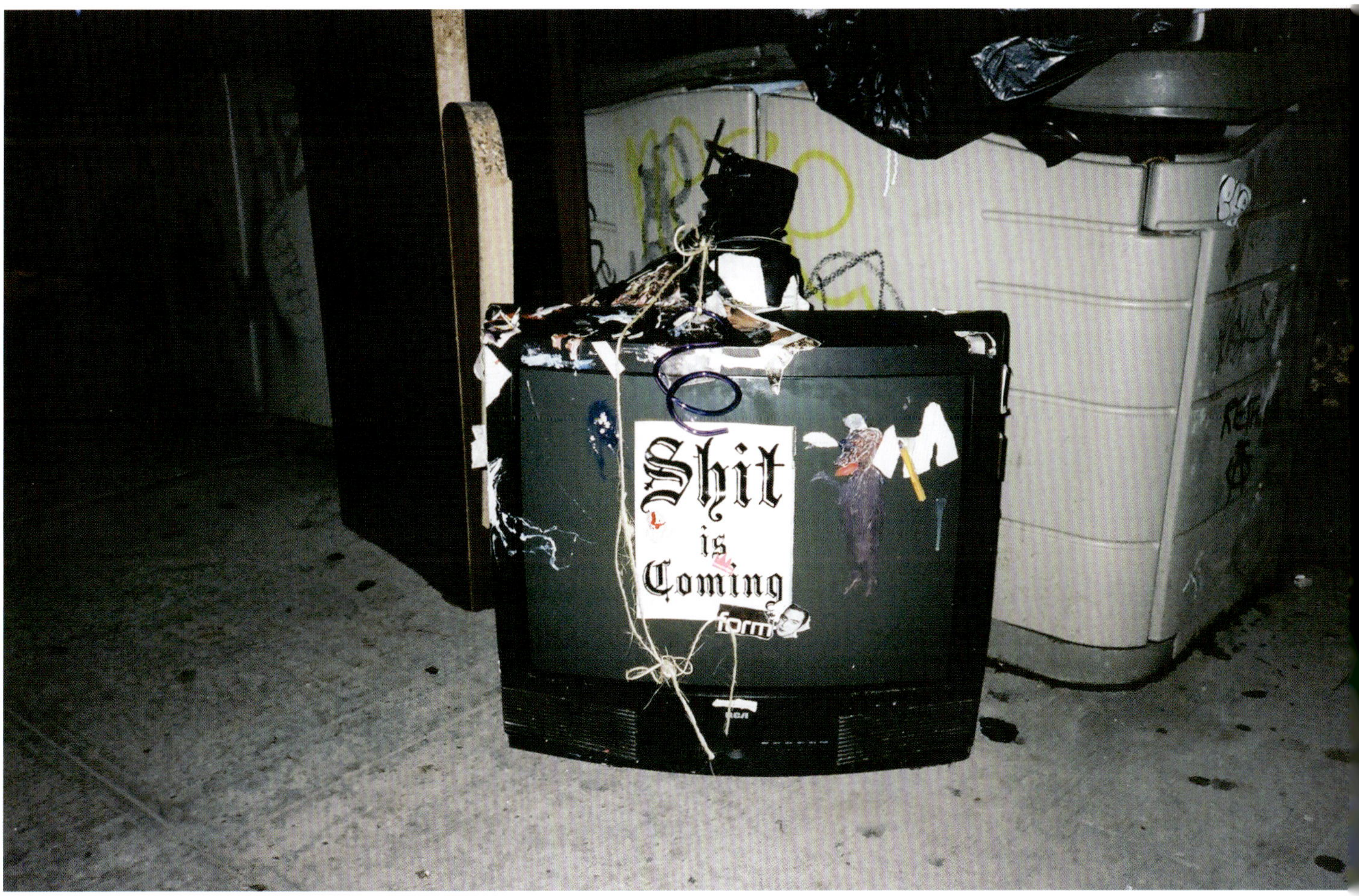

USA

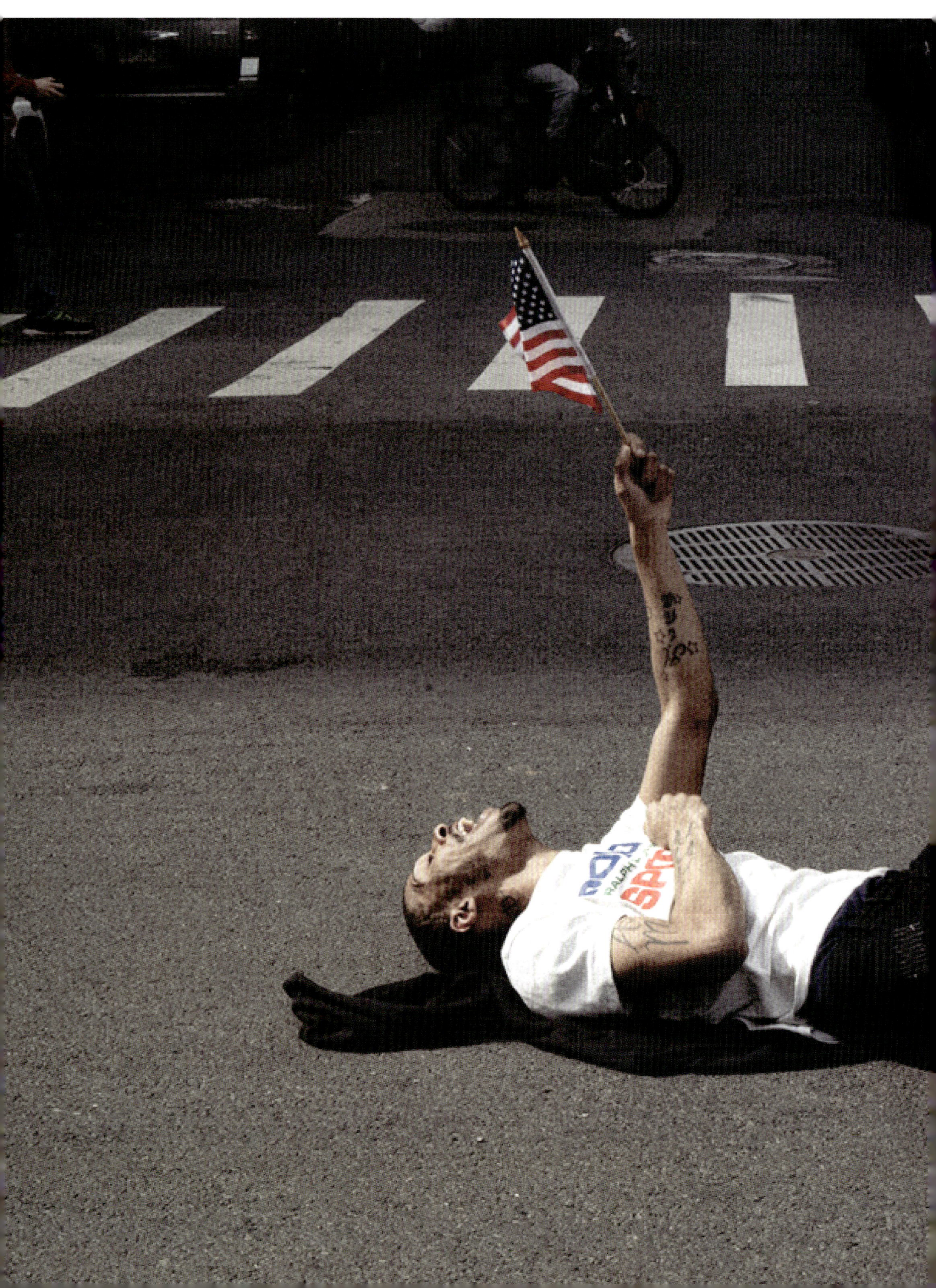

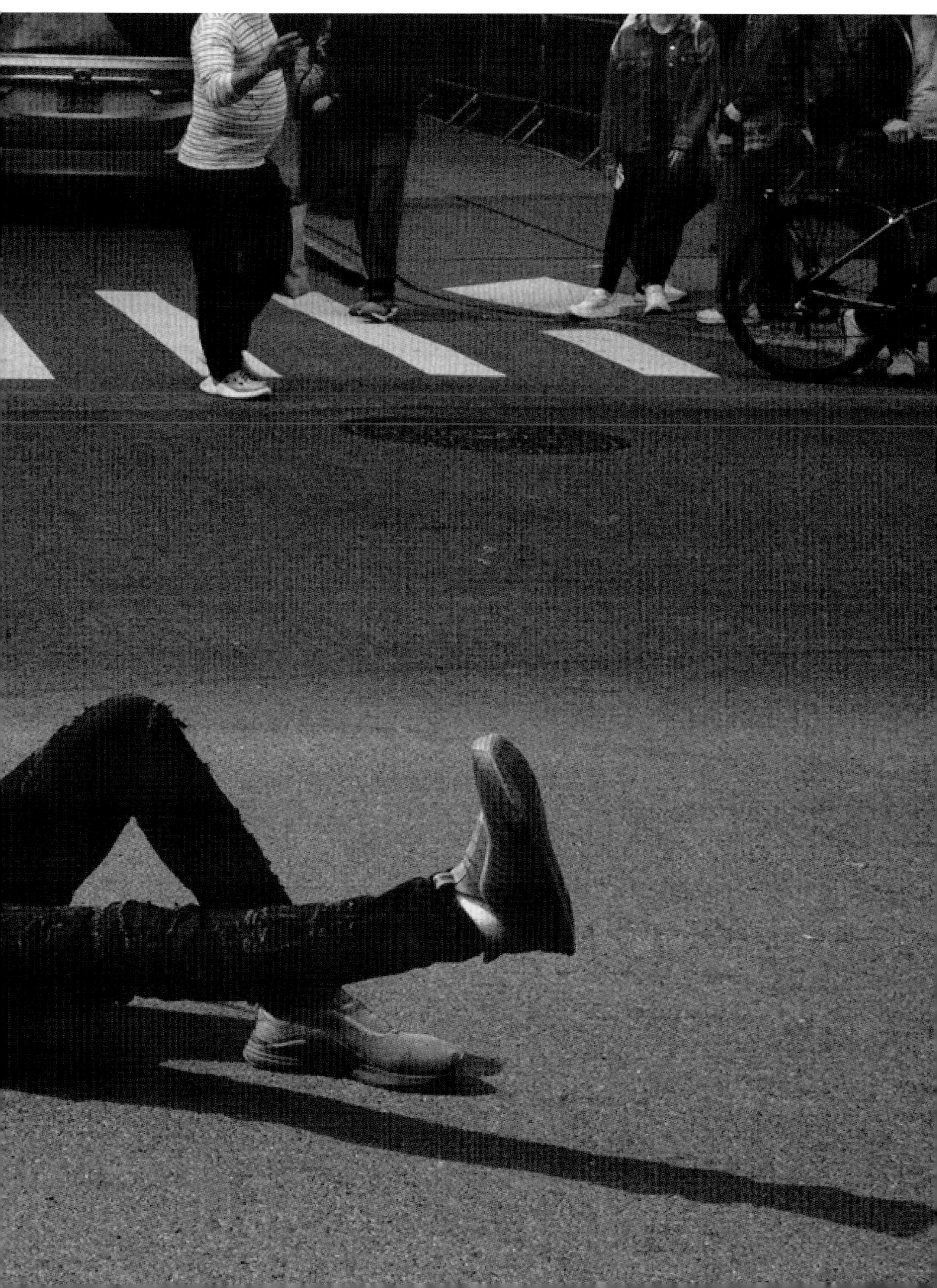

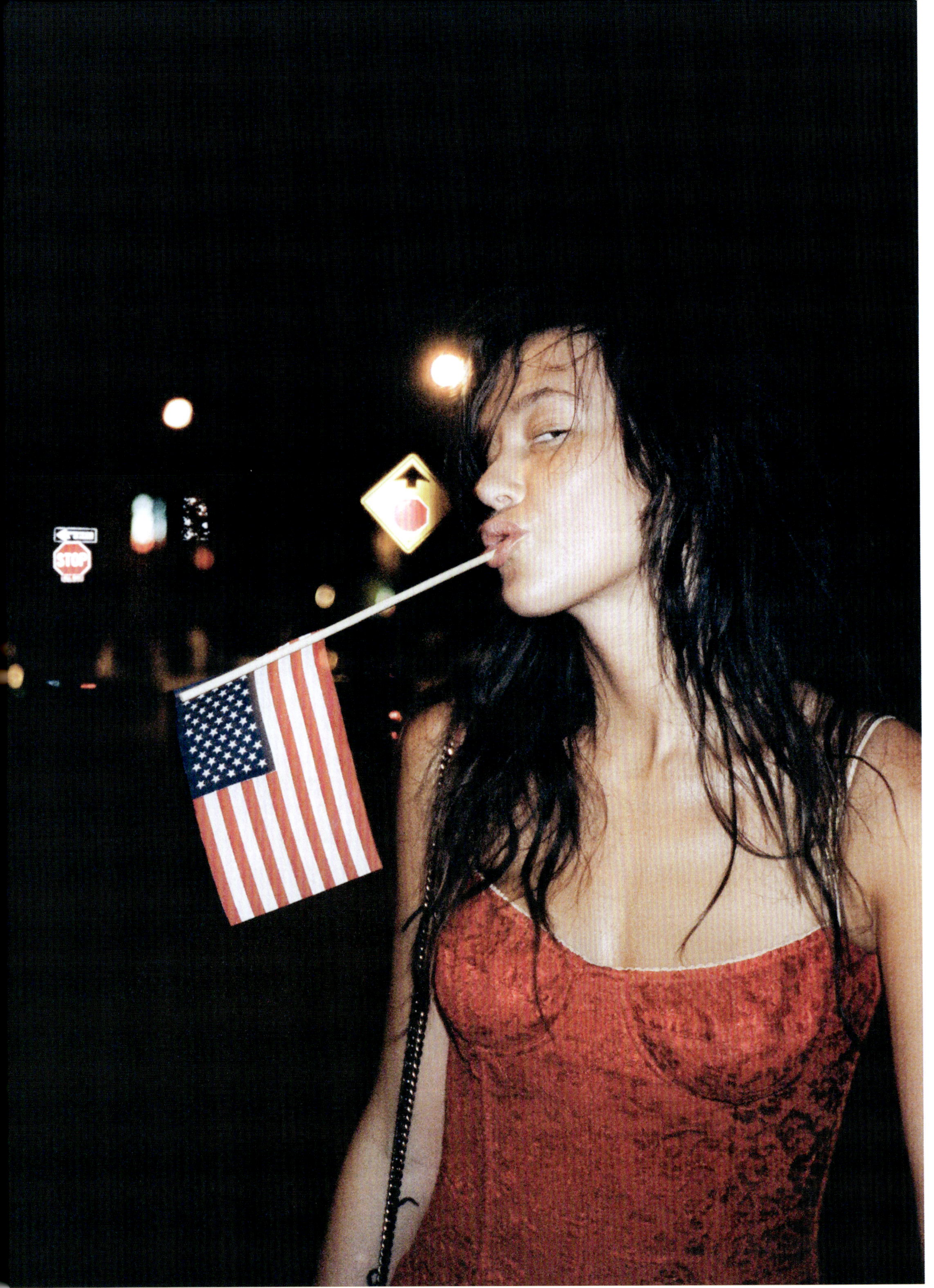
STOP

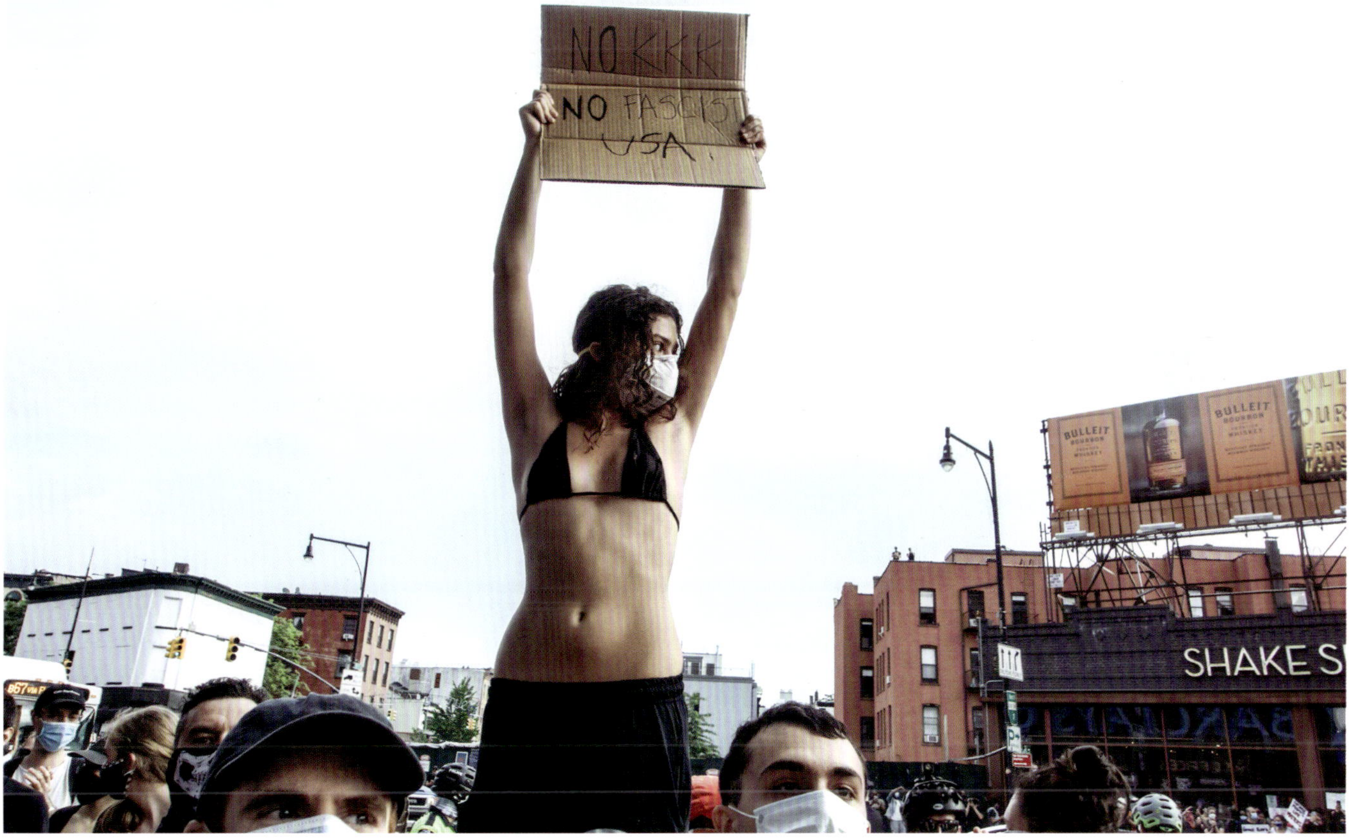
NO KKK
NO FASCIST
USA
SHAKE S

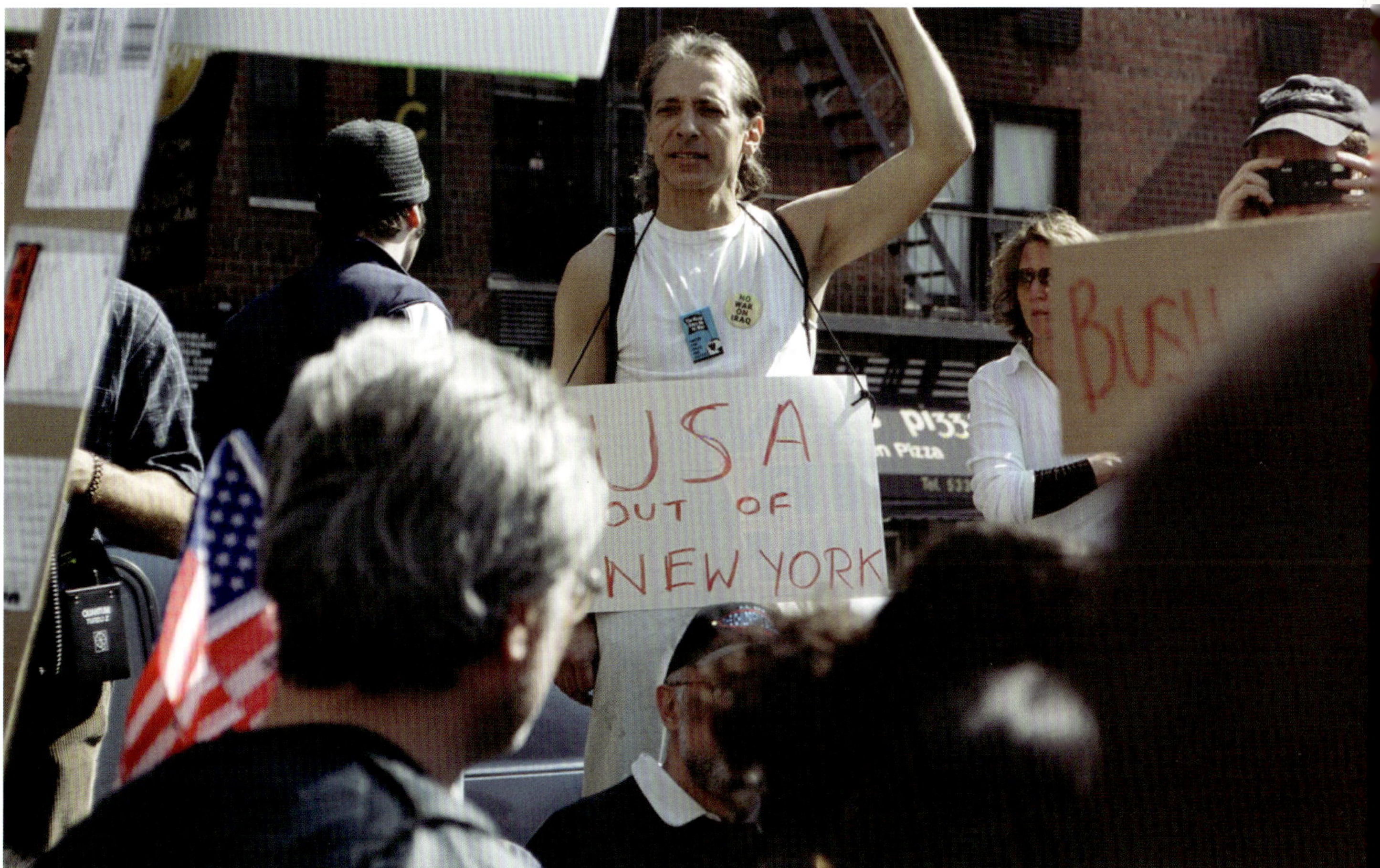
USA
OUT OF
NEW YORK
NO WAR ON IRAQ

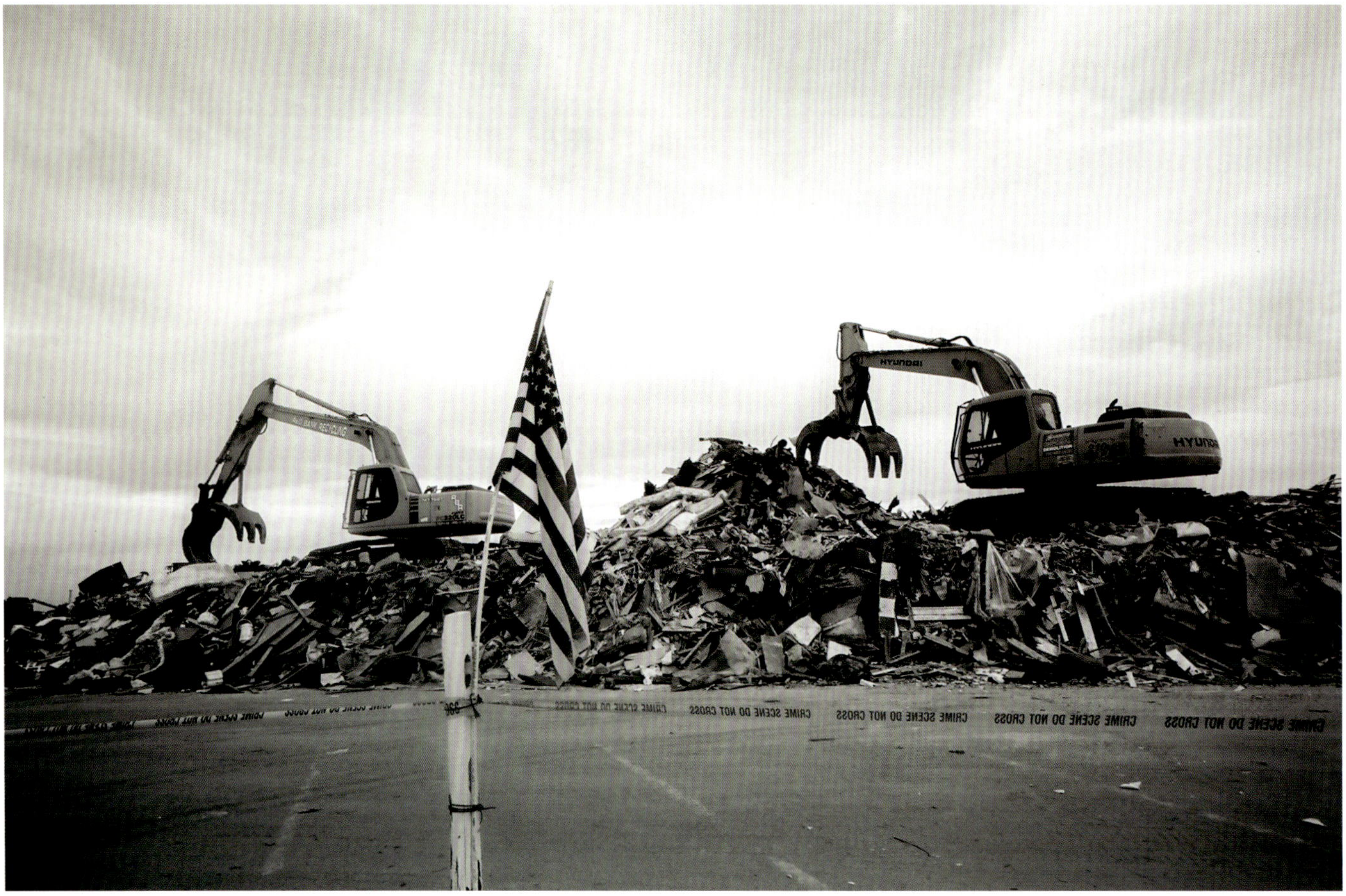
CRIME SCENE DO NOT CROSS
CRIME SCENE DO NOT CROSS
CRIME SCENE DO NOT CROSS
CRIME SCENE DO NOT CROSS

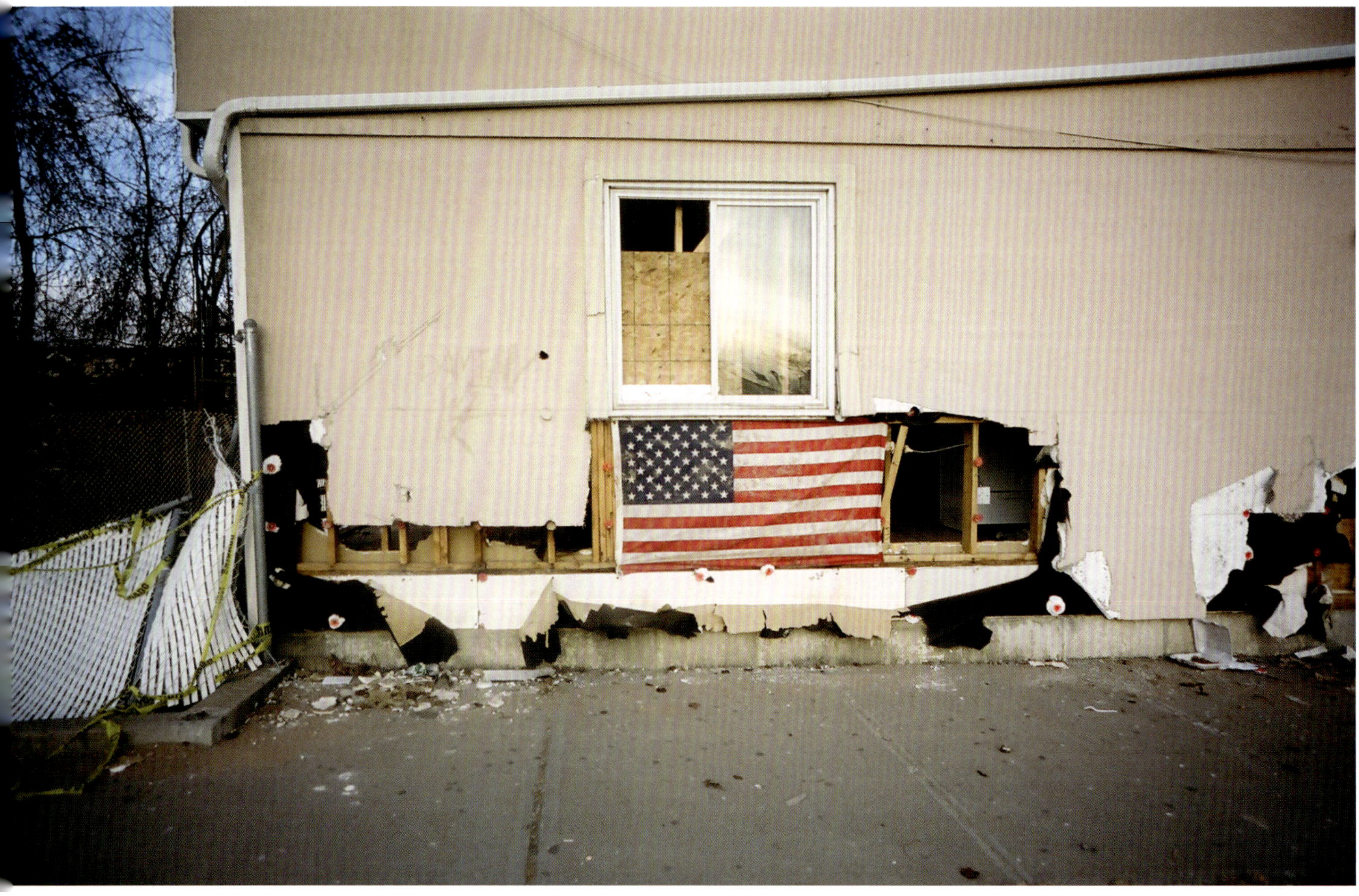

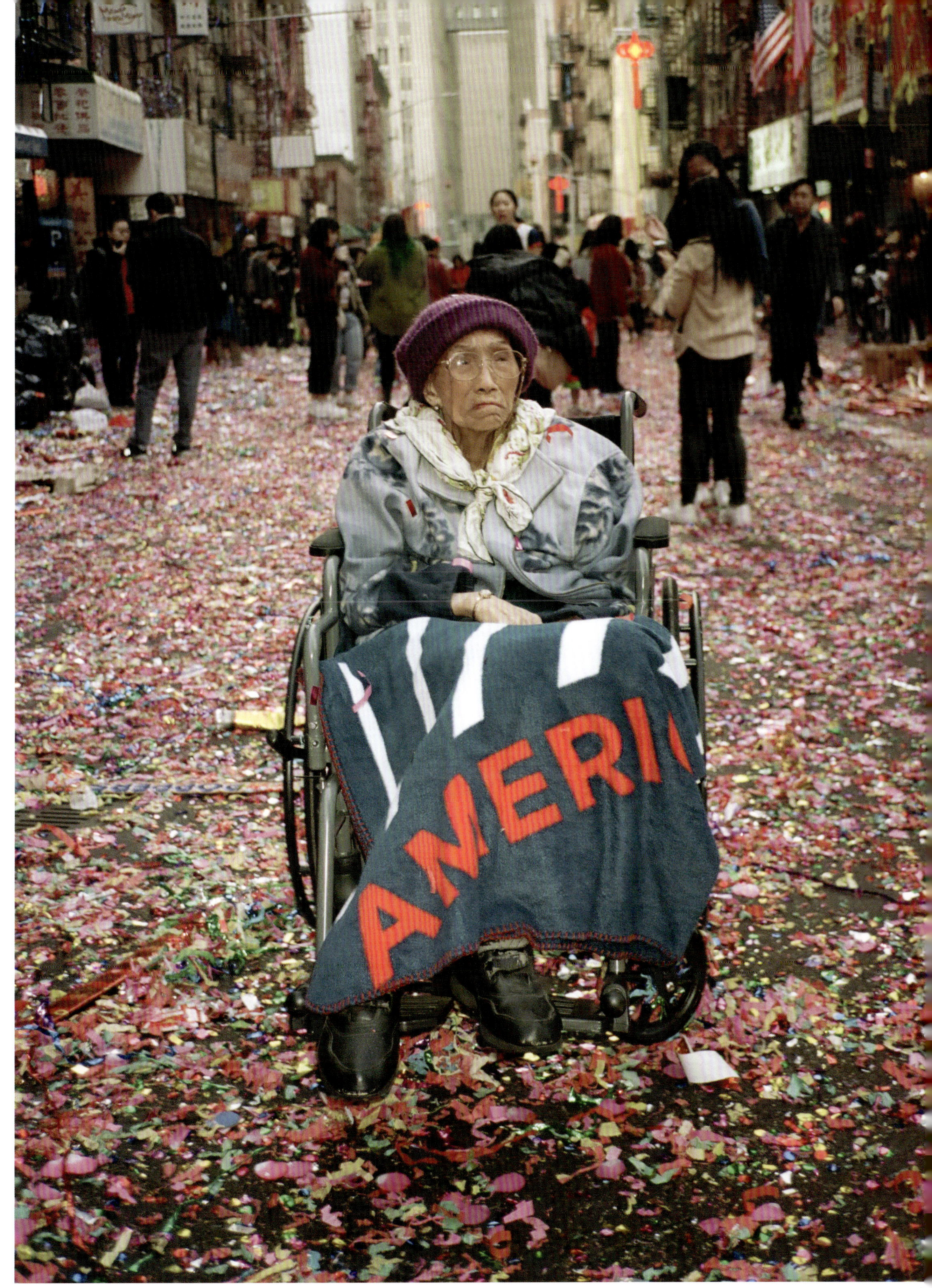
AMERI

WET

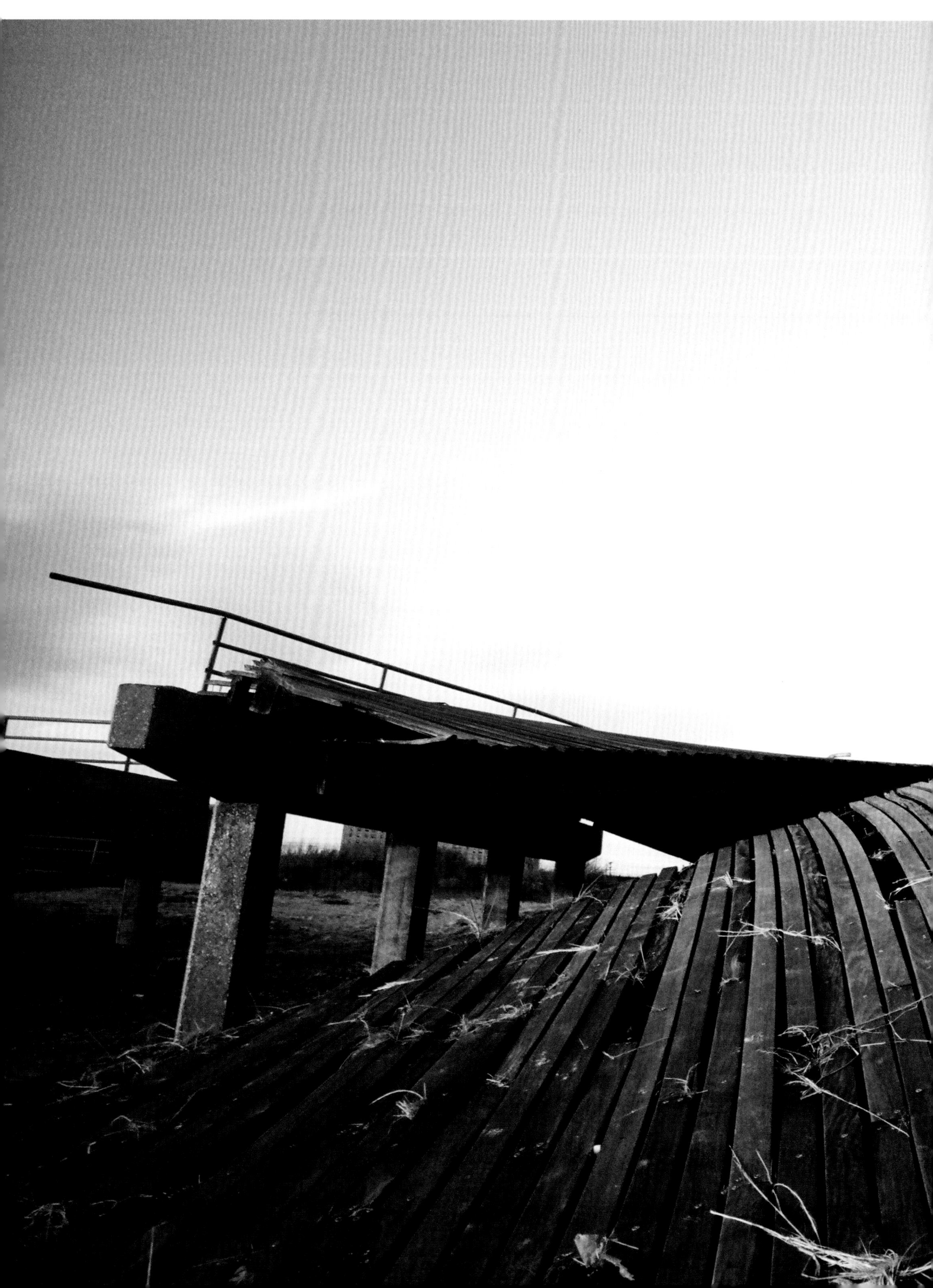

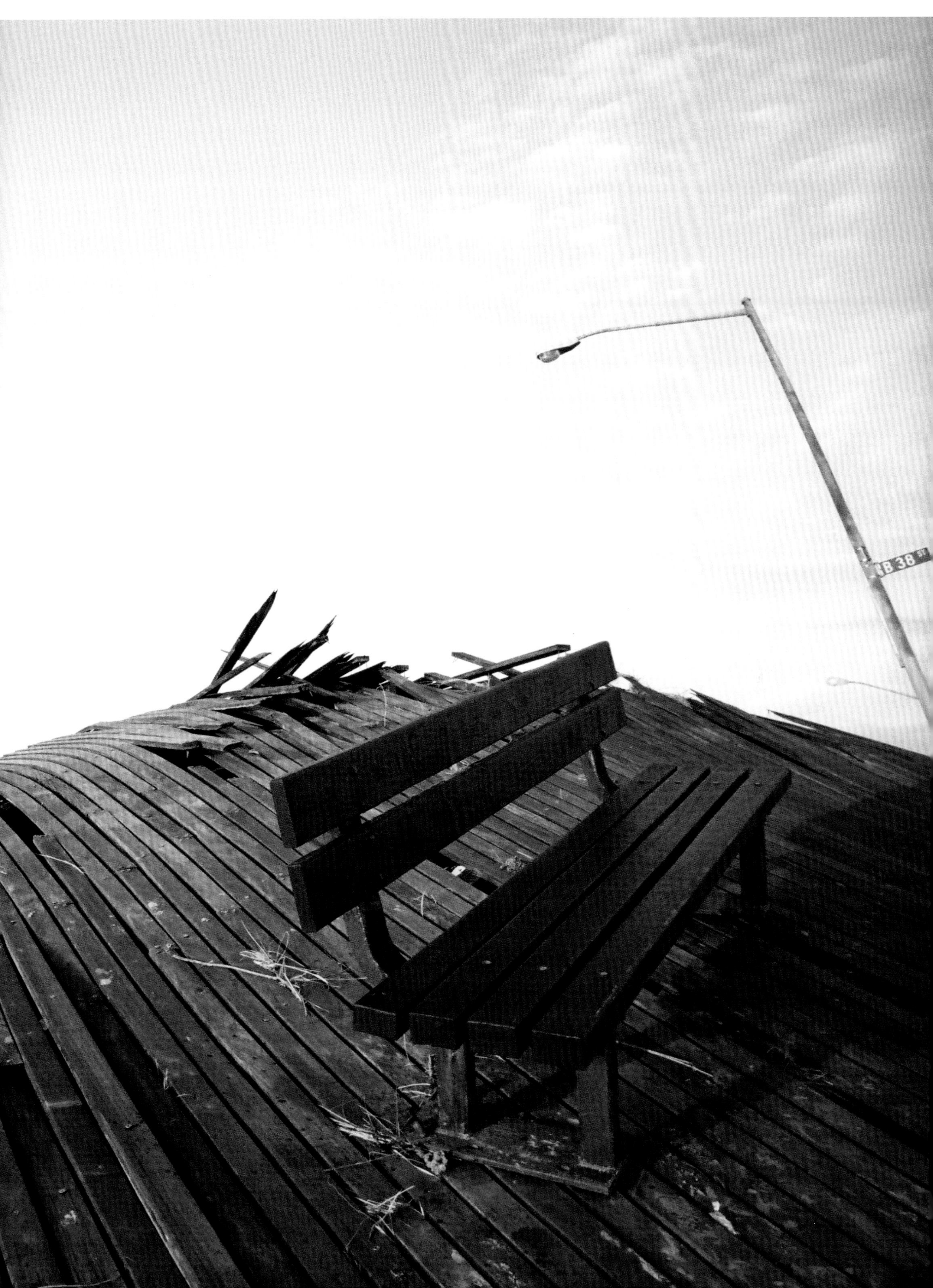
B 38 ST

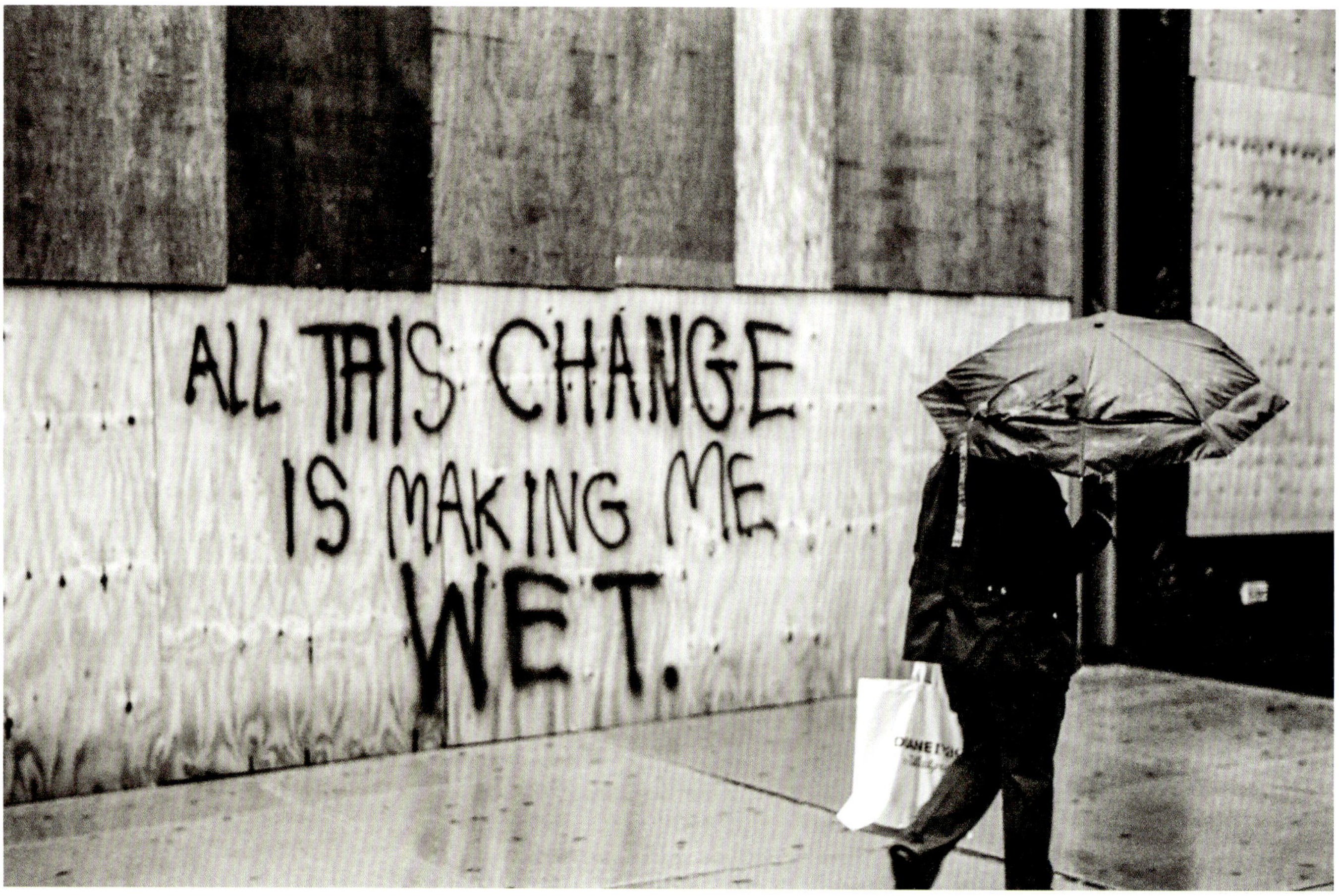
ALL THIS CHANGE
IS MAKING ME
WET.

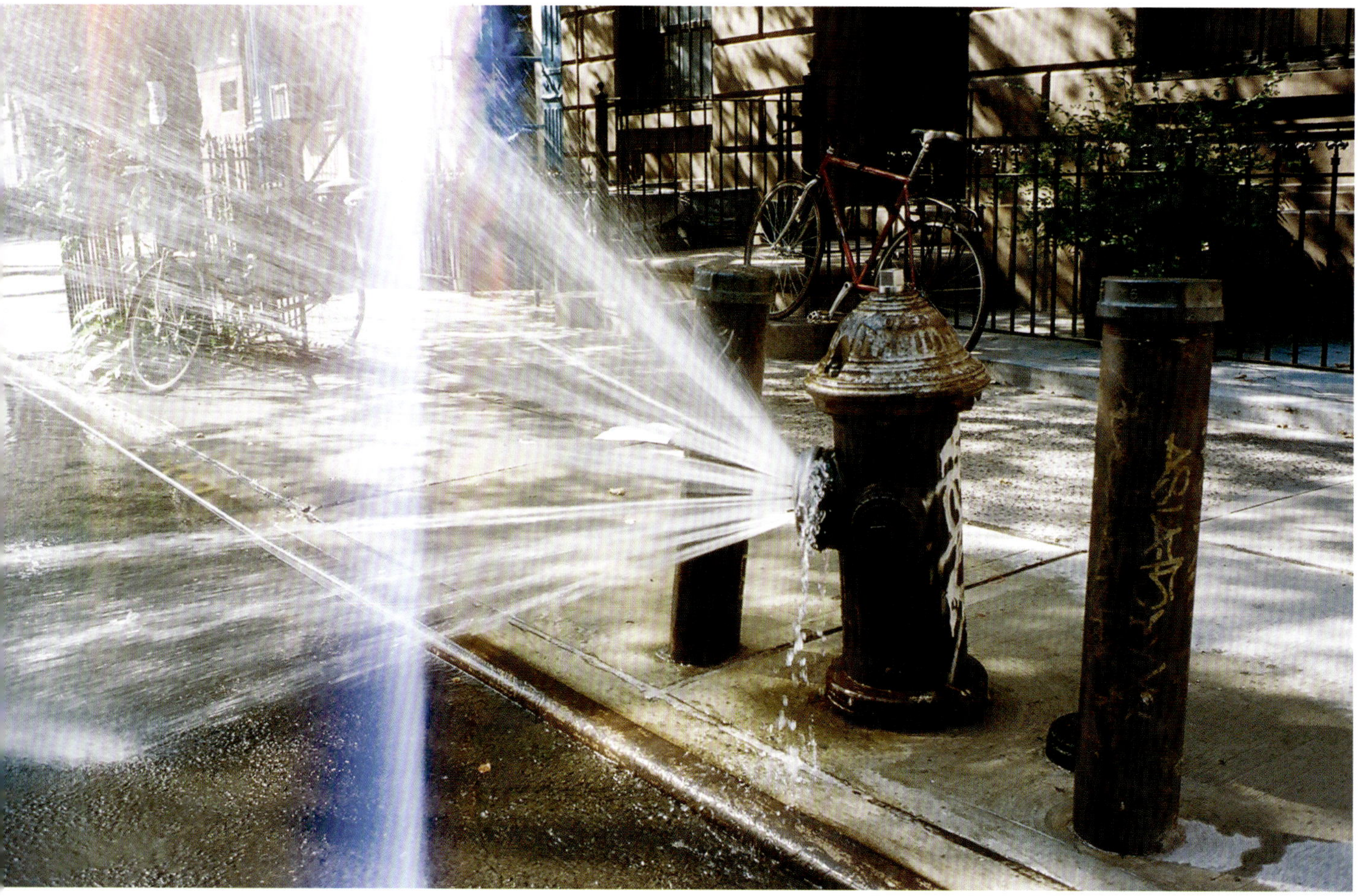

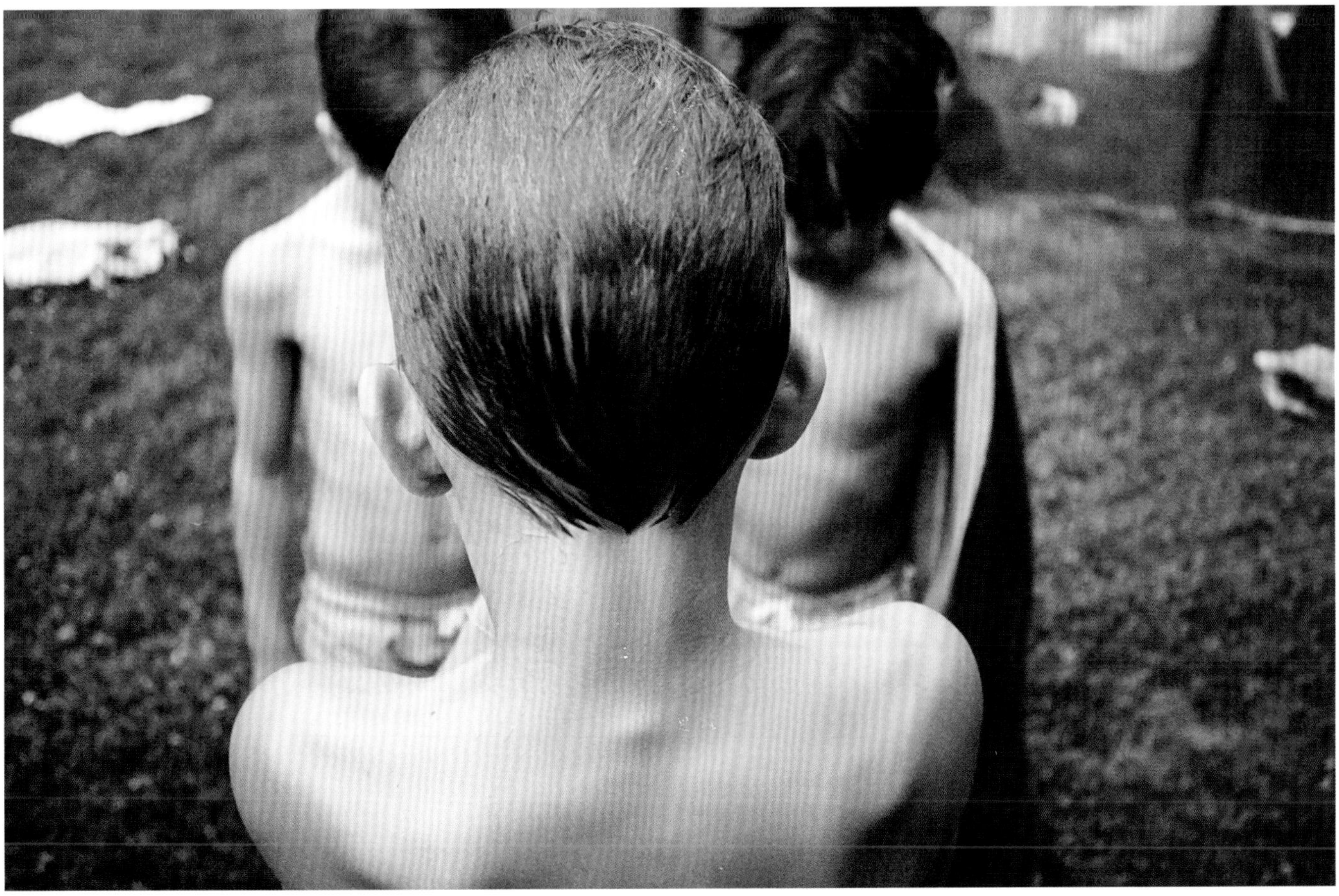

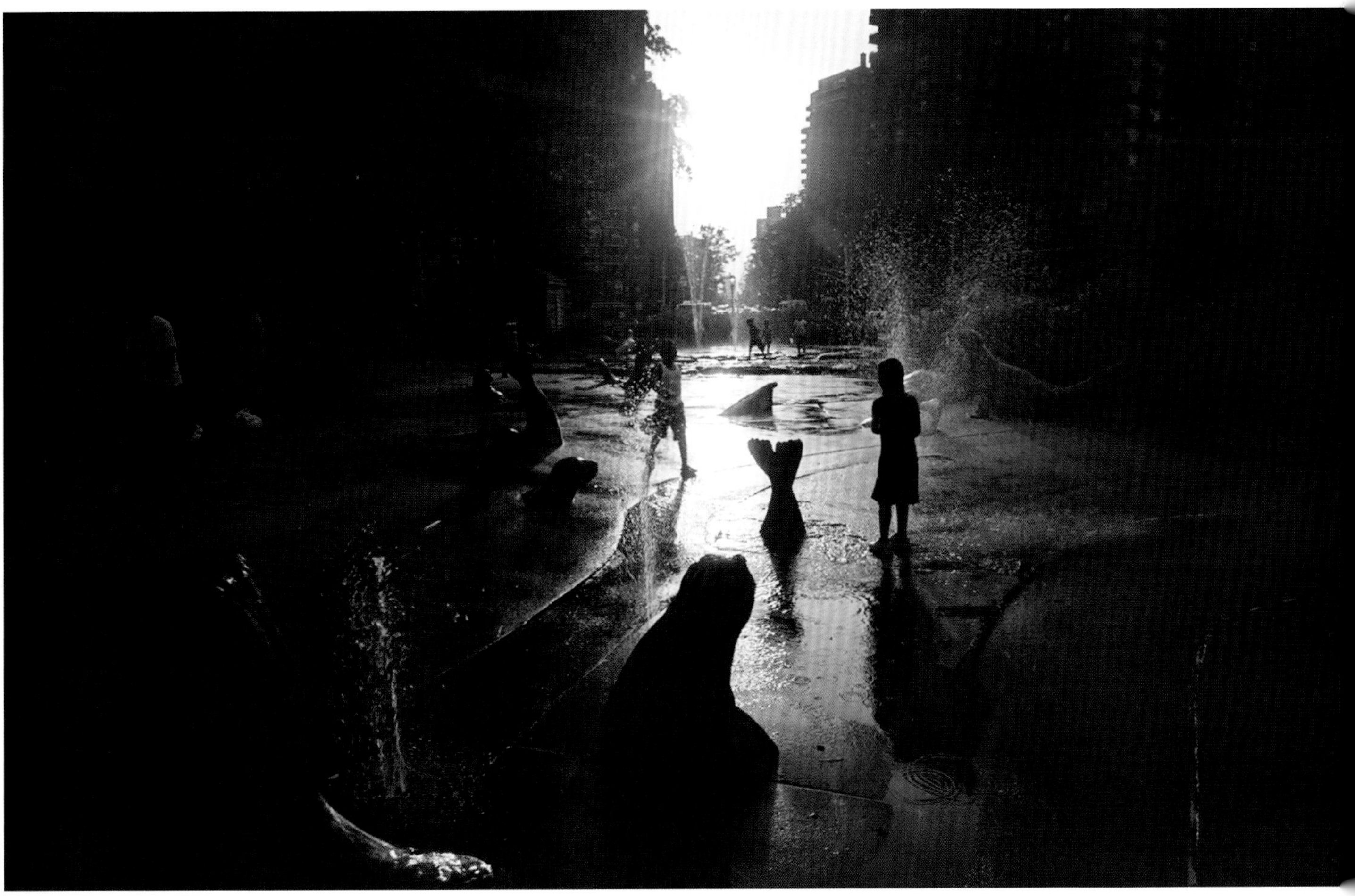

YANKEES

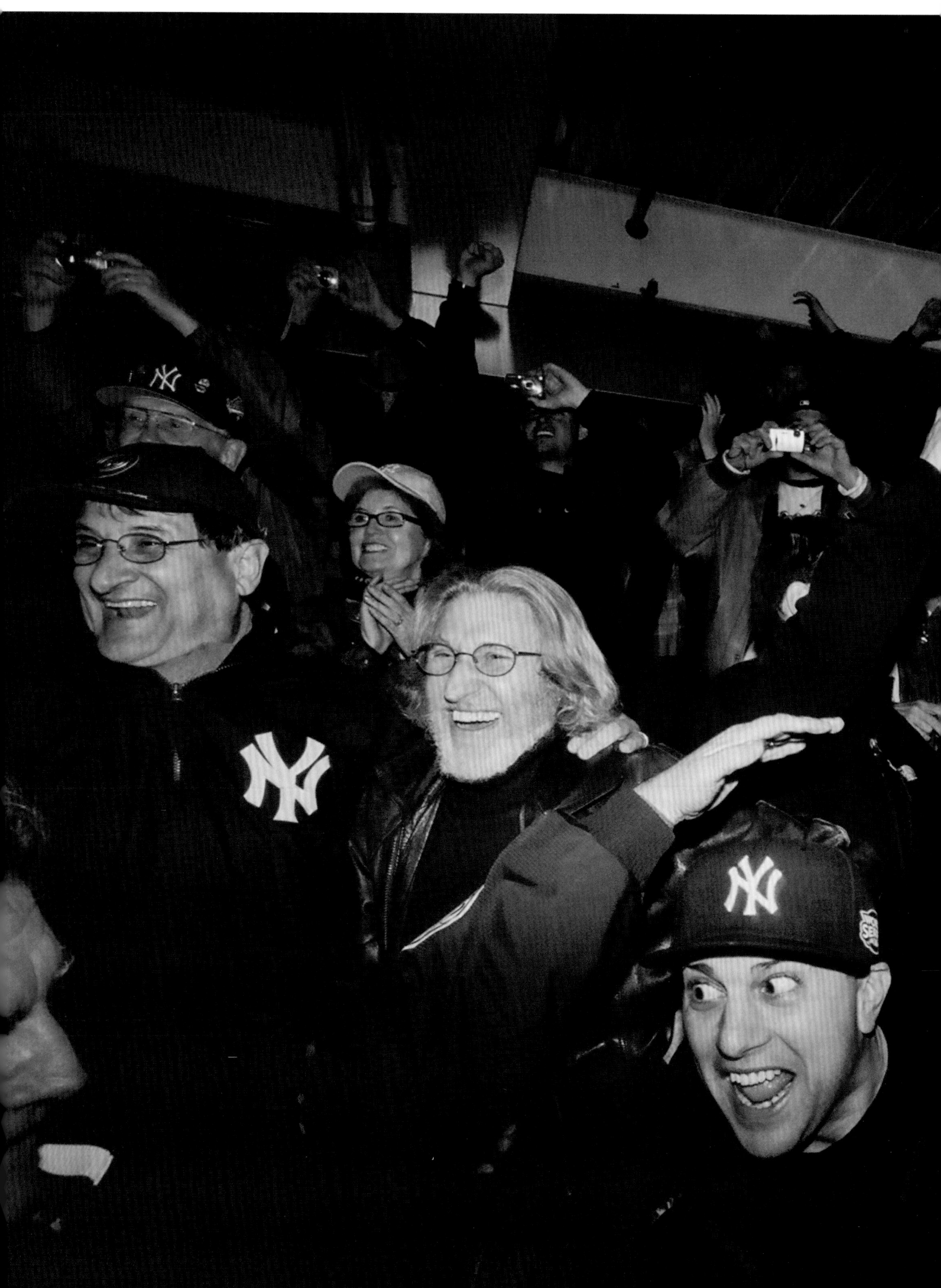

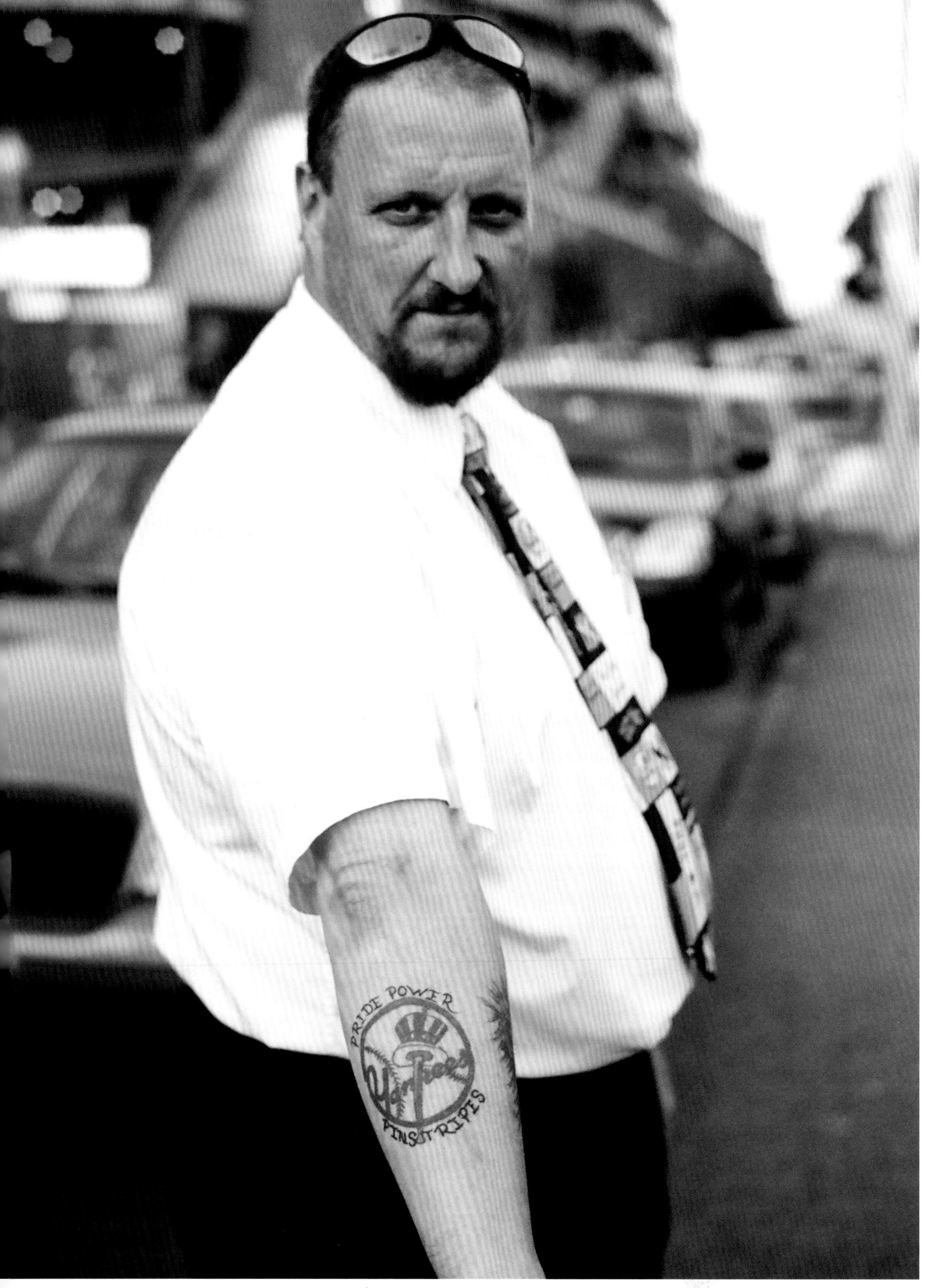
PRIDE POWER
Yankees
PINSTRIPES

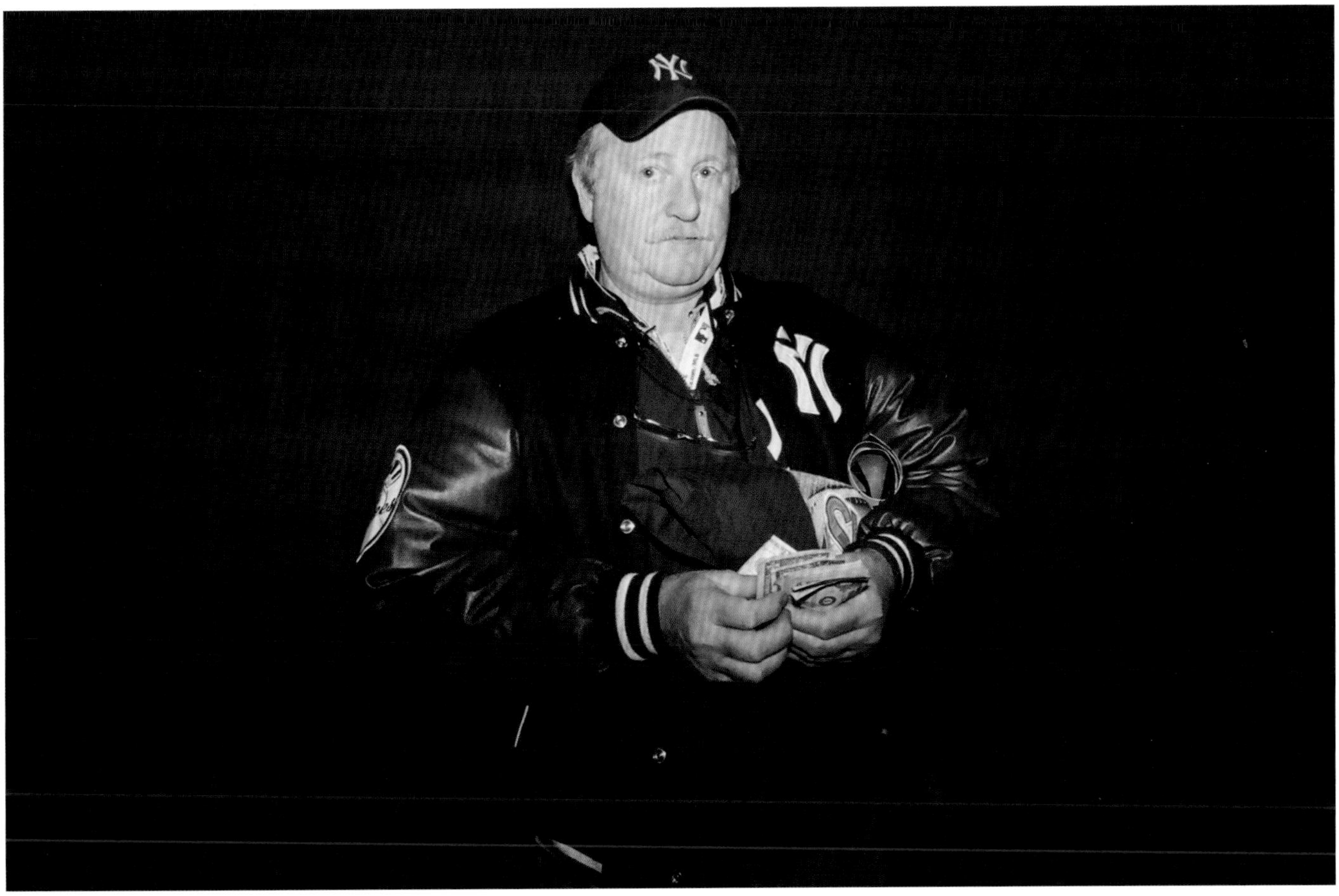

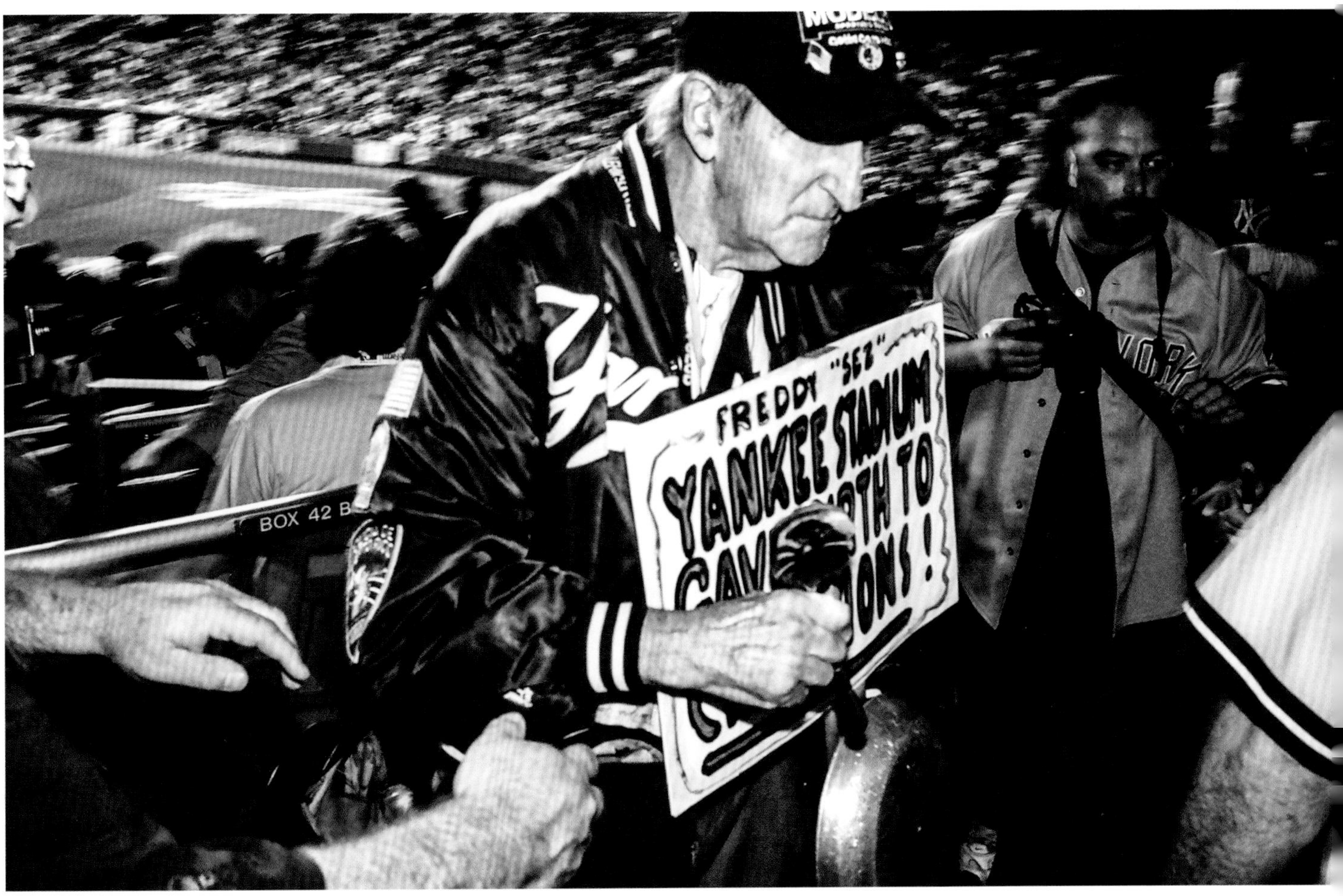
FREDDY "SEZ"
YANKEE STADIUM

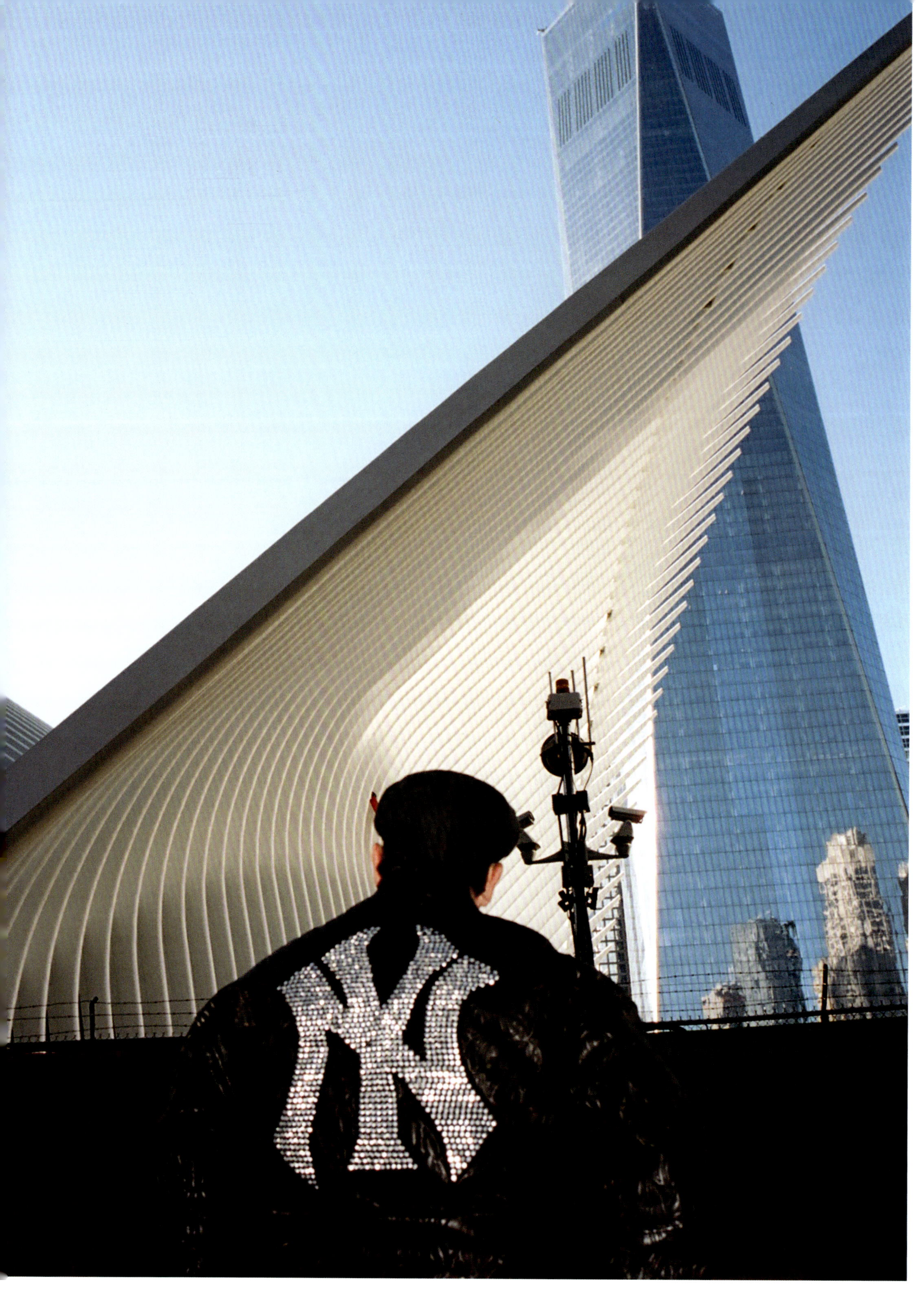

CHERYL DUNN

After 9/11, Lower Manhattan — and all New Yorkers — were forever changed. There's something very specific about a New Yorker, someone that tells you to fuck off one minute and then picks you up off the ground the next. This book, and this image of a bedazzled, Yankees jacket against what I call "the wing building," rising from the dust of the World Trade Center, symbolizes to me the tenacity and resilience it takes to live, survive, and thrive in this city. It's not for everyone, but those who hang in there are a special breed.

They create a rhythm uniquely their own within the caverns of these skyscrapers, where dramatic light ricochets from metal to glass, from river to sky.

I lived on Maiden Lane in the financial center, a block from the World Trade Center for half of my life. When it came down, we returned there as soon as we could, finding it difficult to be around people that did not have like experiences of that day. One of my most distinct, positive memories in the aftermath was the Yankees in the playoffs. We did not win that year, but it was a simple thing that gave a community of people that had just been shot in the heart some hope, some lightness, and some togetherness. As we walked uptown to Tribeca to find a bar that we could watch the game, we traversed on wooden, raised platforms that twisted and turned at each corner. On every block there was a police officer with a transistor radio listening to the game, each updating us on the score. Small gestures — smiles, nods, and the unspoken acknowledgment that we were on the same team: a team of New Yorkers. Bonded, diverse, yet fundamentally alike. When I travel abroad and someone asks if I'm American, I simply reply... "I'm a New Yorker."

PAGE

002 FIRE ESCAPE SHADOW / LES NYC 2025

006 BIRDS OVER FIDI / COURTHOUSE NYC 2013
008 PIDGEON COOP / OCEAN HILL BROOKLYN 2021
PIDGEONS OVER DELANCEY / LES NYC 2007
009 SELFIE IN MAX FISH TOILET / LUDLOW ST NYC 2013
DEAD BIRD BY CURB / EAST VILLAGE NYC 2015
010 DUCK TRUCK AND MAN WITH ICE CREAM / FIDI NYC 2017
PARROT ON SHOULDER / GREENWHICH VILLAGE NYC 2022
011 DEAD PIDGEON WITH SLEEPING MAN / EAST RIVER PATH NYC 2014

012 BOXMAN / 195 BROADWAY STEPS FIDI NYC 2005
014 SUMMER BOX / LES NYC 2023
SPIKE JONES AND JAMES MURPHY PUNCH / UPTOWN NYC 2015
015 AVE C FUN TUSSLE / AVE C. NYC 2010

016 TALL BIKE ON BILLBURG BRIDGE / WILLIAMSBURG BRIDGE 2010
018 VOTE ON BRIDGE / WILLIAMSBURG BRIDGE 2021
CUPCAKE BIKE / WILLIAMSBURG BRIDGE 2015
019 COUPLE ON THE BRIDGE / WILLIAMSBURG BRIDGE 2015
WHERE'S THE KID / BROOKLYN BRIDGE 2021
020 RED HAIR BLUE BRIDGE / EAST RIVER 2019

022 BED ON BROADWAY / BROADWAY FIDI 2017
024 IN FINANCIAL PROBLEM / BROADWAY FIDI 2018
025 DEAD PLANET / BROADWAY FIDI 2011
LIVING ON A PRAYER / BROADWAY FIDI 2010
026 RED SHIRT ON FIRE HYDRANT / EAST BROADWAY NYC 2021

028 BUNNY IN THE MOSH PIT / THOMPKINS SQUARE PARK 2024
030 VET WITH BUNNY EARS / 5TH AVE NYC 2015
031 BUNNY MOSH / VICE PARTY BROOKLYN 2009
MAN ON KNEES WITH BUNNY / 5TH AVE NYC 2019

032 CALL ME - ANDEE AND BILL / MAIDEN LANE NYC 2019
034 CALL ME WHEN IM DEAD / BUSHWICK BROOKLYN 2019
035 WOLF MAKES CALL / GREENWICH VILLAGE NYC 2016
HUH CALL / LES NYC 2021

036 SUPERMAN AND COP / DT BROOKLYN BLM PROTEST 2020
038 COP POINTS AT SUPER MAN / DT BROOKLYN BLM PROTEST 2020
STAY BLACK / DOWNTOW BROOKLYN BLM PROTEST 2020
039 ANGRY PACIFIST / BROADWAY FIDI 2015

040 PUDDLE CROSSWALK / ALLEN ST. NYC 2023
042 WOMAN WITH STIGMATA / 5TH AVE NYC 2017
CROSSWALK - NIGHT / CANAL ST. NYC 2023
043 LOST BIRD IN CROSSWALK / LES NYC 2021
DOUBLE STRIPE CROSSWALK / LES NYC 2024
044 DEAD OR NOT ALIVE / BROADWAY & MAIDEN LANE FIDI NYC 2011
045 BIG CIGAR IN THE CROSSWALK / GRAND ST. NYC 2023
046 CHAIN LINK VIEW CROSSWALK / NYC 1990'S
047 SURFBOARD IN CROSSWALK / CHURCH ST. NYC 2019
PINK CAST YELLOW DRESS OJ IN CROSSWALK / MIDTOWN 2019
048 TROPHY CROSSWALK / GREENPOINT BOOKLYN 2019
LEOPARD COAT IN THE CROSSWALK / WATER ST. NYC 2019

049 HORNS SCOOTER CROSSWALK / CANAL ST. NYC 2023
BROKEN NOSE / PARK AVE. NYC 2019

050 DOG WALKER WITH TRAILS / EAST VILLAGE NYC 2009
052 CRUSTY DOG / ST. MARKS PLACE NYC 2017
053 NO DOGS ALLOWED / ORCHARD ST. NYC 2019
DOG WITH BALLOONS / TRIBECA NYC 2019
054 DOG GRAFF BY LOOTED STORE / SOHO NY 2020
HOMELESS DRUMMER WITH DOGS / FIDI NYC 2018
055 GUARD DOGS AT SAKS 5TH AVE / 5TH AVE. NYC 2020

056 WILL EAT 4 FOOD / EAST VILLAGE NYC 1980
058 I DONT THINK I LIKE YOU / EAST VILLAGE NYC 2009
SKULL CAR LIFE / EAST VILLAGE NYC 1986
059 THE RAMONES / EAST VILLAGE NYC 1995
060 DRAG QUEEN WIGSTOCK / AVE A. NYC 1995
RAINBOW CAT MASK / EAST VILLAGE 2010
061 PACMAN PLYWOOD / EAST VILLAGE 2025
062 LUCIEN WITH CANDY DARLING / EAST VILLAGE NYC 1980
I LOVE BINGO / EAST 10TH ST EAST VILLAGE NYC 2017
063 SPILT CARDS / EAST VILLAGE NYC 2018
2 CATS WALK / EAST VILLACE NYC 2016

064 MORNING FOG / FIDI NYC 2020
066 TOWERS ON FIRE / FIDI NYC 9/11/2001
067 ME AND MK SELF PORTRAIT 911 DUST / MAIDEN LANE NYC 2001
068 TICKERTAPE BUILDING / FIDI NYC 1996
069 RONNIE SPINS IN STREET / FIDI NYC 1998
070 INTERESTED / FIDI NYC 1998
071 HI-TOP FADE & RED CUBE / FIDI NYC 2016

072 FIREWORKS FROM HENRY ST. / CHINATOWN NYC 2017
074 GRAMPS SHOOTING FIREWORKS / CHINATOWN VIEW NYC 2017
RED FIREWORKS IN RAIN / 6TH AVE GREENWICH VILLAGE 2008
075 MAN POINTS AT FIREWORKS / DOWNTOWN NYC 2017
ROOFTOP FIREWORKS / BUSHWICK BROOKLYN 2018

076 THE FLASH INN / BRONX NYC 2016
078 BROADWAY FLASH / FIDI NYC 2019
GIANT FLASH VICE PARTY / BROOKLYN 2009
079 GRANDMASTER FLASH / MAIDEN LANE NYC 1990'S

080 GIRL ON CANAL STREET WITH SKATEBOARD / LES NYC 2023
082 PINK GIRL AT MOMA WITH CIG / MIDTOWN MANHATTAN 2019
083 SIDE EYE WHITNEY BIENNIELLE / UPPER E SIDE NYC 2008
RUNNING GIRL / LES NYC 2021
084 GIRL READING ON THE GROUND / EAST VILAGE NYC 2016
086 BILLY'S TOPLESS / SOUTH OF CANAL NYC 1999
087 PASSED OUT GIRL / LES NYC 2015
CHIC GIRL MIDTOWN / GARMENT DISTRICT NYC 1999

088 LOOTERS WILL BE CRUCIFIED / ROCKAWAY NYC 2012
090 THANK GOD I'M GAY / WASHINGTON SQUARE PARK NYC 2021
WINES AND LIQUORS THANKS GOD / BUSHWICK AVE. BK 2019
091 EXALT THE LORD / BROAD ST. NYC 1995
GOD GIRL WITH STIGMATTA / 5TH AVE NYC 2017
092 MESSIAH AT THE EASTER PARADE / 5TH AVE NYC 2016

093 NO HELP OK GOD - JIM JOE / EAST VILLAGE NYC 2011
GOD CO-PILOT / NYC 2014

094 COMPANION COVERS EYES / THANKSGIVING PARADE NYC 2012
096 IGGY WITH HANDS / ATP CATSKILLS NY 2010
098 HAND PRINTS ON WALL / DOWNTOWN MANHATTAN NYC 1980
LOOKING AT THE WTC DESTRUCTION / FIDI NYC 2001
099 RAISED HAND / BROOKLYN NY 2020
HAND SIGN / WASHINGTON SQUARE PARK NYC 2020
100 PATTY CAKE / BRONX NYC 2009

102 JIM JOE BIG / EAST VILLAGE 2011
104 JOE COLEMAN AND WHITNEY WARD / BROOKLYN HEIGHTS 1999
105 FUCKS COFFEE / LES NYC 2024
RATS AND CUP OF JOE / EAST VILLAGE NYC 2008

106 LONE MAN IN THE DUST 911 / MAIDEN LANE NYC 9/11 2001
108 GO HILLARY IM LONALY / MAIDEN LANE NYC 2016
LONE GORILLA BRONX ZOO / BRONX NYC 2012
109 KATY PETTY WALKS ALONE AS A HAMBURGER / MEAT PD NYC 2019

110 LOVE ME ON THE J TRAIN / BROOKLYN 2018
112 LOVE TATT MAX FISH / LUDLOW ST NYC 2013
LOVE PORTAL UNION SQ. / 14TH ST NYC 2019
113 EVERYONE LOVES ME / DIMES SQUARE 2023

114 SLEEPREME MATTRESS / ALLEN ST. NYC 2021
116 WRECKED HOUSE WITH MATTRESS / STATEN ISLAND NY 2012
MATTRESS FACE / EAST VILLAGE 2012
117 I AM YOUR WORST FANTASY / MUGGERS ALLEY NYC 2019
BEG BUG MATTRESS MOVE / EAST VILLAGE 2014

118 REVS AND RATS AND ME / BENSONHURST BROOKLYN 1996
120 RAT STORY HOTLINE / LES NYC 2024
121 THE RATS DO RUN THE CITY - MAYOR / EAST VILLAGE 2023
122 PIZZA RAT WALKING / VILLAGE NYC 2019

124 ROOFTOP CHINATOWN DOWN VIEW / HENRY ST. NYC 2019
126 CHRIS ROBINSON WITH 40 ON THE ROOF / TIMES SQUARE 1994
127 CHARLOTTE PAINTING ON ROOF/ BUSHWICK BROOKLYN 2025
DASH ON CHINATOWN ROOF / CHINATOWN NYC 2006
128 CLAUDIA ON ROOFTOP / CANAL AND DIVISION ST. 2025
130 MICKEY WITH CROSS ON ROOF / EAST BROADWAY NYC 2025
MICKEY IN CHAIR ON ROOF / EAST BROADWAY NYC 2025
131 CHRIS CHILLS ON ROOF / BUSHWICK BROOKLY 2025

132 JUSTICE SIGN / BARCLAYS CENTER DOWNTOWN BK 2020
134 RESIST AND PERSIST SIGN / WASHINGTON SQ. PARK NYC 2017
135 NOW SIGN / CITYHALL NYC 2020
TRUMP MASK ON EYES SIGN / BROOKLYN NAVY YARD 2020

136 SLEEPING MAN WITH WHITE HAT / MAIDEN LANE NYC 1998
138 MAN SLEEPS ON BASKETBALL / THE BOWERY NYC 2010
SLEEPING MAN WITH LAP OF MONEY / LES NYC 2024
139 MICHAEL LOST KEYS / EAST VILLAGE NYC 2015
SLEEPING GOLD MAN / UNION SQUARE NYC 2020
140 SUBWAY SMILE / DELANCY ST. NYC 2022

142 DIE ANTWOORD SMILE - ALEXANDER WANG PARTY / NYC 2025
143 LESBIANS FOR BUSH SMILE / 5TH AVE NYC 2023
BIDEN WINS BIG SMILE / WASHINGTON SQ. PARK NYC 2020

144 TICKER TAPE ON FIRE WITH SMOKE / FIDI NYC 1999
146 SMOKING GIRL WITH FLASH / EAST VILLAGE NYC 2017
SMOKING VAPES TIME SQUARE ST. PATS / MIDTOWN NYC 2024
147 DASH SMOKING IN ABANDONED BLDG. / MAIDEN LN NYC 2000
LEO, RYAN, SPENCER, MATT, JR SMOKING / DOWNTOWN NYC 2015

148 SPILT PAINT ON CAR / EAST VILLAGE NYC 2009
150 TIPPING TRUCK - STREET MARKET SHOW / SOHO NYC 2000
SPILT ICE CREAM / EAST VILLAGE NYC 2014
151 PAINT SPILL AND CONE / EAST VILLAGE NYC 2015
SPILLING RED. 5TH AVE BLM PROTEST 2020

152 MAN PULLS TIRE DOWN / EAST 7TH ST. NYC 2009
154 BIKER WITH TIRE ON HEAD / GREENWICH VILLAGE NYC 2024
BIKE REPAIR MAN WITH TIRES / EAST 7TH ST NYC 2009
155 TIRE TUBE ON HEAD / EAST VILLAGE NYC 2005
HEARSE WITH FLAT TIRE / BUSHWICK NY 2020
156 DOODLE BUG - DIGABLE PLANETS / FORT GREENE BK 1990'S
157 TOWER OF TIRES / EAST VILLAGE NYC 2010

158 CANNER WITH TRAILS / EAST VILLAGE NYC 2025
159 GIRL IN DIMES SQUARE WITH TRAILS / LES NYC / 2024
160 LEO DANCING TO THE STROKES / DOWNTOWN NYC 2007
SNL AFTER PARTY - KENAN & MICHAEL / MIDTOWN NYC 2019

162 TVS IN MAGIC HOUR / BUSHWICK BROOKLN 2020
164 DON'T WATCH ME TV / LES NYC 2021
TINA WITH TV / BUSHWICK BROOKLYN 2017
165 TV ON THE RADIO 2014
SHIT IS COMING TV / EAST VILLAGE NYC 2013

166 MAN WITH FLAG - COURTHOUSE / DOWNTOWN NYC 2023
168 PAZ WITH FLAG 4TH OF JULY / WEST VILLAGE 2011
169 NO FASCIST USA / BARCLAYS CENTER PROTEST BK 2020
USA OUT OF NYC / MIDTOWN MANHATTAN 2004
170 SANDY DEBRIS WITH FLAG / ROCKAWAY NY 2012
FLAG HOLE PATCH / ROCKAWAY NY 2012
171 100 YEAR OLD WOMAN CHINATOWN NY 2019

172 ZIPPER BOARDWALK POST SANDY / ROCKAWAY QUEENS 2012
174 MAKING ME WET / SOHO NYC 2020
HYDRANT SQUARTS WATER / EAST VILLAGE 2010
175 WET BOYS / NOFO NY 2024
WATER PARK EAST RIVER / EAST VILLAGE NYC 2017

176 YANKEES WIN THE WORLD SERIES 1ST YEAR NEW STADIUM 2017
178 YANKEE TATTOO /NEW YORKER IN BOSTON 2019
179 SCALPER / BRONX NY 2009
FREDDIE SAYS / BRONX NY 2008
180 WING BUILDING WITH YANKEE JACKET / FIDI NYC 2025
184 SECONDA DIANA FORZANI [NANA] - CONEY ISLAND 1915

COVERS FRANKIE'S SNOW SMILE 2007

THANKS

DAVID WANG FOR STARTING THIS PROJECT WITH ME, MICHAEL KARBELNIKOFF, OLIVIA GIDGEON THOMAS, TONY ARCABASCIO, D.V. De VINCENTIS, DB BURKEMAN, SEAN JOHNSON, TO MY IMMIGRANT ANCESTORS WHO ARRIVED IN NY HARBOR AND HELPED BUILD THIS CITY, AND TO ALL THE PEOPLE THAT WERE COOL WITH ME TAKING THIER PICTURE [AND THOSE THAT HAD NO IDEA].

ART DIRECTOR
TONY ARCABASCIO

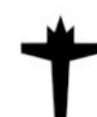

EDITORIAL DIRECTOR
CHERYL DUNN

ARCHIVISTS
VIOLET CHEVEREZ
CLAUDE COBBS

OPENING WORDS
D.V. De VINCENTIS

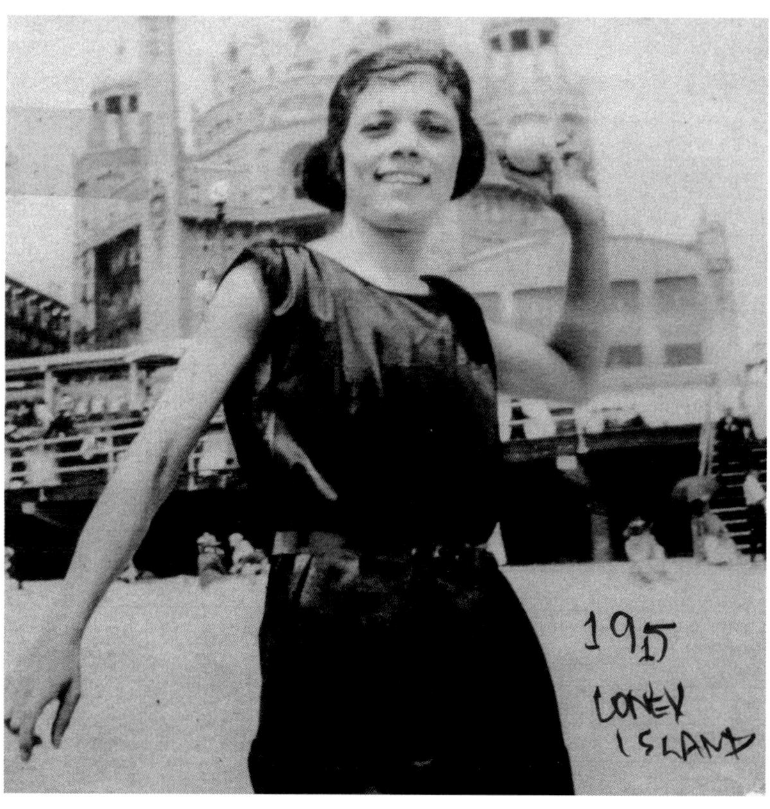

SECONDA DIANA FORZANI [NANA] WHO FLOATED TO NYC FROM ITALY FOR A BIGGER LIFE